WOMEN and MEDIA:

CONTENT, CAREERS, and CRITICISM

women

AND

media

CONTENT, CAREERS, and CRITICISM

Cynthia M. Lont

GEORGE MASON UNIVERSITY

WADSWORTH PUBLISHING COMPANY

A Division of International Thomson Publishing

Belmont • Albany • Bonn • Boston • Cincinnati • Detroit • London • Madrid • Melbourne
Mexico City • New York • Paris • San Francisco • Singapore • Tokyo • Toronto • Washington

In loving memory of Lucy

MEDIA STUDIES EDITOR:	Todd Robert Armstrong
EDITORIAL ASSISTANT:	Laura Murray
PRODUCTION EDITOR:	Carol Carreon Lombardi
MANAGING DESIGNER:	Ann Butler
INTERIOR DESIGN:	Cloyce Wall
PRINT BUYER:	Diana Spence
PERMISSIONS EDITOR:	Robert M. Kauser
COPY EDITORS:	Cheryl Ferguson, Bernie Borok
COVER DESIGN:	Lisa Berman
COMPOSITOR:	T:H Typecast, Inc.
PRINTER:	Malloy Lithographing, Inc.

Library of Congress Cataloging-in-Publication Data
Lont, Cynthia M.
   Women and media : content, careers, and criticism / Cynthia M. Lont.
      p. cm.
   Includes bibliographical references and index.
   ISBN 0–534–24732–6
   1. Mass media and women.   I. Title
P94.5.W65L66   1995
305.4—dc20   94-36309
                                          CIP

For more information, contact Wadsworth Publishing Company:

Wadsworth Publishing Company
10 Davis Drive
Belmont, California 94002, USA

International Thomson Publishing Europe
Berkshire House 168-173
High Holborn
London, WC1V 7AA, England

Thomas Nelson Australia
102 Dodds Street
South Melbourne 3205
Victoria, Australia

Nelson Canada
1120 Birchmount Road
Scarborough, Ontario
Canada M1K 5G4

International Thomson Editores
Campos Eliseos 385, Piso 7
Col. Polanco
11560 México D.F. México

International Thomson Publishing GmbH
Königswinterer Strasse 418
53227 Bonn, Germany

International Thomson Publishing Asia
221 Henderson Road
#05-10 Henderson Building
Singapore 0315

International Thomson Publishing Japan
Hirakawacho Kyowa Building, 3F
2-2-1 Hirakawacho
Chiyoda-ku, Tokyo 102, Japan

contents

PREFACE   XI
INTRODUCTION   XV

Part One

NEWSPAPERS: FRONT-PAGE NEWS BURIED IN THE WOMEN'S PAGES   3

1 WHAT'S NEWS?
M. Junior Bridge   15

2 ACTIVISM THROUGH
JOURNALISM: THE STORY OF
IDA B. WELLS-BARNETT
Jane Rhodes   29

3 *OFF OUR BACKS*
Jennie Ruby   41

4 WRINKLING THE FABRIC OF
THE PRESS: NEWSPAPER OPINION
COLUMNS IN A DIFFERENT VOICE
Norma M. Schulman   55

Part Two

WOMEN'S MAGAZINES: WOMEN WITHIN A WOMEN'S MEDIA FORM   69

5 SOCIALIZATION MESSAGES IN
SEVENTEEN AND *'TEEN* MAGAZINES
Kate Peirce   79

6 "Be Somebody":
Ruth Whitney of *Glamour*
Barbara Straus Reed 87

7 Would the Real Women's
Magazine Please Stand Up . . .
For Women
Linda Steiner 99

Part Three

THE ROLE OF WOMEN IN ADVERTISING 111

8 "You're Not Getting Older
. . . You're Getting Better!"
Tina Pieraccini and Robert Schell 121

9 Caroline Jones: Advertising
Agency Executive
Jannette L. Dates 131

10 Women For Sale
Ann J. Simonton 143

Part Four

PRIME-TIME TELEVISION: FROM LUCY TO MURPHY 167

11 Content Analysis of
the Image of Women on
Television
Sally Steenland 179

12 The Debbie Allen Touch
Bishetta D. Merritt 191

13 Prime-Time Feminism:
Entertainment Television
and Women's Progress
Bonnie J. Dow 199

Part Five

TELEVISION NEWS: WOMEN ON THE FRONT LINE   219

14   WOMEN CORRESPONDENTS
     AND THE EVENING NEWS
     Joe S. Foote   229

15   JENNIFER SCHULZE: FROM
     WINDOW DRESSING ON THE SET
     TO WGN-TV NEWS DIRECTOR—
     A 15-YEAR ODYSSEY
     Susan J. Kaufman   239

16   WOMEN IN BROADCAST NEWS:
     MORE THAN WINDOW DRESSING
     ON THE SET, LESS THAN EQUAL
     WITH MEN
     Sue A. Lafky   251

Part Six

FILM: THE CELLULOID FEMALE   263

17   AFRICAN-AMERICAN WOMEN
     AND THE OSCARS
     Mary Frances Stubbs   273

18   THE NATIONAL FILM BOARD OF
     CANADA'S STUDIO D: FEMINIST
     FILMMAKERS
     Anita Taylor   293

19   NOT "KNOWING HER PLACE":
     THE NEGOTIATION OF
     CULTURAL IDENTITY IN FILMS—
     ASIAN/PACIFIC AMERICAN WOMEN
     Lynda Goldstein   309

Part Seven

ROCK MUSIC AND MUSIC TELEVISION 321

20   MUSICAL GENRE, "GIRL
CULTURE," AND THE FEMALE
PERFORMER: THE ROOT OF
VARIATION BETWEEN MUSIC
VIDEOS
John Tapper and David S. Black   331

21   "THE HERO TAKES A FALL":
THE BANGLES AND '80S POP
Shari Zeck   349

22   "YOU'RE NOT RID OF ME": RIOT
GRRRL BANDS AND NEW ROLES
AND OLD ROLES IN THE WORK
OF FEMALE PERFORMERS
Alan D. Stewart   359

CONCLUSION   373

BIBLIOGRAPHY   379

VIDEOGRAPHY   400

INDEX   403

preface

The intention behind *Women and Media: Content, Careers, and Criticism* is simple—to provide a solid foundation for courses about women and media and for those interested in women and media issues. It brings together, in a structured manner, fundamental research, ideas, and history.

STRUCTURE OF THE TEXT

Women and Media: Content, Careers, and Criticism is organized as its title suggests. The seven parts each highlight a different area of media: newspapers, women's magazines, advertising, prime-time television, television news, film, and rock music. Each part includes an introduction, a content analysis, a history of a woman or group within the media, and a critical essay about the media. The subjects vary, but the structure remains the same.

The introduction to each part details the history of the media form, the portrayal of women by that media form, and the employment of women within the same media form. For readers with a background in mass communication or journalism, this information may be familiar. For readers with little or no background in mass communication or journalism, this information provides a basic foundation.

At the end of each part introduction are lists of women in the media and of women's media organizations to encourage readers to look beyond the few discussed within the chapters. Due to space constraints, the lists are limited to twenty individual women and five women's media organizations. In order to take full advantage of students' research on specific women (either those in the list at the end of each part introduction, mentioned within the chapters, or assigned by the instructor), it is strongly suggested that each student present a five-minute oral report on her/his chosen woman or organization in the media, thus exposing the entire class to details of women's lives and organizations not covered within the scope of the text. In addition, each part introduction includes project ideas for use as assignments, discussion questions, outside activities, or in-class presentations. At the end of the book, an extensive bibliography and videography, organized by media form, is available for further reading and research.

Content   In each part, the introduction is followed by a content analysis or a meta-analysis that quantifies the role(s) of women in media. Some chapters' data are from one specific time period (television advertisements in the 1993 prime-time season) while other chapters focus on women's role(s) in the media over several years (on television or in newspapers), thus presenting patterns or trends over time.

Careers   Each content chapter is followed by a chapter containing a descriptive history of a specific woman or a specific women's media group that has affected the medium. Some chapters focus on historical figures (Ida Wells-Barnett), while others describe the lives of more contemporary women: some well known (Debbie Allen or Ruth Whitney) and others less known (Caroline Jones or Jennifer Schulze). Three chapters describe women-only groups, two of which produce media predominantly for women (*off our backs* and Studio D) and another which, at one point, produced media for mainstream audiences (The Bangles). In general, the intention of this section is to introduce readers to historical figures, discuss the work of contemporary women in the media and/or detail the work of media groups. These chapters are not meant to cover all media women and groups but to present a sampling of those who have contributed to the development of media.

Criticism   The final chapter in each part is a critical essay or thinkpiece. Once readers understand the history of a media form, understand data concerning the roles of women in media, and read about women who developed media, they are ready to deal with more thought-provoking issues. Each critical essay is distinct in style and format while challenging readers to think about women and media in new and different ways. For example, Linda Steiner in Chapter 7 questions exactly what is a "women's magazine." Is it *Cosmo, Ms.*, or *Good Housekeeping*? In Chapter 13, Bonnie Dow discusses the way in which prime-time television portrays "feminism," whether through portrayals in *Mary Tyler Moore* or *Murphy Brown*. Readers may not always agree with the author's point of view, but the critical essays are certain to bring forth an active discussion.

THE CONTRIBUTORS

The study of women and media is broad in scope but the number of scholars studying women and media issues is relatively small. During the 1994 National Speech Communication Association (SCA) convention, more than 700 panels were presented. Of those, seven dealt specifically with women and media; five others dealt with African Americans, Asian-Americans, and Latinos and the media (some were women); and one panel dealt with gay men and lesbians and the media. During the 1994 National Convention of the Association for Education in Journalism and Mass Communication (AEJMC) there were more than 250 panels. Out of those, seven dealt specifically with women and media, five others dealt with "minorities" and the media, and two panels dealt with gay men and lesbians and the media. The point is that there is not a lot of research currently conducted on women and the media. Therefore, I sought contributors from every avenue available to me. I called on scholars whose articles I used in my women and media class. I searched library databases to identify scholars with published work in a specific area. I contacted colleagues whom I knew were studying certain areas of women and media and asked for suggestions of others in the field, and I made endless calls to various women's media organizations. Some sections of the book filled up quickly with more than one potential contributor. In other sections, my network was stretched thin seeking out the right contributor. I sought diversity across professions, wanting to include academics, media writers, and activists; scholars from small universities and Big Ten schools; women and men. I also sought content that would reflect all women in the media: young women, older women, African-American women, Asian women, Latina women, lesbians, and the economically disadvantaged. In many cases I was successful. In others, I was not. In the long run, a network of scholars interested in women and media provided the foundation for this textbook. Many of these contributors have been studying women and the media for years; others have just begun.

ACKNOWLEDGMENTS

This book was made possible by the work of many. To all of the authors, I give thanks not only for their contributions to this book but, more importantly, for their continued work in this field. The success of this book is built on their efforts. My job as editor was merely to build a frame around the chapters and provide some structure for the very important material presented here.

In addition, feedback from outside reviewers strengthened and focused the book in many ways: I thank Bette Kauffman, Pennsylvania State University, and Marion T. Marzolf, University of Michigan, for their time and attention to detail. My thanks also go to the production staff at Wadsworth. My thanks to JoEllen, Tricia, and Sheryl, who supported my effort; to Florence and Leo, Susan and Stephanie for the many hours of time they gave me to work on the book; and to the students at George Mason University who helped in the formation of this book through their participation in my Women and Media class over the past ten years. Last, my heartfelt thanks to Dan, Bekah, Mary, Alex, Lucy, and Maggie—for giving up time together, sleep, and many walks so I could complete this book.

ABOUT THE EDITOR

Cynthia M. Lont, Associate Professor of Communication at George Mason University, earned her Ph.D. from the University of Iowa. Her research interests include women's music, subcultural theory, and women and media. Her latest publications include *Beyond Boundaries: Sex and Gender Diversity in Communication* with Sheryl Friedley, "A Feminist Critique of Mass Communication" in Bowen and Wyatt's *Transforming Visions: Feminist Critiques in Communication Studies*, and "Women's Music: No Longer a Private Party" in Garofalo's *Rockin' the Boat: Mass Music & Mass Movements*.

INTRODUCTION

WHEN YOU THINK OF WOMEN AND MEDIA, WHAT COMES TO MIND? Women as the subject of the media? Women as media producers? How women are portrayed in the media? In fact, the expression *women and media* is broad, encompassing all the above and more. In this book, we'll examine media content related to women, women as producers of media (directors, editors, and so on), the roles assigned to women in the media, and the media messages sent to women, sometimes subtly and sometimes not so subtly, as to what a woman should be.

There are many ways to study the content of the media and their relationship to women. Some researchers count the number of newspaper stories written by women versus written by men. Others add up the amount of time spent on issues relating to women in television newscasts. Some researchers study what approach is taken when reporting news items related to groups of women or a single woman. For example, are media reports about Hillary Rodham Clinton different from reports of past first ladies? Some may see her first-lady status and question whether she should be head of the National Health Plan, preferring her to work with charities or children's issues. Others may view her as a qualified individual whose talents should be used. In what ways are these media items affected by our conceptions of what a woman should do when her husband is elected president? Are our perceptions affected by past stories about Nancy Reagan's red dress and her purchase of new china for the White House, or Barbara Bush's charitable work? In what way(s) does Hillary Rodham Clinton break these stereotypes, and how do the media deal with her?

A second approach to women and media goes beyond content to the creators of media. This approach focuses on little-known women in the present or the past who produced media content. As early as the 1700s, women were part of the U.S. publishing business, reporting stories and working as printers. With the advent of new media forms, women created radio programs and later directed television programs. While many know the name Edward R. Murrow, few have heard of Mary Marvin Breckinridge, hired by Murrow to broadcast CBS' *World News Roundup* in 1957. Some know Ida Lupino as a film actress, but few realize she directed television shows such as the *Untouchables* in the 1960s. Focusing on historical women in media reclaims these noteworthy producers of media.

When most hear the term *women and media*, they think of the roles assigned to women in the media, especially television. Many content analyses count how many women are seen within a television program when compared with men and what role(s) each plays within the program. The conclusion of these analyses have prompted many a battle over the effect that negative or positive portrayals of both women and men have on the audience, especially on children. The battles are not just about the roles assigned to women; all groups, such as African Americans, Asian Americans, Latino Americans, and the elderly, are concerned with their group's media portrayal. Many believe the negative portrayal of a group, when observed repeatedly, will affect how viewers treat members of that group in real life. Although researchers set out to prove this theory, there is little consistent evidence. Nonetheless, many feel that negative portrayals must have some effect.

The last way people think about women and media relates to the sometimes subtle and sometimes not-so-subtle messages sent to women in the audience. If advertisements tell women that they need to use makeup, lose weight, splash on a certain perfume, or purchase certain clothes to be happy, how do these messages affect a woman's self-concept or self-esteem? In an era when food disorders, adolescent suicides, and divorce rates are on the upswing, do media messages contribute to these problems? Although the answers to these questions are not scientifically discoverable, they are nevertheless interesting issues for discussion.

The intention of *Women and Media: Content, Careers, and Criticism* is to ask questions by intertwining various perspectives throughout its chapters—the portrayal of women, women as media makers, and the critical analysis of women in the media—to give an integrative approach to the study of women and media.

Jessica Lee, *USA Today* senior Washington correspondent, this May was inducted into the Gridiron Club of Washington, D.C. She is the first female African-American member of the 108-year-old journalists' society. (*People*, 1993, p. 9)

one

NEWSPAPERS:

Front-Page News
Buried in the Women's Pages

HISTORY

Newspapers have been a significant means by which Americans obtain news since their early days when newspapers were merely newsletters. In essence, they were "short, periodic report[s] for business and government leaders to keep them informed of shipping and financial transactions and important political events" (Becker & Roberts, 1992, p. 105). One of the first newspapers, *Publick Occurrences Both Foreign and Domestick*, was published in Boston in 1690.

Most newspapers were "published with authority" (that is, they were approved by government officials), they were often run by postmasters (because postmasters could mail items without charge), and they focused on business and commerce (DeFleur, 1991, p. 76).

The *New York Weekly Journal* was among the few newspapers not published with authority. John Peter Zenger established the *Journal* in opposition to the "officially authorized" newspaper, the *New York Gazette*. Zenger's paper ran articles critical of New York Governor William Cosby and his policies. In 1734, Zenger was thrown into jail for "seditious libel." *Sedition* is promoting disaffection with government (DeFleur, 1991, p. 77). *Libel* is the act of printing a falsehood. While Zenger was in jail, his wife, Anna Zenger, continued publishing the newspaper. Zenger's lawyer successfully defended Zenger using truth as a defense, and though his case set no legal precedent, it strongly influenced Americans' feelings about the importance of freedom of the press (Becker & Roberts, 1992, p. 106).

Journalism in the United States changed a great deal between 1830 and the 1860s, as did the country itself. The Industrial Revolution and the increase in urban population opened up a new audience for newspapers. "The number of daily newspapers published in the United States grew from 65 in 1830 to more than 350 in 1861. Total circulation increased from 78,000 to 1,478,000" (Stovall, 1991, p. 123). In large part, it was the publication of the penny press that affected society and journalism. The penny press provided the news of the day at affordable prices for an urban middle class. With an eye on the new and larger audience, penny-press newspapers focused less on shipping reports and business activities and more on events of the day (crimes, sports, and foreign news). The number of readers grew, and so did the influence of newspapers in general.

The penny press was followed by a heavily sensationalized form of journalism known as *yellow journalism*. In the late 1800s, Joseph Pulitzer and William Randolph Hearst (competing publishers) printed stories about the unusual: stories with a slant to them, often focusing on violence, crime, scandal, gossip, stunts, or personal crusades. Their intention was to attract readers, increase sales, and beat out the competition.

In reaction to intense criticism of yellow journalism and tabloid journalism, newspapers turned to more objective reporting of the news in the 1930s. Reporters tried to be observers, reporting just "the facts." This is still the standard today, but most realize that although newspapers try to present a story that examines many sides of an issue, no journalist is or can be completely objective. Everyone brings a unique perspective to an event, and journalists are no different. Also, there are exceptions: features, foreign correspondence, news analysis, and sports, to name the most obvious.

Between 1910 and 1930, many small newspapers were consolidated into large newspaper chains. More and more newspapers were published under fewer and fewer owners. Around World War I, the American newspaper reached its peak in terms of number of readers and subscribers per household. Newspapers touched everyone. "During those years, more newspapers were sold per household in America than at any time before or after; ever since, newspaper reading has declined on a per capita basis" (DeFleur, 1991, p. 85). This decline occurred in large part because of competing media (radio, then television), both of which attracted audience's time and advertising dollars away from newspapers.

Today, many large newspapers such as the *New York Times, Washington Post, Chicago Tribune,* and *Los Angeles Times* market to general audiences, whereas other newspapers such as the *Village Voice* seek smaller, more narrow audiences. In fact, there is a newspaper to fit every kind of audience: minority papers, foreign-language papers, suburban weeklies, college newspapers, alternative press, throwaway shoppers, and supermarket tabloids.

Among the most recent trends in newspapers is the electronic one, offering delivery via FAX or computer-generated electronic mail (e-mail). Extended information is available for readers who want to know more about a story than what is printed in the newspapers. Since stories are edited because of limited space, much information is "left on the cutting-room floor." Readers who want to know more about certain stories may be able to access, via a computer modem, further information not included in the hard copy of the story. There are positive aspects to this new way of delivering news (elimination of paper waste, speed of news, specialized ads, and more in-depth information). However, there are also reasons why readers may be reluctant to change. These include people's reading habits, price of hardware to access information, and a limit on where one can read.

PORTRAYAL

By the 1890s, the "women's pages" were part of large newspapers. Editors realized that women readers would increase circulation. Topics in the women's pages included fashion, food, love, health, etiquette, homemaking, interior decoration, and family. These were subjects publishers believed were of interest to women and not offensive to advertisers. Although the late 1800s and early 1900s brought the women's suffrage movement to the forefront of the news, even after women won the right to vote, most news that related to women continued to be located in the women's pages of the newspaper.

With the advent of World War II, women replaced men at the workplace—and, to some extent, on the front page. For example, there were stories about women handling "men's jobs" and keeping the home fires burning for their soldiers. But the end of World War II saw newspaper stories and advertising encouraging women to return home. In fact, recipes and instruction in home care and child care made the homefront appealing to many women.

Articles that had to do with women or that were about a woman were returned to the women's pages. As feminists in the 1960s and 1970s pointed out, placing a story in the women's pages made a difference in who read it and how it was perceived. The "ghettoization" of women's pages diminished the worth of the story, indicating it was meant only for women and was of no concern to men (Epstein, 1978, p. 221). Stories about family life fell into the women's pages, signaling men that this subject didn't concern them.

The women's liberation movement of the 1960s and 1970s raised issues about the women's pages. Newspapers began to rethink their purpose. With increased attention on women's news and the portrayal of women, newspaper editors were pressured to pull the news for and about women out of the women's pages (out of the ghetto) and integrate it into the body of the newspaper. In 1969, the *Washington Post* pioneered this approach by moving stories about women into other parts of the newspaper and creating a new section called "Style."

In 1972, the Northern Virginia Chapter of the National Organization for Women (NOW) studied eight newspapers, including the *Washington Post,* and found:

- Hard news about women often appeared on the women's pages instead of in the appropriate news section.

- Of all the news photos, 30 percent were of women, 81 percent were of men (11 percent included both women and men, hence the total exceeding 100 percent).

- More photos of men appeared on front pages (90 percent), inside news section (86 percent), in business section (94 percent), in sports (95 percent), and in entertainment (78 percent). In the "Style" section, men and women were shown equally (50 percent).

By 1977, the editors of the *Washington Post* "Style" section believed they had eliminated the old stereotypes about "Style" being the "women's pages" when they discovered that 45 percent of the readers were male, compared to only 5 percent male readership when "Style" was labeled the "Women's Pages" (Marzolf, 1977, p. 214–215).

But in 1989, women continued to be underrepresented in major newspapers. In a study of front pages of ten major newspapers, women represented 27 percent of the bylines, 24 percent of the photographs, and 11 percent of the people quoted in stories (Unabridged Communications, 1990).

Focusing on newspaper sports sections, The Amateur Athletic Foundation of Los Angeles released a study in 1990 of four newspapers and their sports coverage. Stories on men's sports outnumbered women's sports 23 to 1. "Even when all men's basketball and football stories were eliminated from the total number of men's stories, men's stories still outnumbered women's stories by an 8.7 to 1 margin. . . . Photographs of male athletes outnumbered those of female athletes 13 to 1" (Newspaper Sports Staff Continues to Slight Women, 1991, p. 3).

In 1994, a new study showed that "women's presence in the news is growing and changing" (Unabridged Communications, 1994, p. 1). The annual *Women, Men and Media* report found the highest percentages for references and photos of females on the front page in six years. On average, women were 25 percent of the front-page references, 33 percent of front-page bylines, and 39 percent of front-page photos. Another important change is that women were portrayed, in most cases, as more than "appendages to men and/or as victims of some abuse" (Unabridged Communications, 1994, p. 1). The study suggests the media should receive credit for reflecting more of what the United States looks and sounds like in all its diversity,

> nonetheless, the study showed that 1994 was a year when American readers and viewers learned more about ice skaters Nancy Kerrigan and Tonya Harding after an assault than in all their years of competitive skating. Despite the increase in references to females on newspaper front pages, many of the nation's leading women in government received scant attention from the print and broadcast media. (1994, p. 3)

The 1990s find fewer women reading newspapers, although women continue to purchase more women's magazines and books. This trend alarms newspaper publishers because women also purchase more products and more expensive products such as new cars. To bring women back to newspapers, editors are re-creating "women's pages." Most editors are not returning to the 1950s-type of women's pages, however. They are looking to create sections targeting women that put a different spin on news stories. Reporters are assigned new beats such as "day care" or "women's health care." Other newspapers are moving away from a "just-the-facts" perspective and writing stories that "get to people." Nancy Woodhull, a full-time consultant to newspapers seeking to win back women readers, is among those who believe having more women in upper management may help. "A newspaper is put out from the gut of the editor. If the editor's gut is not in tune with the issues of some readers, they're not going to get in the paper" (*News, Inc.,* 1992, p. 28).

Mindi Keirman, former managing editor of the *St. Paul Pioneer Press* and a member of Knight-Ridder's Women Readers Task Force, believes women are reading newspapers less because the material is not of interest to them. "The problem is not with women . . . but with newspapers themselves. If editors really want to stem the decline in women's readership, they must look within—and be prepared to make some sweeping reforms" (*News, Inc.,* 1992, p. 22). The task force found similar responses from individual women it interviewed: "Women want more on education, social welfare,

safety and health, personal finance, parenting and family, and ethical issues; more profiles on successful women; and shorter and more useful stories throughout the paper" (*News, Inc.*, 1992, p. 28).

EMPLOYMENT

Women have always been part of the publishing business. In colonial times, widows, daughters, and
sisters published newspapers when their male relatives were unable to do so (because of death, illness, imprisonment, traveling, and so on). For example, in 1739, Elizabeth Timothy of Charleston,
South Carolina, became the first American woman newspaper editor of the *South Carolina Gazette*
when her husband died (Hedgepeth, 1991, p. 91). It was acceptable for women to run businesses
when men were unable, but if these women remarried or male relatives wanted the businesses,
women were expected to relinquish control.

During the American Revolution, Mary Katharine Goddard ran the *Maryland Journal* and printed
the first copy of the Declaration of Independence. Both she and her mother, Sarah Updike Goddard,
ran businesses owned by Mary Katharine's brother, William Goddard, while he traveled (Beasley &
Gibbons, 1993, p. 8). The business was considered a family enterprise, and women were allowed to
continue the enterprise for male relatives.

With the advent of urban daily newspapers, "grimy, noisy downtown offices and printing plants"
were "off limits for women, who were expected to conform to the prevailing ideal of 'the lady'"
(Beasley & Gibbons, 1993, p. 8). Yet some women continued to write in their homes and sell their
stories, poetry, and literary works to newspapers. Margaret Fuller, for example, was employed by
Horace Greeley for the *New York Tribune* in 1844. She is thought to be the first woman staff member
on a major newspaper, the first woman foreign correspondent, and the first woman war correspondent
(Beasley & Gibbons, 1993, p. 9).

Women reported the news from the nation's capital as early as 1870. At first, four women
reported from the congressional press gallery. By 1879, 20 women were admitted. The following year,
Congress enforced a rule limiting the number of reporters from each newspaper to enter the gallery.
Since most women were part-time reporters, this limit kept women out of the press gallery.

By the late 19th century, women in newspaper journalism increased. Stunt girls, like Elizabeth
Cochrane (best known as Nellie Bly), were joined by "sob sister" journalists (Marie Manning, known
as Beatrice Fairfax, and Elizabeth Meriwether Gilmer, known as Dorothy Dix), "who specialized in
gushy, tearful accounts of pathos and romance" (Beasley & Gibbons, 1993, p. 10).

By 1900, only 2,193 out of 30,098 journalists were women. Women's press clubs were organized alongside men's press clubs because men excluded women from theirs. These sex-segregated
press clubs continued until the late 1960s (Beasley & Gibbons, 1993, p. 10).

Investigative journalists such as Ida Tarbell joined the journalistic ranks of such women as
Ida Wells-Barnett, who used her writings to protest the lynching of African-American men.

Although our focus has been on mainstream newspapers, it should be noted that alternative
newspapers grew and continue to grow out of many political and cultural movements, such as the
suffrage movement and the abolitionist movement. For example, *The Revolution* (1868), co-edited by

Elizabeth Cady Stanton and published by Susan B. Anthony, supported "the equal rights efforts of women on all fronts" (Beasley & Gibbons, 1993, p. 81). The *Woman's Journal* (1869), edited by Lucy Stone, provided a more moderate stance toward suffrage.

African-American women's entrance into journalism was marked by Mary Ann Shadd Cary, publisher of a Black abolitionist newspaper in Canada (1850s). Black women, realizing the power of newspapers to move audiences, used the print medium to reach those who could not be reached face to face. "Unlike Black men, however, African-American women's protest extended beyond the horrors of slavery and discussions of race and education to the issues of sex, gender, and class" (Rhodes & Calloway-Thomas, 1993, p. 662).

In general, the alternative press offered a voice to women who would not have had a voice within mainstream newspapers, provided an opportunity for many women to work their craft (writing, photography, editing, and so on), and most often focused on women as the primary audience rather than as an afterthought.

In mainstream newspapers, "the 1930s marked the first major turn in the fortunes of women reporters . . . and the force behind that turn was Eleanor Roosevelt" (Mills, 1988, p. 36). The then–First Lady's activities ensured newspapers' interest, and she insisted that only women be allowed to her news conferences. This demand guaranteed that all major newspapers covering Washington would have to retain one woman to cover Mrs. Roosevelt's news conferences at a time (during the Great Depression) when women were the first to lose their jobs (Mills, 1988, p. 36).

During World War II, more opportunities were open to women. Women set type, ran presses, wrote copy, and became news editors. The Washington United Press Bureau staff jumped from 1 woman to 100 women. When peace returned, jobs were reshuffled, and many women lost their jobs to men or quit. Those who retained their jobs were considered less of an oddity than they had been before the war. Women had earned the right to be reporters, but only of some subjects. Not all beats were open to them, and there were still only a few women in newsrooms.

Throughout the 1950s, the increasing trend in the number of women reporters slowed. By 1960, women held approximately 37 percent of the jobs in book, magazine, and newspaper publishing (Marzolf, 1977, p. 74). These numbers increased little as women moved back into the home. Many explanations were given for keeping women out of news gathering: Women shouldn't be out at night; women shouldn't go certain places; and women will only get married, get pregnant, and leave their jobs with all that training going to waste.

In the late 1960s and early 1970s, however, there was a substantial increase in the number of women in newspaper newsrooms. The increase came from pressure by the women's liberation movement, an expanding economy, and the jobs available to women working in newspapers. Beasley and Gibbons state that "according to the 1970 U.S. Census, women in journalism were outnumbered 2:1 by men and confined to the lower ranks" (1993, p. 24). Yet feminist activism helped more women gain entry into places that were previously men-only (local press clubs, journalism schools, and national journalism organizations). By 1978, women comprised 53 percent of the student body in journalism programs (Peterson, 1979, p. 3).

The 1980s was not considered a decade of progress for women. A 1989 poll compared answers from women working in print and broadcasting with those from 1979. In general, the data showed women in the field of journalism were more convinced than ever that the women's liberation movement helped, but it was still more difficult for women than men to get ahead in the field (Media Women Poll, 1990, p. 13).

— The perception that women have a harder time gaining recognition and promotion is validated by a 1990 study that found women and men were on an unequal footing in terms of jobs and salary. Although women and men entering the job market in 1990 received similar salaries (women received 91 percent of what men earned), as each climbed the ladder to management, women fell behind. For example, 14 percent of all editors in 1990 were women, earning 61 percent of what men in the same position earned. During that same year, 7 percent of all general managers were women, earning 52 percent of what men in the same position earned. At the very top, women comprised 6 percent of all newspaper publishers, presidents, and vice presidents, earning 83 percent of what men in the same position earned (Women in Communications, Inc., 1990, p. 10).

Where are women the majority in the newspaper industry? They can be found most often in business (75 percent), advertising (60 percent), and administration (55 percent) (Women in Communications, Inc., 1990, p. 11). Women, therefore, continue to "support" the newspaper system in the lower paid, less visible, and less powerful positions within the newspaper work force.

In a 1993 panel discussion at the convention of the Asian American Journalists Association, Sharon Stewart, an editorial writer for the Long Beach *Press-Telegram,* asked, "Why aren't 50 percent of the expert sources we contact for stories or editorials women? . . . Why is it that when a woman becomes a publisher, executive editor or city editor, she is still a 'pioneer'?" (Stein, 1993, p. 50).

Why is it important to have women and minorities in all aspects of the newspaper business? Different people ask different questions, hear the same things with a different ear, and, as editors, determine different news as important enough to position on the front page. "Women and minorities offer the promise of more thorough coverage of ever-changing communities and, through that improved coverage, improved circulation and advertising prospects in a world in which many other media compete for the newspaper reader's time and money" (Mills, 1988, p. 334).

REFERENCES

Beasley, M. H., & Gibbons, S. J. (1993). *Taking their place: A documentary history of women and journalism.* Washington, DC: The American University Press in cooperation with the Women's Institute for Freedom of the Press.

Becker, S. L., & Roberts, C. L. (1992). *Discovering mass communication.* New York: HarperCollins Publishers.

DeFleur, D. (1991). *Understanding mass communication* (4th ed.). Boston, MA: Houghton Mifflin Company.

Epstein, C. F. (1978). The women's movement and the women's pages. In G. Tuchman, A. K. Daniels, and J. Benet (Eds.), *Hearth and home: Images of women in the mass media* (pp. 216–221). New York: Oxford University Press.

Hedgepeth, J. A. (1991). Women in media, 1700–present: Victims or equals? In W. D. Sloan (Ed.), *Perspectives on mass communication history* (pp. 91–103). Hillsdale, NJ: Lawrence Erlbaum Associates.

Marzolf, M. (1977). *Up from the footnote: A history of women journalists.* New York: Hastings House.

Media report to women. (1993, Spring). *People,* 9.

Media women poll: 1980s not a decade of progress. (1990, February 10). *Editor & Publisher,* 13, 51.

Mills, K. (1988). *A place in the news: From the women's pages to the front page.* New York: Dodd, Mead.

National Organization of Women (1972). Arlington, VA.

News, Inc. (1992, September). 4, 8, 22–28.

Newspaper sports staff continue to slight women in their coverage. (1991, March/April). *Media Report to Women,* 3.

Peterson, P. V. (1979, January). Enrollment surged again, increases 7 percent to 70,601. *Journalism Educator, 33,* 3.

Rhodes, J., & Calloway-Thomas, C. (1993). Journalism. In D. C. Hine, E. B. Brown, & R. Terborg-Penn (Eds.). *Black women in America: An historical encyclopedia* (pp. 662–666). Brooklyn, NY: Carlson Publishing.

Stein, M. L. (1993, September 11). Unwelcome gender politics: Female panelists say it still pervades newsrooms. *Editor & Publisher,* 13, 50.

Stovall, J. G. (1991). The penny press, 1833–1861: Product of great men or natural forces? In W. D. Sloan (Ed.), *Perspectives on mass communication history* (pp. 123–138). Hillsdale, NJ: Lawrence Erlbaum Associates.

Unabridged Communications. (1990). *Women, men & media:* Alexandria, VA: M. J. Bridge.

Unabridged Communications. (1994). Arriving on the scene: Women's growing presence in the news. Alexandria, VA: M. J. Bridge.

Women in Communications, Inc. (1990). *Women, men & media: A women in communications resource kit.* Arlington, VA.

PROJECT IDEAS

1　Contact a local newspaperwoman who works as a reporter or in a management position at a newspaper. Interview her or invite her to speak to your class. What is her background? What paths did she take to obtain her current position?

2　Newspaper consultants, helping large newspapers regain women readers, suggest that news stories are *not* of interest to women. In what ways might you redesign a newspaper to regain women readers?

3　Using Chapter 1 as a guide, evaluate your local newspaper. Whose stories are on the front page? How many photographs of females and males are there on the front page? How many times are women experts versus men experts cited within the stories on the front page? How might the absence of women on the front page be connected to the loss of women newspaper readers?

4　Select a newspaper (local, regional, or national) with content that relates directly to women and their interests. Examples are *off our backs, Media Report to Women, National NOW Times,* or *Womanews*. How do these newspapers differ from the general circulation newspapers such as the *New York Times*? Look at their content, layout, front-page stories, photographs, and advertisers.

NAMES

The following list identifies some of the women who have been or are currently part of the newspaper industry. Women who were previously mentioned in this introduction are not duplicated in this list.

Christine Brennan—First woman sportswriter for the *Miami Herald* (1981). First female reporter assigned to cover the Washington Redskins (1985).

Marge Henderson Buell (Margé)—Cartoonist and creator of "Little Lulu" (mid-1930s).

Mary Ann Shadd Cary—Believed to be the first Black woman newspaper publisher and editor in North America (1850s).

Charlotte Curtis—First woman to have her name on the *New York Times* masthead (1974).

Edwina Dumm—Believed to be the first female editorial cartoonist (1915).

Katherine Fanning—Former editor of the *Christian Science Monitor* and the first woman to serve as president of the American Society of Newspaper Editors (1987).

Doris Fleeson—First female political columnist and known as one of the toughest journalists in Washington, DC (1940s–early 1960s).

Mary Garber—One of the first woman sports editors (1940s).

Katharine Graham—Publisher of the *Washington Post* (1965–1979).

Katherine Beebe Pinkham Harris—Reporter for Associated Press (1932–1959).

Marguerite Higgins—Won a Pulitzer prize (1951) for her reporting of the Korean War.

Jennie June (Jane Cunningham Croly)—Women's page writer (1860s) who wrote on fashion, drama, straight news, and advice for over 40 years. She also began the Women's Press Club of New York (1889).

Minna Lewinson—First woman hired by the *Wall Street Journal* (1918).

Anne O'Hare McCormick—First woman to win a Pulitzer prize for foreign commentary reporting (1937).

Judith Martin—*Washington Post* reporter (1960–1978) and columnist, "Miss Manners" (1978–present).

Dale Messick (Dalia Messick)—Syndicated cartoonist. Creator of "Brenda Starr" (1940).

Lucy Morgan—First woman to win a Pulitzer prize in the investigative reporting category (1985).

Jane Swisshelm—Editor of the *Pittsburgh Saturday Visiter*, an abolitionist newspaper. First woman to sit in the Senate Press Gallery (1850).

Helen Thomas—United Press International reporter and one of the first women to gain the White House as her assignment (1960).

Dorothy Thompson—Prominent foreign-affairs journalist of the 1930s.

ORGANIZATIONS

Association for Women in Sports Media
P.O. Box 355
Alameda, CA 94501

JAWS (Journalism and Women Symposium)
P.O. Box 3100
Estes Park, CO 80517

National Federation of Press Women
Box 99
Blue Springs, MO 64015

Women In Communications, Inc.
3713 Columbia Pike
Suite 310
Arlington, VA 22204

Women's Institute for Freedom of the Press
3306 Ross Place, N.W.
Washington, DC 20008

These lists were, in part, derived from Mills (1988), *A place in the news: From the women's pages to the front page,* New York: Dodd, Mead, and Company, and Beasley & Gibbons (1993), *Taking their place: A documentary history of women and journalism.* Washington, DC: The American University Press in cooperation with the Women's Institute for Freedom of the Press.

When females are described by their physical appearance, their clothes and hairstyles, and their marital and parental status whereas males are described by their accomplishments and status, what is the message sent?

1

Content

WHAT'S NEWS?

M. JUNIOR BRIDGE

M. Junior Bridge is President of Unabridged Communications, a research and education company located in Alexandria, Virginia, focusing on cultural behavior and attitudes. Bridge has published annual reports on societal roles assigned to women and men as reflected by print and broadcast media since 1989.

Traditionally, females have not been considered newsworthy. Even today, despite the many legal and cultural strides forward made by women, media coverage and media images of females are woefully inadequate and often misleading.

When the front page of a newspaper contains not one reference to a female, not one female byline, and not one photo of a female, what is the message sent about females? When major stories about war, the economy, social issues, or other topics of great import appear day after day devoid of female references and images, what is the message sent about females?

When females are described primarily by their physical appearance, their clothes and hairstyles, and their marital and parental status whereas males are described by their accomplishments and status, what is the message sent?

The message sent is a misleading, erroneous one: Females are saying and doing nothing of importance, nothing worth reporting. Their intellect, their skills, their perspective, their ideas, their accomplishments are devalued by underrepresentation and invisibility in the news.

WOMEN'S PLACE IN THE NEWS

Beginning in 1989, newspaper coverage of and by women was tracked in an annual survey conducted by the Women, Men and Media Project (WMM). In 1991, a television news component was added to the survey.

Coverage, on average, was found to be extraordinarily poor. Females were significantly underrepresented in newsrooms and in news stories across the country. Yet, women were and remain the majority of the country's population.

WMM was founded by Betty Friedan, noted feminist, author, and lecturer, and Nancy Woodhull, a founder of *USA Today*. Currently, Woodhull is president of her own media consulting firm, Nancy Woodhull and Associates, Inc.

The project is housed at the University of Southern California and New York University. Funding for WMM is provided primarily by The Freedom Forum, an international organization dedicated to free press, free speech, and free spirit for people throughout the world. WMM's primary goal is to examine and document diversity in news coverage.

Initially, the month-long news survey examined the front pages of ten major-market, general-interest newspapers, drawn from geographically diverse areas. It has since been expanded to include more pages—the first local page and the opinion-editorial (op-ed) or equivalent page—and ten smaller-market, general-interest papers, also geographically dispersed. The circulation of the smaller-market papers ranged from 20,000 to 50,000. The survey also contains a network television nightly news component, but this chapter will focus on the newspaper content audits.

The major newspapers reviewed included the *Atlanta Constitution, Chicago Tribune, Houston Chronicle, Los Angeles Times, Miami Herald, New York Times, Seattle Times, St. Louis Post-Dispatch, USA Today,* and *Washington Post.*

The smaller-market papers examined were the *Albuquerque Journal* (New Mexico), *Beacon-News* (Aurora, Illinois), *Courier* (Findlay, Ohio), *Daily Camera* (Boulder, Colorado), *Enid News and Eagle* (Oklahoma), *Joplin Globe* (Missouri), *News-Times* (Danbury, Connecticut), *Pine Bluff Commercial* (Arkansas), *Sun-Journal* (Lewiston, Maine), and *Tuscaloosa News* (Alabama).

WHOSE NEWS?

The January 1993 study (released in April 1993) showed that men were referred to or solicited for comment 85 percent of the time in front-page news stories. Men wrote 66 percent of the front-page stories and appeared in 73 percent of the front-page photos (see Figure 1.1).

References to and comments from female leaders and experts in a variety of fields were conspicuously low or missing altogether from many major stories and commentaries. Unless the news was negative, stories about female leaders were largely relegated to lesser inside news pages, if they were carried at all.

On the opinion pages, men wrote 74 percent of the commentaries. On the first pages of the local sections, men were solicited for comment or referred to 77 percent of the time. They wrote 59 percent of the articles. One or more males appeared in 71 percent of the photos on these pages.

Despite the discouragingly low percentages of female bylines, references, and appearances in photos, these numbers were the highest recorded on the front pages in five years. Steady increases in the percentages—some small, some substantial—were recorded for many of the individual news outlets studied as well.

In 1989, the percentage of female references on the front pages of the ten newspapers examined was 11 percent. By 1993, the number had gradually increased to 15 percent in the 20 papers studied. Female bylines were 27 percent of the total in 1989, rising to 34 percent in 1993. The percentage of front-page photos containing one or more females rose from 24 percent in 1989 to 34 percent in 1993.

Part of this increase is due to the inclusion of smaller-market papers, which, in general, hire more female reporters and cover women better than the larger-market papers. One consistent finding, however, throughout the five years this survey was conducted is that just because a female byline appears on a news story doesn't mean that there will be more female references in the copy or in the accompanying photos.

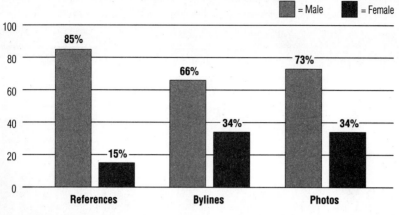

Newspapers: Front Page Averages*

■ = Male ■ = Female

*Based on study of 10 major and 10 smaller-market, general-interest newspapers from across the United States

Figure 1.1

The Face of the News, January 1993

SOURCE: Unabridged Communications for Women, Men and Media Project, 1993.

THE GOOD NEWS AND THE BAD NEWS

To the credit of the news industry, it is clear from these surveys that efforts—some better than others—are being made to expand gender diversity in both coverage and reporting. More stories are appearing in the news overall about women and their accomplishments; more that contain commentary from female sources; and more females are reporting the news.

Examples of some of the positive changes include the following: In the 1993 WMM survey, the highest number of op-eds written by women was 40 percent in the *Atlanta Constitution*. This was an increase of 20 percent over the paper's percentage in 1991, when bylines on the op-ed pages were first counted. The *Enid News and Eagle* had a surprisingly large number of female bylines on its front pages in 1993: 92 percent.

References to females on the front pages of the *New York Times* rose from a low of 5 percent in 1989 to 13 percent in 1993. When questioned by a reporter from another major newspaper about the lack of females on these pages, *Times* executive editor Max Frankel said, "If you are covering local teas," more women would appear on the front page.

In this one testy comment, Frankel belittled and insulted the wisdom, talents, and contributions of women, ranging from unpaid mothers to highly salaried Pulitzer prize-winning scientists, from local politicians to world leaders. Yet, the attitude expressed by Frankel is not uncommon in the news world and in society in general.

THE MEDIA MIRROR

In a free society such as the United States, the way the media cover the news provides an excellent cultural looking glass. The attitudes, values, biases, strengths, and weaknesses of the society covered by the media are reflected in the media mirror. Simultaneously, the media, by the way they report the news and by the way they define what is newsworthy, influence the society they cover.

Content audits are useful for documenting those reflections and potential influences. The documentation can then serve a number of purposes, such as stimulating dialogue on the adequacy and accuracy of news reporting or the impact of news reporting on individuals or certain groups within society.

The content audit methodology developed for the WMM surveys to track gender diversity in print media news reporting relied on a two-pronged approach. The first employed a simple quantitative technique: counting. Female and male names in headlines, copy, and captions were counted, as were female and male bylines and the number of times one or more females and males appeared in photos. These findings have already been discussed.

The second prong involved a more detailed look at the context of the news such as the descriptors, the topics, the placement of stories, the commentary, the use of pronouns instead of proper names on successive references, the emphasis, who is covered (where and how) and who isn't. Some examples of these findings follow.

Pronouns and Prefixes

When the WMM survey first began, survey monitors discovered that when a female was referenced in a news article, her name was seldom repeated. Instead, if referenced again, pronouns were used instead of the female's name. For males, it was a different story. When males were mentioned in news copy, their names were repeated throughout the story.

To illustrate, a story with a male reference would read something like this: John Doe saved the life of little Johnny and Mary Smith today when their boat overturned in the river. Doe said . . . Doe did . . . Doe received . . . Doe helped . . .

The same story with a female reference, if it appeared at all, would have more likely been written as follows: Mary Smith saved the lives of two children today. She said . . . She did . . . Her actions . . . She helped . . .

The problem appeared to be one of discomfort and confusion about how to refer to a female. Society, and the media, were used to encouraging men to take risks and great strides, were used to robust discussions about men and their exploits, and were used to referring boldly to men solely by their last names.

Females, on the other hand, were expected to be more demure and quiet, to be discussed in more "hushed" and "reverent" tones, and to be referred to by a title that indicated their marital status, as though their marital status was of primary importance to them and to society.

One glaring example of this was found in the *Joplin Globe* (Missouri) in the 1991 WMM survey. In succeeding references to Kansas Governor Joan Finney, she was referred to as "Mrs. Finney," never "Governor Finney" or just "Finney," as a male in the same position would have been. The same was true for other females, regardless of their accomplishments or positions.

State Representative Gracia Backer was consistently referred to in the *Globe* as "Mrs. Backer." Again, seemingly to temper accomplishment by emphasizing gender in a descriptor, the *Globe* referred to another woman as "Erike Braun, *manageress* of City Jeans." (Emphasis added.)

In 1989, when not relying on pronouns, most newspapers insisted on using a prefix that indicated marital status before a woman's name in subsequent references. It was "Mrs." or "Miss" Jones. Men were most often just referred to by their last names, and occasionally by the marital neutral "Mr." In a few rare instances, reporters were allowed to use the female equivalent of "Mr." and refer to a woman as "Ms."

By the time of the 1993 study, most of the newspapers studied had dropped the prefixes and were simply using last names by themselves. At the same time, it was noted that as the prefixes were dropped, women's names, rather than pronouns, were being used more in subsequent references.

Descriptors

The emphasis on female marital status did not end here, however. It is still common to find adult females described first, if not entirely, by their marital and parental status and their looks. One of the most severe examples of avoidance of emphasis on female accomplishment was found in a story carried in the *Washington Post* (August 26, 1992) about Lynn Yeakel.

Yeakel, a political unknown, had challenged one of the most powerful men in Congress, Republican Arlen Specter. Specter was not only powerful, but he was also the leading political fundraiser. Rather than focusing on her credentials, opinions, and capabilities, the article talked mostly about the men in Yeakel's life, as though by defining them, she was defined.

She was referred to as a "feisty and feminine 50-year-old with the unmistakable Dorothy Hamill wedge of gray hair and the dazzling silk suit of lime, tangerine and blue . . . a congressman's daughter . . . an unlikely standard-bearer . . .

[with] a wardrobe befitting a First Lady . . . married to a once-Republican stockbroker . . . a former full-time mother. . . ."

It wasn't until the last part of the lengthy feature piece that the things that really mattered about her candidacy—her ability, her opinions, her commitment—were mentioned.

On the following day, a feature article about Specter appeared in the *Post*. It started out by describing him as the former "crime-busting district attorney and mayoral hopeful." He was not defined by the women in his life, and there was not one word in the entire article about his hair color or his wardrobe.

Illinois's Carol Moseley-Braun, the first African-American woman to be elected to a U.S. Senate seat, was subjected to similar media treatment. In *The New York Times* (July 29, 1992), Moseley-Braun and her male opponent were described thusly:

> The two cut strikingly different images on the campaign trail: she is commanding and ebullient, a den mother with a cheerleader's smile; he, by comparison, is all business, like the corporate lawyer he is. . . .

It wasn't until the 20th paragraph that the writer mentioned that Moseley-Braun is not only a lawyer, but also a former federal prosecutor and state representative.

During her Senate campaign, Moseley-Braun's home state newspaper, the *Chicago Tribune* (August 30, 1992), described her as "a stunningly successful newcomer to state . . . politics." She had served ten years in the state legislature; a newcomer to state politics she was not.

Women's Issues—Men's Voices

When the story broke in 1992 about the disastrous side effects of silicone gel breast implants, the WMM survey found that most of the people quoted in these stories were males. When females were referenced or quoted, they were most often victims suffering the ills of the implants.

This was consistent with WMM survey findings from the beginning. Men were portrayed most often as the "movers and shakers"; women as appendages (Mary, the wife of . . . , Sue, the daughter of . . .) or victims of crime and other abuses.

The men quoted in the breast-implant stories were described as CEOs, chief scientists, plastic surgeons, university professors, program directors, or technical directors. Descriptors of the few professional females quoted or referenced were primarily limited to "spokeswoman."

A curious descriptor was applied to Nancy Dubler by the *Washington Post* (February 21, 1992). Dubler was described as a "researcher." In fact, at that time, Dubler was the director of the division of legal and ethical issues on health care, department of epidemiology and social medicine at the Montefiore Medical Center in New York.

She was also a voting member of the nine-person Food and Drug Administration panel that was charged with holding hearings, listening to evidence presented on the safety of the breast implants, and advising the agency on the fate of the product.

Also worth noting was that the panel was chaired by a woman, Dr. Elizabeth Connell, and five of its voting members were female. References to and quotes from Connell and her prestigious female colleagues were rare in the articles reviewed during the WMM survey. In only one article in the *New York Times* (February 21, 1992) were the names and affiliations of the panelists given.

More often, the articles contained all male quotes or references, such as the story in the *Seattle Times* (February 11, 1992) titled "Dow files show years of complaints on implants." This article contained 17 references to men, none to women.

Comments from female professionals—plastic surgeons, physicians, academicians, health experts, and government officials, to name a few—were missing in almost all the articles on the breast implants.

Missing in Action

During the 1991 WMM survey, stories about the Gulf War dominated the front and inside pages of the nation's newspapers. War affects every member of society—men, women, children. Yet at the height of the Gulf crisis, with more American women than ever participating in a violent conflict and with women constituting more than half of the country's population, they were largely ignored or treated lightly by the media.

The vast majority of the war stories were about men, their jobs, their weaponry, their opinions. When stories about female soldiers appeared, which was rare, they most often centered on the women's parental status. Photos of females during the reporting period were most frequently of women at home showing concern for or grieving over loved ones who were involved in the Middle East conflict. There were almost no pictures of women with their weapons or performing their military duties or making policy decisions.

Another curious finding was the editorial and news-copy fervor over the impact on families of women going to war. Although most such articles were critical of mothers going to war and expressed extreme concern about the impact on children, there was not one article or editorial on the impact of a father leaving his children to go to war.

Yet another finding was that female reporters tended to be assigned to write local or home stories. In general, males covered the war. Again, consistent with WMM survey findings, a female byline on a story did not mean the story would contain a different perspective or more references to and photos of females.

Newsworthiness

As previously mentioned, unless the stories are negative, such as the Zoe Baird saga (the Clinton administration's failed nominee for U.S. attorney general), stories about females and their accomplishments are usually carried on inside pages and treated as features, if they are carried at all. Stories about successful businesswomen are more likely to be found in lifestyle-type sections rather than business sections where profiles of men and their business accomplishments are located.

Issues of particular concern to women, such as abortion and breast cancer research, usually contain more references to males than females. Sports sections are dominated by male sports stories and dramatic shots of male athletes—almost to the exclusion of female athletic skills and accomplishments.

During the 1992 WMM survey, there was extensive coverage of the Olympics. Female athletes from the United States performed outstandingly, substantially outshining the men. Of the 11 medal winners, 9 were female. It was, according to the *Albuquerque Journal* (February 24, 1992) "the best U.S. winter performance on foreign soil since its 11-medal showing in Oslo in 1952."

The coverage, however, was predominantly on males. It was more common to find a story about a male who lost than a female who won. During that period, the *Seattle Times* (February 24, 1992) ran a story titled "Showing their medal: Why did U.S. women outshine the men?"

Automotive sections are written almost exclusively by men for men. However, even the automobile industry admits that most car-buying decisions in this country are made directly or are heavily influenced by females.

Photographs containing females usually fall into one of three categories: group shots, most often with family; emotional shots, such as a grieving widow; or "cheesecake" shots, with women as sex objects. Photographs of males, on the other hand, are mostly dramatic portraits and action shots, and they are predominantly located on key news pages.

Whether the story is about war, social conflict, the economy, science, agriculture, the environment, or any other issues, female voices and strong images are frequently absent or minimal. Women play major roles in all these arenas, and they are certainly affected by actions taken on such subjects. Women constitute 45 percent of the paid labor force, and that number is growing. Women make most of the consumer decisions. There are more female voters than male. Women own most of the agricultural land in this country. By 1993, women-owned small businesses employed more people than the Fortune 500 companies combined. Females are the majority of the U.S. population. Why, then, is the face of the news male?

THE MEDIA'S MESSAGE

By minimizing or ignoring altogether the voices and strong images of females, the message sent by the media is that the contributions, talents, opinions, and activities of females are not of value. Is this true? Of course not, but the way the media report the news denigrates a major segment of the population.

The impact of this fleeting attention and outright invisibility of females in the news is lowered self-esteem in females. It is common knowledge that low self-esteem affects performance. Does the media deliberately degrade females? In general, no. However, the inadvertent effect of some of its traditional practices is degrading.

As mentioned earlier in this chapter, there are efforts underway by the newspaper industry to hire and promote more female journalists and to improve coverage of females. Content audits, such as the WMM studies, are being used both by analysts within and outside the industry to help guide news managers in these efforts. In addition, you can conduct your own study to determine how well you think newspapers are doing in repairing past inequities.

DO-IT-YOURSELF NEWSPAPER STUDY

The following explains the methods used to do the WMM annual surveys on gender diversity in newspapers. The methodology was developed by Unabridged Communications, a research and education firm located in Alexandria, Virginia. Simple techniques are used so as to encourage others to conduct similar studies.

Study Period

Select a one-month period during which to conduct your survey and make arrangements to get the final edition of each newspaper you decide to monitor for every day during that time.

Basic Materials Needed

You will need four different-colored highlighters, tally sheets (see Figure 1.2), pencils, pocket calculator, and newspapers to be monitored. Your tally sheets should show the daily counts for male and female references; male and female bylines; total number of times one or more males appear in photos per page, and the total number of times one or more females appear in photos. At the bottom of your tally sheet, there should be space to total the daily counts and note the month's percentages for each category.

PAPER: _____ **MONTH/YR:** _____

Day	REFERENCES					BYLINES					PHOTOS			
	M	F	Total	%F		M	F	Total	%F		M	F	Total	%F
1														
2														
3														
4														
5														
6														
7														
8														
9														
10														
11														
12														
13														
14														
15														
16														
17														
18														
19														
20														
21														
22														
23														
24														
25														
26														
27														
28														
29														
30														
31														
Totals														

Figure 1.2
Media Study

What to Monitor

Three select pages are included in the WMM news surveys: the front page, the first page of the metropolitan section, and the op-ed or equivalent page. You must determine which page or pages are relevant to your study, then pull those from each of the newspapers you are monitoring.

Whatever page or pages you choose (with the exception of editorial or op-ed pages), you will be examining three items quantitatively, as mentioned previously. In the WMM surveys, only the gender breakdown of bylines is tabulated for the op-ed pages.

Methodology: References

1. Use one color of highlighter for male names, another color for female names. Whichever colors are chosen, be sure all monitors use the same designated colors for the specified category being counted.

2. Mark proper names of human beings only (*no* pronouns) in story copy, headlines, or photo captions (do not mark ads or jumps). For example, do not count "Walt Whitman" Freeway; do count "Clinton" administration. Do not count "God," "Devil," or proper names of cartoon characters, fictional characters in plays, books, and the like. Remember to mark repeated use of the same proper human name.

3. Count your totals and mark them at the bottom of the news page (so they can be double-checked or spot-checked at a later time) and on your tally sheet.

4. At the end of the study period, the totals should be computed and the percentage of times female names appear figured. For example, if male names total 523 and female names total 467, female names represent 47 percent of the total references (523 plus 467 = 990; 467 divided by 990 = 0.4717 or 47%).

Methodology: Bylines

1. Use one color highlighter for male names, another color for female names (obviously, these should be different colors than the ones used for the references).

2. Only mark story bylines (whether at the beginning or end of a story), not photo credits.

3. Count the totals and mark them at the bottom of the news page and on your tally sheet.

4. At the end of the study period, as you did for references, compute the totals and the percentage of times female bylines appear. For example, if there are 45 male bylines total and 35 female bylines, female bylines are 44 percent of the total bylines (45 plus 35 = 80; 35 divided by 80 = 0.4375 or 44%).

Methodology: Photos

Count all photos and record total at bottom of news page and on tally sheet, *in addition to* counting the number of photos in which one or more males and one or more females appear. For example, there might be four photos on a page. One woman appears in one picture, two women appear in another, three men and one woman appear in the third. The fourth photo is of an airplane.

Therefore, the count for the day would be a total of four pictures, with females in three and males in one. If this were the total count for the study period, then the percentages would be as follows: females appear in 75 percent (three out of four) of the pictures, and males appear in 25 percent (one out of four).

This is the only category where the total number in the male column and the total for females will *not* necessarily equal the total number of pictures, as with the other two categories tabulated. This is because one photo containing both a male and a female (or multiples thereof) will be counted twice, once for males and once for females.

Context

Beyond these simple counts and for further amplification, examine the context of articles and commentaries. Here are some sample questions to help you start:

- How are females described—by their marital/parental status, by their appearance, by their occupation? How are males described?

- In what kinds of stories are females quoted or referenced or left out? In what kinds of stories are males quoted or referenced or left out?

- How are females portrayed in photographs? Are males portrayed differently? If so, is there a valid reason for the differences?

- Are proper names or pronouns used for repeated references to a female in the same proportion as are references to males?

- Are there pages with no female references, bylines, or photos? Are there pages with only female or predominantly female references, bylines, and photos?

- Are issues of special concern to women, such as reproductive rights or breast cancer, being covered? If not, why not? If covered, is it adequate coverage? Where is such coverage—in news briefs, in major articles; in editorials or commentaries; in cartoons? In what sections of the newspapers are they covered?

- In news of general interest, such as the economy, the job market, war, day care, and education, are women's viewpoints, experience, and expertise included? Is female commentary being sought out as frequently as male commentary? Are males excluded in the coverage of certain topics, such as teenage pregnancy and child care? If so, why?

- Are the accomplishments of females covered in the news? If so, how and where? How does this coverage compare to coverage of the accomplishments of males?

- Are female reporters assigned to all topic areas? If not, what are they reporting on, and why are they limited to certain subjects? What are the subjects?

As you answer these questions and others, be sure to record examples found in news stories.

The Results and Their Utility

Your findings will provide a good indication of whether or not the newspaper(s) you are monitoring are doing a fair job in their news coverage of and by females. Also, your results can be compared to the national results compiled in such studies as the WMM surveys to determine similarities and differences.

Content audits give you concrete information to use in discussions with news managers and to pursue changes where appropriate. Additionally, your findings will be useful in stimulating public and academic dialogue on gender diversity issues in your community as well as in the media.

News reporting is in a state of flux, as is the surrounding culture. Content audits, no matter what the focus (gender diversity, multiculturalism, violence, or political coverage, for example), help the news media and their respective audiences to clarify what is covered and what is not, and the impact.

The news industry—whether it is print or broadcast or some other form—cannot report on all people and their issues all the time. It can, however, do a better overall job in reporting the news as if all people mattered.

2

ACTIVISM THROUGH JOURNALISM:

The Story of Ida B. Wells-Barnett

JANE RHODES

Jane Rhodes is an Assistant Professor in the School of Journalism at Indiana University, where she teaches a course on *Race, Gender and the Mass Media,* as well as media and society, media history, and news reporting. She earned her bachelor's and master's degrees from Syracuse University, and a doctorate from the University of North Carolina at Chapel Hill. Rhodes's previous work includes "Falling Between the Cracks: Studying Women of Color in Mass Communication" in Creedon's *Women in Mass Communication: Challenging Gender Values* and "Mary Ann Shadd Cary and the Legacy of African-American Women Journalists" in Rakow's *Women Making Meaning: New Feminist Directions in Communication.* Rhodes's upcoming book on Mary Ann Shadd Cary, the first African-American woman to publish a newspaper, is forthcoming from Indiana University Press.

Ida B. Wells-Barnett used her skills as a journalist to uncover the horrors of lynching and racial violence.

Arican-American women have had a long and distinguished history as journalists in the United States in the face of struggles against racial and gender discrimination. Throughout the years before the Civil War, African-American women served as writers, editors, and columnists for the approximately 40 African-American newspapers that were sporadically published. Many of these women were in the forefront of the movement to abolish slavery, and were well-known literary and political figures. But it was not until Reconstruction that African-American women journalists were recognized for their accomplishments and influence in the Black press. The most famous of these women was Ida Bell Wells-Barnett.

The practice of journalism during this period was very different from today's professional definitions. The emphasis was not on some vague notion of objectivity, but on using the press to disseminate distinct ideas and perspectives to a large audience. For African Americans, women, and other groups who were generally ignored by the press, becoming a journalist was a way to get a point of view into print, and to mobilize individuals and communities to action. Ida Wells-Barnett combined her writing with political and social leadership to transform key social issues of the late 19th and early 20th centuries.

EARLY YEARS IN THE SOUTH

Ida Bell Wells was born on July 16, 1862, in Holly Springs, Mississippi, the oldest of six children. Her parents, Jim Wells and Lizzie Warrenton, had met and married while they were slaves. Their first daughter was born as the War Between the States gained momentum. After emancipation, Ida's father supported the family as a carpenter and became active in Reconstruction politics. Her parents considered education for their children to be an important tool for their improvement and survival. As a child, Ida witnessed her parent's determination to improve their lives within the confines of rural, segregated Mississippi, and she was taught that knowledge was essential for poor, disenfranchised African Americans.[1]

Ida Wells attended Shaw University in Holly Springs, a school established to educate freedmen after the Civil War. Here she acquired the basic education and skills that would one day transform her into an international figure. Tragedy struck the Wells family in 1878, however, and forced Ida to rely on the strength of her parents' teachings. That year, when she was just 16, Ida's parents and her youngest brother died in a yellow-fever epidemic, and she was thrust into the role of caretaker for the rest of her family. She dressed herself to appear older, passed the local teaching examination, and was hired at a school six miles from her home. For the next two years, Ida Wells was her family's sole supporter, and she demonstrated the grit and determination that would mark her later career as a journalist and activist. The young schoolteacher rode a mule to the schoolhouse where she taught during the week and came home on the weekends to tend to her siblings. When an aunt living in Memphis, Tennessee, offered to care for her two youngest sisters, Ida moved to the big city, leaving her two brothers working on a farm.

Memphis was a thriving, segregated, southern city, considered to be the economic and cultural center of the mid-South. Her new home offered Ida Wells broader opportunities for employment and education than rural Mississippi. She enrolled in the LeMoyne Institute and earned the certification necessary to teach in the Memphis public schools, and she continued her education with summer courses at Fisk University, one of the nation's first colleges for African Americans. She attended plays and concerts and took elocution lessons for self-improvement. Black teachers were poorly paid, and Ida struggled to send money to her brothers, help her aunt, and pay her own bills. Yet teachers were held in high esteem as learned members of the Black community, and Ida B. Wells became part of this small group. She joined a lyceum—or reading group—of public schoolteachers, which published a small newsletter of current events, called the *Evening Star*. Her career in journalism began when she was asked to edit the little newspaper for the group.

FIGHTING BACK WITH HER PEN

The 1880s—a period aptly called Redemption by historians—was a frightening era in which many Whites sought to reaffirm their social and political supremacy in the South. Many of the successes of Reconstruction, such as the election of Black public officials and Black access to public services, were gradually eroded

---

1. Biographical information was obtained from sources listed at the end of this chapter.

by intimidation, violence, and the passage of Jim Crow laws. In 1884, Ida Wells witnessed this process firsthand when a railroad conductor insisted that she move from the first-class ladies' coach to the segregated smoking car of a train owned by the Chesapeake and Ohio Railroad. Wells was outraged. She had frequently ridden in the ladies' car when she traveled between Memphis and Woodstock, Tennessee, and she refused to leave her seat. When the conductor tried to force her to move, Wells fought back. It took three men to drive her off the train while White onlookers cheered. An angry Wells brought suit against the railroad company, charging that her civil rights had been violated. To the surprise of many Blacks and Whites, Wells won the case and $500 in damages, instantly making her a well-known figure across the country.

The editor of a small Baptist weekly, the *Living Way*, asked Wells to write an article about her successful suit, based in part on her growing reputation as editor of the *Evening Star*. Before long she was writing a regular column for the paper, and eventually she became its editor. By the time Wells was in her early 20s, her weekly columns, published under the pen name "Iola," reached Black and White readers in the city of Memphis and surrounding rural areas. She was outspoken in her criticism of the oppressive racism that Blacks encountered in the South, and she encouraged the Black community to become educated and financially independent. Her reputation spread beyond Memphis, and she began to contribute articles to some of the nation's best-known African-American newspapers like the *New York Age* and the *Indianapolis World*.

The press was a powerful outlet for Wells, who was quickly becoming a polished and persuasive writer. But it offered little financial reward. Most African-American newspapers were then shoestring operations and often could not pay their correspondents. Wells' diary from the period reveals that she buried herself in her work, constantly composing and refining articles and stories for African-American papers like the *Fisk Herald* and the *Detroit Plaindealer*. Sometimes the results were encouraging, such as when the editor of the *A. M. E. Church Review* asked her to send in an article from "her brilliant pen." But her prolific writing was still a sideline to her full-time job as a teacher, and she constantly worried about how to cover her debts when papers like the *Indianapolis World* paid her with a free subscription rather than cash.

Wells was particularly disturbed by the violence against Blacks that was becoming a daily occurrence across the South, and she saw her writing as a way to bring attention to the problem. It was risky for a Black woman to be such an outspoken critic of the racial order, but Wells was undaunted. For example, in September 1886, she heard about the lynching of a Black woman who had been accused of poisoning a White woman. The lynching victim had been stripped and shot, and her body left in public view. In the pages of her diary, Wells mourned for the woman and decried the horror and injustice of such an atrocity. She also made sure her concerns made their way into print:

> Wrote a dynamite article to the G[ate] C[ity] Press almost advising murder! My only plea is the pitch of indignation to which I was carried by reading an article concerning a great outrage in Jackson, Tenn. . . . It may be unwise to express myself so strongly but I cannot help it. (Sterling, 1984, p. 489)

Within a year of her journalistic debut, Wells had written more than 200 columns and her views were widely disseminated. She was still quite young, however, and a series of events would transform her outlook and propel her into making activist journalism her lifelong work. In the spring of 1887, Wells suffered both a personal and political setback; her suit against the railroad was overturned by the Tennessee Supreme Court. The court ruled that Wells's lawsuit was not in good faith, but rather an attempt to harass the railroad company. In private, the judge admitted that the other justices let their personal prejudices outweigh the merits of her case. Wells, in a state of despair, wondered if African Americans would ever be treated with fairness and equity in their own country:

> I felt so disappointed, because I had hoped such great things from my suit for my people generally. I have firmly believed all along that the law was on our side and would, when we appealed to it, give us justice. I feel shorn of that belief and utterly discouraged, and just now if it were possible would gather my race in my arms and fly far away with them. O God, is there no redress, no peace, no justice in this land for us? (Sterling, 1984, p. 493)

Wells' faith in the legal system had been shattered, but her faith in the power of journalism seemed to find new energy. She continued to uncover instances of social injustice, both in Memphis and other regions of the deep South. In 1889, she was invited to edit another Baptist weekly, the Memphis *Free Speech and Headlight*. Wells agreed, and scraped together the funds to purchase a one-third interest in the paper. She also began to attend meetings of Black journalists and was elected assistant secretary of the National Afro-American Press Convention in 1887. Two years later, she was elevated to secretary of the organization. Her colleagues dubbed her the "Princess of the Press."

Her sense of outrage and purpose attracted the attention of many, including T. Thomas Fortune, the editor of the *New York Age* and a prominent Black journalist. Fortune and his contemporaries admired Wells' skillful writing and political commentary, and welcomed her into the mostly-male fraternity of Black journalists:

> She has become famous as one of the few of our women who handle a goose-quill, with diamond point, as easily as any man in the newspaper work. If Iola were a man, she would be a humming independent in politics. She has plenty of nerve, and is as sharp as a steel trap. (Quoted in Penn, 1891, p. 408)

Wells paid a personal and financial price for her hard-hitting journalism. In 1891, she wrote and published a stinging investigation of conditions in Memphis's segregated Black schools, and she was promptly fired from her teaching position by the school board. This meant, however, that Wells could devote all of her energies to reporting and building up her newspaper. She traveled across Tennessee and neighboring states to sell subscriptions to the paper, increasing the circulation by 2,000 readers in one year. The *Free Speech and Headlight*, under her guidance, became an influential publication throughout the Mississippi delta region.

When three Black men who were Wells' friends and colleagues were lynched in Memphis a year later, her response reverberated through the community. One of the victims was a close friend named Thomas Moss; Ida Wells was the godmother of Moss' young daughter. The men had committed no crime other than operating a successful grocery store in direct competition with a neighboring White-owned business. When a group of armed White men approached the store, Moss and the others picked up guns to defend themselves. A flurry of gunfire left several Blacks and Whites dead. For a Black man to kill a White was considered the most heinous crime. The trio were taken from the jail and lynched despite expressions of outrage from the Black community.

Wells lashed back the best way she knew; through her newspaper. She began with an editorial that declared that the law would not protect Blacks' lives in the city of Memphis. Then she urged the city's Black population to move their families and businesses to more hospitable surroundings. The writer and editor might have been surprised by the power of her words. Wells' columns sparked an exodus of hundreds of African Americans from Memphis to settle in the Midwest and West. The flight of Memphis' Blacks hurt the city's economy, and for the first time, Wells was courted by White leaders anxious to reverse the process. Wells was unmoved by their conciliatory gestures, and she initiated a Black boycott of the city's trolleys to protest segregation and unfair treatment of Black passengers. Wells' tactics were effective; the power structure of Memphis began to understand the economic role of the city's Black population. But they had no intention of dismantling the system of racial segregation that gripped the South. Wells was an influential messenger for African Americans, but in the process she attracted the hatred of local Whites.

Finally, in the spring of 1892, this outspoken African-American woman journalist wrote an editorial that cut to the heart of Southern racism and violence. Later she would explain that her writing was inspired by ". . . the many inhuman and fiendish lynchings of Afro-Americans which have recently taken place . . ." in Arkansas, Georgia, and Louisiana. "Eight lynched in one week and five of them charged with rape!" she exclaimed (Wells, 1969, p. 5). Wells' outrage spilled over into the pages of the *Free Speech*, a move that would profoundly change her life.

> Nobody in this section of the country believes the old thread-bare lie that Negro men rape white women. If Southern white men are not careful, they will over-reach themselves and public sentiment will have a reaction; a conclusion will then be reached which will be very damaging to the moral reputation of their women. (Wells, 1969)

The White residents of Memphis were infuriated by the editorial, and turned their threats of lynch mobs against Wells and her newspaper. One of the city's leading papers, the *Daily Commercial*, retaliated by reprinting her editorial, and the following charges:

> The fact that a black scoundrel is allowed to live and utter such loathsome and repulsive calumnies is a volume of evidence as to the wonderful patience of Southern whites. But we have had enough of it. There are some things that the Southern white man will not tolerate, and the obscene intimations of the foregoing have brought the writer to the outermost limit of public patience. (Wells, 1969)

Another local paper was even more direct when it suggested that Whites should capture the author of the article—who they assumed to be a man—and "brand him in the forehead with a hot iron and perform upon him a surgical operation with a pair of tailor's shears."

Wells had become the object of the very violence that she had fought against in her writing. A group of Whites, led by some of Memphis' leading businessmen, descended on the offices of the *Free Speech*, seized the printing press and other supplies, and closed down the paper while they issued threats against Wells and her associates. Ironically, Wells was attending a convention in Philadelphia as these events unfolded. T. Thomas Fortune learned of the violence in Memphis and warned Wells not to return to her hometown. Thus, at the age of 30, Ida B. Wells was exiled from the region of her birth, and it would be several decades before she again set foot on southern soil. Instead, Wells went to New York, where she became a regular correspondent for Fortune's *New York Age*. A month later, the *Age* published a seven-column article on lynching written by Wells, and distributed 10,000 copies to cities around the country, including Memphis (Thornbrough, 1972, p. 125). Shortly afterward, Wells sold her subscription list to the *Free Speech* in exchange for one-fourth ownership in the *Age*.

A NEW VOICE IN THE NORTH

Wells no longer had to worry about her personal safety in her northern refuge, and she had the influence of a well-known newspaper behind her. After her article was published, she traveled the lecture circuit to educate Northerners about the realities of lynching. In October 1892, a group of influential African-American women in New York City held a testimonial dinner in Wells' honor to help raise funds to publish her work. The result was a 24-page pamphlet titled *Southern Horrors: Lynch Law in All Its Phases*, which expanded the *Age* article to include Wells' latest research on the subject. She waged a tireless campaign in print to refute the myth of Black men as rapists and to demonstrate that lynching was a conscious practice of control and intimidation. That same year, and again in 1894, she was invited to lecture in England by the British Anti-Caste Society, where she was able to instigate international condemnation of American racial violence. The small-town reporter from Mississippi rose to worldwide prominence as she impressed audiences with her command of statistics, her inexhaustible energy, and her commitment to ending lynching.

Her tours through England and the United States were grueling but seemed to be having some effect. In 1893, the number of lynchings was beginning to decline. Yet, Wells continued to read about further atrocities committed against Blacks in the South, prompting her to embark on a three-year investigative journalism project. In one instance, she hired a private detective to research the facts of a particularly heinous lynching in Paris, Texas. She also began collecting accounts of lynchings published in the nation's mainstream press, particularly the *Chicago Tribune*. The results appeared in her second pamphlet, *A Red Record*, published in 1895.

The book began with a tabulation of the lynchings carried out between 1892 and 1894, and then offered graphic details of some of the incidents. A central theme in the study was the frivolous nature of the charges against most of the victims, highlighted by the titles of each case: "Hanged for Stealing Hogs," "Lynched for No Offense," "Lynched Because They Were Saucy," or "Lynched for a Quarrel." Wells complained that although the lynchings took place in public and were often reported in the press, White Americans had done little to stop them.

> It is his [the Negro's] regret, that, in his own defense, he must disclose to the world that degree of dehumanizing brutality which fixes upon America the blot of a national crime. . . . It becomes a painful duty of the Negro to reproduce a record which shows that a large portion of the American people avow anarchy, condone murder and defy the contempt of civilization. (Wells, 1969, p. 14)

Ida Wells also took her campaign for racial justice to other arenas. In 1893, she was among a group of African-American women who traveled to Chicago to protest the absence of positive examples of African-American heritage at the World Columbian Exposition. The event, a precursor to the World's Fairs of later years, sparked criticism by influential Black leaders such as Frederick Douglass for ignoring African Americans except as gross racial stereotypes. Wells joined forces with Ferdinand L. Barnett, publisher of Chicago's Black weekly the *Conservator*, to publicize these complaints. She published a pamphlet titled *The Reason Why the Colored American Is Not in the Columbian Exposition*, which decried the hypocrisy of an international event designed to celebrate the progress of American society. When the exposition officials sponsored a "Colored American Day" to appease the Black protestors, Wells wrote a column in the *Conservator* to denounce the event for displaying watermelons and other negative images of African Americans.

Two years later, Wells returned to Chicago, where she married Ferdinand Barnett and became editor of the *Conservator*. The two seemed an ideal pair;

Barnett had founded the *Conservator* in 1878 and was in the forefront of the quest for civil rights in Chicago (Kreiling, 1978).

WELLS-BARNETT AND POLITICAL ACTIVISM

Ida Wells-Barnett also played a leading role in the formation of local and national organizations, known as the Black Women's Club Movement. Throughout the 1890s, many African-American women had been outspoken in the dual struggles for racial equality and women's rights. In 1896, Wells-Barnett was present at the formation of the National Association of Colored Women in Washington, D.C., and her first son, Charles, was named "Baby of the Association."

In addition, Wells-Barnett continued her customary hard-hitting journalism and attacks on racial prejudice until 1897, when her second child was born. Wells-Barnett cut back on writing and traveling, but she did not hide in the shadow of her children and domestic life. Shortly after the birth of Charles, she traveled and made speeches on behalf of a Republican women's campaign committee, with a nurse provided to care for her son. The Barnetts sold the *Conservator,* but Ida Wells-Barnett continued to write regularly for the paper, and they retained some financial and editorial control of the paper. And though she tried to retire from public life when her second child was born, she could not resist the call to remain involved in anti-lynching and other public activities. Wells-Barnett was clearly torn between the social expectations that she remain in her place as wife and mother and her commitment to public action. For the rest of her life, she struggled to strike a balance between the two.

The fiery journalist never relented in her calls for militant protest against racism. She constantly exposed atrocities in the pages of the Black press. In 1900, she published yet another exposé of racial violence: *Mob Rule in New Orleans: Robert Charles and His Fight to the Death.* Using accounts from the New Orleans daily newspapers, as well as from her independent research, Wells-Barnett told the story of a week-long rampage in that city in which Black men and women were assaulted and killed. She concluded with an update of her accounting of lynchings through 1899, noting that "the Negro asks only for justice and an impartial consideration of these facts" (Wells, 1969, p. 48).

Her insistent calls for justice placed her at odds with one of the period's most influential Black figures, Booker T. Washington. The founder of Tuskegee Institute and a proponent of social separation of the races and tactful, nonconfrontational politics, Washington seemed to argue against Wells-Barnett's strategies. Her old friend T. Thomas Fortune had become aligned with Washington and refused to publish Wells-Barnett's criticism of Washington's tactics. She turned, instead, to the pages of the *Conservator,* where she could have her say. Not surprisingly, Washington was angered by her criticism. A long and acrimonious feud began between the two, and soured her relationship with Fortune. One of Washington's strategies for silencing opposition was to purchase and control influential Black newspapers. The *New York Age*, in financial straits, became a mouthpiece for Washington, and he set his sights on quieting the *Conservator*, as well. Eventually, the Barnetts gave up their interest in the newspaper, and Washington took control in 1908.

Wells-Barnett also was an active and influential member of the Afro-American Council, a forerunner of the National Association for the Advancement of Colored People (NAACP). She founded the Negro Fellowship League, which aided Black migrant workers, and the Ida B. Wells Club of Chicago, which worked to establish Black cultural and educational institutions under her leadership. However, her myriad involvement in such organizations was not without controversy. When she was elected financial secretary of the Afro-American Council, some Black men protested her visible role in the organization. She also clashed with Margaret Murray Washington, wife of Booker T. Washington, who played a prominent role in the National Association of Colored Women.

Despite the obstacles, Ida Wells-Barnett was active in the formation of the civil rights movement of the 20th century. She was one of two Black women to participate in the founding of the NAACP in 1909. She eventually sided with the more radical politics of W. E. B. DuBois, who led one faction of the organization in opposition to the accommodationist stance of Booker T. Washington and his followers. She was enthusiastic about the formation of a national organization of influential Blacks and Whites who would act together to end racial violence and discrimination. In her later years, however, she would criticize the NAACP for not taking strong enough stands on many issues, especially on getting Congress to pass a national anti-lynching law.

Wells-Barnett was also an active supporter of women's suffrage. She argued that the best course for social and political equity was for Black women, as well as men, to be able to participate in the political process. To this end, she organized the Alpha Suffrage Club in 1913, the first African-American women's suffrage organization in Illinois. That year she represented Illinois in the National Woman Suffrage parade, but left the event when she discovered that Black women involved were asked to march at the end of the procession. Wells-Barnett would often be frustrated by the racism she found among White women who rallied for the right to vote.

As the years passed, Wells-Barnett reluctantly took a back seat to younger Black activists, but she never ceased to use her pen as an instrument for change. She became a contributor to the Chicago *Defender*, which was founded in 1905 and was one of the nation's most effectual African-American newspapers. In 1917, she wrote a series on a race riot in East St. Louis reminiscent of her reporting about social conditions in Memphis 40 years earlier. The series was widely read and spurred an investigation into the conviction of one Black man imprisoned during the riots. She also reported on racial unrest in other American cities and was considered a soothsayer by some when she practically predicted an outbreak of racial violence in her hometown of Chicago. Not content to observe the events unfold, she also organized a protective association for the city's Black residents.

By the time she was a grandmother, Ida Wells-Barnett had been associated with the most influential African-American leaders of the early 20th century, including W. E. B. DuBois and Marcus Garvey, whom she represented at the Paris Peace Conference of 1919. Indeed, Wells-Barnett was a leader in her own right, who used journalism to needle and cajole the American public to openly confront racism and eradicate its worst manifestation in the form of lynching. Her uncompromising positions, which alienated many public figures, were a product of her life's experience. Since her days in Memphis, she had found that the most effective means of achieving social change was to confront problems directly and mobilize people to act in an affirmative matter. Throughout her life, she would have little patience for those people, White or Black, who appeared to accommodate injustice or make concessions in the face of insurmountable odds.

Wells-Barnett's journalism was solidly grounded in the colorful polemical writing of the late 19th century. Years before Ida Tarbell, Lincoln Steffens, and other muckrakers became famous, Wells-Barnett plied the trade of the investigative journalist. She spent months, and sometimes years, gathering data, conducting interviews, and exploring every seamy detail of the lynching incidents she documented. Once her work was published, Americans could no longer deny the violence committed against African Americans occurring across the South. But her fame would always be limited by the fact that many Americans would discount the words of an African-American woman, and much of the nation's press could choose to ignore or suppress her work. Nevertheless, Ida Wells-Barnett proved that activist journalism was part of a proud tradition in American history that, at its best, could enhance the social and moral fabric of society.

REFERENCES

Duster, Alfreda M. (Ed.). (1970). *Crusade for justice: The autobiography of Ida B. Wells.* Chicago: University of Chicago Press.

Giddings, P. (1984). *When and where I enter: The impact of Black women on race and sex in America.* New York: William Morrow.

Hendricks, W. (1993). Ida Bell Wells-Barnett (1862–1931). In D. C. Hine (Ed.), *Black women in America: An historical encyclopedia* (pp. 1242–46). Brooklyn: Carlson Publishing.

Holt, T. C. (1982). The lonely warrior: Ida B. Wells-Barnett and the struggle for black leadership. In J. H. Franklin and A. Meier (Eds.), *Black leaders of the twentieth century*. Urbana: University of Illinois Press.

Krieling, A. (1977–78). The rise of the Black press in Chicago. *Journalism History, 4,* 132–136, 156.

Sterling, D. (Ed.). (1984). *We are your sisters: Black women in the nineteenth century* pp. 481–495. New York: W. W. Norton.

Thornbrough, E. L. (1972). *T. Thomas Fortune: Militant Journalist.* Chicago: University of Chicago Press.

Wells, Ida. (1969 rpt.). *On lynching and a red record.* New York: Arno Press.

3

Career

OFF OUR BACKS

JENNIE RUBY

Jennie Ruby earned her M.A. degree in Women's Studies at George Washington University. Her master's thesis is titled "The Anti-pornography Movement: A Study of the Coverage in *off our backs*" (1989). Ruby has been a member of the *off our backs* collective since 1989. Her research interests include gender studies, environmental issues, and philosophy.

Off our backs (*oob*) is a collectively run, radical-feminist monthly news journal based in Washington, D.C. The paper was born, with the women's liberation movement, out of women's dissatisfaction with the failure of the civil rights and antiwar movements of the late 1960s to adequately address women's issues. The founders chose the name *off our backs* "to connote that men should 'get off our backs' and that women should 'get off our backs' and work for our liberation" (Douglas, 1990, p. 15). Founded in 1970, *off our backs* is now the longest running national feminist newspaper in the United States.

OVERVIEW OF *OFF OUR BACKS*

Off our backs covers news about women and events that affect women, as well as news about the feminist movement. Long-time collective member Carol Anne Douglas (1989) said, "Our 'mission' is to cover all the news of the feminist movement and all the news affecting women . . . and to be the journal of record for all the actions and ideas of the women's movement."

Coverage of news about women is important as a counter to the primarily male-oriented mainstream news media that minimize events important to women's lives. According to long-time collective member Lorraine Sorrel (1989),

> a recent conference of journalists here in Washington said that 21 percent of the stories in the newspapers were either by or about women. It's really a male media. The news is about events happening to and by male leaders of patriarchal countries. Any news about what is happening to women is on back pages and very rarely seen and picked up. So it is very important to have [it] picked up, condensed, and analyzed. That's what the news section of *off our backs* tries to do.

Off our backs makes a specific effort to cover violence against women. "I don't think women want to read about atrocities against women," said collective member Debbie Ratterman (1989), "but I think it's really important that what happens to women doesn't go unnoticed because it's in a little corner of the *Washington Post* or some local paper so that we think it is some minimal thing, that it doesn't happen a lot. I'm really proud of our work on that."

Off our backs also covers "political developments both on a state and a federal level that affect women, and even on the local level when there is something exceptional, such as a pornography ordinance," says Douglas (1989). In sum,

Thanks go to Angela Johnson for help in compiling the highlights and for reading a draft and to Farar Elliott for her love and support.
Correspondence concerning this article should be sent to Jennie Ruby, 18 N. 30th Street, Richmond, VA 23223.

according to Douglas, "We are a newspaper trying to bring feminists basically all the news they will need about women for that month" (1989).

The news in *oob* includes both original reporting and compilations from other sources. International women's news is an important area of coverage. Feature articles, book reviews, commentary, interviews, conference coverage, and letters make up a significant portion of the paper. Upcoming events and conferences, publications available, publications seeking material, and opportunities for activism are listed in the monthly "Chicken Lady" column. Advertisements appear in a section at the back of each issue.

Off our backs is part of the alternative press; that is, it provides an alternative to traditional mainstream newspapers that claim global objectivity. *Oob* speaks from a particular point of view, a feminist one, and does not purport to be objective in that sense. However, within the feminist context, the paper does attempt to preserve its independence from any one point of view or position. *Oob* is an independent paper, which means it is not owned by a larger corporation and it is not affiliated with any particular political organization. Its independence is a policy that has been maintained throughout its existence. In 1972, for example, *oob* withstood pressures to join with the Washington D.C. women's center in moving into a building with them (Douglas & Moira, 1993).

In covering "all the news affecting women," *oob* provides a service that is not present in the mainstream news media. In some instances, *off our backs* has provided original reporting on current world events. In February 1993, for example, it was the first to report that Croatian women's groups had retained attorney Catherine A. MacKinnon in order to seek legal remedies and immediate relief for Croatian and Muslim women raped by Serbian soldiers in "ethnic cleansing" actions. In others, *oob* has provided space for a point of view not found in other media coverage of news. An article defending alleged serial killer Eileen Wuornos and justifying her self-defense plea was a direct counter to coverage in other media outlets that looked askance on her self-defense arguments and drew parallels to male serial killers. Wuornos, a prostituted woman accused of killing six men who fit the profile of johns, stated over 50 times during her taped confession that she killed the men after they became violent with her and she feared for her safety and life. The *oob* article documents the multiple rapes and beatings that pimps, johns, and other men routinely perpetrate on female prostitutes. In this context, the acts of violence Wuornos says the six men committed are believable, and they justify her plea of self-defense (Chesler, 1993; Hamilton, 1993).

In addition to providing space for alternative news and news analysis, *off our backs* gives women whose stories are not publishable elsewhere an outlet. An article in the February 1993 issue on the (fairly unusual) occurrence of lesbian rape is probably such an article.

The commentary and letters pages of *off our backs* provide an important forum for debate among feminists and other women. During 1982 through 1984, for example, intense debates over what, if any, actions women should take against pornography raged in the pages of *oob*. In providing space for these kinds of discussions, *oob* enables many women who are scattered throughout the country and in nonurban centers to learn about and participate in feminist political movements. Coverage of conferences held on topics of interest to women also performs this function.

Off our backs forms part of a national and international network of feminist and alternative publications. Exchange subscriptions between *oob* and publications such as *Mother Jones, Ms., The Guardian, Sojourner, The Advocate, The Washington Blade*, and many other alternative newspapers and journals assure that the staffs of these publications are aware of what is in the pages of papers covering related and overlapping subjects. The information can then be shared with readers when relevant.

HISTORY

Marilyn Webb, Heidi and Nan Steffens, Norma Lesser, Nancy Ferro, Marlene Wicks, and Coletta Reid conspired to produce the first issue of *off our backs* in late 1969. When that first issue was published on February 27, 1970, it was the first national feminist newspaper in the United States. The publications *Ain't I a Woman* and *Rat* appeared shortly afterward, but it would be two more years before *Ms.* was produced (Douglas & Moira, 1993; Webb, 1993). The money to print the first issue had been saved by Webb and Margie Stamberg during the summer of 1968 for the purpose of opening a GI coffeehouse to provide a forum where peace activists could talk with GIs about the Vietnam war. The coffeehouse plan was dropped because of the paucity of GIs in Washington and the prohibitive cost of licensing. In addition, Webb and Stamberg's interests were changing to a focus on the lives of women (Webb, 1993).

Webb and Stamberg were both "loosely affiliated" with Students for a Democratic Society, a civil-rights group that by 1968 was working on antiwar demonstrations. Webb had also been organizing high-school teachers for Vietnam Summer, a "national antiwar organizing effort" (Webb, 1993, p. 124). Both women were writing for alternative newspapers; Webb for the *Guardian*, covering Washington, and Stamberg for *Quicksilver Times* and for the Liberation News Service. Although Stamberg had left Washington by the time planning for *off our backs* was in the wind, she okayed the use of the money she and Webb had collected (Webb, 1993).

The mailing lists for the first issues were to Webb's contacts from Vietnam Summer and to lists of women from the antiwar movement who had started meeting in consciousness-raising groups in New York, Chicago, San Francisco, and other places. The women on the mailing list from the 1968 women's conference also received *oob*. The initial mailing recorded a response rate of nearly 100 percent (Douglas & Moira, 1993, p. 108; Webb, 1993).

Abortion, the pill, how to use a diaphragm, and International Women's Day were among the topics covered in the first issue of *off our backs*. Reproductive health and rights remained a strong focus throughout the early years of the paper and are still covered extensively. The first volume of the paper included several special issues that focused on women and ecology, women and the media, women and class, women and work, women and the church, and women and imperialism (produced by another collective). The Vietnam War and demonstrations against it and the relationship between the women's movement and the left were frequent topics in the first years.

Webb left the paper in the fall of 1970 because of pressures within the collective. She was apparently seen as having a disproportionate amount of power, compared with other members of the collective, because of her experience in journalism and her position as a founder of the paper. Other collective members did not have journalistic experience, and there was an emphasis on allowing them to develop those skills rather than having an informal leader emerge (Douglas & Moira, 1993; Webb, 1993).

Another bout with leadership and the question of having editors occurred in 1973–74, when the collective member who had been coordinating a section on culture surreptitiously renamed the section "Culture Vulture" and placed her name on that section as its editor. She initiated the new pull-out section in the middle of the night before the paper went to press, so that other collective members did not know about it in advance. When she said she would only continue to coordinate the section if her name remained as editor, the collective agreed. The section lasted only a few months because other collective members felt that their book reviews and movie reviews were "no longer to be writ[ten] for *off our backs*, but rather for an individual's enterprise" (Douglas & Moira, 1993, p. 113).

Since that time the newspaper has been run collectively by a constantly changing group of women. One current collective member has been with the paper since 1973, and two others have been involved for more than ten years. The remaining members have been on the collective from one to five years. New members join the collective by first working with the collective as a friend, then interviewing with the collective to become a member. Each new member affects the newspaper in a unique way. "*Off our backs* is always whoever is on the collective," said one member (Sorrel, 1989). "I think that where the paper goes depends tremendously on who's on the collective, and what women are willing and able to do," said another member (Lootens, 1989). "The personal is political, the political is personal. It is really going to depend on who's working on it."

Some highlights from 23 years of feminist publishing:

• In 1970, *oob* designed a spoof center spread for "Butterballs, the genital deodorant for men"; the photo was of two naked men with daisies shielding their genitals. The regular printer refused to print it and the paper had to be taken to New York to be printed.

- In 1972, *oob,* along with nine other media organizations in D.C., was sent the key to a bank vault containing a bomb. The action was arranged to demand the release of political prisoners. Unfortunately, no one got around to opening the mail until the story had been broken by the *Washington Post.*

- In 1974, an editorial lamented that "women with a feminist consciousness who were ready to take direct action against the state had no place within the women's movement" (Moira and Douglas).

- In 1975, an essay on the pages of *oob* accused Gloria Steinem of having ties to the CIA, and said that getting killed was an occupational hazard for rapists.

- In 1976, *oob* praised the recognition that we are "more than intellectual beings" provided by the spirituality movement, but "called goddess worship a sham" (Douglas and Moira, 1993, p. 108).

- In June 1979, the collective turned over resources to the group *Ain't I a Woman,* to put out a special issue on imperialism.

- One specialty of *oob* is the coverage of international women; in 1980, among other topics, the following were covered: movements in Egypt to return women to wearing the veil; arrests and expulsions of Soviet feminists; Sandinista women in Nicaragua; and women freedom-fighters in Zimbabwe.

- In 1981, the most-requested special issue ever was put out: women and disability.

- In 1983, in the midst of the sex wars, *oob* examined the practice of sexual sado-masochism within the context of feminism.

- In 1984, the idea of confrontation as a response to rape and an anti-rape tactic was explored on the pages of *oob,* in addition to the new right-wing tactic of bombing abortion clinics and pro-choice offices.

- In 1985, after months of fundraising, *oob* sent a reporter to the U.N. Conference on Women in Nairobi, a mid-decade examination of the U.N. Decade of Women.

- In 1986, *oob* covered the resistance by Navajo women to relocation from Big Mountain, Arizona, where the U.S. government had first drawn arbitrary lines between Navajo and Hopi land and then attempted to enforce those boundaries.

- In 1987, an issue was put together with a focus on prostitution, including coverage of the Second International Whores' Congress, prostitution in Southeast Asia, and The Red Thread, a Netherlands prostitute group.

- In 1991, the issue published immediately after the outbreak of the Gulf War was devoted to a feminist analysis of the U.S. involvement in the conflict between Iraq and Kuwait.

- In 1992, members of the *oob* collective had the privilege of talking with one of the founding members of SPEAK, the South African women's journal, along with two other African feminist journalists from Namibia and Uganda. Also in 1992 *oob* ran what proved to be a very popular cover: a woman holding the American flag, taken from a patriotic poster from early in this century, with the caption, "Does anyone have a match?"

- In 1993, bell hooks was the focus of a cover story on feminism and Black liberation.

POLICIES AND POLITICS

The organizational structure of *oob* is closely tied to its feminist politics and its roots in the early women's liberation movement. *Off our backs* is run collectively by a group of six to ten women who share responsibility for all aspects of its operation. Business, production, and editorial decisions are made by consensus. One collective member is employed by the paper to staff the office. Other collective members give time to the paper on an unpaid volunteer basis.

Collective structure and consensus decision making distribute the responsibility for and control of the paper evenly among the individuals who run the paper. There is no one leader or editor-in-chief. The nonhierarchical structure reflects feminist "ideology, which inspires women to be autonomous, take responsibility, make decisions, and develop their own positions" (Gelb & Palley, 1982). Consensus decision making assures that the points of view of all collective members are reflected in all collective decisions. This is quite different from, for example, majority-rule decision making, where the voice of the minority is silenced because decisions reflect only the views of the majority.

The *off our backs* policy on remaining an independent paper was spelled out in a 1972 editorial (vol. III, no. 1):

> Producing a women's paper that [does] not shrink from evaluating women's theories and actions necessarily entail[s] that a certain distance be maintained from all institutions, albeit feminist. . . . We have, on occasion, been admonished for "failing to develop a consistent politics." This fact is not a failure, but rather a conscious decision that any line would destroy our ability to view critically what we are covering, would, in fact, predetermine what received space in this newspaper, what was trashed, and what we proselytized. We are not an organizing tool for any one tendency in the women's movement—or for any one women's organization (Douglas & Moira, 1993, p. 122).

More recently, the collective has considered applying for nonprofit tax status for financial reasons, but many members are cautious about the strings that may come attached to any grant money that might become available to a nonprofit *oob*. (*Oob* does not make a profit; it just barely breaks even on overhead and production costs each fiscal year.) "In real terms we wouldn't want to compromise ourselves, and most funders do require that, whatever they say," said collective member June Thomas (1989). That feeling was seconded by Tricia Lootens (1989): "I think the paper has survived this long by very conservative management, and that has ensured its integrity. I don't want to worry about outside forces slipping in through the back door in a grant."

Closely related to the insistence on nonhierarchical structure and shared decision making is an anti-"star" value system. Bylines are placed at the end of articles in *off our backs*, rather than at the beginning, as in traditional newspapers. This emphasizes the content of the article over the identity of the author. Lootens (1989) said,

It's done by a group of women who do it because they love the movement and love the work, and not particularly because they want to be stars. There's a long tradition of not even signing their own names. [Although signed articles are important in terms of accountability,] I kind of like the old sense that it doesn't matter who is saying this, it is someone from the movement and this is another woman and you ought to listen to her. Not because you loved her last book, and not because you know she's associated with X crowd, but just because.

Some feminists have been critical both of the consensus decision making process and the rejection of leaders or "stars." Sara Evans (1980), for example, says that for many radical feminist groups, "the anti-leadership consensus proved inadequate as a basis for organization. A preoccupation with internal process—the effort to live out the revolutionary values of egalitarianism and cooperation within the movement itself—took precedence over program or effectiveness" (pp. 222–223).

Because production of a monthly newspaper demands a certain level of effectiveness, *off our backs* has apparently managed to hold this tendency at bay. Said collective member Ratterman (1989), "It is not like a regular political group where you can waste six months talking about planning to do something and never get around to it. We can't. We've got to get out that paper every month." Nevertheless, collective members do value the process of working collectively and using consensus. According to Angela Johnson (1989), "the paper is very much something I do to prove that you can have a different kind of life and you can have a different kind of society. . . . It is very important to me to work collectively and by consensus, and I don't see how the paper serves anyone if it doesn't serve the people that are most connected with it."

The participatory politics of feminism extends beyond the collective at *oob*. The paper is still manually laid out, and a number of women, credited as "friends" on the masthead, come in during one weekend to type, design, and lay out each issue of the paper. Student interns are also a routine part of the *oob* staff.

Rejection of leaders and the star system, although criticized by some feminists as a route to mediocrity through descent to the lowest common denominator (see, for example, Berson, 1993), has served to give *oob* a uniquely powerful place as the voice of a social movement. The newspaper is not identified with the point of view of one particular editor or with a particular city.

Part of what gives it its grassroots flavor is its being carried on by a group of women whose paid work, professional lives, [and] identities are somehow separate, so that when you think of *off our backs,* you think of the paper, not necessarily any individuals. That's an indication of how well over 18 years the collective has worked. . . . From the outside it is perceived as a unified entity. *Off our backs* takes this position, *off our backs* is powerful. What happens behind the scenes is there are all these different women taking all these different positions. None of them feels personally particularly powerful. There is more division, there is less of a sense of power. (Lootens, 1989)

Another factor in the paper's identity as a grassroots product is the fact that so much of the content of the paper comes from outside the collective. One-half or more of each issue of the paper is made up of unsolicited contributions by readers or activists in the feminist movement. Many of the news items are compiled from news clippings mailed in by readers. A large part of the work of the collective is reviewing the submitted materials, deciding what pieces to publish, and determining the specific contents of each issue.

Of this work by the collective on other writers' materials, Lootens (1989) commented, "There's a very nice sense that I felt when I was at the paper that we really were providing a service to the movement. That we really were there to get the word out. I would take as much care laying out some unknown woman's article as I would laying out my own article [or] as I would laying out a star's article, and so did everyone else."

Although the collective members strongly influence the direction and identity of the paper through their writing and through editorial decisions, the flow of articles from outside the collective makes the paper much more than the sum of the collective. Sorrel (1989) discussed this aspect of the paper:

> I learned as an insider . . . that the collective members are more open to different ideas than some of the people who write articles for us, and the articles themselves may come across in a very strong, very angry way . . . [They] are not toned down and not rejected because they are valid points that are being raised, and there's really no other forum that is going to be accepting some of these views by women about oppressions. So the paper serves as a means for some people who would never get anything of their voice or their message across to get that there.
>
> As a consequence, I think sometimes the readers think that all the collective members on *off our backs* are these incredibly ill-dressed ideologues who are always 100 percent politically correct . . . whereas the truth is that people at *off our backs* are probably so overworked they probably don't have time to contact [other feminists], but they are not particularly ideologues at all, and are interested in what is happening in all parts of the world.

Despite Lootens' reference to the apparent unity of the collective, political divisions among feminists, and thus among members of the collective, are a common occurrence. What happens when there is division on the collective? Until about 1974, the collective hammered out editorial positions that they could all endorse (Douglas & Moira, 1993). By the late 1970s, the collective found it more workable for those who had opposing opinions to write signed commentaries indicating their position, while the paper carried a notice that signed articles indicated the position of the person, not of the newspaper as a whole. This handling of disagreement is in line with *oob's* practice of publishing articles by women with differing opinions on the same topic. Because of *oob's* refusal to choose sides in these disputes, those who see one of the sides as the only correct side have often criticized *oob* for not taking their position. "We usually see the fact that both sides of an issue are annoyed at us as a sign that we are doing a good job," said Douglas and Moira (1993, p. 114)) in their history of *off our backs.*

In the interest of making sure that both, or many, sides of an issue are covered, *off our backs* has a policy of publishing all letters in full. There are several notable exceptions to this. On occasions when *oob* has received numerous letters with very similar wording, one has been published with a note that other similar letters were received. In these cases, it seemed evident that a form letter was being circulated. Another is that during the so-called pornography wars of the early 1980s, *oob* received and published several letters signed by long lists of individuals and made an editorial decision not to continue publishing lists of names. The collective published a statement explaining: "We feel a long list of signatures turns a letter or response into a petition that serves more to identify who's on what side than to explore issues . . . [and] changes the focus from what's said to who said it, which *oob* would like to avoid in the future." Letters that might be libelous or that contain personal attacks on individuals rather than on their ideas are also avoided. In another instance, discussed in the next section, *oob* discontinued publishing letters replying to one particular article when it appeared that no new arguments were forthcoming.

CONFLICTS AND CONSENSUS

The politics of the collective have sometimes been questioned by readers. In 1971–72, for example, *oob* covered the formation of the Women's National Abortion Action Coalition in Washington, D.C. During its formation, there was a split between women who favored a single-issue national organization and those who did not. Those who favored a single-issue group were mostly socialists belonging to the Socialist Workers Party (SWP) or the Young Socialist Alliance. When an article in *oob* favored the single-issue organization, the collective member who wrote it was accused by readers of being an infiltrator from SWP (Douglas & Moira, 1993). However, according to Douglas and Moira, the newspaper was in fact moving away from any socialist point of view, as was the women's movement itself:

> During that period the pages of the paper reflected the growing awareness of women around the country that SWP tactics of bloc voting and of working with women to increase its own numbers and further its interests made working in groups with SWP women self-defeating. Independent women were developing ways of functioning that did not include majority rule or a follow-the-leader philosophy. *Oob* articles reflected this change in women's consciousness. (p. 111)

The "pornography wars" of the early 1980s also brought the question of the paper's politics to the fore. Individual collective members wrote against banning or censorship (Kelly & Moira, 1979), against sadomasochism and an exclusive focus on sexual liberation (Douglas, 1980; Dejanikus, 1980; Moira, 1982), and in guarded support of some of the analytical claims of anti-pornography feminists (Douglas, 1980). In 1982, readers criticized the paper's coverage of the Barnard conference—from both sides of the conflict. Alice Henry (1984), a collective member, wrote an article critical of the Minneapolis anti-pornography ordinance, setting off a deluge of letters to *oob* that continued well into the next year and prompted *oob*'s only refusal to continue to publish letters on a single topic. The collective decided to stop printing "letters directly responding to a particular article by Alice Henry," but did not cease to publish letters and commentaries on the topic of pornography. Douglas (personal communication, 1989) noted that the decision was made that no more space in the paper should be given when nothing new seemed forthcoming.

Not every woman on the collective published in *oob* on the topic of pornography. Editorial statements indicate more division than appears in the writing by collective members in *oob*'s pages. "Although everyone at *off our backs* agrees on the need to fight pornography, we have strong disagreements. . . . This has often taken concrete form in arguments not only about the content, but about the length of our coverage" (Collective, 1982, p. 9). The point of consensus decision making is that it is not likely that a certain point of view would be completely overridden and not appear in the paper.

There is an interesting point at which the question of censorship and consensus decision making can come into conflict. In consensus decision making, every individual has the power to veto a decision, or "block consensus." The question of what this means on a collective where many of the decisions made are on whether to publish an individual's writing is a difficult one. If an individual collective member blocks publishing of a certain article, then that individual effectively censors that piece of writing. Publishing decisions are routinely made on the basis of appropriateness to *oob*'s audience, quality of the writing, factuality of the information, and whether the point of view is feminist in a very broad sense. Censorship could become a question if within the broad politics of feminism a certain point of view is blocked from publication in the paper. Collective members recognize the seriousness of this type of decision, and I have known of only one article, in 1992, that was not published because consensus was blocked. The hope is that by operating the newspaper by consensus, a broader range of opinion is covered than would be the case if a single editor or owner controlled the paper's content.

LOOKING AHEAD

In 1993 *off our backs* was in the peculiar position of being viewed as an institution among alternative papers. Young women are producing 'zines that have a more raw, more grassroots feel even than the homemade-looking *oob*. Because of the play on our name, *off our backs* is sometimes seen as the anti-sex, more conservative journal that the lesbian sex publication *On Our Backs* sets itself up against. It is a challenge for the paper to not allow itself to be frozen into an aging and more conservative niche relative to these newer publications. In 1993, *oob* ran articles on and by the Riot Grrrls, a collective of women in their late teens and early twenties organizing in Washington, D.C., and other cities. With a double special issue on sex, the paper has provided space for a new generation of feminists to explore current thinking on this topic. With its broad base of readership in the United States and abroad, *oob* remains a powerful vehicle for communication between feminists.

"I feel that we are vital in that we can, for those who read us, tie everything together, and give them a sense of action in a time when they might feel there isn't much," said Douglas (1989). "In terms of keeping feminist activists in small towns in touch with the movement, and in that sense holding the activist part of the movement together on an intellectual level, in that kind of a forum, yes I think it is still working," agreed Lootens (1989). Well into its third decade, *off our backs* continues to keep alive the connections between women that were forged in the early women's liberation movement and to provide an alternative to the mainstream suppression of women's news, women's actions, and women's lives.

REFERENCES

Berson, Ginny Z. (1993). The Furies: Goddesses of vengeance. In K. Wachsberger (Ed.), *Voices from the underground*, (Vol. 1, pp. 124–130). Tempe, AZ: Mica Press.

Chesler, P. (1993, June). A woman's right to self-defense: The case of Eileen Carol Wuornos. *off our backs, XXIII*, 6–7, 12–15.

Collective. (1982, June). [Editorial]. *off our backs, XIV*, 9.

Dejanikus, T. (1980, November). Our legacy [commentary]. *off our backs, X*, 19–20.

Douglas, C. A. (1980). Sex and violence: Titillating or depressing? *off our backs, X*, 17.

Douglas, C. A. (1989). [Interview]. In Ruby, J., *off our backs: A case study*. Unpublished manuscript.

Douglas, C. A. (1990, February). Looking back on the last 20 years. . . . *off our backs, XX*, 15.

Douglas, C. A., & Moira, F. (1993). *off our backs:* The first decade (1970–1980). In K. Wachsberger (Ed.), *Voices from the underground,* (Vol. 1, pp. 107–124). Tempe, AZ: Mica Press.

Evans, S. (1980). *Personal politics: The roots of women's liberation in the civil rights movement and the new left.* New York: Random House.

Gelb, J., & Palley, M. L. (1982). *Women and public policies.* Princeton, NJ: Princeton University Press.

Hamilton, A. (1993, June). Phyllis Chesler on Eileen Wuornos [interview]. *off our backs, XXIII,* 8–9, 22.

Henry, A. (1984, November). Porn is subordination? *off our backs, XIV,* 26.

Johnson, A. (1989). [Interview]. In Ruby, J., *off our backs: A case study.* Unpublished manuscript.

Kelly, J., & Moira, F. (1979, January). A clear and present danger. *off our backs, IX,* 7.

Lootens, T. (1989). [Interview]. In Ruby, J., *off our backs: A case study.* Unpublished manuscript.

Moira, F. (1982, June). Barnard finale. *off our backs, XII,* 23–24.

Ratterman, D. (1989). [Interview]. In Ruby, J., *off our backs: A case study.* Unpublished manuscript.

Sorrel, L. (1989). [Interview]. In Ruby, J., *off our backs: A case study.* Unpublished manuscript.

Thomas, J. (1989). [Interview]. In Ruby, J., *off our backs: A case study.* Unpublished manuscript.

Webb, M. S. (1993). *off our backs* and the feminist dream [appendix]. In K. Wachsberger (Ed.), *Voices from the underground,* (Vol. 1, pp. 124–130). Tempe, AZ: Mica Press.

Women political columnists have written for newspapers in the United States since 1856, when Fanny Fern began writing for the *New York Ledger,* but few have attained the status of the best-known male columnists.

4

WRINKLING THE FABRIC
OF THE PRESS:

Newspaper Opinion Columns in a Different Voice

NORMA M. SCHULMAN

Norma Schulman currently teaches mass communication at George Mason University. She has published articles on a variety of mass communication topics in the *Canadian Journal of Communication, Southern Humanities Review, Hebrew University Studies in Literature, Journal of Popular Film & Television,* and elsewhere. Her work includes "A Narrative Theory to Understanding News and Journalistic Form" in *Ecquid Novi.* She received a Ph.D. in mass communication from the University of Iowa and a doctorate in English from Tufts University.

The detective's voice was patronizing each time he repeated the now-famous line from *Dragnet*: "Just the facts, ma'am." He seemed to say it at least once in every episode of the television show. His intonation never varied. He'd tilt his head down slightly, as if speaking to a younger, smaller, less-focused person—his hands poised motionlessly above his note pad—while an overwrought female character blurted out what she knew.

The woman the detective admonished was different every week—sometimes a "girl Friday," sometimes a cousin, sometimes a neighbor of the deceased. But one thing remained constant on the *Dragnet* that I remember: She was always too emotional, too illogical, and too unobservant to illuminate much of anything.

Except when Detective Joe Friday had the uncanny good sense to find a clue in all the disconnected particulars that poured pell-mell out of her mouth as she recalled the events of the day in question. Her train of thought was a hail of inference, spiced with minutiae: what the cat ate, how she needed silk stockings, why the paper boy liked her yard.

Watching this as a girl growing up before the women's movement of the sixties, I thought she seemed to become giddy at the unaccustomed pleasure of being listened to by a serious-looking man who, as he explained by flashing his credentials, was there on official business. Her desire to please came through loud and clear, but her answers to questions were heavily qualified, tentative, or downright vague. When she was specifically asked, on occasion, to describe something concrete, her answers were as flat and unselective as the text of a Sears-Roebuck catalog read aloud. Otherwise she emoted, she free-associated, she wandered far afield of "just the facts."

What bothered me then, and what bothers me more now, both as a journalist and as a woman, is central to the concerns of this chapter on newspaper opinion columns written by women. In the world of my own private *Dragnet*, women seemed to be looked down on as being incapable of separating fact from inference—a separation that somehow proved quite unproblematic to the detective and his (all-male) law enforcement team. In the detective's world, which was the larger, public world, only facts mattered—impressions, opinions, and intuitions merely hindered the pursuit of authoritative and unimpeachable Truth. A single correct version of events existed. Exposing it—with its pristine, unambiguous outlines intact—was Detective Friday's sole function in life. And everything he did—every quizzical arch of his eyebrows—seemed to contribute to achieving this purpose.

What was offensive to me, though I was not fully conscious of it then, was the stereotypical representation of women as receptacles of unadulterated emotion, incapable of the kind of rational analysis that is necessary to draw logical conclusions from a mass of isolated details. Or, as the journalistic version would have it, incapable of letting the (real) story "tell itself," without the contagion of a subjective point of view muddying the picture.

The primary purpose of journalism was, after all, "getting it right," as almost any editor would tell you in the early 1960s, when I first tried my hand at it. Analogies were made between newswriting and stenography, a skill at which many female college graduates of my generation were destined to become more proficient than they wanted to be. "Transparent prose" was a phrase often quoted by my mentors. To say that one's own writing voice was to be toned down would be a vast understatement.

OVERVIEW OF WOMEN AS COLUMNISTS

It was no accident that when women began entering newspaper journalism in substantial numbers in the late 1960s and early 1970s, they gravitated, or were propelled, toward so-called soft news or human-interest features rather than hard, event-oriented stories on topics of social and political import. It was no accident that the terms used to describe effective prose were then, and are now, perilously close to terms of approbation used to describe the male sex: "lean, dry, terse, powerful, strong, spare, linear, focused, explosive," as DuPlessis (1985) has noted.

A well-written news story is supposed to externalize its point; provide a liberal amount of attributed "proof" in the form of authoritative quotes; employ argument as the preferred mode for discussion; focus on concrete actions, instead of cognitive states or emotion; and offer grounds for objective conclusions, if not outright closure.

Women who grew up in the first half of the century were not generally given much encouragement to focus on these writing techniques. Moreover, these techniques necessitated the use of predictable story structures and forms of organization that actually got in the way of presenting open-ended, perceptual frameworks—frameworks that raise important questions about the human condition, rather than claiming to definitively answer them; or that call attention to the *process* of working through the ambivalence and confusion of actual experience to arrive at fuller understanding.

The sudden, unaccountable insights into other people that can sometimes come from observing human interaction or mulling over anecdotal detail are constricted by such prescribed journalistic modes of communicating information. Linear and oriented toward logic, they are incapable of rendering the fluidity of consciousness or the illogic of feeling.

Modern American mainstream journalism has largely relinquished those virtues it had in centuries past when news writing was an epistolary art. It has lost much of its intimacy, responsiveness, involvement, metaphorical language, capacity for subtle nuances of feeling and tone, and distinctive, personal voice.

These attributes have now come to be regarded as the major strengths of "woman's writing," although it is certainly not the intention of this essay to suggest "biology is destiny" when it comes to the written word.

However, what does underlie the critical analysis in this chapter of newspaper opinion columns by women is a notion of what Mary Ellman has called "the sex of the writing," as opposed to the sex of the writer. The sex of an author is biologically determined. The sex of the writing, on the other hand, reflects the particular way culture has conditioned the author to think, feel, and communicate.

Gender roles constitute an important part of cultural conditioning, but they are not, at least from the perspective of this chapter, determinant. Individual tendencies and attributes play an important part as well. As a consequence, there are women whose writing is more "masculine" than "feminine," as well as men who adopt ways of expressing themselves more often associated with the female sex.

In the last few decades, women newspaper columnists such as Mary McGrory, Ellen Goodman, and Anna Quindlen have initiated a refreshing new trend—one that already shows signs of spreading to their male colleagues: integrating commentary on public affairs with insights into the human condition. The newspaper columns that do this successfully provide both food for thought and an emotional aftertaste that can linger for years. They are at the same time both informative and meaningful, with the impact of actual, powerful experience because they go beyond "just the facts."

Unlike other journalistic forms, the newspaper column allows for self-reflection, the full range of emotional tones, the distinctive (even idiosyncratic) authorial voice, and the progressive discovery-by-analogy that mark some of the most outstanding examples of women's journalism in the United States today. Moreover, personalization of the author's informed, lively perspective is integral to the popularity of newspaper columns, which regularly appear in the same part of a newspaper and prominently display the writer's byline. In the past, it was customary for newspapers to include a picture of the author to increase reader identification, but the practice appears to be gradually disappearing, especially from major metropolitan dailies.

Presentation of individual opinion, however personal or subjective, is acceptable in this part of the newspaper. By definition, it makes no claim to be objective or to reflect the ideas of anyone but the writer. Progressively, an effective columnist develops a reputation for informative, interesting, illuminating observations on issues that range from international events to the kind of mundane domestic matters that female columnists have, unfortunately, been disproportionately associated with.

Even today, close to a quarter of a century after the women's pages supposedly became gender-neutral sections with names like "Style" or "Lifestyles," female authors of serious opinion columns are remarkably few, even at elite papers like the *New York Times*. The roster of names of prominent, widely read, nationally syndicated columnists indicates that serious print journalism continues to overrepresent male concerns and male points of view on current issues of public importance. And college journalism texts, directed at the would-be reporter, prove no significant exception to the rule.

Women political columnists have written for newspapers in the United States since 1856, when Fanny Fern began writing for the *New York Ledger*, but few have attained the status of the best-known male columnists. Even the fact that Eleanor Roosevelt wrote a syndicated newspaper column before, during, and after she lived in the White House is rarely noted. And it is no wonder. President Roosevelt sorely minimized this accomplishment by telling reporters that his wife "simply writes in a daily diary" (Braden, 1993, p. 5).

Typically, 20th-century newspaper columns written by women in the United States have not been forums for short essays of opinion or commentary, like Eleanor Roosevelt's eventually became, but have been confined to areas traditionally defined as "women's turf": society, fashion, gardening, the home, gossip, cooking, child-rearing, or "advice to the lovelorn." Names like Hedda Hopper, Louella Parsons, Emily Post, and Erma Bombeck, as well as pseudonyms like Ann Landers and Abigail Van Buren, have long been synonymous with journalism in a much lighter vein than the nationally syndicated newspaper columnists discussed in this chapter.

MARY McGRORY

The purpose of a newspaper opinion column is not merely to inform a reader, but to evoke a reaction or response. As a consequence, virtually any device is permissible that causes a reader to connect emotionally as well as intellectually with the content: anecdote, real or hypothetical example, dialogue, humor, or extended metaphor. For example, Mary McGrory, a 1975 Pulitzer prizewinner and nationally syndicated political commentator for the *Washington Post*, used allegory to elicit reactions to her July 9, 1989, column titled "Ingrate Flowers and Drunken Squirrels." Her column began with what appears to be fairly straightforward discussion of her attempts to rid her garden of squirrels and slugs. Gradually, almost imperceptibly, she moved from literal description to satire of the Washington political scene:

> My guess is that the slugs hired the squirrels as consultants, and that I now am like so many people in Washington—fighting an unseen enemy that has unlimited resources and no conscience. I can go on putting out melons and beer until the squirrels get so fat they can't function. Or else I can face the fact that the only thing I can grow is impatiens and learn to love Franco-American spaghetti.

McGrory became especially well-known for scathing criticism of the Reagan administration, but her columns have usually cleaved to somewhat more traditional modes of political commentary. She is the oldest and most traditional of the three columnists we will examine. McGrory was one of the first women in the Washington press corps. Her characteristically well-researched, iron-clad arguments—effectively buttressed by a lively writing style and succinct, colorful quotes—enable her to be taken seriously as a thinker by readers of both sexes. Perhaps this is also because she tends to maintain somewhat more of a distance from her own particular personal experience in her newspaper pieces than other opinion columnists such as Ellen Goodman and Anna Quindlen.

On the other hand, the relative absence of overt expressions of emotion in McGrory's columns has, undoubtedly, contributed to the frequent characterization of her commentary as "hard-boiled" or "sharp-tongued"—two of the many gender-linked epithets hurled at female journalists as though they were still the kiss-of-death in a country where women were once explicitly socialized to be gentle and submissive.

There are, however, many subtle ways in which restrained emotion plays a role in making McGrory's writing truly "androgynous" from the standpoint of customary, gender-linked categories and approaches to the world. On November 26, 1963, a few days after the death of President John F. Kennedy, her column "The Funeral Had That Special Kennedy Touch . . . ," resurrected the essence of the man at the same time as it described his funeral, tempering the somberness of its content with playful, imaginative conjecture. The column begins with a lead that is risky because it is pure inference—"Of John Fitzgerald Kennedy's funeral it can be said he would have liked it"—but concludes on a traditional, elegiac note:

> It was a day of such endless fitness, with so much pathos and panoply, so much grief nobly borne that it may extinguish that unseemly hour in Dallas, where all that was alien to him—savagery, violence, irrationality—struck down the 35th president of the United States.

Well under the usual newspaper column length of 750–1,000 words, it is one of the enduring masterpieces of this exceedingly brief and subjective journalistic form. With style and grace, it articulates loss while lavishing praise on the much-admired late president:

> [The funeral] had that decorum and dash that were his special style. It was both splendid and spontaneous. It was full of children and princes, of gardeners and governors.

McGrory's feminist proclivities are frequently implicit in her choice of topics,[1] though the targets of her political invective are selected with more explicit

---

1. For example, during July and August 1993, she wrote spiritedly about allegations of sexual harassment ("Tales of Mistreatment at NIH," August 17, 1993); urged intervention to bring injured Bosnian children to hospitals in the United States ("Babes, Not Arms," August 15, 1993); and applauded Sen. Carol Moseley–Braun's successful protest against a patent perpetuating the use of Confederate flag insignia ("Freshman Turns Senate Scarlet," July 27, 1993).

regard to their (conservative) ideology than to their gender. One of the things that *does* mark her writing as feminine, despite its propensity to heavily deflect emotion, is the particular content of the extended metaphors she sometimes uses to articulate her political perceptions. For example, in her June 17, 1993, nationally syndicated column titled "Clinton Unbridled," she uses the details of a homey, elaborated conceit to convey a mixture of wariness and awe toward the new president. Characteristically avoiding the kind of first-person commentary she is more inclined to include in her heavily mannered, satirical pieces, McGrory utilized a quotation from the White House press corps as an objective peg for what actually turned out to be her own view of what it is like to "live with" such a person:

> He is, one of them said, "a work in progress." Living with him is like having a teenager in the house. It is never certain whether he will total the family car or bring home a national merit scholarship.

The content of the metaphor objectifies what is actually a very shrewd and analytical political assessment in terms so graphically domestic that it is easy for a reader who has ever been, or ever parented, a teenager to relate to her perceptions. This builds rapport with readers—something an effective newspaper column must do—by reminding us that the columnist's perspective, just like our own, is rooted, in the final analysis, in the vicissitudes of real-life experience.

ELLEN GOODMAN

When comparing McGrory's approach to current issues and her choice of topics with Ellen Goodman's, one must take into account that nearly a generation intervened between the time the two authors began to practice their craft. McGrory was already a seasoned journalist when the women's movement of the 1960s came into being; whereas Goodman, who is in now in her early 50s, was at the beginning of her career as a columnist and was one of the early champions of the social changes the movement labored to bring about.

Of the two, it is Ellen Goodman who, both by historical accident and by design, has turned out to be the architect of a new type of newspaper column that bridges the gap between personal experience and the larger arena of social, cultural, and political analysis. In 1980, Goodman won a Pulitzer prize for commentary. She has noted that news is the "starter dough" for her columns. An examination of the expansive range of her numerous columns—many of which have been collected and published in book form—shows this playful self-analysis to be appropriate. She uses the imagery of everyday domestic life to "bring home" the impact of social structural changes on individuals—often she uses representative personifications to communicate in visceral and psychological terms.

Goodman works for the *Boston Globe*, but her newspaper columns are nationally syndicated. In her columns, Goodman's perspective is rather consistently on women's issues, but her ideological focus is almost never polemical. Although she is a strong supporter of feminist concerns and is sensitive to the many different ways gender inequities play themselves out, she does not usually advocate a particular position. Rather, she tends to unexpectedly illuminate the flip side of a "politically correct" position, implicitly generalizing her own mixed feelings to illustrate that things are not as simple as our social and political agendas may sometimes make them seem. It is a gutsy move. For she runs the risk of appearing to "backslide" in the face of change if she fails to make the psychological nuances of the conflict clear and convincing.

An example of how she successfully does this appears in a June 1988 (Father's Day) column titled "The New Father and The Mother's Secret." In it, she concludes that, ironically, "women have also given up something," because those "new fathers" have begun to assume some of the burdens of child-rearing:

> It turns out that sharing the work of raising children also means sharing the power over children's lives. Sharing the power—even the kind you didn't fully recognize—is harder than expected. Letting go of child power, giving up the central role in a child's life, can be as hard as letting go of purse power. It doesn't sound like a dramatic struggle. But it can come with a sudden, internal wrench.

Ultimately, Goodman suggests that though pain is an inevitable accompaniment of "letting go" of children even under such ideal circumstances, women should not feel that they must "hide their ambivalence [from their husbands] as if it were a dirty little secret." Engaging the reader in a dynamic process of analysis, she works to validate such emotion as a natural accompaniment of shifting maternal and paternal roles, even though the implications of such "reactionary" feelings might be unsettling to women who have so unequivocally allied themselves with altering the domestic status quo.

A skilled aphorist when she wants to be,[2] Goodman tends to save her carefully crafted metaphors and often witty punch lines for less serious topics on which she can give a column closure without oversimplifying the issues. For example, in her August 15, 1991, syndicated column "A New Parental Battle: Countering the Culture," Goodman concluded that raising children properly in a TV-culture is like "trying to get your kids to eat their green beans after they've been told all day about the wonders of Milky Way."

---

2. One of my favorite examples of this is her satirical observation that "ours is an era of marriage until love do us part." The line appears in an August 1988 column with the title "A Little Romance." A close second is Goodman's "wedding wish" for Sarah Ferguson in a July 1986 column on "Fergie's Famous Hips": "May her happiness spread. May she broaden the image of women. Even, verily, unto a size fourteen." Or the concluding line of "Dick and Jane Play Tennis," her spoof on the fitness craze that appeared in August of 1986: "Dick and Jane are willing to sacrifice every bone in their body in order to stay healthy."

Thematically and stylistically then, this versatile author has two major modes of column-writing. The first delves under the surface of the deceptively simple observational world, uncovering a tangle of emotions and refocusing a perspective that seemed at first relatively clear-cut. The second, used for less personal, less subjective, and less volatile material, works in the opposite direction to sharply focus and distill the essence of specific people, places, or events in a way that is culturally meaningful.

The first type of column tends to emanate from transitional moments in the life cycle of a woman or in the "life cycle" of the social order as a whole. The more personal examples, which generally are written in the first person, may start with a pivotal event like the birth of a child, the departure of a teenager for college, or the death of a loved one.

In the second type of column, the "starter dough" is not usually a deeply felt personal experience, but "news": that is, the more external emblems of the public world of famous people—often celebrities or well-known politicians. She uses them as icons through which to communicate carefully deflected and focused social commentary, as she does in her January 1989 column "Exit Ron Reagan: Stage Right":

> So, as the credits start to roll on his last hours in office, this is the Reagan I take away: A man who followed and recreated a great American story line. A man who thought of us as an audience rather than a citizenry. A man who elicited goose bumps more often than action. He projected an image on the screen to make us feel as good as we did at a Saturday matinee, when everybody knew the good guys from the bad and the good guys always won. The End.

Goodman used essentially the same technique of externalization to make her own serious comment on the battle between Clarence Thomas and Anita Hill, since it (like the movie) exhibited moral polarities she perceives to be clear-cut. In this column, too-current events provided an objective scaffold, illustrating the powerful hold staged images seem to exert over U.S. culture as she sees it. Except that in this real-life scenario, the plot line vindicates the wrong side of what ignorant observers mistakenly viewed as just a "he-said, she-said sort of thing," or, as Goodman wryly put it, "the 'reverse discrimination' story line[s] of the time, the female pit bull attack on the ankle of innocent man." Nonetheless, she concluded on an upbeat note, in the flat, unadorned prose that is often the key to history-making, empowering events in her lexicon:

> At the 11th hour and the 59th minute these senators finally heard, loud and clear, the voices of women. The women they represent. His word, her word. This is our word to Congress: Listen up. ("Few Doubting Thomases in the Senate," October 10, 1991)

ANNA QUINDLEN

In her November 22, 1990, column, *New York Times* syndicated columnist Anna Quindlen repeated a remark a newspaper editor once made to her in earnest: "I'd love to run your column, but we already run Ellen Goodman." Quite understandably, Quindlen interpreted this as evidence of the existence of an informal "quota of one" serious woman columnist per newspaper. I totally condemn such sexist reasoning; however, it is fair to say that these two brilliant columnists happen to have many outstanding attributes in common.

Both Goodman and Quindlen successfully fuse personal anecdotes and concrete description with commentary on a range of topical and enduring issues that tend to concern women more profoundly than men in our society—issues like parenting, child care, abortion, sexism, human-rights violations, or media violence. Both sort out and suffuse experiential facts with meaning, as well as grapple with current policy issues. Both are oriented toward process, not conclusion; toward rendering the questions and confusions of life in modern American culture, not merely using their progressive, liberal convictions to ward off uncertainty as new situations unfold.

Anna Quindlen received a Pulitzer prize for commentary in 1992. She is the youngest of the three opinion columnists discussed in this chapter, and her columns most precisely reflect the distinctive tenor of the times. Her pieces have displayed a special sensitivity not only to issues of gender, but to those of class and race as well. Compared with Goodman's columns, hers deal more with issues of social conscience than interpersonal relationships or social change. Quindlen tends to reflect on the plight of oppressed groups—gays, Blacks, abused children—rather than render the nuances of cross-gender communication that Goodman articulates so beautifully.

Many moving anecdotes and vignettes in her columns—such as those written in the aftermath of the 1992 Los Angeles riots—communicate her deep sense of the injustices minority groups continue to endure in our society. In columns like "The Great White Myth" (January 15, 1992), she attacks as a cultural "myth" a notion often used as a rationale for opposing programs like affirmative action: the belief that "the world is full of black Americans prospering unfairly at white expense."

Quindlen is particularly adept at combining "hard news" with an imaginary construct or "frame"[3] in order to force readers to contemplate acknowledged facts from the vantage point of a fresh perspective. She does this in "Across The Divide," written shortly after the violence in Los Angeles erupted (May 3, 1992):

> No matter how many times I watch the four police officers beat up Rodney King, it still
> looks indefensible to me, and to the eight-year-old, too. Three times he watched the video-

---

3. For further discussion of news as "constructed reality" see Gaye Tuchman, *Making News* (1978).

tape and three times he brought his arms over his head in a double arch, as though to ward off the baton blows. And finally he said, "Are they really allowed to do that?" It broke my heart, but it could have been worse. I pictured a mother and an eight-year-old watching the same clip, both of them black, the son asking the same question, the mother forced to reply, "Yes, baby, they are."

In this example, the hypothetical scene she imagines taking place (as a Black mother and child watch the videotape of Rodney King's beating the way she and her son have just done) is what functions to draw new meaning out of a set of brutal acts that, by now, are familiar to most American television viewers. Her point here appears to be that not even the acutest empathy can ever really surmount the racial differences that constitute an impenetrable "barrier" between different groups of people. Skin pigmentation has arbitrarily "divided" us, not just visually but experientially, into two distinct camps: the oppressors and the oppressed. And not even the deepest sensitivity can ever completely enable one race to "cross the [racial] divide" to the life the other leads.

In a parallel (though less purely imaginative) fashion, Quindlen depicts gender as another source of divisiveness in one of her columns on the Clarence Thomas hearings:

The absence on the panel of anyone who could become pregnant accidentally or discover her salary was five thousand dollars a year less than that of her male counterpart meant that there was a hole in the consciousness of the [Senate judiciary] committee that empathy, however welcome, could not entirely fill. The need for more women in elective office was vivid every time the cameras panned that line of knotted ties. ("Listen To Us," October 9, 1991)

Proficient in many different modes of writing, Quindlen is also adept at making her political points satirically. For example, the contradiction-in-terms that constitutes the recent change in policy on gays in the military is something she mocks in a barbed one-liner: "Homosexuals will be tolerated as long as they don't homosex" ("Another Kind of Closet," June 27, 1993). And her ability to caricature many different voices and tones is reflected in one of her columns on the Persian Gulf War—in the crude, inarticulate put-downs of teenagers, who are trying to be cool: "'Saddam Hussein, man,' they would say, if they could talk. 'He's toast.'" She parodies "the angle for kids" in this military confrontation with imaginary dialogue: "Saddam Hussein is Bart Simpson cubed. Bad attitude, dude" ("The Invasion Vacation," August 19, 1990).

On the other hand, Quindlen writes on matters of sentiment in a personal voice that sometimes recalls Goodman's. For example, in this (Mother's Day) reflection on how quickly young children mature:

They are not long, the days of construction paper and gilded rigatoni. That's why we save those things so relentlessly, why . . . those of us who can instantly make friends with a stranger by discussing colic and orthodonture, have as our coat of arms a sheet of small handprints executed in finger paint. ("The Days of Gilded Rigatoni," May 12, 1991)

Quindlen is one of the few people writing newspaper columns today capable of moving into registers that are truly lyric. "The Lightning Bugs Are Back," written before she began her more impersonal column "Public & Private" for the *New York Times* op-ed page in 1988, is about as far as it is possible to go from traditional "hard news" writing. In it, she uses an image that starts off as a "bug" and winds up as "the glow and not the dark" to communicate a desire to recapture her own childhood experience by watching her own child find "magic" in the spectacle of the fireflies. An attempt is made here to communicate through readers' imaginative not intellectual faculties. Only someone susceptible to being thus beguiled can possibly be capable of joining the author in re-experiencing the mystery of the life cycle, once their own childhood perceptions have "died" out in the sealed jar of adult life:

> This is why I had children: to offer them a perfect dream of childhood that can fill their souls as they grow older, even as they know that it is only one bone from a sometimes troubled body. And to fill my own soul, too, so that I can relive the magic of the yellow light without the bright white of hindsight, to see only the glow and not the dark. Mommy, magic, those little flares in the darkness, a distillation of the kind of life we think we had, we wish we had, we want again. (*Living Out Loud,* "The Lightning Bugs Are Back," 1988, pp. 3–5)

At their most illuminating, women's opinion columns have come to stake out new territory in American newspapers at a place Quindlen has called "the intersection of the private and the public." Against the proverbial feminist rallying cry, "The personal is the political," this essay suggests that these two realms can be, and have been, worlds apart; that the art of column-writing, at best, involves *bringing the two together,* just as the women's movement itself involves bridging the prototypical gender gap.

As Quindlen has put it, "the personal without the political [is] not telling enough." This is the realm that has, for much of this century, been regarded as stereotypically feminine—both off and on the women's pages. It has sometimes been too strictly an autobiographical place, limited to a single hearth and a single home, on one particular day-in-the-life of one particular writer at play in the fields of people and places that do not resonate beyond back fences and driveways.

On the other hand, McGrory, Goodman, and Quindlen, along with other emergent women writers of serious journalism, help make the point that public policy issues, like trends, social problems, or social change, are meaningless as narratives, delivered by some faceless, omniscient "hit-and-run driver" grazing the surface of the facts; that news events have *embodiments* that resonate all the way from the august corridors of power to the familiar, down-to-earth details of daily domestic life.

REFERENCES

Braden, M. (1993). *She said what: Interviews with women newspaper columnists.* Lexington, Kentucky: University of Kentucky Press.

DuPlessis, R. B. (1985). For the Etruscans. In Elaine Showalter (Ed.), *The new feminist criticism: Essays on women, literature, and theory.* New York: Pantheon Books.

Goodman, E. (1989). *Making sense.* New York: Penguin Books.

Goodman, E. (1979). *Turning points.* New York: Doubleday & Co.

Quindlen, A. (1988). *Living out loud.* New York: Random House.

Tuchman, G. (1978). *Making news: A study in the construction of reality.* New York: The Free Press.

Looking at the field, we realized that the whole category of women's service magazines tends to address women with certain assumptions as to who these women are, but the assertions may not be valid for baby boomers, who tend to see themselves as more fully empowered adults. We are adjusting our editorial voice in a way that will be comfortable with this generation of women. (Michael Golden, *McCall's* publisher, as reported in "U.S. Women's Magazines," 1990, p. 5)

two

WOMEN'S MAGAZINES:
Women Within a Women's Media Form

The women's magazine is one of the few media forms to attract a primarily women-only audience. The success of this particular medium in attracting a large women's audience for more than 200 years may be attributed to two factors. First, the publication of a monthly medium is more easily supported through subscription fees and advertising revenues than a weekly or daily schedule. Second, the print medium, in general, is more accessible and less costly than other forms such as radio, television, or film. Because women's magazines are one of the few media to "speak" to women, it should not be surprising that from their inception, women's magazines have helped shape the ways in which women and men see the ideal woman. In many ways, women's magazines have been a constant voice to women.

HISTORY

The first American magazine appeared in 1741. Forty-three years later the first women's magazine, *Gentlemen and Lady's Town and Country,* was published. Although that magazine folded one year later, other women's magazines followed.

One of the most well known of the early women's magazines was *Godey's Lady's Book.* Sarah Josepha Hale merged her nine-year-old publication, *The Ladies Magazine,* with its competitor, *Godey's Lady's Book,* in 1837 and was hired as editor. She retained that position for more than 40 years.

Godey's Lady's Book focused on the manners, morals, and tastes of its readers. Although Hale fought for higher education for women, property rights for married women, and improved health care, she did not support the suffrage movement (women's right to vote), nor did *Godey's.*

During the 1880s and 1890s, the number of women's magazines greatly increased, reaching middle-class women, predominantly homemakers. The magazines offered lower subscription prices to gain large circulation because advertising rates were circulation-based. The most successful women's magazines of the time included *Delineator* (1872), *Ladies' Home Journal* (1883), *Good Housekeeping* (1885), *The Woman's Home Companion* (1897), *Pictorial Review* (1899), and *McCall's* (1897). Referred to as the "Big Six," they focused on homemaking, entertainment, fiction, and social reform.

During this same time, African-American women's magazines became popular. African-American "women and their interests had always been a significant part of the Afro-American periodical press" (Bullock, 1981, p. 166), and although men edited most of the African-American magazines, women writers contributed to these periodicals, thus reflecting African-American women's concerns of the time. One periodical targeting women was *Our Women and Children* (1888), published and edited by two Baptist ministers, Charles Parrish and William Simmons, but staffed by women writers and department heads. Another periodical, *Ringwood's Afro-American Journal of Fashion* (1891), on the other hand, was published and edited by Julia Ringwood Coston, wife of an African Methodist Episcopal minister. While *Ringwood's Afro-American Journal of Fashion* highlighted the latest fashions, love stories, and makeup hints, the *Woman's Era* (1894), published a few years later, provided a different kind of women's periodical.

Mrs. Josephine St. Pierre Ruffin helped establish the Women's Club, an active civic organization "engaged in the study of current issues and the support of education and charitable causes" (Bullock, 1981, p. 189). The Woman's Era Club was "not necessarily a colored woman's club but a club started and led by colored women, organized not for race-work alone, but for work along all the lines that make for women's progress" (Bullock, 1981, pp. 189–191). The Woman's Era Club publication, the *Woman's Era,* was published by Mrs. Ruffin and soon became the journal of women's clubs across the nation. Its columns included "Literature," "Women at Home," "Chats With Girls," and "Social News." The *Woman's Era* highlighted information on prominent women, music, drama, health issues, domestic science, and education (Bullock, 1981, pp. 192–193). The periodical was devoted to the interests of women, "especially the black educated woman who was hemmed in by 'the limitations of her surroundings and the circumscribed sphere in which she must move'" (Bullock, 1981, p. 192).

Another women's magazine reflecting subtle changes in society was *The Woman's Home Companion,* a competitor of *Ladies' Home Journal.* Its title, *The Woman's Home Companion,* pointedly refused to refer to females as "ladies," as most magazines up to this point had done. The editors of *The Woman's Home Companion* believed the word *lady* had been abused and that "the noblest ambition of our end-of-the-century femininity is to be a 'woman.' . . . The use of 'lady' as a synonym for 'woman' is vulgar" (Tebbel, 1969, p. 160). Gertrude Battles Lane, editor, said that she tried to keep in mind "the housewife of today as I see her. She is not the woman who wants to do *more* housework, but the woman who wants to do *less* housework so that she will have more time for other things. She is intelligent and clear-headed; I must tell her the truth. She is busy; I must not waste her time" (Tebbel, 1969, p. 160).

During the 1930s, magazine sales declined. Some believed this decline was due to a saturated market with too many magazines and too few readers and advertisers. The increased competition pushed editors and publishers to limit women's portrayal to the traditional roles of homemaker and sex object. Others criticized women's magazines for their lack of practical information during a time of economic depression (Fishburn, 1982). Two of the Big Six (*Delineator* and *Pictorial Review*) folded.

By the 1940s, having learned a lesson from the 1930s, women's magazines confronted issues dealing with World War II and real women's concerns: working women, the war effort at home, and women awaiting male relatives serving in the war. Unfortunately, with the end of World War II, these more diverse women's roles and topics were ignored, and the general direction of women's magazines went back to the 1930's homemaker/sex object portrayal. *Ladies' Home Journal, Better Homes and Gardens* (1922), *Family Circle* (1932), *Good Housekeeping, McCall's, Redbook* (1929), and *Woman's Day* (1937) became known as the "seven sisters" because of their similar content and audience. By the 1950s, readers, unhappy with the limited perspective of women's magazines and attracted to the new media form, television, purchased fewer magazines.

Yet women's magazines continued to wield considerable influence over society's views on women. In the 1960s, this influence was questioned. Betty Friedan argued in her book *The Feminine Mystique* (1963) that women were brainwashed by women's magazines into thinking their "highest value" was in their femininity (p. 37).

In response to the traditional roles assigned women by the seven sisters, new women's magazines were published to reflect the viewpoints of younger female readers (18–34 years old). The feminist press entered the magazine marketplace, seeking fewer but more homogeneous readers. *Essence* (1970) targeted urban Black women, *Ms.* (1972) focused on those interested in the women's movement, and *Self* (1979) targeted readers concerned with women's physical and emotional fitness.

Women were no longer associated only with the kitchen or the home. With changing interests, the seven-sisters-type magazines refocused their content in order to compete. Some were more successful than others in their quest for the new woman.

In 1980, the top-ten list of all magazines (based on total revenue) included *Woman's Day* and *Better Homes and Gardens.* Of the top ten consumer magazines, the list included *Better Homes and Gardens, Family Circle,* and *McCall's* (Taft, 1982, pp. 27–28). Although on the surface these statistics look good, the seven sisters suffered a serious decline in readership in 1980 and 1981 while fashion and beauty magazines *Vogue, Mademoiselle,* and *Glamour* grew (McCracken, 1993).

By the mid-1980s, the seven sisters were back on track; some with new publishers or new owners. In general, they focused on all aspects of women's lives (day care, maternity leave, health, environment, and career topics) while food and crafts were deemphasized.

Into the 1990s, the seven sisters continue to seek and hold a mass audience. Other publications, realizing that they can't attract a *mass,* seek a narrower *class* of women with high potential buying power. Magazines that attract women with high buying power also attract a greater number of advertisers seeking to reach these women.

Specialized magazines have been successful when they don't target too narrowly and are able to attract an audience sufficient to keep the publication alive. Other women's magazines in the 1990s have failed because they were "founded by individuals or small groups with minimal capital, or, when backed by large corporations, failed to attain enough ad revenue and circulation to turn a profit" (McCracken, 1993, p. 288). In magazine publication, as with most media, the bottom line is profit.

PORTRAYAL

Few would argue that women's magazines were key in the socialization of women and the creation of the image of the idealized American woman. Although the content of the magazines has changed from decade to decade (at times emphasizing the traditional roles of mother and wife; at others, the nontraditional roles of "Rosie the Riveter"), many women and men believed their happiness could be found by being or finding the "perfect woman" as portrayed in women's magazines.

For example, *Godey's Lady's Book* helped in socializing American women by creating an image of the happy American woman as a homemaker, serving her family and community needs.

In the 1920s, the portrayal remained much the same but included more romance. Johns-Heine and Gerth, studying women's and men's magazines from 1921 through 1940, found more stories that emphasized love themes in women's magazines than in men's magazines and found more success stories in men's magazines than in women's magazines (1949). Women's magazines portrayed women as concerned with love, whereas men's magazines focused on personal and professional success.

In a ten-year study of *Ladies' Home Journal, McCall's,* and *Good Housekeeping,* Lefkowitz (1972) found that stories about heroines with careers decreased from 9 percent (in 1957) to 4 percent (in 1967). In fact, heroines with careers were portrayed as unwomanly and a threat to the marriages of nonworking women. The stories portrayed marriages as happier if women did not have careers: 81 percent (in 1957) and 93 percent (in 1967).

The portrayal of happy women in the home is a concept that was reinforced by a study of fiction in women's magazines from 1940–70. Franzwa (1974) found that few married women were portrayed as working outside the home, and of the women who did work, 51 percent had low-status jobs. Women who were portrayed as working did so to find a husband, and they quit upon their marriage. Those who did work after marriage did so because they lost their husbands or had unhappy marriages.

> For years leading magazines aimed at women have had long-range effects in creating stereotypes in their readers' minds. The American female, from young girlhood on, has been encouraged by these periodicals to believe in certain circumstances as normal and to be taken for granted—for example, that the primary goal is to be taken care of by a man, preferably through marriage. In any case, to achieve the goal in one manner or the other it is necessary to be physically as attractive as possible (Wolseley, 1973, p. 109).

Clark (1980) examined how women living alone were portrayed in issues of *Glamour, Ladies' Home Journal, McCall's, Ms.,* and *Redbook.* In 1978, 62 percent of the single-person households in the United States were maintained by women, and 24 percent of all American women lived alone. Women's magazines "devote less than 12% of their nonfiction to matters related to women alone.

When the magazines do address living alone, they generally depict it as a less desirable lifestyle in comparison with marriage" and something a woman must "live through" (p. 293).

Loughlin (1983) analyzed issues of *Good Housekeeping, Ladies' Home Journal,* and *McCall's* from 1979 to 1981 and found the typical adult female character to be attractive and happily married, between 26 and 35, with two children living in a house in the city. She was college-educated, middle-class, held a job outside the home, and was concerned "with family-oriented problems that were psychological in nature" (p. 140). The job outside the home was considered secondary and, in fact, was often not identified at all. "In general, fictional characters are younger, better educated and have fewer children than their real life counterparts" (p. 141).

An interesting pattern emerges as one looks at the portrayal of women in *Good Housekeeping* and *Ladies' Home Journal* from 1954–62, 1964–72 and 1974–82 (Demarest & Garner, 1992). As one would expect, the 1954–62 era was predominantly filled with the images of women as efficient homemakers, with approximately 70 percent of the articles concerned with marriage and family. After the publication of Friedan's book in 1963, women's magazines began to include other themes concerning politics, social awareness, and career development. Conversely, the happy homemaker portrayal decreased. By 1982, approximately 58 percent of the number of articles dealt with traditional themes (marriage and homemaking) (p. 362).

On the other hand, Flora (1979) found that women's portrayal in women's magazines (1970–75) aimed at working-class women did not change and continued to portray women as passive and traditional (1979). Most of the content analyses discussed previous to Flora were completed on magazines aimed at middle-class women.

EMPLOYMENT

Although female editors were somewhat common in the early days of women's magazines, there is little statistical data to indicate how common. Women were always and continue to be the bulk of staff writers and advice columnists. By the 1960s, women were replaced by men as editors of many of the women's magazines. Of the seven sisters, five were edited by men. In a 1973 study of magazine editors, Seaver found men edited the well-known women's magazines. This trend reversed, and by the 1980s, only two of the seven editors of the seven sisters magazines were men.

In 1989, a photograph titled "The Sisters' Brotherhood" identified seven male publishers of the seven sisters (Fannin, p. 39). Although men publish the seven sisters, predominantly women (five out of seven) served as their editors in 1994 (Ulrich, 1993–94).

In the 1990s, the trend is for editors, both men and women, to migrate freely between women's magazines and general interest magazines. Gone is much of the stigma once associated with editing a "women's magazine"; many women's magazines continue among the top ten in terms of advertising and circulation. For many editors, perhaps it is not whether one is editing a women's magazine (noting all the positive and negative aspects of it) but the size of the publication and its potential audience.

REFERENCES

Bullock, P. L. (1981). *The Afro-American periodical press 1838–1909.* Baton Rouge, LA: Louisiana State University Press.

Clark, R. L. (1980). How women's magazines cover living alone. *Journalism Quarterly, 58,* 292–293.

Demarest, J., & Garner, J. (1992). The representation of women's roles in women's magazines over the past 30 years. *The Journal of Psychology, 126,* 4, 357–369.

Fannin, R. (1989). The growing sisterhood. *Marketing and Media Decisions,* pp. 38–44.

Fishburn, K. (1982). *Women in popular culture: A reference guide.* Westport, CT: Greenwood Press.

Flora, C. G. (1979). Changes in women's status in women's magazine fiction: Difference by social class. *Social Problems 26,* 558–569.

The Folio: 400. (1983). p. 82.

Franzwa, H. H. (1974, spring). Working women in fact and fiction. *Journal of Communication,* 104–109.

Friedan, B. (1963). *The feminine mystique.* New York: Dell.

Johns-Heine, P., & Gerth, H. H. (1949). Values in mass periodical fiction, 1921–1940. *Public Opinion Quarterly,* 105–113.

Lefkowitz, M. (1972). The women's magazine short-story heroine in 1957 and 1967. In C. Safilios-Rothschild (Ed.), *Toward a Sociology of Women* (pp. 37–40). Santa Barbara, CA: Wiley.

Loughlin, B. (1983). The women's magazine short-story heroine. *Journalism Quarterly, 60,* 1, 138–142.

McCracken, E. (1993). *Decoding women's magazines: From Mademoiselle to Ms.* New York: St. Martin's Press.

Taft, W. H. (1982). *American magazines for the 1980s.* New York: Hastings House.

Tebbel, J. (1969). *The American magazine: A compact history.* New York: Hawthorn Books, Inc.

U.S. women's magazines: In search of an audience. (1990, September/October). Media Report to Women, 5.

Ulrich's international periodicals directory (1993–94). New Providence, NJ: R. R. Bowker.

Wolseley, R. E. (1973). *The changing magazine: Trends in readership and management.* New York: Hastings House.

PROJECT IDEAS

1 Select one of the seven sisters magazines. Seek out an issue from 10, 20, or 30 years ago. What are the subjects of the articles? What products are advertised? What roles are women assigned? Now look at a copy of the same magazine from this year. What differences do you find? What similarities do you find?

2 Obtain two magazines that target the same basic demographic group but of a different sex. For example, look at *Vogue* and *GQ*. You might not be able to find the exact same demographics, but get as close as you can. First, look at the articles. What are the subjects? Can you categorize them? Health? Fashion? Self-improvement? Sports? Come up with your own categories. Is there a difference in the types of articles in the "women's" magazines versus the "men's" magazines?

3 Who edits and writes for magazines targeting males and targeting females? Although many would assume that women write for women's magazines, that's not always the case. Compare the number of women and men who write for a women's magazine to the number of women and men who write for a men's magazine. In some cases, such as *Ms.*, the editorial staff intentionally uses as many women as possible on their staff, but in other magazines, this is not the case. Check to see who the editors of the magazines are and who serves on the editorial board. What impact might this have on magazine content?

4 Standard Rates and Data Service (SRDS) and W. R. Simmons Market Research Bureau, Inc. are references that can be found in a library. Both provide information to advertisers. SRDS provides demographic data, circulation, and magazine type (business, consumer, and so on). W. R. Simmons Market Research Bureau, Inc. audits the magazine industry, providing information on audience composition, demographics, subscription sales, newsstand sales, and the number of readers per copy.

Focusing on the type of store, store location, and the types of advertisements within a magazine, make an educated guess as to the type of reader a particular women's magazine is trying to reach. Think about the age, socioeconomic status, and education (demographics), as well as the lifestyles, attitudes, and hobbies of the readers (psychographics). Once you have thought these out and written them down, check your ideas with SRDS or Simmons or write to the magazine for its advertising or promotional material where it defines its audience and see if you agree.

NAMES

The following list identifies some of the women who have been or are currently part of women's magazines. Women who were previously mentioned in this introduction are not duplicated in this list.

Bettina Ballard—Fashion editor of Paris *Vogue* and American *Vogue* (1930–50).

Bessie Beatty—War correspondent for the *San Francisco Bulletin*, later became editor of *McCall's* (1918–21).

Betsy Blackwell—Editor-in-chief of *Mademoiselle* (1937–71).

Mary Kay Blakely—Writer for *Ms., Vogue, Lear's,* and *Working Woman* (1970s–present).

Myrna Blyth—Editor of *Ladies' Home Journal* (1981–present).

Helen Gurley Brown—Editor of *Cosmopolitan* (1965–present).

Pat Carbine—Editor and publisher of *Ms.* (1971–87).

Edna Woolman Chase—Fashion editor of *Vogue* (1895–1952).

Vera Leona Connolly—Editor and writer for *Good Housekeeping, Delineator,* and *Pictorial Review* (1920–40s).

Jane Cunningham Croly (Jennie June)—Chief staff writer for *Mme. Demorest's Mirror of Fashions,* later known as *Demorest's Monthly Magazine* (1860–87).

Marcia Ann Gillespie—Editor of *Essence Magazine* (1970s).

Beatrice Blackmar Gould—Co-edited *Ladies' Home Journal* with her husband, Bruce Gould (1935–61).

Lenore Hershey—Senior editor of *McCall's;* managing editor, executive editor, and editor-in-chief of *Ladies' Home Journal.*

Mrs. Frank Leslie (Miriam Squier)—Editor of *Leslie's Lady's Magazine* and *Leslie's Lady's Journal,* and directed the Leslie publishing empire (1860–70s).

Ellen Levine—Editor of *Redbook* (1991–1994); presently editor of *Good Housekeeping.*

Midge Richardson—Editor of *Seventeen* (1975–present).

Ruth N. Ross—First editor of *Essence* (1970).

Jessie Wilcox Smith—Illustrator for *Good Housekeeping* (1912–1933), *Delineator* (1915), *Harper's Bazaar* (1902–1912), *Ladies' Home Journal* (1896–1915), and *Woman's Home Companion* (1896–1920).

Lucy Wilmot Smith—Editor of the working women department for *Our Women and Children* (1888–unknown).

Diana Vreeland—Fashion editor of *Harper's Bazaar* (1939–62) and editor of *Vogue* (1962–71).

ORGANIZATIONS

Essence
    1500 Broadway
    6th Floor
    New York, NY 10036

Mirabella
    200 Madison Avenue
    8th Floor
    New York, NY 10016

Radiance: Magazine for Large Women
  Alice Ansfield, Editor and Publisher
  Box 30246
  Oakland, CA 94604

Spare Rib
  27 Clerkenwell Close
  London EC1R OAT England

Working Woman
  Lang Communications
  230 Park Avenue
  New York, NY 10169

These lists were, in part, derived from Zuckerman's *Sources on the history of women's magazines, 1792–1960* (1991), New York: Greenwood; Humphrey's *American women's magazines: An annotated historical guide* (1989), New York: Garland; and Bullocks' *The Afro-American periodical press, 1838–1909,* (1981), Baton Rouge: Louisiana State University Press.

Despite a few changes over the years, the ideology remains the same: Teenage girls should be concerned with their appearance above all else, and they should concentrate their efforts on finding a boy—a "guy" in teenmagazinespeak.

5

Content

SOCIALIZATION MESSAGES
IN *SEVENTEEN* AND *'TEEN* MAGAZINES

KATE PEIRCE

Kate Peirce, Associate Professor of Mass Communication at Southwest Texas State University, earned her Ph.D. at the University of Texas-Austin. Her publications include "A Feminist Theoretical Perspective on the Socialization Messages in *Seventeen* Magazine" and "Socialization of Teenage Girls Through Teen-Magazine Fiction: The Making of a New Woman or an Old Lady?" both published in *Sex Roles*. Her research interests include socialization through the media, feminist theory, and sex differences in academe.

Gender-role socialization is the process by which children learn the behaviors and attributes societally sanctioned for each gender. Although there are alternatives, this chapter discusses *traditional* socialization.

The process begins with the mother, who says of the child in her womb, "It's kicking so hard I know it's a boy. Maybe he'll play for the Cowboys." She "knows" this because boys are strong and aggressive, and girls are weak and passive. Imagine her surprise when her little place kicker turns out to be a girl. Let's suppose she has a girl *and* a boy. She believes that her baby boy is stronger, firmer, better coordinated, more alert, and hardier than her baby girl, who is softer, smaller, more inattentive, and more beautiful. She "knows" these things even though there is no evidence that babies—inside the womb or out—differ in any way but visually (Rubin, Provenzano, & Luria, 1974). She will treat the children as if there is a difference by talking to her daughter more and touching her son more during their first three months of life. At six months, she will touch her son less, thus encouraging his independence (Hunter College, 1983, p. 145). Such treatment may act as a self-fulfilling prophecy. Once children are defined as different, they're treated differently, and they develop in ways that confirm and reinforce the expectations of their parents (Denmark, 1977).

When the children are a little older, they will be given gender-appropriate toys to play with: The boy will get a football and be told to play outside, and the girl will get a doll and be told to play quietly inside. Eventually, the boy will help dad in the yard, and the girl will help mom in the kitchen. The boy will learn to be independent, aggressive, and active, and the girl will learn to be dependent, passive, and inactive. Both will learn that there are boy activities and girl activities, boy traits and girl traits.

Although the home is a significant contributor to the socialization process, it is not the only one. Schoolchildren are treated differently simply because they are of different genders. Teachers will call on boys more often than girls and be more specific and intense in their interactions when a boy gives a wrong answer (Sadker & Sadker, 1985). Just as a mother "knows" a boy kick from a girl kick, so do teachers "know" that boys are more mathematically, analytically, and spatially gifted than girls. This message will be passed on to the students even though the evidence suggests that with the proper training there are no gender differences (Romer, 1981, p. 72).

The girl will outperform her brother in elementary school, but by high school he will be outperforming her. Schools encourage the quiet, passive behavior that the girl learns early in life, but it is the boy who can't sit still or keep quiet who receives the attention. Boudreau, Sennott, and Wilson (1986,

A portion of this chapter was based on Kate Peirce's "A Feminist Theoretical Perspective on the Socialization of Teenage Girls Through *Seventeen Magazine*," *Sex Roles*, Vol. 23, Nos. 9/10, November 1990, pp. 491–500. Used with permission by Plenum Press.

p. 125) suggest that the very behavior that allows girls to fit into school more easily also functions to make them less visible, inhibits their learning process, and leads to differences in self-expectancies.

By high school, boy and girl will both understand that their proper gender roles include him being good at athletics as well as math and her being pretty and popular. He will be motivated to achieve by the desire for mastery and other intrinsic rewards, and she will be motivated by the desire for social approval and other extrinsic rewards (Kaufman & Richardson, 1982). Girls are told, by schools, peers, and parents, that the definition of feminine success is being attractive to men, attaining a desirable social status, and marrying the right man (Weitzman, 1979, p. 46). Girls are taught that "femininity" (defined as being attractive to men) and "achievement," both academic and occupational, are at odds because society has attached the words *warm, gentle, tactful, dependent* and *submissive* to women rather than to men. Women should, therefore, be subordinate to men and dependent on them (Hunter College, 1983, p. 190).

While the children are learning gender roles from their families and at school, they are also seeing them reinforced in the media. On television, for example, women are underrepresented, are more often associated with domesticity than with paid employment, are younger than men but age more quickly, are often victims, and are often identified by their relationships to men (Busby, 1985; Signorielli, 1989). Child characters are just as stereotyped as their adult counterparts: Girls play with dolls, play dress-up, help with the housework, and talk on the phone, whereas boys make mischief, play outside, and participate in sports (Peirce, 1989).

Research suggests that magazines are no different from television (Butler & Paisley, 1980). New magazines such as *Working Woman, Ms.*, and *New Woman* have changed the picture of nonfiction content somewhat, offering alternatives to the traditional *McCall's, Good Housekeeping*, and *Ladies' Home Journal*. Even the more traditional magazines have begun to portray women working outside the home although they tend to work in traditionally female occupations (Ruggiero & Weston, 1985).

BACKGROUND

Magazines for teenage girls have not been extensively analyzed, but the analyses so far show that the publications have decidedly traditionalist leanings. One of the first was a 1982 study of *Jackie*, a British teen magazine, in which McRobbie looked at the ideology constructing teenage femininity. She found that a girl's only concerns—according to *Jackie*—are romance problems, fashion, beauty, and pop stars. McRobbie says the magazine is something to be reckoned with by feminists, who must counter its powerful ideological force. I found the ideology constructed in *Seventeen*, an American teen magazine, to be similar to that in

Jackie: fashion, beauty, food, and decorating made up 60 percent of each issue, and relationships with boys made up another 6–7 percent for the years 1961, 1972, and 1985. Although the feminist content was slightly higher in 1972 than it had been in 1961 (at the height of the most recent women's movement it *should* have been), it was slightly *lower* in 1985 than in 1961 (Peirce, 1990). I concluded that although *Seventeen* is a small part of the media and a small part of the socialization of a teenage girl, in conjunction with those other parts, it can be a powerful reinforcer of the traditional ideology of womanhood.

In an analysis of *Seventeen, YM,* and *Sassy,* Evans, Rutberg, Sather, and Turner (1991) found that fashion and beauty dominated all three, that articles on interpersonal relationships meant male–female relationships, and that advertisers capitalized on the fact that teenage girls tend to have negative feelings about their bodies. They also found that the physical beauty theme extends to health and nutrition, that identity themes weren't emphasized despite their importance for that age group, and that ads were generally populated with slim white females, often with blond hair and blue eyes.

I found the fiction in teen magazines to be as traditional as it is in women's magazines. In more than half of the stories in *Seventeen* and *'Teen* for the years 1987–91, the main character did not solve her own problems but depended on someone else to do it for her. Almost half the conflicts had to do with relationships with boys and all but 2 of the 44 occupations mentioned in the stories were stereotypically portrayed (Peirce, 1993).

The purpose of this chapter is to extend my work on *Seventeen's* editorial content by looking at issues from the early 1990s to see if there is a change in the amount of coverage given to various topics. *'Teen* will also be included in the analysis. Two recent articles in which teen magazines were analyzed impressionistically rather than quantitatively offer conflicting ideas about the focus of *'Teen.* Pool (1990) suggests that it is beauty and self-improvement, whereas Massey (1992) says it is beauty and dating. We shall see.

METHODS

The 1990 analysis was an attempt to determine the ideology constructed in *Seventeen,* the ways in which it reinforces traditional ideologies, and whether the feminist movement of the late 1960s and early 1970s affected its content. Content categories were Appearance (fashion and beauty), Home (cooking and decorating), Male–Female Relations (how to get, keep, deal with a boy), and Self-Development (education, occupations, vocations, and health). Those categories, as well as the category Public Figures (stories about male or female performers, primarily), will be used to analyze *Seventeen* and *'Teen* in the 1990s.

The categories were chosen to represent traditional and feminist ideology. Traditional ideology includes the importance of looking good, finding a man, and taking care of a home—thus the categories Appearance, Home, and Male–Female Relations. Self-help represents feminist ideology, which emphasizes independence and self-reliance rather than reliance on a man. Public figures can be traditional or feminist, depending on whether the story is about a male or a female public figure.

A random sample of 12 issues for both magazines was drawn from those dated between January 1990 and June 1993. The number of nonadvertising editorial pages was 866 for *Seventeen* and 623 for *'Teen*. The percentage of editorial pages devoted to each category was determined by dividing the category page total for each issue by the editorial page total. Percentages were then added and divided by 12 to produce an average percentage. Two coders rated each article for inclusion in the categories; intercoder reliability was .89.

RESULTS AND DISCUSSION

Table 5.1 makes it quite clear that Appearance is the dominant category for both *Seventeen* and *'Teen*. From previous research, it is not surprising that more than half the editorial content in both magazines was devoted to fashion and beauty. Somewhat surprisingly, though, the percentage for *Seventeen* has increased by 10 percent since 1985. At 8.5 percent, Male–Female Relations has increased slightly for *Seventeen; 'Teen*, at 7.5 percent, is similar, which suggests that dating is not the magazine's primary focus. The amount of coverage given to public figures is also similar for the two publications. Both cover male public figures twice as often or more than twice as often as they cover females. The difference between past and present is in the category Home. It ranged from 9 percent to 11 percent from 1961–1985, but is now at 3 percent for *Seventeen*. *'Teen*, at .1 percent, rarely covers anything related to home-and-hearth issues. The difference between the two publications is in the Self-Development category. *Seventeen's* 7.5 percent isn't much different from what it was in 1961 or 1985, but *'Teen's* 15.5 percent is much higher than *Seventeen's*. Its figures more closely resemble *Seventeen's* for 1972, which seem to have been an aberration for the magazine. Pool's assessment of *'Teen's* focus—self-improvement—is in line with these figures. We have to keep in mind, however, that by combining the categories Male–Female Relations and Male Public Figures, more than 15 percent of the editorial copy in both magazines is about men.

Despite a few changes over the years, the ideology remains the same: Teenage girls should be concerned with their appearance above all else, and they should concentrate their efforts on finding a boy—a "guy" in teenmagazine-speak. While home-and-hearth messages have decreased, the proliferation of stories about famous guys cancels out the decrease in traditional messages. It also reinforces the idea that men are more important than women. Of course, the editors of teen magazines say (as did one editor in a telephone conversation) that they simply are giving their readers what they want, that teenage girls want to know all about relationships with guys, and that they are interested in knowing all about their favorite actors and musicians. This may be true, but it is also true that underrepresentation of women throughout history has led to a lack of knowledge about their accomplishments and to a false belief in the superiority of men.

Teenage girls will not, of course, become traditional women rather than feminist women just because they read teen magazines. The magazines can have an effect, however. According to DeFleur and Ball-Rokeach's dependency theory (1982), those most affected by a medium are those most dependent on the medium for information and those whose social realities are inadequate. Media dependency is determined by an individual's need for information, ability to get information elsewhere, and interest in the subject. The greater the dependency, the more likely a message is to alter audience behavior in terms of cognitive, affective, or overt behavior. Social realities are the product of the processes by which society socializes people. When people's social realities are adequate and messages aren't linked to dependencies, messages will have little or no alteration effects, the authors say.

Teenage girls may indeed be dependent on teen magazines for information; they aren't going to find as much material targeted solely to them in any other medium. Teens are still learning how to live in the world as well, so it wouldn't be going too far to suggest that the ingredients for message receptiveness are there: inadequate social realities and media dependency. It would also not be going too far to suggest that teen magazines contribute to any stereotypical views its readers hold.

Several solutions come to mind. The most radical solution would be to create a utopia in which no one is allowed to participate in gender-role stereotyping and current teen magazines are replaced with feminist publications for both

Table 5.1

Percentages of Editorial Pages Devoted to Various Topics in *Seventeen* and *'Teen*

	Seventeen				'Teen
	1961	*1972*	*1985*	*1990s*	*1990s*
Appearance	48	52	46	56	53
Home	9	10	11	3	0.1
Male–female relations	7	2.7	6.5	8.5	7.5
Self-development	7.5	16.6	6.8	7.5	15.5
Male public figures				7	10
Female public figures				3.8	2

genders. Such utopias have been created by fiction writers and will no doubt remain the creations of fiction writers for a long time. A more realistic solution would be to create alternative publications. At the moment, no feminist publications are targeted to young people. Although teenage girls are welcome to read *Ms.* and *New Woman*, and many of them do, they are not the target audience for these publications. Feminist publications addressing teenage issues would be ideal antidotes to current teen magazines.

If all of the above is out the question, perhaps the magazines now in existence could examine their behavior and include more feminist content. Children will reject stereotypes if shown counterstereotypes. For example, Schau (1979) found that stories with reversed gender-role stereotypes could reduce occupational gender-role stereotyping in grade-school children. By paying less attention to looking good and getting a guy and more attention to developing self-reliance skills, teen magazines would be offering their readers choices for their lives. By including nontraditional occupations in fiction stories and letting female characters solve their own problems, the magazines would show readers that they are not confined to such occupations as secretary and nurse or to such traits as passive and dependent. It would not be utopia, but it would be a start.

REFERENCES

Boudreau, F., Sennott, R., & Wilson M. (1986). *Sex roles and social patterns.* New York: Praeger Publishers.

Busby, L. (1985). The mass media and sex role socialization. In J. R. Dominick & J. E. Fletcher (Eds.), *Broadcast Research Methods.* (pp. 267–295) Boston: Allyn & Bacon.

Butler, M., & Paisley, W. (1980). *Women and the mass media.* New York: Human Sciences Press.

DeFleur, M., & Ball-Rokeach, S. (1982). *Theories of mass communication.* New York: Longman.

Denmark, F. (1977). "What Sigmund Freud didn't know about women." Convocation Address, St. Olaf's College, Northfield, MN.

Evans, E., Rutberg, J., Sather, C., & Turner, C. (1991). Content analysis of contemporary teen magazines for adolescent females. *Youth and Society, 23,* 99–120.

Hunter College Women's Studies Collective. (1983). *Women's realities, women's choices.* New York: Oxford University Press.

Kaufman, D., & Richardson, B. (1982). *Achievement and women: Challenging the assumptions.* New York: Free Press.

Massey, J. Girl talk mags. (1992, October). *School Library Journal, 54.*

McRobbie, A. (1982). *Jackie: An ideology of adolescent femininity.* In B. Waites, T. Bennett, & G. Martin (Eds.), *Popular Culture: Past and Present.* (pp. 263–283) London: Croom Helm.

Peirce, K. (1989). Sex-role stereotyping of children on television: A content analysis of the roles and attributes of child characters. *Sociological Spectrum, 9,* 321–328.

Peirce, K. (1990). A feminist theoretical perspective on the socialization messages in *Seventeen* magazine. *Sex Roles, 23,* 491–500.

Peirce, K. (1993, July). Socialization of teenage girls through teen-magazine fiction: The making of a new woman or an old lady? *Sex Roles, 29,* 58–68.

Pool, G. *Magazines in review.* (1990). *Wilson Library Bulletin, 65,* 131–132, 135, 159.

Romer, N. (1981). *The Sex Role Cycle.* New York: Feminist Press.

Rubin, J., Provenzano, F., & Luria, Z. (1974). The eye of the beholder: Parents' views on sex of newborns. *American Journal of Orthopsychiatry, 44,* 512–519.

Ruggiero, J., & Weston, L. (1985). Work options for men and women in women's magazines. *Sex Roles, 12,* 535–547.

Sadker, M., & Sadker, D. (1985, March). Sexism in the schoolroom of the '80s. *Psychology Today,* 54–57.

Schau, C. (1978). Evaluating the use of sex-role reversed stories for changing children's stereotypes. ERIC, ED 159494.

Signorielli, N. (1989). Television and conception about sex roles: Maintaining conventionality and the status quo. *Sex Roles, 21,* 341–360.

Weitzman, L. (1979). *Sex role socialization.* Palo Alto, CA: Mayfield.

6

"BE SOMEBODY":

Ruth Whitney of Glamour

BARBARA STRAUS REED

Barbara Straus Reed, Associate Professor at Rutgers University in the Department of Journalism and Mass Media, has long been involved with women's publications. She created a set of 55 slides and lengthy script for Vis-Com, titled "Women's Magazines Today" and "Women's Magazines in the 1970s." To date her work appears in colleges and universities, nationally and internationally. In addition, Reed's chapter about women in the media in Michael C. Emery and Ted C. Smythe's *Readings in Mass Communication, Concepts and Issues* has been well received for almost 20 years, through numerous editions. She has conducted scholarly research about women and magazines for presentations at professional meetings and for publication and has headed the magazine division for the Association for Education in Journalism and Mass Communication and its Commission on the Status of Women.

Ruth Whitney, editor-in-chief, *Glamour*.

Glamour magazine reaches 2.3 million readers every month through subscription and single-copy sales. Its success has given rise to the supposition that no matter how profits fluctuate within Condé Nast (the company that publishes *Glamour* and other magazines), any losses can be covered by *Glamour.* In large part, this supposition is based on the talents of Ruth Whitney, editor of *Glamour* for more than 25 years.

GROWING UP WITH A GOAL

Ruth Reinke (Whitney) grew up in Oshkosh, Wisconsin. Her role model was her father, Leonard G. Reinke, a strong man who brought up three children almost single-handedly. Her mother, Helen, suffered most of her adult life from mental illness, causing numerous hospitalizations lasting years. The Reinke children became accustomed to their mother's relatives living with them at various times—an uncle, an aunt: "Family was always moving in and out, until they got on their feet. These were hard times," Whitney said.

Ruth Whitney did not come from a wealthy family, yet all the Reinke children attended school and later college on scholarships, and all were expected to make use of opportunities and attain an education. The Reinke children were competitive and successful. Her sister, "regarded as the smart one in the family," Ruth said, became assistant provost of City College in Chicago. Her brother became an architect of some renown. Indeed, her father provided the central role model in his children's lives. "Just be somebody," he counseled his children.

This material is based, for the most part, on three interviews with Ruth Whitney in her office at 350 Madison Avenue, New York, in September 1993.

In high school, Whitney's other role models included a Latin teacher and a teacher of creative writing. Whitney stayed in contact with her Latin teacher for years after graduation. "She had extraordinary faith in me," Whitney explained, "and that's, of course, what made her so appealing to me." Whitney edited the high school newspaper and won a couple of minor honorary mentions in national competitions. Her writing teacher encouraged her more than others in the class, Whitney remembered. "By the time I left for college, I knew if I excelled at anything, it was using words and on paper . . . working with words."

After high school, Whitney enrolled at Northwestern University, where she majored in English literature. She selected Northwestern because of its reputation and the generous scholarship she was offered. She didn't enter journalism school because she "got kind of seduced" by a special program, broad and classic in feeling. "People say, 'just an English major' like they say 'just a housewife'; it's terrible," Whitney said. "I don't regret it at all."

Her father felt a lot of consternation "as to what in heaven's name" she would do to support herself when she graduated. Like many fathers of the time, he advised her to go into teaching; indeed, it was "the only thing he could think of," Whitney said, smiling. "Get your teaching degree; you'll have something to fall back on," he admonished. She knew what he did not: that she did not want something to fall back on but wanted to be a career woman.

Following college in 1949, she found a job at Time, Inc. in Chicago, writing sales-promotion letters to motivate and train college subscription agents, all "ghosted" for a male superior. "I got the job because I could write like a man," Whitney stated. She worked with two other women, then was promoted to copywriter, alongside two men. "The two men were hired as copywriters, one probably straight from college. I worked my way up to be a copywriter, and I think both of them were taken more seriously than I was in the assignments they were given: more complicated letters to deal with, more complicated issues to deal with, more important promotional material to handle."

After two years, she received a phone call informing her that her department was being moved to New York and if she wanted to she could move as well. Although the two men holding the same position remained in Chicago, she surprised the staff by moving. She and her husband, whom she had met in college and married after graduation, had dreamed of moving to New York, sharing the belief that succeeding in New York's publishing and advertising industries connoted that one had arrived in one's lifework.

Having a fulfilling career simply meant following her father's "Be Somebody" admonition. "Dad never concerned himself with what I would do; he merely urged me to make my mark," she said. Her father wanted achievement, but he didn't anticipate her move to New York. "He saw a tidy little achievement, preferably back in Oshkosh," Whitney said. "I don't think he ever anticipated that I would go as far as I really went, both in career and distance-wise." (Indeed, she was at her father's funeral when she received a call to be interviewed for the editor-in-chief position at *Glamour*.)

While in New York, Whitney continued working for *Time* but added *Life* and *Fortune* magazines to her letter-writing efforts because the circulation department served all three publications. She graduated from letters into real sales-promotion pieces, the kind sent as a mailing. Officially, she was a copywriter. After a few years, Whitney became restless and bored. She grew sullen and difficult as an employee. "Finally, they had the good sense to fire me," Whitney said, but they encouraged her to seek another job within the company.

FINDING AN EDITORIAL POSITION

Whitney recognized the limitations of being female at a magazine like *Time*, *Life*, or *Fortune*. Editorial writers were male; researchers were female. Even at the women's magazines, editors were male. She ticked off, "The editor of *Woman's Home Companion* was male; so was the editor of *Ladies' Home Journal*. The editor of *Good Housekeeping* still is male." Men held the top jobs.

While unemployed, Whitney came to a turning point in her career. "When you're out of work, you have a real chance to do some real thinking," she said. She realized she wanted to move into the editorial side of magazines. At the same time, she realized she could not make much progress, if any, at general interest or newsmagazines because they were dominated by men.

In 1953, she joined *Better Living*, a magazine for homemakers sold exclusively in supermarkets. "The magazine, published by McCall company, was quite new when I came to it," Whitney said. She continued to write, and the job turned out to be a wonderful spot for her. She had a female boss who encouraged and nurtured her. In three years, Whitney moved from copy editor to copy chief to managing editor. Whitney's boss, Barbara Hewson, worked her hard. "She would ask for not one title to a story but ten titles, and if she didn't like them, she'd ask for ten more, and if she didn't like the third, then she'd ask for ten more," stated Whitney. So she learned a lot about titles, words, and captions. Whitney worked hard and had a lot of fun. "For the first time, I was really beginning to work to capacity. I worked for long hours, rewriting my stuff, and learning at a very rapid clip," Whitney said. She credited Hewson for teaching her the magazine business. "She may have been a taskmaster in terms of demanding high quality, but she was very warm and encouraging, and when you did something right, she was lavish in her praise," Whitney said.

When the editor quit ("She probably knew something I didn't know"), Whitney shocked herself by taking the helm. It was 1956 and Whitney was 27 years old. She became editor-in-chief of *Better Living*, not realizing the magazine was doomed to extinction. The magazine was in great financial difficulty; to this day, Whitney believes the owners hired from within because they knew of the impending demise of the publication.

Although the magazine folded shortly after Whitney assumed editorship, she felt the title looked good on her resume. However, she found she still wasn't hired to write at *Time* or *Newsweek* or any of "those places." It never occurred to her at the time that women should be allowed equal opportunity. "I think that's important to know; you expected your opportunities to be limited and designed by your gender," she said. "You expected a double standard; you saw nothing surprising about that at all. That's the way the world was."

Whitney promoted her skills and was hired as associate editor at *Seventeen*. What she liked about *Seventeen* was the market; she found young people responsive, idealistic, and wonderful as readers. "I could see that a magazine could have importance in a life. That's really why I was so interested in sticking with a young audience," Whitney stated. "I did not feel that you could achieve that, or achieve it as easily if you were talking to women in their 40s or 50s. I really felt that I was making a difference in human lives as an editor there [*Seventeen*]. That's what hooked me to the idea that a magazine could be that important in a reader's life." She made up her mind she would only be happy writing to a young market.

At *Seventeen*, she worked among women. "It was a mainly female ghetto," she stated. By contrast, the same company that published *Seventeen* published *TV Guide*. "I'm sure I never made what Merrill Pannett [the male editor of *TV Guide*] made," she said. Circulation figures for *Seventeen* greatly increased during Whitney's time there, but she credits that, in part, to a rise in the population of teenagers.

Whitney developed as an editor and her self-image grew, as did her respect for other women's talents. "Keep in mind that I had been brought up by a man," Whitney reminded. "I felt more comfortable with men that I did women; it was easier with men than with women," but working at *Better Living* and *Seventeen* changed her perceptions.

Whitney stayed at *Seventeen* for 11 years. In the last few years, Whitney became dissatisfied, wanting a magazine of her own. In New York, however, few top editor-in-chief jobs were available. She also wanted to work on a "young" magazine. The wait proved long, hard, and painful.

Over the course of her years at *Seventeen*, Whitney had become friends with the personnel director at Condé Nast, Mary Campbell. The two friends chatted often about their work and their respective magazines. Whitney, serving as executive editor, was hiring and firing, so she and Campbell shared many problems and solutions. Job opportunities emerged at Condé Nast, but Whitney didn't feel any of these positions were right for her. Then a vacancy for editor of *Glamour* occurred, and Whitney applied. Although men were editors of many women's magazines, such as *McCall's* or *Ladies' Home Journal*, the fashion magazines were primarily women's preserves. Women editors headed *Harper's Bazaar*, *Vogue*, and *Mademoiselle*. At 39, Ruth Whitney was hired as editor of *Glamour*, an indispensable magazine for a growing number of young adult women 18 to 35 years old.

CHANGING THE FOCUS OF *GLAMOUR*

Glamour is the second biggest seller in college bookstores, right behind Helen Gurley Brown's *Cosmopolitan*. *Glamour*'s ad revenues totaled at least $100 million in 1992, a 10 percent increase over 1991. More than half the income from circulation comes each month from single-copy sales, which are certainly more profitable than subscription sales.

Traditionally a fashion magazine, *Glamour*'s name today seems to be almost an anachronism to its mission. When Whitney first took the position as editor-in-chief, she inherited a fashion magazine with white-glove concerns, but Whitney didn't feel hampered. Whitney broadened and deepened *Glamour*'s editorial formula. At *Glamour*, the core of the editorial product was its fashion and beauty pages, "with a little bit of feature material strung out in between." The attitude of the magazine clearly addressed women who were not rich but suggested that if a woman had taste—and she could learn that—she could find the right man and even the right job. Whitney wanted to add some meat to the editorial content. "For the most part," she said, "I left the fashion and beauty pages alone."

Whitney inherited a solidly professional staff that included Gloria Steinem, a contributing editor who gave readers wardrobe and beauty advice; Phyllis Starr Wilson, later founding editor of *Self*, as copy editor; and Midge Richardson, college editor at *Glamour*, later editor-in-chief of *Seventeen*. "It's ironic," Whitney stated, "there were a lot of very strong people when I came."

Whitney challenged the prevailing issues of *Glamour* when she took over. "How to get and keep a man—but was that an issue?" she questioned. "That was service really; that was how-to." Changes in *Glamour* were reflected in some of Whitney's early modifications. For example, she changed the annual best-dressed contest among college-age women to an annual achievement competition. Ten college women were chosen based on their grades and activities rather than on their wardrobes.

Whitney also pushed the limits of what were considered acceptable covers. Eight months after she arrived at *Glamour*, she wanted to run a photo of Katiti Kironde, an African-American woman, on the cover. There was a lot of corporate fear, anger, and consternation at Condé Nast about a Black woman on the cover. "Keep in mind that I had been editor for only eight months, not a long, reassuring record to build their confidence in my judgment," Whitney stated. Because no one had placed an African-American woman on a cover before, no one knew what would happen. Would they lose their wholesale distribution? Would advertisers pull their ads? Would there be a backlash because "we didn't tell anybody"? asked Whitney. The concern about perception overrode others, but financial concerns could not be minimized either. Whitney "thought hard" about the individuals who could approve or deny her decision, and she spoke to each, one by one. "A number of them surprised me," she said. "*Glamour*'s publisher clearly did not relish the risk, but he made it clear he would not try to stop the cover." In August 1968, Katiti Kironde graced the cover of *Glamour*. Quite a few subscribers canceled their subscriptions, but nowhere near the number of new readers *Glamour* won over. This issue sold more single copies than any issue in the entire history of *Glamour*. "Our audience was out there just waiting for it. Women's magazines were so fearful back in those days, just so fearful. And it wasn't a scary thing to do at all once you'd done it," Whitney stated.

Soon, the women's movement made clear many issues that were being ignored. Whitney believes *Glamour* became a "mainstream feminist" magazine, for Whitney sees herself as a mainstream feminist. Issues such as sexual harassment (before Anita Hill), rape, the glass ceiling, equal rights in terms of the law; "We've really dabbled in all this," she said.

During the Equal Rights Amendment vote, Whitney helped organize a massive effort of 39 women's magazine editors—some of them men—who all wrote pieces about the Equal Rights Amendment during the same month. They had a historic meeting and decided on a united effort to push ratification through the remaining states, perceiving that ERA needed one last big push. However, a backlash was building. "We were definitely behind the ERA, and a lot of good it did us," she said sarcastically. Their effort backfired. "People in the heartland of America often see the magazines of the East Coast almost as a conspiracy, and I think the fact that so many magazines all talked about ERA in their July issue struck a lot of people as a conspiracy," Whitney said. "That was a mistake. Looking back on it, we never should have done what we did. It outraged people. That certainly was not our intention."

Glamour received "tons" of mail, and threatening letters went to advertisers. Groups opposed to ERA passage targeted advertisers of participating magazines. Heads of corporations received letters from such groups as Stop ERA, which read in part: "We implore you to withhold your advertising from magazines that make it their policy to . . . espouse the philosophy of feminists, which is anti-family, pro-abortion, and pro-lesbian." All the other magazines experienced the same response. "We never got together as a group effort after that, and I wouldn't today on *any* subject, no matter how deeply I cared about it," she added. Her magazine could take a stand on an issue, but she would never join with other editors in that kind of mass effort because it is self-defeating.

In contrast, the subject of civil rights resulted in positive feedback, as did a very long article on women and AIDS. "It had a tremendous impact on our readers, in the sense that they had never really seen themselves as potential victims, and this brought home to them how dangerous 'unsafe sex' was," she said.

A *Columbia Journalism Review* survey examined the coverage of abortion issues by women's magazines. "Even I was surprised to read that *Glamour* had published 37 articles on the subject from 1972 to 1991, many more than any other magazine," Whitney stated. "Some editors feel that publishing articles on the abortion issue will frighten away advertisers. It doesn't. I can't think of a single advertising page *Glamour* lost over those years because of its editorial coverage."

Another controversial story included "Not Just Another Prom Night," the story of Heidi and Missy, two young lesbians who decided to attend the prom as each other's date. Almost immediately, *Glamour* received close to 50 subscription cancellations, about 100 negative letters, and 40 positive ones. Later, 132 letters arrived, largely positive. Although *Glamour* had published articles about lesbians before, never had a story made this kind of impact.

Whitney has a rule of thumb: If she hasn't offended either her readers or her advertisers in six months—or worse, a year—she is probably not doing her job. "You really have to keep pushing right out there to the edge," she said. She believes magazines do shape opinion, along with other media. But an individual magazine or individual news commentator is muted in power by all the others clamoring for attention.

As for material about beauty issues, Whitney believes the consumer mentality has changed. "The reader today is much more sophisticated, much more knowledgeable, much smarter, much more demanding," she said. The beauty consumer is less preoccupied now with how to put on mascara than how to choose one that will last the longest or not waste her money on one with the wrong brush. "Fashion relating to sociology is more and more complex, and over the years how women have spent their fashion dollar has changed tremendously," said Whitney. "They used to spend it to get a man; then money used to go into dating, clothes, that kind of thing. Now most of the young American woman's fashion goes into getting ahead: She puts her money into getting her work wardrobe. That's what really matters to her, so that's been a real sociological change," said Whitney.

"We try to be as honestly helpful as we can," Whitney said. Young women are faced with a much more complicated life these days, she believes, and "I think women's magazines are pushing women to new rights and new wants and new demands." A lot of change is inch by inch, Whitney said. With a magazine like *Glamour,* "it is difficult to know whether society is moving you or you are moving society, and it's a little bit of each." She explained that topics of nutrition and fitness are concerns of society in general but especially women. Women have much more interest in health, Whitney believes. They are taking control of their own health, and are less reluctant to challenge doctors. "It's a much more take-charge generation, so we are giving them lots and lots of information on health and medical news and fitness information," she said. This is partly self-serving, too, she acknowledged, because using health on magazine covers frequently sells more magazines. "Maybe not as much as the word 'sex,' but almost." And she quipped, "Healthy sex: Now there's a combination!"

Whitney hears from 200 different readers every month. They come from a group, which in turn comes from a pool of people who complete surveys. The group is not randomly drawn, but statistically represents the readership in terms of demographics and psychographics. The group's composition changes all the time; it is not a reader panel. The surveys seek to learn from readers which articles they found to be very interesting, fairly interesting, and somewhat interesting. Respondents are also asked how much they read of a subject. Whitney primarily looks for surprises in the monthly research. "I've been in this job long enough so that I could probably go through an issue and come within five percentage points of what everything should rate," she said.

The magazine's title is one element of readers' concerns because it seems outmoded. Indeed, Whitney says turning out a really serious product with the name *Glamour* to be "something of a hat trick." She said, "I cannot say how many times I have been asked why the magazine has not changed its title, and, of course, the magazine can't possibly change its title; that's its heritage." Mainly, the question comes from college students. "Unless you're familiar with the magazine, and you hear a magazine named *Glamour*, your feeling about what is in that magazine is not going to be an accurate representation of what is actually there, just on the basis of the title," she said. On the other hand, worse titles remain, too, she noted; for example, a magazine called *Good Housekeeping* in the 1990s—she'd rather be editor of *Glamour.*

At *Glamour*, Whitney reviews each piece of artwork and every article; she is a hands-on editor, never content to sit back and make decisions from the top. In fact, she sees articles at various stages of production. At any given time, Whitney is working on three issues at once. She juggles the progress of each, okaying one copy, laying out and placing photographs on a second, meeting to plan the third. Such juggling constitutes the routine of a monthly magazine's schedule.

Whitney meets monthly with every department and always with the art director. They discuss at length the graphics treatment and often work out the title—at least a good working title. "We get a clear picture of what it is we want that piece to deliver," she said. "Sometimes we arrive at an actual title; if we are really lucky we arrive at a cover title."

For years, Whitney wrote all the cover lines herself. "Now I round up a half-dozen of the most creative people on the staff, a cover-writing team, and we thrash out the cover lines together." Usually such a meeting consists of five or six people, not necessarily the most senior, but "the zaniest, the freest, the ones who are most able to put themselves inside our readers' heads. The meetings are loud, funny, raunchy. In about an hour and a half, they accomplish better what used to take me a whole day of agonizing," Whitney said. Whitney changes members of the team, or group. "When people go off [the team] and new people come in, that, too, helps train people," she said. It's a changing circle, too, because of "burnout." It's hard to retain a freshness in that challenging role, she said.

The staff at *Glamour* is almost entirely female. The editorial staff numbers more than 60 and another 40 comprise the business area. "The editorial staff is unusually stable; they like it here," Whitney said. "They have a lot of pride in their work, pride in the magazine itself; it's a good place to work, it really is." She believes in "trading up." "Every time I lose a staff member, I try to hire someone stronger and better for the job than the person who left," she admitted. "This is especially important if your personnel department says you can't increase the body count, because then that is the only way you have to build a better staff."

In Whitney's view, there has never been a better time for aspiring women to become editors. "Just go for it," she advises. "The field is more open than it's ever been." Although most women's magazines have women editors, newsmagazines do not, but Whitney believes that change will occur in time. "Eventually women will make it [those editorial slots in newsmagazines], probably in the future, maybe a long time away," she said. In magazine editing, talent is perhaps foremost, even more important than gender, so opportunities exist now that were never there before, she said. What holds women back are tradition and habit. "The old-boys network is still alive and well," she admitted. "Increasingly, of course, there is an all-girls network, or whatever you want to call it. There are many more women, not only in the pipeline, but also those who are making real strides. It takes a long time, but it's happening," she said.

At Condé Nast itself, working conditions and attitudes have changed. "There were no women publishers until really quite recently; it might have been as recent as five years ago." The publishers of *Vogue, Self, Mademoiselle*, and *Vanity Fair* are all female. "That represents tremendous change."

THE CONSUMMATE PROFESSIONAL

Whitney's tenure at *Glamour* speaks well of her, for it represents an eternity in a line of work known for rapid turnover of editors. In a speech to the editors-in-chief at the American Society of Magazine Editors meeting in 1987, Whitney stated, "I think editors know that a magazine is such a tapestry of skills and experience and hard information and research and industry wisdom and marketing smarts and guesses and gut, that it is as individual as that proverbial snowflake, and as quick to melt."

Although in her mid-60s, Ruth Whitney has no retirement plans. "I'm not ready yet. This is a very exciting job," she said, and she is not receiving pressure from either her husband or from management to step down. "The magazine is going very well, and I come home happy and exhilarated and 'up,'" she said.

Whitney runs *Glamour* by seven rules. They are not universal, and some are specific to women's magazines. "I remind myself of one or the other of these rules almost every working day," she said. The rules are:

1. Beware of editing down to the reader
2. Beware of presenting women as victims
3. Beware of elitism

4. Beware of New York provincialism
5. Beware of fat-catism
6. Beware of resting on past laurels
7. Beware of playing it safe.

Every editorial decision she makes involves marketplace risk, and it is risk that makes the editor's job satisfying to her. "I would not swap the years at *Glamour* for any magazine, for the top job at any magazine," she said. "I think women's lives have changed so much, I think the real excitement has been with women." That's influence. Be somebody, her father told her, and Ruth Whitney is.

From the women's sections of newspapers to soap operas, media for women have been forced to be trivial (since their purpose is always to sell consumption), and then are disparaged for such triviality. So, too, 19th- and early 20th-century critics, for the most part male, disparaged both the concept and the content of women's magazines.

7

Criticism

WOULD THE REAL WOMEN'S MAGAZINE PLEASE STAND UP . . . FOR WOMEN

LINDA STEINER

Linda Steiner, Assistant Professor of Journalism and Mass Media at Rutgers University, earned her Ph.D. from the University of Illinois at Urbana. Her publications include "Finding Community in Nineteenth-Century Suffrage Periodicals" in *American Journalism* and "Oppositional Decoding as an Act of Resistance" in *Critical Studies in Mass Communication*. Steiner's research interests include alternative media and media ethics, both of which she addresses from the standpoint of cultural studies and feminist theorizing.

The January 1993 issue of *Mirabella* described "What Women Want." Among the desirables were, apparently listed in no particular order, 50 female senators, safe sex (and, separately, clever sex), a great haircut under $100, intelligent child care for everyone, first-class medical care for everyone, the same fat cells as men, more time, flannel sheets, aromatherapy in subways, a gal Friday, a manicurist who makes office calls, Jeff Bridges, Denzel Washington, and Anita Hill as chairwoman of the judiciary committee. Lastly, *Mirabella* called for getting "the last word." The 77-item list betrays the casual hodgepodge of interest in sex, celebrities, sexual politics, personal products and services, diets and sexual appearance, and sexual partners that historically and currently dominates what are characterized as "women's magazines." *Mirabella* said nothing about "a great women's magazine."

Attempting a critique of so-called women's magazines forces a confrontation with an entire set of arguments about both popular culture and the standards for criticizing popular culture, and about various concepts of womanhood and feminism. In short, analyzing women's magazines raises questions about the very definition of women's magazines. Is the mere fact that women, but generally not men, read a particular magazine sufficient to establish it as a women's magazine? Are women's magazines necessarily magazines of and for women? As service magazines, which women do they define as deserving service? Finally, if "a great women's magazine" had been included on *Mirabella*'s list, what might it look like? How might it differ from those already on the magazine racks?

OVERVIEW OF WOMEN'S MAGAZINES

Before getting entangled in a web of rhetorical questions, let's review what we know about women's magazines. First, all women's magazines are not the same. From *Allure* to *Women's Household*, they are marked by a certain variety in style and content. Many have responded to perceived (or scientifically studied) changes in the market and to larger social and cultural changes. Indeed, the long-lived ones continually and ruthlessly experiment with format and design. They add, adapt, or drop features and modify editorial philosophy. Their specialization is even more apparent. One could not confuse *The Joyful Woman*, "for and about Bible-believing women who want God's best," with *Self*, with its emphasis on psychological, emotional, and physical well-being. *Ladies' Home Journal* locates itself in dead center, claiming to "reflects the lives of the contemporary mainstream woman and provides the information she needs and wants to live in today's world." But there is also *Mademoiselle*, directed to college-educated, unmarried working women 18 to 34; and *Lady's Circle*, directed to middle- to low-income midwestern homemakers. According to the recent volume of *Writer's Digest*, a reference book geared to freelancers, every submission to *Redbook*, with its circulation of 4 million young mothers (all circulation figures are from the 1993 edition of the *Standard Periodical Directory* published by Oxbridge), must explain why "it's right for only *Redbook*." Magazines are available for large women, Black women, business women, New Age women. Furthermore, magazines for adolescent girls, who devour their highly detailed instructions on how the use of female products can help negotiate the complexities of growing up female, also provide an early introduction to the habit of consuming women's magazines.

Of course, despite the vast array of specialized women's magazines and their close attention to the evolving needs of readers, there is not a magazine for "every" woman. Only readers who represent markets desirable to advertisers are served. Women buyers are the ones who have been treated as business opportunities. The A&P chain, for example, established *Woman's Day*, selling it at grocery-store check-out stands. Women's magazines are created and adapted, then, as the market research indicates, to attract those readers—and only those—who have significant, active purchasing power.

Second, both as a genre and by individual example, women's magazines have exploited the entire range of organizational strategies in order to enjoy a relatively long history of financial success and hefty circulation. The stories of individual specimens show skillful, if brutal, deployment of the magazine industry's repertoire of devices to gain commercial advantage and ensure profit. This includes mergers, chain and corporate takeovers, name and format changes, transformations of editorial policy, and specialization. James McCall, not the first tailor to establish a magazine simply to promote his tissue-paper patterns (the credit for this goes to Ebenezer Butterick, with his *Delineator*, begun in 1872), started *The Queen* in 1873, later renamed it *McCall's*, and sold it in 1913 to a banking company involved in several publishing ventures. Since then, *McCall's* management has periodically studied ways to attract readers. One such experiment was the three-way makeup introduced in the late 1920s; that is, the division of the magazine into three parts, each with its own cover. Its circulation has significantly fallen since its height in the 1960s. Nonetheless, 5 million women a month still buy *McCall's* for advice on food, household management, fashion, beauty, and decorating, with a healthy dose of self-help narratives and features on relationships. *McCall's*, the magazine's staff now says with all seriousness, "carefully and conscientiously services the needs of the woman reader—concentrating on matters that directly affect her life and offering information and understanding on subjects of personal importance to her." What more could a woman want?

Women's magazines are attractive to publishers because they are attractive to advertisers. But how do they command their large circulations—with *Woman's Day* at 6 million, *Good Housekeeping* at 5 million, *Glamour* at 2.1 million? Largely, by doing what they promise to do, no more, no less. Since 1770, when the British publication *The Lady's Magazine* claimed to combine "amusement with instruction," these magazines have promised to include an array of recipes for life. This includes both readily understood and immediately applicable recipes as well as more complex recipes for fantasy and dreams. Therefore, they offer both pragmatic advice and instruction and "mental chocolate," as the writer for some British magazines put it.

I would argue that women's magazines see their major function as providing moments of pleasure. They create opportunities to avoid, perhaps to escape or even to transcend, more mundane responsibilities of domestic and work life. When flipping through the glossy pages of these magazines, one is not cleaning, cooking, typing, teaching, lawyering. One is not attending to others, not catering to others' needs or problems, perhaps not even aware of others' presence. One is spending time on oneself. Indeed, although women's continuing protests about pornography make my next suggestion controversial, one might speculate that the head-on, close-up, cosmetically made-up, air-brushed photographs of beautiful women (or, more often, of erotic "pieces" of women's bodies) in fashion layouts and advertising even provide flashes of sexual pleasure for women consumers. It might be argued that women's magazines combine certain advantages and luxuries offered by a range of popular culture products. They offer the portability of paperbacks, the accessibility of newspapers. Would-be readers without subscriptions can easily find them in various reception rooms. And at $1 to $3 a copy, they are relatively cheap. They carry the rich, visual glamour of feature films, the variety and ease of consumption of television. One can save and re-read, or not. One can devour at leisure in bed, or during odd moments while waiting for appointments.

Meanwhile, these magazines offer the perfect excuse for consistent consumption: They teach. Their recipes and patterns are not simply for chicken casseroles and afghans, but for finding and keeping husbands, managing efficient households, rearing children. Perhaps they do not provide all the important information of newspapers, but neither do they smudge one's fingers with ink. If all that relevant information in the feature articles, often written by or with credentialed experts, weren't enough, the fiction offers useful insights about people. Advertising educates about new products. The checklists determine the degree to which one fits neatly within a "type" or if one needs to invest in professional care. According to readers, the poetry is inspiring, the advice columns applicable, the profiles motivating.

However, the "instruction" almost invariably has a specific subtext. A good part of the editorial content is dictated by the interests of advertisers. The editorial product often explicitly pushes either particular products and services of advertisers ("complementary copy") or general categories of products. The rest is directly authorized by advertisers or at least heavily influenced by their agenda. Advertisers advise magazine staffs on how to show readers that their problems, deficiencies, and failures can be addressed by consumer products and services. Conversely, advertisers often have explicit rules about unacceptable content. Maidenform does not want any "editorial adjacencies" with a negative tone, since, they explain, their underwear appeals to positive emotions. Procter & Gamble, for another example, reserves the right to pull its ads from magazine issues that mention witchcraft, gun control, abortion, or contraception. An article in the first ad-free issue of *Ms.* (July/August 1990) exposed the long, seamy relationship of women's magazines and advertisers. Gloria Steinem quoted a former *Redbook* editor asserting that advertisers have historically been able to dictate to women's magazines (in ways and to an extent not possible with other advertiser-subsidized formats) "because of the general disrespect they have for women."

From the women's sections of newspapers to soap operas, media for women have been forced to be trivial (since their purpose is always to sell consumption), and then are disparaged for such triviality. So, too, 19th- and early 20th-century critics, for the most part male, disparaged both the concept and the content of women's magazines.

Is there a way to critique these magazines without denying the very real pleasure women take from the magazines and the very real need for private time and space? Specifically, can we construct such a critique without resorting either to the highly mechanistic effects model (an invalid theory that sees readers as passive, vulnerable dupes of media messages) or to an excessively activist model (which assumes that, since readers make their own oppositional meanings, all popular cultural artifacts are potentially equally satisfying and valuable)?

CRITERIA FOR WOMEN'S MAGAZINES

I'd like to propose several criteria for women's magazines and then contrast that admittedly highly idealistic prescription with a description of women's magazines. I grant that these magazines give pleasure. (Indeed, this fact can be somewhat frustrating for women who are alienated by these magazines and who are therefore summarily dismissed as not properly or sufficiently feminine). Nonetheless, pleasure is not a sufficient condition.

Feminist activist and writer Gloria Steinem raises some provocative, if rhetorical, questions in her new collection of essays, *Moving Beyond Words:* "What could women's magazines be like if they were as editorially free as good books? as realistic as the best newspaper articles? as creative as poetry and films? as diverse as women's lives? What if we as women—who are psychic immigrants in a public world rarely constructed by or for us—had the same kind of watchful, smart, supportive publications on our side that other immigrant groups have often had?" (1994, p. 163). That is, what else, ideally, might women's magazines at least try to do?

Express Readers' Interests in Their Own Voices

The issue of voice, much less authentic voice, is difficult, especially inasmuch as women do not speak with a single voice. To my ears, however, while not all magazines are equally flippant or "sophisticated," women's magazines as a group increasingly tend to share a modern, homogeneous editorial and visual style. This erases the otherwise differing voices of real people and reduces cultural and political differences to matters of fashion preference. Their professional writers, editors, and publishers have uniformly adopted a standardizing corporate language.

Meanwhile, the magazines' interest in appearing friendly, accessible, and positive mitigates against resonating with readers' larger and deeper fears and concerns. Their quick, casual patter grabs readers' attention without engaging it. They certainly do not want to be provocative. Instructions for freelancers that *Country Woman*, circulation one million, provided for *Writer's Market '93* included a charge to submit "something that feels like a reward." It mentioned the adjectives "positive," "light," "entertaining," and "upbeat" to describe what it looks for in nonfiction and fiction. Likewise, *Woman's World*, a national weekly covering "controversial, dramatic, and human-interest women's issues," requires that nonfiction stories about romance present "tender, beautiful, touching and unusual love stories." Furthermore, every fiction piece must have a light romantic theme, a protagonist no older than 40, and a positive resolution "that clearly states the villain is getting his or her come-uppance."

Encourage Women to Control Their Own Expressive Media

Historically, women's magazines have not been marked by gender-specific control or editorial authority. These days, the people most intensively involved in the editing and writing of women's magazines are usually women careerists. On the other hand, few publishers maintain a formal policy of training women at all levels of magazine production, mentoring women, or bringing women up the editorial and management ranks. The publishers are still often male, as are the owners of the corporations that own the magazines.

Inspire Women to Act to Improve Women's Lives

Not all women's magazines are as interested in self-improvement as *New Woman Magazine* (1.4 million circulation), whose prime focus is on "self-discovery, self-development, and self-esteem." Instead, across women's magazines there is an emphasis on changing the self to accommodate the world. They recommend individualistic solutions that mitigate against seeing problems as systematic or structural and, therefore, in need of collective action. That some problems are not the fault of individuals and that lives might be more productive in a changed society are seldom acknowledged.

Ironically, at the same time the official voice is cheerful and intimate, they encourage an obsession with one's own flaws and a panicky search for quick fixes. The beneficiary of this is, again, the magazine industry. Readers come to depend on magazines to identify problems (many of which they would not otherwise think existed) and solutions (often consumerist). Even magazines that most vociferously proclaim the importance of self-esteem may actually be promoting neuroses, or at least widespread "nervousness."

Empower Women to Improve the Condition of Others in Need

"True" women's magazines need to deal with the real problems of the oppressed. But even the magazines claiming to be provocative want only to provoke purchases. They smooth over any subversive edge, unwilling to upset readers (who might, therefore, be too distraught to shop). Some might be willing to criticize men. But capitalism? Never. They want to cause some tension—but only the amount and kind that can be resolved with purchases. They create problems that can be cured by consumption. Accounts or pictures of people who are suffering horribly are conspicuously absent—they might depress women (and thereby depress shopping). *Bridal Trends* makes this very clear in advising writers (*Writers's Market '93*) that it emphasizes the use of wedding consultants, gift registries, floral designers, caterers, and travel agents. In other words, women's magazine writers are compelled to write about people who will take your money.

Celebrate Women's Collective Struggle and Success

To their credit, women's magazines honor some heroines (remarkably, Princess Di still among them). But whether in first person "triumph over tragedy" stories or the newest diet, the emphasis on self-improvement and personal relationships reinforces an ideology of ego. This is marked even on the covers, which almost invariably show one person—indeed, one with perfect teeth. Women's magazines of a century ago honored social reform efforts to a much greater extent than does the current crop, which essentially ignores the hard work of women's groups and organizations as such.

Respect Women's Intelligence and Take Risks on Their Behalf

Women's magazines' preference for a casual mix of extremely brief articles; short poems and condensed short stories; lists and hints; and abstracted quizzes may be a realistic concession to the frenzied way women often live. Perhaps it also represents a patronizing and even invalid assumption that women cannot maintain interest in a long, thoughtful piece. It is also an issue of money, since in-depth, researched articles by serious thinkers cost more and take up more space. Some recent research indicates that newspaper readers, including women, will read long, complex articles, even while drinking their morning coffee. The same may be true of magazine readers. For all their diversity, why do no women's magazines run stories the length of those in, say, the *New Yorker* or even the *Atlantic*?

Recognize and Appreciate Diversity among Women

Magazines can help readers articulate and cultivate various definitions of womanhood as these emerge from their specific positions, experiences, and problems. Yet, the homogeneity within any particular magazine is remarkable. One needs to go to *Essence* to see Black women. With Frances Lear's 1994 decision to shut down the magazine bearing her name, older women will again not see themselves on a women's magazine cover. More critically, the entire industry speaks for middle-class, heterosexual, youthful, politically mainstream women. For the most part, any woman who does not speak their voice, who does not and cannot look like their cover girls, does not count. This erases lesbians, poor women, disabled women, as well as all other seemingly minor differences. It authoritatively enforces its own version of womanhood, which is casually treated as global, as normative.

Avoid Harming Women's Interests

I put this last, given its negative construction. Yet the point is that even magazines subsidized by advertising could establish policies that prefer advertising for products and services that serve women, and exclude advertising for products and services that directly harm women as individuals or that essentially install or confirm gender-specific barriers. Even more easily, they can encourage advertisers to produce visual and verbal texts that respect women's minds and bodies. They can choose to exclude ads that trivialize women, that objectify and dehumanize women, and that sanction violence against women.

COMPARISON TO THE CRITERIA

It may be argued that these criteria are impossible to satisfy or that these expectations are unreasonable. I concede that this list is more platonic than practical. Nevertheless, I articulate these high standards for several reasons. First, magazines are a medium uniquely able to meet the challenges implied here. Magazines (and newspapers) are the primary mechanism by which groups of people can come together to redefine themselves and their world. Unlike television, for example, magazines are not economically compelled to sell to huge audiences or earn huge audiences. Technically and technologically, they are fairly simple and accessible. As they have been for 200 years, magazines are still constituted, at least hypothetically, so as to allow groups of people to come together to renego-tiate their identities, to stake out claims to a meaningful life, and to articulate and dramatize their hopes and goals in uniquely expressive language. That is, I offer these criteria because there is no reason why women's magazines could not meet the challenges and because the challenges are worth meeting. Even an earnest effort is better than nothing.

Readers can and should choose their own criteria and then judge for them-selves whether or not their magazines satisfy those criteria. They can examine what or who is on the cover, who is posing in other photographs and in what poses; what kinds of products are advertised and how they are advertised; what problems are discussed and how; whose problems they are, and who is dis-cussing them. Some readers may indeed be content with "mental chocolate." Others may desire something more substantial and, to stretch this metaphor one more time, something more nutritious, less sugary.

These points are starkly illustrated by comparing all these magazines to *Ms.*, which, although by no means perfect, is engaged in an ongoing struggle to serve diverse women's interests. Few people are likely at first glance to regard *Ms.* as a "women's magazine" because it does stand apart from the rest, essentially in a category by itself. Even its cover—often pure text, sometimes leavened with a gritty photography of a group of activists—illustrates how *Ms.* upsets the con-ventions and expectations of women's magazines. But as a product of the women's liberation movement (published since 1972) and judged by the criteria suggested above, it counts as an "authentic" women's magazine. Robin Morgan, its editor-in-chief from 1990–93, quotes a feminist proverb to explain its risk-taking: "Only she who attempts the absurd can achieve the impossible."

Since 1990, *Ms.* has been "liberated" from advertising; with *Mad* and *Con-sumer Reports*, it is now one of three ad-free magazines published nationally. The bimonthly "magabook" carries no glossy photographs, horoscopes, or recipes for lo-cal chocolate cake. Rather, it takes up the issues of the feminist move-ment, including structural reform; indeed, it takes them up at length in serious prose. It looks out for the diversity of its readers regardless of sexual orientation, class, age, physical ability, race and ethnicity (and geography, for that matter, given a board of international advisors who ensure its sustained attention to global developments). *Ms.* listens to readers, taking sincerely their needs and their interests. It does not sugarcoat its politics. If nothing else, its circulation of 500,000 (relative to *Ladies' Home Journal*, circulation over 5 million) suggests the extent to which many women may be put off by dense text and spare graph-ics, or, more likely, its unadulterated politics. In serving the varying interests of more women, *Ms.* gives pleasure to fewer women, thereby inverting the formula of the traditional women's magazines. Ironically, recognizing that some women will need to go elsewhere for a medium through which to sustain and clarify their identities, *Ms.* also publicizes the work and efforts of other feminist peri-odicals and liberation media. It's a gesture of modesty and generosity not made by traditional women's magazines.

Ms.'s opportunity to be honest is certainly intimately connected to its refusal to accept advertising. Many readers and not a few researchers had noticed that by the 1980s the magazine, then still in its previous advertiser-subsidized incarnation, had yielded on some of its founding principles, apparently falling down the slippery slope greased by advertisers. Despite its early promises to the contrary, it began to run advertising for products that before were deemed harmful to women, as well as for the same cosmetics advertised throughout the rest of the women's magazine industry. Not coincidentally, *Ms.* began running more complementary copy, more glossy photographs of smiling celebrities, more fashion news.

Is the implication that only feminist magazines are authentic women's magazines or that only ad-free magazines can afford to refuse to pander to readers? Perhaps this is true, at least at this point. What we see on the racks at bookstores and pharmacies are magazines about fashion and beauty, work and family, self-help and self-esteem (in the narrow sense of these words). And they are read by women. But not until they try to do more for their readers will they be truly women's magazines.

Without denying their pleasure, albeit a temporary palliative, they are "women's magazines" merely by virtue of their being directed at women who are objects of corporate interests. One looks to *Ms.* and its sisters for models of publications that are produced by women whose interest is communicating with women.

How serious does it have to get before things change?
You don't see any more little black Sambo ads.
You don't see the Frito Bandito or Aunt Jemima.
Women are oppressed by their sexuality in a way other minorities are not. Why is it still politically correct for an advertiser to be a sexist pig? (Lori Peterson, attorney representing women workers at Stroh's brewery suing that the "Swedish Bikini Team" advertising campaign encourages harassment at their workplace, "Briefs," 1993, p. 8)

three

THE ROLE OF WOMEN IN ADVERTISING

Advertising is the economic glue that holds together the media system in the United States. Much of the cost of producing newspapers or magazines is covered by the money advertisers pay to run advertisements. The subscription costs you pay are a small part of the revenue necessary to produce a newspaper or magazine.

The same advertising system pays for the television programs you see and the radio programming to which you listen. You also receive free material through advertising. Pencils, pens, matchbooks with the company or establishment name on them, and T-shirt giveaways from radio stations are all examples of free items that advertising pays for.

HISTORY

Advertising has been in existence for a long time. The first advertisement appeared in 1477 in Britain when William Caxton posted written handbills on doors to promote a book.

In 1704, the first paid newspaper ad in America was printed. This simple ad sought a buyer or renter of real estate. Ads during this time had no pictures; it wasn't until 1765 that an ad in the United States included a design (*Advertising Age,* 1976, p. 7).

Ad agencies were first created by Volney B. Palmer, known as the "father of the agency business," in the 1840s. His agency differed greatly from the agencies we know today. Instead of helping clients create and locate appropriate publications in which to place their ads, he helped newspapers locate advertisers to place ads. He didn't deal with ad design or copy. By the Civil War, there were 30 advertising agents in the United States following Palmer's footsteps. Soon after, advertising agencies included copywriting and design in their services.

In the 1890s, J. Walter Thompson persuaded U.S. magazine publishers to allow ads in their pages. Thompson bought ad space and made a great deal of money by using it for his own clients and selling it for a high price to competing agencies. "As late as 1898, Thompson continued to control all the space in most of the women's magazines as well as in the general monthlies" (*Advertising Age,* 1976, p. 12).

Between 1900 and World War I (1914–18) there was great growth in the advertising business. Advertising possibilities included newspapers, magazines, and outdoor advertising. Auto manufacturers turned to ad agencies to help increase sales. Even into the 1920s, advertising continued to be a healthy investment.

With the Depression came the end of a golden era for advertising. The public sought reforms in advertising, and even pushed for ads to be completely banned. The government gave the Federal Trade Association the task of overseeing advertising.

By the late 1940s and early 1950s, the advertising industry regained some of its previous power and wealth. The economy turned around and television, a new vehicle for advertising, entered the media arena.

Computers and media analysis had become an integral part of the advertising industry. Research ranged from the testing of advertising messages and commercials to the analysis of specific audiences. Research firms studied who listened to what radio stations, read what newspapers and magazines, and watched what television programs. Advertisers determined which radio stations, newspapers, and magazines were good "buys" (that is, which stations, magazines, or newspapers had the audience who was most likely to purchase their product). This move from the shotgun approach (scattering your advertising message across various media, hoping it hits a person who is a potential purchaser) to a rifle approach (targeting potential purchasers by using the media they use) became more critical as advertising costs increased.

Although the research methods became more sophisticated, the messages did not. In a bicentennial book by *Advertising Age,* the editors wrote:

> The changes in advertising during the past 40 years have been largely superficial, and haven't kept pace with the changes of people. We're saying exactly the same kind of things to an entirely different kind of person—a wary, sophisticated, skeptical human being (1976, p. 93).

The 1970s was the decade of mergers within advertising. Smaller agencies gave way to larger, less intimate places to work. Many people, men and women, left the business. Although advertising grew and prospered in the 1980s, it seemed to have lost its edge (Fox, 1984, p. 328). By the 1990s, it had become an integral part of the economic machinery that keeps this country functioning, but with less influence.

Advertising is big business in the United States and supports most media. Newspapers bring in the most advertising dollars, followed by television and direct marketing. Television ad time is the most expensive, but many advertisers use it to seek national audiences. Newspapers, on the other hand, are used more often for local audiences and, therefore, take in more advertising revenue.

There are records of women in advertising as far back as 1867. One or two owned ad agencies, others were hired as freelance writers by ad agencies such as J. Walter Thompson Company. By 1903, the advertising field was known as a place in which women of ability were offered opportunity (Fox, 1984, p. 285). There were a few well-known women in the field, but most were hidden in support roles and not credited for their creative contributions (*Advertising Age,* 1976, p. 31).

In 1911, the first women's advertising club was formed with 200 "advertising girls" from across the United States (McBride, 1948, p. 203). While still "temporary tokenists" by the 1920s, women were "hired for specific tasks (such as 'influencing' decision makers of [a] client or prospect) or more often anonymous footsloggers who rarely made it to title or stockholder" (*Advertising Age,* 1976, p. 30).

J. Walter Thompson Company was the exception. Headed by Helen Lansdowne Resor, a skilled, well-paid female staff was established (*Advertising Age,* 1976, p. 31). Resor was not only a great copywriter, she was also very good with clients, explaining how specific ads would appeal to women consumers. In 1911, Procter & Gamble broke with a 20-year tradition and hired J. Walter Thompson to introduce its new product, Crisco. "On five occasions Lansdowne appeared before the P&G board of directors—the first woman to do so—to explain the advertising" (Fox, 1984, p. 81). J. Walter Thompson Company also was the first agency to promote women to major positions and "one of the first to elect a woman [Ruth Waldo] vice-president" (*Advertising Age,* 1976, p. 31).

Between World War I and World War II, the number of women in advertising increased to 3,000, which appears to be a large number until compared to the 32,000 men in advertising during the same period. During World War II, twice the number of women entered the advertising field but they were "still outnumbered by men at least five to one" (McBride, 1948, p. 204).

Although World War II opened up the field of advertising to women, they were still a small percentage. Women appeared to gain the most "advertising" experience as advertising managers for department and specialty stores. In 1931, 44.5 percent of the ad managers in New York stores were female (Fox, 1984, p. 290). For example, Bernice Fitzgibbon wrote advertising copy for Macy's and then Gimbels (1920s). She was responsible for the slogan, "Nobody, But Nobody Undersells Gimbels" (*Advertising Age,* 1976, p. 32). Years later, Fitzgibbon was awarded Business Woman of the Year (1954) and ranked among *Fortune*'s seven top businesswomen (1964) in the United States (*Advertising Age,* 1976, p. 32).

After World War II, advertising agencies were surveyed to discover how managers believed women they hired had performed. Seventy-five percent had hired at least one woman during the war. "One-third stated that the girls had done their work as well as the men; and half that many (one-sixth of the total) said the girls were, on the whole, more satisfactory" (McBride, 1948, p. 206). Most employers felt women would succeed in advertising if they stuck to specializing in fashions, food, beauty aids, and home products (McBride, 1948).

McBride discussed the limitations women confronted in the field of advertising in her 1948 book *How to Be a Successful Advertising Woman.* "Few advertising agencies outside the big cities have more than one woman copywriter, if any, and large department stores, where girls do most of the writing and illustrating, usually have men advertising managers" (p. 204). In the 1950s, women in advertising were often the brains behind the boss. Some advertising presidents wouldn't hire women as account executives because they didn't think a man–woman rivalry was good within the company (Fox, 1984, p. 292). Women were often in the creative staff. Three women art directors were the first elected to the New York Art Directors Club in 1950 (Fox, 1984, p. 293).

The women's movement in the 1960s affected advertising, in part, by focusing on women's lack of advancement in the advertising industry. Old barriers broke down and women were hired in all aspects of the industry. Doyle Dane Bernbach (DDB), among other agencies, led the way. DDB hired their first woman account executive, Marcella Rosen, in 1962 and introduced her as "the first goddamned woman account executive we've ever had" (Fox, 1984, p. 295). Later that year, another agency hired their first woman art director and McCann-Erickson promoted 6 women to their staff of 100 vice presidents (Fox, 1984, p. 294).

During the 1970s and 1980s, women continued to gain strides in the advertising industry. Fewer young women entered the field by accepting positions as receptionists or secretaries. More women entered the field as account executives.

Although women in the 1990s continue to work in the advertising field, Jean Craig, president of the Los Angeles Kresser/Craig agency, stated the "paucity of women running advertising agencies is shocking" ("Briefs," 1992, p. 8). Bruce Horowitz, marketing columnist for the *Los Angeles Times,* stated "senior-level women ad executives seem to be declining in number even as more junior women are working their way up the ranks." Fewer than 2 percent of the top slots are filled by women (Horowitz, 1992).

Many women, having gained experience in larger advertising agencies, form smaller, independent agencies. Some argue that these smaller agencies are the wave of the future as the role of agencies changes in the 1990s. Although large agencies (Ogilvy and Mather, Inc., J. Walter Thompson Company, or Young and Rubicam) still exist, smaller agencies are attracting clients. In the current economic climate, smaller agencies do more for their clients than merely create advertisements and purchase time and space on the media. Smaller companies become "communication" agencies, helping their clients with everything from the design of their letterhead to their store displays; small things larger advertising agencies of the past didn't do. As advertising dollars become tight, ad agencies offer more personalized services.

PORTRAYAL

In 1906, the first ad using sex appeal appeared in copy written by Helen Lansdowne Resor. The product was Woodbury soap; the copy, "the skin you love to touch."

The 1920s saw an increase in the number of women in ads but their portrayal remained the same (homemaker or sex object). "From its inception, advertising was directed at the woman who, wishing only to catch and keep her man, was willing to reshape and clothe her body to please him" (Fishburn, 1982, p. 161).

Although women were the "shoppers of the world . . . buy[ing] from 80 to 90 percent of the things in general use" (Naether, 1928, p. 4), the author of *Advertising to Women,* written in 1928, was disrespectful of women's intelligence and individuality, believing that women are only concerned with their "desire to look young and sexually appealing" (Fishburn, 1982, p. 163).

Through the 1930s, advertisements continued to portray women as homemakers or objects of sexual desire. The first advertisement with a nude was a color ad for Cannon towels in 1933, revealing the backside of a woman's body.

From the 1940s through the mid-1960s, women's roles in advertising patterned the roles portrayed in media programs. During World War II, women were portrayed as effective, efficient workers, taking care of business while men were at war. With the end of World War II, many women left the job place and returned to the home. Advertising's 1930s portrayal of women returned.

When Betty Friedan's book, *The Feminine Mystique* (1963), focused on women's portrayal in media, attention was paid to the portrayal of women in all advertising forms. Yet changes in the portrayal of women were slow to come. Courtney and Whipple found in 1974, "There is little evidence in the world of TV commercials to show that the family structure may be changing or that women are capable of performing responsible tasks other than those associated with the family and home" (p. 116). Males dominate TV commercials; more male characters than females characters are seen in ads, and there are more male voice-overs than female voice-overs. Women who work outside the home are "still virtually ignored" (Courtney and Whipple, 1974, p. 116).

The women's movement sparked rising criticism about the portrayal of women in advertisements, which forced industry leaders to review their work. A report by *Advertising Age* acknowledged the misrepresentation of women in advertisements, noting that women were too often portrayed as housewives and sex objects to the exclusion of other roles, such as working professionals (1975). In addition, homemaker characters in ads had a "warped sense of values" and were portrayed as stupid and in need of men to solve all their problems ("Advertising portraying or directed toward women," 1975, p. 75). The report stated the problem would not go away by itself and that in order to help correct the problem, the advertiser must ask, "How would I like to be depicted that way?" (p. 76).

Erving Goffman, perhaps one of the most recognized names in any discussion of women in advertisements, gave readers a new way in which to analyze advertisement photographs (Goffman, 1979). Goffman noted that in many advertisements women appeared helpless, often appear smaller than men, are shown most often in family scenes, are framed in such a way as to appear subordinate to men, are instructed by men, and have their hands positioned differently than men's (not firmly grasping objects).

In a study comparing ads within major general-circulation publications in 1973 and 1986, Lazier-Smith found little improvement in the portrayal of women over 13 years. The 1973 data showed that 75 percent of the ads fell into two categories: "Put her down," portraying women as helpless or decorative; and "Keep her in her place," portraying women in traditional roles as wives and working women (nurses, secretaries, and teachers). Nineteen percent of the ads fell into the category, "Fully equal," and 2 percent at the "Nonstereotypical" level. The 1986 data used the same categories and found that images of women did not significantly change (1989, p. 256).

In a study of general circulation magazine advertisements, Klassen, Jasper, and Schwartz found a "disproportionately high number of advertisements that portrayed women in 'traditional' poses relative to advertisements that showed women and men together as equals" (1993, p. 36). The researchers also found that the traditional depictions of women have been decreasing since the 1980s and "that 'equality portrayals' are on the rise" (1993, p. 36).

Although there seems to be some indication that advertisers are portraying women less traditionally, advertisers continue to ignore "feminist" views of women. Between the treatment of Anita Hill at confirmation hearings for Supreme Court Justice Clarence Thomas and the publication of Susan Faludi's best-selling book, *Backlash: The Undeclared War Against American Women,* more women's attention focused on their portrayal in advertisements (Mlller, 1992, p. 1). Judith Langer's survey, distributed through *Self* magazine, found "that women had 'much less patience' with ads that they found demeaning to women" (Miller, 1992, p. 1). Advertisers don't want to deal with feminist issues but are finding women are angry about ad portrayal of women. "Advertisers are scared of it at this point and they're still avoiding it," stated John Ford, chairman of Old Dominion University's Marketing Department (Miller, 1992, p. 2).

Although many advertisers may be steering away from "less traditional" ad portrayals, some are slowly testing new waters. Maidenform moved from the "woman in a bra" ad to an ad that shows a chick, a doll, a tomato, and a fox. The copy states, "While the images used to describe women are simple and obvious, women themselves rarely are. Just something we like to keep in mind when designing our lingerie." Nike follows suit with ads to which the response has been "phenomenal," according to Lisa DeNeffe, Nike's PR manager (Miller, 1992, p. 2). One Nike ad shows a young girl with a softball mitt, asking "Did you ever wish you were a boy?" Others demonstrate the strength of being a woman (in Nikes, of course).

Most in the advertising field believe the days of the overtly sexist ads are in the past, but that doesn't mean the portrayal of women as "mere bodies" is over. Jean Kilbourne accuses the advertising industry of "trivializing and co-opting" feminism in ads that show women in positions of power but still overconcerned with physical perfection (Miller, 1992, p. 18).

If adults are concerned with the portrayal of women in advertisements, what might the advertiser have to contend with in the upcoming generations of consumers? In an article in *Advertising Age,* Emily Hume (age 11) compares television commercials and how they portray boys and girls. First, she notes, "Boys are clearly favored in commercials" (1993, p. S6). In one of the few examples in which boys and girls are equally shown playing a game, Hume writes:

> At the end [of the commercial] the boy wins and gleefully shouts, "I win! I win!" while clapping his hands. My mouth fell open when I saw this commercial. Not only was this kid rude, but he sounded annoying! (1993, p. S6)

Hume found one commercial in which a girl won the game. The girl's reaction is of surprise. Hume stated, "I'm not surprised that she's aghast [that she won] because there are so many sexist commercials!" (1993, p. S6). If advertisers find upcoming generations to be as aware and critical of advertisements as Emily Hume, they have a lot of homework to do.

REFERENCES

Advertising Age. (1976). *How it was in advertising: 1776–1976.* Chicago, IL: Crain Books.

Advertising portraying or directed to women. (1975, April). *Advertising Age, 46,* 16, 72, 75–76.

Courtney, A. E., & Whipple, T. W. (1974, Spring). "Women in TV commercials." *Journal of Communication,* 110–118.

Fishburn, K. (1982). *Women in popular culture: A reference guide.* Westport, CT: Greenwood Press.

Fox, S. (1984). *The mirror makers: A history of American advertising and its creators.* New York: William Morrow.

Goffman, E. (1979). *Gender advertisements.* New York: Colophon.

Horowitz, B. (1992, March 3). Marketing column. *Los Angeles Times.*

Hume, E. (1993, February 8). Blame it on the boys. *Advertising Age, 64,* S6.

Klassen, M. L., Jasper, C. R., & Schwartz, A. M. (1993, March/April). Men and women: Images of their relationships in magazine advertisements. *Journal of Advertising Research,* 30–39.

Lazier-Smith, L. (1989). Advertising: Women's place and image. In P. J. Creedon (Ed.), *Women in mass communication: Challenging gender values* (pp. 247–260). Newbury Park, CA: Sage.

McBride, M. M. (1948). *How to be a successful advertising woman.* New York: Whittlesey House: A Division of McGraw-Hill.

Briefs. (1992, Spring), *Media Report to Women,* 8.

Briefs. (1993, Spring), *Media Report to Women,* 8.

Miller, C. (1992, August 17). Liberation for women in ads: Nymphettes, June Cleaver are out; Middle ground is in. *Marketing News, 26,* 1–2, 18.

Naether, C. A. (1928). *Advertising to women.* New York: Prentice-Hall.

PROJECT IDEAS

1   Obtain two magazines that target the same basic demographic group, but different sexes. For example, look at *Vogue* and *GQ.* You might not be able to find the exact same demographics, but close is fine. Look at the advertisements in both magazines. Look for a product type (liquor or fragrance) advertised in each magazine. Does the advertiser try to sell the same product type differently to women and men?

2   If advertisers are targeting specific groups such as African Americans, Asian Americans, or Latino Americans, how might they target women within a specific group? Are stereotypes of women from a specific group reinforced in advertisements? Seek out the advertisements targeting a specific ethnic group. How are women portrayed? Do they reflect women you know?

3 Content-analyze advertisements on children's programs. What advertisements target young girls? What advertisements target young boys? How did you determine this breakdown? What products are less stereotypically female or male? What percentage of girls and boys (or adult females or males) are in these advertisements?

4 Examine magazines aimed at teenage females (*Seventeen* or *'Teen,* for example). What products are advertised? Based purely on the ads, what do they tell you about the type of person who reads this magazine? What interests her?

NAMES

The following list identifies some of the women who have been or are currently part of the advertising industry. Women who were previously mentioned in this introduction are not duplicated in this list.

Mary Ayres—First women to serve on the board of directors of the American Association of Advertising Agencies (AAAA) (1971).

Amelia Bassin—Advertising director for Fabergé, started her own agency, and received the Advertising Woman of the Year Award from the American Federation of Advertising (1970).

Charlotte Lenore Beers—Senior vice president at J. Walter Thompson (1969–1979) and chair and chief executive officer at Ogilvy & Mather (1979–present).

Helen Gurley Brown—Copywriter and Account Executive at Kenyon & Eckhardt (1958). Later became editor of *Cosmopolitan.*

Louise Taylor Davis—First woman copy supervisor and vice president at Young & Rubicam, Inc. (1925–1946).

Dorothy Dignam—Writer for N.W. Ayer & Son, Inc. (1930s).

Lois Geraci Ernst—Creative director of advertising to Women, Incorporated (1970s–1980s).

Lucille Goold—Vice president at Ogilvy Agency (1955).

Mabel Hill—a copywriter at N.W. Ayer who started her own agency in New York (1920s).

Ethel Holm—Member of J. Walter Thompson Company (1940s).

Reva Korda—Chair at Ogilvy & Mather (1975–1980).

Annie Liebowitz—Fashion photographer (1970s–present).

Nedda McGrath—First woman art director at a major advertising agency, Blackman (1924).

Shirley Polykoff—Voted National Advertising Woman of the Year (1967); owner of her own agency, Shirley Polykoff Advertising (1971).

Barbara Proctor—Founder, chief executive officer, and president of Proctor and Gardner Advertising, the second largest Black-owned ad agency in the mid-1980s (1970–present).

Erma Perham Proetz—First woman inducted into the Advertising Federation of America's Hall of Fame (1920s).

Alice Stoddard—Hired by J. Walter Thompson Company in the 1880s to sell ads.

Jane Trahey—Worked for Neiman-Marcus, then owned her own advertising agency (1958–1970s).

Mathilde C. Weil—Ran her own agency, M.C. Weil agency (1867).

Mary Wells (Bunny)—Highest paid executive in advertising (1969) and co-founder of Wells Rich Greene Advertising Agency.

ORGANIZATIONS

Advertising Women of New York, Inc.
153 East 57th Street
New York, NY 10022

Los Angeles Advertising Women
5518 McLennan Avenue
Encino, CA 91436

Media Watch
P.O. Box 618
Santa Cruz, CA 95061–0618

Women's Advertising Club of Chicago
820 South Michigan Avenue
Chicago, IL 60605

Women In Communications, Inc.
2101 Wilson Boulevard
Suite # 417
Arlington, VA 22201

These lists were, in part, derived from *How it was in advertising: 1776–1976* (1976), Chicago: Crain Books; Fishburn's *Women in popular culture: A reference guide* (1982), Westport, CT: Greenwood Press; McBride's *How to be a successful advertising woman* (1948), New York: Whittlesey House; and Fox's *The mirror makers* (1984), New York: William Morrow and Company, Inc.

There has been no shortage of criticism of the treatment of women in advertising over the decades. A review of relevant literature reveals several studies that charge high levels of gender stereotyping both in television and magazine ads.

8

"YOU'RE NOT GETTING OLDER . . . YOU'RE GETTING BETTER!"

TINA PIERACCINI AND ROBERT SCHELL

Tina Pieraccini is an Associate Professor of Communication Studies at the State University of New York, College at Oswego, where she teaches courses in broadcasting, public relations, and communication. She earned her B.A. in Speech from the University of Rhode Island and her M.A. in Mass Communication at the University of Massachusetts at Amherst. Her research interests include children's television and the portrayal of women and minorities in the media.

Robert E. Schell is the Associate Dean of students at the State University of New York, College at Oswego. He is responsible for the research and assessment studies in the Division of Student Services. In addition to his administrative responsibilities, he teaches courses in developmental psychology and multivariate statistics. Schell earned his B.S. in Secondary Education from East Stroudsburg University and his M.A. in Guidance and Counseling from Montclair State College, and has taken further graduate studies at Syracuse University. Schell's research interests include studies of person–environment interaction, program assessment, and applied statistical models. Schell worked for a number of years in commercial radio as an announcer, disk jockey, and copywriter.

Women in advertising have often been portrayed with exaggerated stereotypes, misconception, and distortion. In the 1950s, TV ads mirrored the prime-time portrayals of home-and-hearth images. In the 1960s, the women's movement began, and popular Virginia Slims ads promised, "You've come a long way, baby." Women were seen outside the home more frequently in TV ads. The 1970s boasted change, but in reality presented Superwomen, the distortion no woman could achieve. The 1980s saw more varied roles for women, yet continued to perpetuate a narrow distortion of the career woman and stereotypes continued through television ads. It seems true that in the 1990s, women aren't getting older, they're getting better—at least on prime-time television advertising.

HISTORICAL PERSPECTIVES

Throughout the 1950s most television advertisers portrayed women in the kitchen—cooking, cleaning, and doing laundry. The message was clear: Women belonged in the home. "The image of woman as homemaker had become a cultural stereotype that limited women to housework, and advertising had unwittingly perpetuated the stereotype" (Randazzo, 1993, p. 125). The 1960s saw some change but continued to stereotype and present women as homemakers and sex objects.

The 1970s, however, saw the first comprehensive studies and content analyses of the portrayal of women in advertising. The interest and criticism were reflective of the women's movement and created increased awareness, sowing the seeds for change. Cancian and Ross document "a striking association between media coverage of women and the strength of the woman's movement" (1981, p. 11). Other studies agree. One study, titled *A Woman's Place*, found women almost exclusively in home settings, dependent on men, unable to make decisions, and treated as sex objects (Courtney & Lockeretz, 1971).

Also, during the 1970s, women's groups organized the first protests against advertisers. The most well known of the protests were by the National Organization for Women (NOW). NOW's "Barefoot and Pregnant Award" was systematically presented to advertisers that ran offensive and sexist ad campaigns. *Ms.* magazine similarly ran its "No Comment" page spotlighting offensive and sexist ads. Women Against Pornography gave Zap awards for sexist advertising. The efforts of these women's groups all contributed to public awareness of sexism in advertising.

The 1980s saw some minor improvements, but criticism continued, as did stereotypes and distorted images. Sex dominated, and sexual fantasy became highly successful in brand-name recall (Yovovich, 1983). Jeans advertisers in particular went to the limits in the 1980s depicting sexual fantasy to sell jeans. The most controversial ads were for Calvin Klein jeans.

One improved, but still offensive, stereotype of the 1980s was "Betty Briefcase." No matter where she was, the career woman in the advertising world always wore a tweed suit and carried a briefcase. A 1985 study by Olgilvy & Mather Advertising Agency found that 68 percent of women were offended by the Betty Briefcase television ads (Alrop, 1985, p. 31). By 1989, advertisers had heard the criticism and the response was the demise of Betty. "In the past, ads have portrayed working women in severe suits clutching briefcases. Today, the best ads show that success outside the home doesn't mean women have to relinquish femininity or romance" (Piirto, 1989). Piirto's article, "Romance Sells," suggests that today's working mothers want romance more than sex and ads targeted to baby boomers are reflecting the need.

There has been no shortage of criticism of advertising and women over the decades. A review of relevant literature reveals several studies that charge high levels of gender stereotyping in both television and magazine ads (Kovacs, 1972; McCarthy, 1981; Richmond & Hartman, 1982). Compared to magazine ads, however, television has fared better. For example, in the early 1980s several campaigns for Calvin Klein jeans were banned from television by the networks themselves, while they continued to be seen in abundance in magazines. Compared to ads on children's programs, prime time has fared better. Ads on children's shows are highly sex-typed (Eaton & Dominick, 1991, pp. 67–75).

ADVERTISING MYTHS ABOUT WOMEN

Many studies and content analyses have come to the same conclusion: Women have traditionally been exploited by some advertisers to sell products. And in the process, myths about women have been reinforced. Advertisers have sold us the myth that all women must be thin. Advertisers have sold American women the myth that the ideal woman is blond. Media campaigns have reinforced the myth that women must remain youthful to be desirable. The myth communicated is that product use makes a woman sexy. The reality is that sex sells.

Forbes explained it this way: "Women would pay 25 cents for a bar of soap that made their hands clean, but $2.50 for a bar of soap that promised to make them beautiful" (Trachtenberg, 1987, pp. 134–138). Advertising reflects myths and distorts reality.

Although a great deal of progress has been made in the last ten years, *Media Studies Journal* (Winter/Spring, 1993) concludes that images of women in the 1990s still have a long way to go. Sanderson (1990) wrote, "All too often, the woman depicted in ads and commercials is a lifeless mannequin, a fantasy unattainable by most of the billions of women in the world" (p. 91).

After two decades of slow progress, popular books like *Backlash: The Undeclared War Against American Women* and *The Beauty Myth* suggest a retreat of the gains of the women's movement. Beer commercials and fashion ads in particular are targets of criticism. Betty Friedan, author of *The Feminine Mystique* and leading figure in the women's movement, takes a strong view of this advertising. She said, "Sexist ads are retribution for the gains women made in the 1970s" (Scott, 1991).

The chapter's researchers asked the following questions to determine the status of women in advertising in the 1990s. Our purpose was to determine just how much sexism still exists and what elements lead to the perception of stereotypes.

1. Does television advertising create stereotypes, distortions, and exploitative images of women on prime-time television?

2. What elements lead people to perceive television commercials as sexist?

3. How are these elements related to show genre on which the commercial was aired, the scheduled time the commercial was aired, and the network on which the commercial was aired?

METHOD AND DESIGN

Students in an advanced broadcasting course were trained to monitor prime-time programs over an eight-week period during the Spring 1993 television season. The students received training in the procedures and definitions of the variables under analysis to ensure an initial level of reliability before coding the ads into the main study. Monitored programs were prime-time programs representing various genre. All four major networks—NBC, CBS, ABC, and FOX—were included. The sample did not include cable or independent networks. A total of 715 ads sampled from January through March 1993 were analyzed.

The sample was chosen to represent the most pervasive time period—prime time. Programs on which the ads were monitored were categorized by program genre and network aired. To assure a balanced sample, programs were chosen to represent those appealing to both men and women and young and old viewers. To guarantee balance, all program genre types were represented.

The study was primarily concerned with measurement of sex-role portrayals. Students were instructed to observe the ads and make notes of the following:

- sex of the announcer
- who the ad was aimed at with regard to gender
- people on camera with regard to gender, roles, and speaking roles
- any sexist word usage

- stereotypes
- any omission
- physical exploitation

The following definitions were used by all monitors:

Word usage was defined as language that is patronizing or demeaning to women. Examples would include terminology such as *girl*, *baby*, or physical descriptions such as *blond* and *slim*.

Omission was defined as an ad where women are obviously excluded from the commercial or they are present in the ad but do not speak, whereas the men in the ad have speaking roles. Also included as omission was when an ad is clearly directed to women but the voice-over is a man.

Stereotypes were defined as any ad where women are portrayed in typical, so-called women's roles. For example, they are seen as homemakers, nurses, secretaries, or victims. Also included as a stereotype is a situation where a woman is portrayed as not being in charge when men are present, or is presented simply as a nag or scatterbrain.

Physical exploitation was defined as women's bodies being exploited by the camera. In particular would be a scene where the men in the ad are fully clothed while a woman is scantily clad or when the dress is inappropriate for the occasion.

The data were collected for eight weeks for a comprehensive evaluation of television ads in 1993. The observers were asked to watch the advertisements on the programs that had been selected and to record their observations on standard coding sheets according to the definitions given. In addition to the advertisement data, observers were instructed to name the program and record the time and date of the observation and the network watched. These data were transformed to computer-readable form and entered into the *Statistical Package for the Social Sciences*.

Since the primary purpose was to describe the depiction of women in contemporary television advertising, the data were analyzed by means of simple tabulations. The number and percent of observations in each response category are shown in Table 8.1. The conclusions reached were based on a simple examination of the observation percentages.

Observers watched advertisements on the major networks in the following proportions: ABC (35%), FOX (27%), CBS (21%), and NBC (16%). They watched advertisements on 21 different programs. Observers indicated that they had viewed advertisements for more than 500 different brands or products. Although the range of observations was not exhaustive, the sample of advertisements appeared to be representative.

Data were analyzed to test the contention that television advertising still creates stereotypes, distortions, and exploitative images of women during prime-time programs.

DISCUSSION AND ANALYSIS OF FINDINGS

The contention that advertisers create stereotypes, distortions, and exploitative images of women in prime-time programs was not supported. The areas monitored supported a positive image of the women represented in the ads monitored. Fewer gender-linked stereotypes and, in general, a more balanced picture were seen than in the studies from previous decades. The specific findings are outlined as follows.

Table 8.1
Portrayal of Women in Advertising

	Number	Percent		Number	Percent
Observed TV Commercials					
Sex of Announcer			**Female Speakers**		
Both	45	6.3	None	516	72.5
Female	159	22.2	One	155	21.8
Male	491	68.7	Two	34	4.8
Neither	20	2.8	Three or more	7	1.0
Target Audience			**Word Usage**		
Both	412	57.8	Not patronizing/demeaning	645	90.3
Female	204	28.6	Patronizing/demeaning	69	9.7
Male	97	13.6	**Omission**		
Number of Males on Camera			Not excluded	606	84.9
			Excluded	108	15.1
None	280	39.5	**Stereotypes**		
One	293	41.4			
Two or three	114	16.1	No typical role	496	69.5
Four or more	21	3.0	Typical role	218	30.5
Number of Females on Camera			**Physical**		
			No exploitation	576	80.7
None	241	34.1	Exploitation	138	19.3
One	336	47.5			
Two or three	111	15.7			
Four or more	19	2.7			
Male Speakers					
None	515	72.2			
One	151	21.2			
Two	35	4.9			
Three or more	12	1.7			

Sex of Announcer

Although nearly 70 percent of the announcers on the ads monitored were males, this represents an improvement over previous decades. Traditionally, male voice-overs have been at the level of 85 percent and more.

Target Audience

Prime-time television targets both males and females in the majority of ads. An analysis of the data further suggests that women are targeted more frequently than men when the ads geared only to women are taken into account. Only 13 percent of ads were directed only to men, whereas 28 percent were directed only to women. We conclude that there is no apparent discrimination in television advertising with regard to gender and target market.

Number of Males versus Females on Camera

The data support the conclusion that there is no significant difference regarding gender and on-camera presence. This is a positive finding for women in that, traditionally, men have outnumbered women on camera as much as three to one.

Speaking Roles

The data support no significant difference regarding gender and speaking roles. In fact, the data show men and women are equally assigned speaking roles on television ads. Traditionally, men were more likely to have speaking roles, whereas women often appeared on camera but did not speak. This previous inequity was not supported by this study.

Word Usage

The study found very little sexist language use. In fact, more than 90 percent of the ads monitored found no incidence of patronizing or demeaning language.

Omission

Women were not excluded from television advertising. Eighty-five percent of the ads analyzed did not exclude women.

Stereotypes

Nearly 70 percent of the ads did not stereotype women. This clearly supports the conclusion that advertisers are reflecting societal change and acceptance of women as equal to men, at least during prime-time television. The women in the ads were portrayed in diverse roles and in charge. Traditionally, this has been the strongest area of criticism. This study suggests that advertisers have responded to earlier criticisms.

Physical Exploitation

Traditional criticism of cheesecake shots in advertising was not supported by the data. This study found that more than 80 percent of the ads monitored did not exploit women's bodies. However, nearly 20 percent still do physically exploit women's bodies, and even though an improvement, there is still room for change.

CONCLUSION

Because the way women are depicted on prime-time television contributes to and reinforces society's views and attitudes about women, this study is significant in 1993. Sexism is still present in many media forms and television advertising still perpetuates to some degree unfair and stereotypical images of the women the ads claim to represent.

However, the contention that television advertisers still contribute to stereotypes, distort images, and exploit women physically was not fully supported. There were examples in the ads monitored of sexism, but the sexist ads were clearly the minority. This study suggests much progress in that overall sexism has decreased in the 1990s in prime-time television advertising. The data support that advertisers have responded to earlier criticism. The television ads monitored more realistically reflect societal views and more realistically portray women in television ads. A 1960s ad for Clairol said it best—"You're Not Getting Older . . . You're Getting Better!"

REFERENCES

Alexander, W., & Judd, B. (1978, February). Do nude ads enhance brand recall? *Journal of Advertising Research, 18,* 47–50.

Alrop, R. (1985, August 1). Despite less blatant sexism, ads still insult most women. *Wall Street Journal,* p. 31.

Anderson, D. (1981, April). My side. *Working Women, 120,* 118.

Bartos, R. (1982). *The moving target.* New York: The Free Press.

Belkaovi, A., & Belkaovi, J. (1976, May). A comparative analysis of the roles portrayed by women in print ads. *Journal of Marketing Research, 13,* pp. 168–172.

Cancian, F. M. & Ross, B.L. (1981, January/March). Mass media and the women's movement: 1900–1977. *Journal of Applied Behavioral Science,* 9–26.

Conant, J. (1986, September 15). Sex does it. *Newsweek*, 62–64.

Courtney, A. & Whipple, T. (1983). *Sex stereotyping in advertising*. Lexington, MA: Lexington Books.

Courtney, A. & Lockeretz, S. (1971, February). A woman's place: an analysis of the roles portrayed by women in advertising. *Journal of Marketing Research, 8*, pp. 92–95.

Eaton, C. & Dominick, J. (1991, Spring/Summer). Product-related programming and children's programming: A content analysis. *Journalism Quarterly*, 67–75.

Foltz, K. (1985, March 11). A kinky new Calvinism. *Newsweek*, 65–66.

Frons, M. (1980, October 6). The jeaning of America. *Newsweek*, 81.

Gross, M. (1985, July/August). Sex sells. *Saturday Review*, 50–52.

Hartman, T., & Richmond, D. (1982, October/November). Sex appeal in advertising. *Journal of Advertising Research, 22*, pp. 53–61.

Hennessee, J., & Nicholson, J. (1972, May 28). NOW says commercials insult women. *New York Times*, VI p. 12.

Kanner, B. (1980, March). She brings home the bacon and cooks it. *Ms*, 104.

Kovacs, M. (1972, July 17). Where is a woman's place? Homes, say ads. *Advertising Age*, 48.

Liebert, R. Sprafkin, J. N., & Davidson, E.M. (1982). *The early window* (pp. 187–207). New York: Pergamon Press.

McCarthy, E. J. (1981). *Basic marketing.* (7th Edition) Homewood, IL: D. Irwin, Inc.

Marin, A. (1980). *50 years of advertising as seen through the eyes of Advertising Age*. Crain Communication Inc., Chicago, IL.

Marquardt, D. (1987, May). A thinly disguised message. *Ms*, 33–34, 71–72.

Media Studies Journal. (1993, Spring).

Moyer, D. (1983, October 3). Breaches of bad taste label some overseas jean ads. *Advertising Age, 54*, M40.

Ogilvy, D. (1983). *Ogilvy on advertising*. New York: Crown Publishers.

Piirto, R. (1989, August). The romantic sell. *American Demographics*, 38–41.

Randazzo, S. (1993). *Mythmaking on Madison Avenue*. Chicago: Probus Publishing Company.

Richmond, D. & Hartman, T. (1982, October/November). Sex appeal in advertising. *Journal of Advertising Research, 22*.

Sanderson, S. (1990, November 11). You've come a long way, baby—or have you? *USA Today*, pp. 59–61.

Scott, J. (1991, November 24). Selling with sexism. *Atlanta Journal*, p. 12.

Trachtenberg, J. (1987, March 23). Beyond the hidden persuaders. *Forbes*, 134–138.

Trachtenberg, J. (1985, May 5). It's become part of our culture. *Forbes*, 134–135.

Yovovich, B. (1983, May 2). Sex in advertising—the power and the perils. *Advertising Age, 54*, M4–5.

Zinn, L. (1991, November 4). This Bud's for you—no not you, her. *Business Week*, 86–90.

In the 1990s, there are fewer African Americans in advertising than there were in the 1970s. For 20 years, mainstream advertising agencies, reflecting the climate of the times, have turned their backs on equal employment opportunity thrusts.

9

Career

CAROLINE JONES:

Advertising Agency Executive

JANNETTE L. DATES

Jannette Dates, Acting Dean and Associate Professor in the School of Communications at Howard University, earned her Ph.D. from the University of Maryland at College Park. Her publications include *Split Image: African Americans in the Mass Media,* which won the Gustavus Myer Award for the best book written in the United States in the area of human rights. Currently, Dates is working on a book titled *Image Shapers: African Americans in Advertising and Public Relations.*

Caroline R. Jones, president of the Caroline Jones Agency, is an outspoken critic of the advertising field's record on diversifying its workforce and its products.

In the 1990s, African Americans were younger, tended to spend a higher percentage of their money on consumer goods than their White counterparts, showed a preference for top-line merchandise, and demonstrated a willingness to try new products. In other words, they were a marketing executive's dream. In addition, according to the 1990 Census, minorities had become the majority in 21 U.S. cities and the dominant group in 30 more. *Business Week* reported that the African-American population was growing twice as fast as the White population and would swell the 18- to 35-year-old group, so coveted by merchandisers, as the average age of Whites grew older (Mallory & Anderson, 1992).

Moreover, in 1990, African Americans collectively earned $263 billion, making them a market too large to continue to ignore. Yet, at many levels the advertising industry continues to act as if this market does not exist. Some argue that the advertising industry in the 1990s is much like the auto industry of 20 years ago—uninterested in making a fundamental change that is required of them if they are to survive (Simpson, 1992).

ADVERTISING AND BLACK MARKETS

Research findings of the 1990s indicated that African-American households, the largest demographic minority group targeted by advertisers, watched 23 hours more television than other households each week. Thus, it was economically sound for advertisers on television to include Black models in their general ads. However, although more Black models were included in the 1990s than at any point before, they were typically assigned minor and background roles (Whittler, 1991).

In the 1990s, although African Americans have spent nearly $300 billion annually on consumer goods, advertisers have spent only $736 million annually to reach them—a mere 2 percent of the dollars spent on annual advertising. African-American marketing executives argue that comparatively little was spent on this consumer group to get to know them—what they buy, why, and what induces them to change brands.

White researchers had noted that collecting data about Black consumers was more difficult than for the general populace. They argued that African Americans were more likely to have unlisted phone numbers and were less cooperative with researchers' questions. Those in business were sometimes unable to afford accountants, so their invoices were not up-to-date. Also, researchers were often afraid to visit homes in urban neighborhoods.

On the other hand, however, Black marketing executives suggested that more resourcefulness by marketers could have helped. For example, researchers could schedule focus groups in community centers, schools, and churches, instead of relying on door-to-door surveys and they could use telephones in a more resourceful manner. Some argued that Black people were not randomly distributed, but clustered in communities, and that Black people were suspicious of those seeking personal information. Thus, alternative collection systems were not only desirable, but indispensable for accurate assessments of minority consumption patterns (Hume, 1991; Phillips, 1993).

In 1993, *Black Enterprise* noted that after years of defining beauty standards with White models, *Cover Girl* was sporting a fresh, new face—that of tawny-toned model Lana Ogilvie—and courting a brand-new customer: the African-American woman. The *BE* article argued that Black female consumers were being courted by numerous general-market cosmetics companies as never before. It predicted that by 1997 a total of $732 million would be made in annual sales of ethnic beauty products. The Black woman thus became the new darling of the $4-billion beauty industry, and she was younger, better educated, and more affluent than ever before.

During this period, Prescriptives Inc., a subsidiary of Estee Lauder, began marketing its *All Skins* line of cosmetics targeted to Black women, who spent $600 million annually on such products. As a result, *All Skins* accounted for a 45 percent increase in Prescriptives' sales in the first half of 1992. Other companies began targeting Black women consumers, as well, including Maybelline, J. C. Penney, Mattel, Pillsbury, and Quaker Oats.

Ironically, in the 1970s African-American-owned firms that catered to Black women had sprung up because of prejudice against African Americans. Fashion Fair, for example, emerged directly from the refusal of White cosmetics firms to target Black women consumers or acknowledge that such a market existed. John Johnson, founder and chief executive officer of Johnson Publishing Company—publishers of *Ebony*, *Jet*, and *Ebony Man*—approached the Revlon Corporation in the 1970s urging them to go after the Black woman by advertising in Ebony magazine. Revlon said no. In response to this rejection, Johnson established

Chapter 9   Caroline Jones

Fashion Fair. By 1993, with his daughter Linda Johnson Rice serving as president, Fashion Fair had built its line to 310 products, selling in 2,000 stores internationally, with revenues between $60 million and $100 million annually. In the 1990s, Fashion Fair and other Black-owned cosmetics firms prepared for war with the mainstream cosmetics firms that now wanted to target their market. Many feel confident that they will prevail with Black women consumers (Clarke, 1993).

Through the years, the advertising industry had not targeted African Americans in mainstream publications, and they were also reluctant to use available Black media to approach this market. For example, most African-American-oriented magazines found that despite a steady increase in readership, they could not increase the number and types of advertisements in their publications. *Essence*, the lifestyle magazine targeted to African-American women, appeared on newsstands in 1970. Its circulation soared from 50,000 in its first months, to 450,000 in the mid-1970s, to nearly a million in the 1990s. The number of advertising pages in *Essence*, however, stagnated in the 1980s and declined in 1989 and 1990, following a trend in the magazine industry that slumped across the board at 3.5 percent. In 1990, advertising fell 7 percent in *Essence*, 12.1 percent in *Jet* magazine, and 4.2 percent in *Ebony*.

Through these years *Essence* magazine was unable to attract cosmetics companies, despite studies showing that African-American women bought more cosmetics than the average general-market female consumer. The cosmetics companies argued that *Essence* magazine's insistence on including Black models in their advertisements was an obstacle. Further, they stated that they could easily reach Black women consumers through mainstream publications by putting African Americans in general-market publications, and without alienating their other target markets. Many African-American marketers disagreed, however, noting that "although you find us reading other magazines, we don't *act* until we see it in our own" (Masterson, 1990).

After the 1990 census report, in addition to cosmetics companies, other marketers also focused their attention on the growing importance of minorities. Beginning in the 1970s, leaders in targeting the Black consumer had been soft drinks, fast foods, alcoholic beverages, and then automobile companies. But, for the first time in the 1990s, numerous major companies such as Toys-R-Us, K mart, and Pillsbury hired Black-owned agencies to assist in the development of campaigns to customize their products and "pitch" to suit Black tastes (Simpson, 1992).

Douglass Alligood, an African American who was vice president of special markets at Batten, Barton, Durstine, and Osborn Advertising (BBDO) in 1992, argued that his study and report on Black popular reading and viewing habits showed that "if you're an advertiser with a message targeted to Blacks, it is wise to consider the Black top-rated media. However, if Blacks are a part of the overall audience you're trying to reach, then it's still most effective to use national (general market) top-rated media" (Alligood, 1993).

Many among African-American market advertisers disagreed. They saw this as self-serving data collection that was interpreted to retain or increase the power and influence of general-market agencies over Black consumers, and as another way to complete an end run around Black advertising agencies.

They believed that segmented marketing had been established as the most effective way to reach consumers and that returning to mass-market appeals was counterproductive to their interests and to Black consumers' interests. They believed advertisers should come through Black agencies, the experts on the Black consumer market, to reach and appeal to Black consumers. In addition, mass marketing had diminished over the previous ten years. It appeared to Black experts that when the African-American consumer was involved, marketers wanted to return to mass marketing despite widespread proof that target marketing was more efficient and effective.

Ken Gilbert, a Black senior executive at the mainstream firm Messner, Vetere, Berger, McNamee, and Schmetterer, observed that "since African Americans set the tone for creativity as defined by pop culture, then you'd think most ad agencies would get smart and hire more Blacks to create ads and direct campaigns," but they don't (Alligood, 1993). Even in the 1990s, most top executives view the issue of hiring more African Americans into mainstream corporations as politically motivated rather than business-necessity-driven, just as they gave short shrift to Black-owned agencies.

There were, however, some Black owners—determined fighters—who had vowed to make things different and more inclusive in the advertising/marketing arena and who fought daily to achieve this end. Enter Caroline R. Jones.

CAROLINE R. JONES AND ADVERTISING

Caroline R. Jones, the eldest daughter of ten children, grew up in Benton Harbor, Michigan, where her father, an auto worker, and her mother, a homemaker, devoted their time to raising their large family.

In the 1960s, Jones, one of the few Black students studying at the University of Michigan, had attended an assembly where a recruiter from J. Walter Thompson Company described the advertising game at the world's largest advertising agency. The recruiter's enthusiasm about advertising was contagious. An honor-student English major, Jones talked at length with the recruiter and began corresponding with her about advertising. After graduation, Jones took a job as a secretary (as did all women) at J. Walter Thompson, where she quickly rose through the ranks, as major corporations finally began to "allow" women to compete for nontraditional jobs.

Through the years, Jones had no Black mentors to help her negotiate her way through the system. In fact, she became one of the pioneers in the corporate world who served as a mentor to many others.

In 1975, Jones had become the first African-American woman elected vice president within a major advertising firm when she joined Batten, Barton, Durstine, and Osborn, Inc. (BBDO) as vice president and creative group supervisor. Then, in 1977, after 13 years in mainstream corporate advertising, Jones and Frank Mingo opened Mingo-Jones Advertising Agency, Inc. Mingo had been a senior vice president at McCann-Erickson Advertising, but both had become disillusioned with mainstream advertising agencies.

They each believed that the system had kept them from rising to their full potential, restricted other capable African Americans from participating, and systematically diminished the importance of Black consumers as a market. Within seven years, New-York-based Mingo-Jones Advertising (MJA), specified as a general market agency, had acquired 30 percent general billings, 10 percent Hispanic billings, and 60 percent African-American-oriented billings. The company included among its clients Heublein, Kentucky Fried Chicken, Seagrams, Miller Brewing Company, Phillip Morris, Goodyear Tire and Rubber, Liggett & Myers Tobacco, and Westinghouse Electric.

MJA developed the premise that American cities were a distinctive target market and that Black agencies were uniquely capable of servicing them. They called it their "urban marketing concept." It was both a crafty trend analysis and defensive positioning for an agency that targeted culturally and linguistically diverse population groups.

Jones and Mingo realized that much of the advertising that was originally designed to reach consumers in so-called minority markets reached the mainstream and became a part of the broader popular culture. They hoped to win "big" as their campaigns became popular in both the minority target market and the general mass market. And they did—in a way.

In the early 1980s, one of the company's general accounts included the New York region advertising account for Kentucky Fried Chicken, with billings of about $3 million. For the assignment, MJA came up with the theme "We do chicken right." It became highly successful far beyond the Black community. MJA wanted to visibly and dramatically move to a new plateau, reaching beyond the minority advertising mold with that slogan. Jones and Mingo campaigned with the decision makers at Kentucky Fried Chicken (KFC), requesting to take the slogan and a larger campaign into the mainstream. KFC declined, however, and gave the slogan to their large mainstream agency. MJA thus lost a great opportunity to make a lot of money from their own creativity and hard work. It was extremely difficult for Mingo and Jones to watch a mainstream agency reap financial rewards and recognition based on MJA's creativity. Frank Mingo was so furious at first that he thought seriously about getting out of advertising forever. In time, however, he became determined not to let these types of frustrations overwhelm him (S. Chisholm, personal communication, Spring 1992).

In 1984, MJA began its first corporate campaign for Walt Disney Productions. At that time, they contracted to do advertisements for the general market that were designed to increase the number of African-American customers of Disneyland, Walt Disney World, and their other products, as well.

In 1987, Caroline Jones left the Mingo-Jones Advertising Agency to start her own firm—Caroline Jones Advertising, Inc.—which quickly became a full-service agency with international and domestic clients in advertising, promotions, and public relations. MJA changed its name to The Mingo Group (TMG). As the years passed, Jones served on numerous industry-related boards, lectured across the country, and received constant recognition for her work. In 1982, for example, she received the prestigious Foremost Women in Communications Matrix Award for Advertising, from Women in Communications. In 1990 she was named "Advertising Woman of the Year" by the Advertising Women of New York, Inc.

CJA is one of the few firms owned by an African American that consistently obtains general market accounts as well as African-American–targeted accounts. Always outspoken about her views of society's problems, Jones realizes that as a double minority—female and Black—one of the biggest hurdles she faces is the existence of castes within society, business, and advertising. Jones publicly addresses such controversial issues.

VIEWPOINTS ON AFRICAN AMERICANS AND ADVERTISING

I talked with Caroline Jones in the fall of 1992 as one of the people I interviewed for a forthcoming book about advertising and public relations. I asked Jones questions about how she achieved success, who had helped her, how being an African American affected her, how race affected the industry, and the like. It is clear that Caroline Jones has strong opinions on many issues. She discussed them with candor.

Regarding the advertising industry, Jones argued that this is a very complicated business because it deals with money, attitudes, images, and an "underground system." It is an underground business because advertising agencies promote products and services and not themselves. It is complicated, with many agencies and support systems, but with ten major agencies controlling the vast majority of advertising dollars.

On Black politicians, she applauded the efforts of leaders such as Rev. Jesse Jackson who, during his days at Operation PUSH in Chicago, had led the fight for the inclusion of campaigns developed by Black advertising and public relations agencies in the work of national advertising agencies, particularly as they targeted Black consumers. Jones noted, however, that those activist tactics were not successful strategies for the 1990s. She believed that in the 1990s people have other things on their minds, while many Black politicians kept taking the same steps and making the same statements, erroneously believing these strategies will continue to work because they worked in the past. She blamed this inability to get things done on the fact that Black leaders do not understand the advertising, public relations, and marketing industries because of their "underground" existence. Such leaders, she observed, might compensate for this lack by doing their homework and by calling on the skills and expertise of African Americans within the advertising and marketing industries.

On language, she had great concern about the use of a capital letter to spell the word *Black* in reference to Black people. She believes that major newspapers such as the *Wall Street Journal* used a lowercase *b* to write the word *black* when referring to African Americans who, in turn, allowed them to get away with it. She dislikes seeing a series such as Hispanic, Asian American, American Indian, and Italian capitalized, but the word *black* appearing with a lowercase *b* in reference to African Americans.

On the term *general market*, Jones noted that the term has been used to mean the majority of consumers, "which to marketers meant only White people, and they didn't intend to have Black people thrown in—even a little bit, most of the time." The general market always should mean the inclusion of people in "general"—including Black people.

On Black men, she believes that they have suffered from all the problems Black women face, but that Black men carry the additional burden of trying to make it in the United States without being perceived as a threat. She is convinced that part of the reason for their exclusion from the advertising industry lay in White people's fear of Black men, a fear created, in part, by the media industry—newspapers, television, and motion pictures—to instill and perpetuate fear-invoking perceptions.

On the scarcity of African Americans in advertising, she noted that in the 1990s, there were fewer African Americans in advertising than there had been in the 1970s. For 20 years, mainstream advertising agencies, reflecting the climate of the times, have turned their backs on equal employment opportunity thrusts. They have systematically designed hiring and promotion practices favoring those who come from their own backgrounds—most often White and male.

On the term *target marketing* in the 1990s, when issues were raised concerning target marketing of segmented consumer groups as a subject of national debate, Jones argued that all marketing is targeted. She believes that budget constraints have always forced each corporation to have primary, and then other targets—a concept and strategy that J. Walter Thompson Company used with all its employees for many years. Noting that the so-called full-service agencies clearly were *not* full service, she believes that specialists, such as CJA, are needed to complete the job that "full-service" companies neglect. Thus, racial targeting is not racist, as charged, but a necessary and sensible approach to court and welcome purchasers to products or services.

Jones believes it is redundant to use the term *target marketing* in advertising, anyway, since no marketing/advertising business wants *un*targeted marketing.

The object of marketing is selling, so you target those most likely to purchase your product. Targeting Black consumers became necessary precisely because White people would not include people of other colors in their advertising—regardless of what the demographics or psychographics revealed.

When some in the general advertising and public relations community raised the issue about not needing to target Black consumers, arguing that Black people could see advertisements on television just like everyone else, Jones responded, "That is racist! Turn it around. Can you imagine launching a product for all consumers on a TV campaign that included only Black actors? How many White people would think, 'This product is for me'?" "Further," Jones argued, "different ethnic groups spend their money differently, based on accessibility, price, sophistication, knowledge of brand names, and the deal offered. You can design a program to sell more to different groups, but only if you admit that there are differences." Jones believes that public relations overtures and campaigns, followed by direct advertising to Black consumers, are simply common-sense approaches in businesses that depend on the public for their success (Rothenberg, 1991).

On African Americans in corporate advertising, Jones said that in the 1990s, the position of Black people in the advertising/public relations field is steadily declining on a number of levels, as those in the so-called general market agencies make across-the-board cutbacks, and as those Black people who own their own companies continue to receive small budgets from these industries. For example, she said that the advertising/marketing industry fail to use the services of Black-owned agencies for minority-targeted or general market accounts unless there is heavy pressure on them from various sources.

In addition, "In the 1990s, senior African-American professionals (who had entered advertising in the 1970s) were being 'cut back' at corporate advertising agencies, in what was a 'Catch-22' for those few African Americans who had survived the system." Jones described a colleague, an African-American man with 18 years of experience in advertising production who was highly touted in the industry as the finest producer at one of the major agencies. Despite his strong record and outstanding reputation, he was let go in late 1992 in what was termed "cutbacks." Jones argued, however, that this extremely talented man, who had paid his dues as he worked his way up the ladder, was never promoted as his White counterparts of equal and lesser abilities were. "He never got to be in charge of a department, so that instead of being able to hire and fire others, he was the one they let go," she maintained.

On why the advertising industry's record is so bad, Jones believed things are worse in the industry in the 1990s for Black people because African Americans have let the larger society get away with their unfair, unequal practices for so many years. The reason: Black people are so busy trying to take care of the basic necessities, like obtaining food, clothing, shelter, keeping the kids in school, and watching out for drugs, that they fail to police the elements that impacted on their "image" in society.

During the 1980s, most people did not see how actions by political types could affect them directly, she observed. She believes that the fallout from the Reagan and Bush White House years was far more devastating than people at first realized. "We didn't want to pay attention because it was painful; but by not paying attention, we lost a lot of ground. Because African Americans did not continue their criticisms and push for fairness and inclusiveness, the so-called backlash really happened without many of us realizing it. White America and corporate America were primarily Republican in the 1980s and 1990s. They embraced the subtleties about not having to work on affirmative action, since this country did not want to discuss racial issues. White people wanted to be in charge and have everybody else just watch what they said and not what they did," she observed.

"Many White people thought of White people who supported minority causes as 'nigger lovers.' It didn't have to be stated in so many words; but when one said, 'Why are you bringing that up again?' or 'I don't want to hear that again,' you're sending a subtle message, such as: 'Who do you love—us or them?' It's complicated because it's subtle in its code words, but everybody in the game understands it," Jones noted. Further, "Many Black conservatives made it look as if it was okay to maintain the status quo. A few powerful conservative Black people were in positions to write articles in major publications which were mainly read by White people. Many readers then thought that if Black people believed and were writing in this manner about such issues, it must be okay to leave things as they were." She believes these conservative viewpoints severely damaged the cause of social equity.

On the issue of targeting Black consumers, Jones believes that advertising cannot make anybody buy anything they don't want to purchase—twice. "It's out of the question. People won't even take something free if they don't want it, and Black people are no more persuaded by advertising than anyone else. In fact, we have less advertising aimed at us than do White people—across the board," she argued. Since cigarettes and alcohol are considered bad by some people, the issue of whether cigarettes and alcoholic beverages should be legal products—particularly cigarettes—for anyone to use, could be debated. "It has nothing to do with whether or not they're advertised to Black people."

Believing that many people were swept up in the belief that Black people were being swamped by advertisements of unhealthy products, she argued, "If all the cigarette brands spent all this money on Black people, I would be rich just doing cigarette advertising, but they do not spend great sums targeting Black consumers. It's a drop in the bucket compared to the billions of dollars spent on advertising to the general market."

Jones is concerned that advertisers, who have always been reluctant to spend money to target the Black community, will use the uproar caused by the aborted plan to introduce Uptown cigarettes and Power Master malt liquor to cut advertising spending again, using the two companies (R.J. Reynolds Tobacco Company and G. Heileman Brewing Co.) who had been so denounced for targeting African-American consumers as scapegoats. Jones called it "a dangerous and divisive time," particularly with the government taxing cigarettes and liquor, and the advertising industry backing away from the Black consumer market. Jones resented the paternalism implicit in this proposed action.

When Black people told cigarette and liquor companies not to do anything special to target them, what public relations, promotion, and advertising programs were developed to replace them? Jones asked. "Before something of value is removed, you must have a game plan for replacement. If, for example, you take down the billboards advertising cigarettes and alcoholic beverages, what do you put in their place? You're left with a still blighted neighborhood with no billboards! What have you replaced them with? Do you have schools for the kids and clothes for the kids? What have you done, except tear down some billboards?" Jones argued that the offended community should simultaneously request different advertisements to replace those they considered offensive billboards.

In 1989, in an effort to help the Black ministers who had concerns about offensive billboards, Jones analyzed the billboard advertisements then found in New York's Black neighborhoods, and examined the multinational companies that placed them there. She selected R.J. Reynolds, Anheuser-Busch, and Philip Morris for careful scrutiny and noted all the other products that these companies made, other than cigarettes and liquor, and those that had higher Black consumption than other consumer groups. Jones advised one of the campaign leaders, Reverend Calvin Butts, that when he urged for the removal of cigarette and alcoholic beverage billboards, he suggest they be replaced by some of the product brands with high Black consumption rates, also made by the same companies.

The numbers Jones cited in this report were indisputable evidence of Black consumer power. She had selected product brands that represented Black consumption that was much greater than consumption by White people. Jones knew that the companies that produced these products clearly understood what such numbers meant to their bottom line. She distributed copies of her research findings to organizations and campaigns focusing on this issue, giving them what she called "a game plan." According to Jones, the jury is still out "on how effective these billboard replacement requests were with the major corporations."

Jones believes "you have to tell people what the alternatives could be. We're too used to being mad all the time and complaining about things. But we don't spend enough time on solutions. The truth is White people really do want to do right if they don't have to work too hard at it. So we have to do some of the work for them." She said she was willing to do the work because it was her job.

Jones did not claim to have all the answers, but she and her staff used what Jones viewed as "balanced judgment and principles" as operating codes. Aware that this philosophy does not always work to her financial advantage, but undeterred, Jones pushes her staff, firm in the belief that they can "always hold their heads up when their work [is] completed." She believes that if the system had truly worked for them, CJA would have been among the wealthiest agencies in America. "Instead," she observed, "we are inching along, but we're retaining what I think is important—our accountability, credibility and our reputation" (C. Jones, personal communication, Fall 1992).

REFERENCES

Alligood, D. (1993). Special report: Black television viewing—1991–92. *BBDO Special Markets* (Media Department).

Chisolm, S. (1992, Spring). Personal communication.

Clarke, C. V. (1993, June). Industry overview: Redefining beautiful—Black cosmetics companies and industry giants vie for the loyalty of Black women. *Black Enterprise*, 243–252.

From minority to majority (1992, July 6). *Boston Business Journal*.

Hume, H. (1991, July 1). Marketing to African-Americans: Barriers to data remain high. *Advertising Age*, 20.

Jones, C. (1992, Fall). Personal communication.

Mallory, M. & Anderson, S. (1992, March 23). Marketing demographics: Waking up to a major market. *Business Week*, 70–72.

Masterson, P. (1990, July 2). Should marketers target Blacks more? *Advertising Age*.

Phillips, C. (1993, Feb. 19). Data Gap: When it comes to understanding Black consumers, most companies are surprisingly ignorant. *The Wall Street Journal*, p. R18.

Rothenberg, R. (1991, July 23). Blacks are found to be still scarce in advertisements in major magazines, *New York Times*, p. A18.

Simpson, J. (1992, August 31). Buying Black. *Time*, 52–53.

Whittler, T. E. (1991). The effects of actors' race in commercial advertising review and extension, *Journal of Advertising 20*, 1, 54–60.

10

Criticism

WOMEN FOR SALE

ANN J. SIMONTON

Ann Simonton is a former top model who appeared on the cover of *Sports Illustrated, Seventeen,* and in dozens of national television commercials before turning her back on this lucrative career to dedicate her life to exposing the media's role in exploiting women. Simonton is an international lecturer on the effects of media images and has been arrested and jailed 11 times for her nonviolent and often humorous protests. She is the founder and director of Media Watch, an educational nonprofit organization working to help people become critical viewers of the media. Simonton was awarded the Feminist Heroine of the Year, is listed in 1993's *Who's Who,* and has garnered national acclaim through her educational videos. The latest, *Don't be a TV: Television Victim,* received the Silver Apple Award from the National Educational Video and Film Festival. Her autobiographical writings have been published by HarperCollins in *I Never Told Anyone* (1983) and *Her Wits About Her* (1986).

According to the United Nations, "The images of women in the media (and its advertising) are among the main obstacles to eliminating discrimination against women" (Wyndham, 1987, p. 52). Creating a world where women's health, human rights, and safety are championed is not feasible in a society where images of women for sale litter every billboard, every street corner, and every newspaper. Eliminating these images won't create social equality overnight. The deleterious effects of transforming real human beings into consumable objects is likely to remain with us for many generations. Lasting social change will involve active, informed participants who take the media's imagery bombardment seriously. It is time for the advertising industry and the corporations they represent to move over so the silenced members of our culture can speak up.

THE AD ATTACK

There is little doubt that advertising is effective in persuading viewers of all ages to purchase products (Huston, Donnerstein, Fairchild, et al., 1992). A more troubling effect of ads is the difficulty that viewers have when distinguishing ads from television shows, ads from movies, ads from editorial copy, ads from news, or ads from music. The cumulative effects of all these ads, like a constant haze of mental pollution, is desensitizing our culture. Human beings are being used like experimental guinea pigs in the media's ever-expanding marketplace. No known civilization in the history of humankind has previously been subjected to as many as 3,000 marketing messages a day (Collins & Jacobson, 1990).

The job of singling out problems specifically related to sexist advertising is difficult because most advertisers still claim that sexism doesn't exist. Their standard responses are, "It's sexist, but it sells," or dismissal of all complaints, saying they come from a few feminist ratbags who fuss about trivia (Wyndham, 1987, p. 52). Some advertisers are beginning to reshape the way they advertise to women not because they suddenly believe women deserve more dignity but because their economic bottom line is being affected. Women's presence in the work force has changed material realities, and this will eventually force a change in the reality of advertising. While these changes take place, a continual flood of old-guard images still abound.

Imagine the impression a space alien might have upon landing in a major metropolis in front of the following clothing ad that appeared on many bus stops: An angry, unshaven man brutally shoves a woman's face against a wall, yanking back her hair. The ad copy reads, "KIKIT." The alien might easily imagine that all women or, at the very least, *this* woman, had been bad and deserved his angry treatment, as well as public animosity. Why else would this image appear so prominently? Then this same alien could look down the street to see a giant image of a second female, her breasts and body outlined in lights, her nipples flashing on and off. The adjacent sign reads, "Live Sex Shows, Totally Nude, Girls, Girls, Girls." A group of jovial men try to corral the alien inside. At this point the alien might conclude that females were a sort of unruly sex beast, bred for male entertainment. However, needing to confirm these assumptions, the alien radios a friend who has landed near a highway in an Iowa cornfield. The friend confirms that, adjacent to the highway, a billboard displays a nearly nude woman's body and the words "Coors Silver Bullet." Later that day, the alien opens a local newspaper. A full page of headless women in bras is found next to stories of a kidnapped girl, a strangled wife, and a female injured in an auto accident who is then raped by a passing male motorist. The alien concludes that female humans are dangerous, sexual beasts, needing public humiliation and only the most severe violence to make them behave.

Most people would find the alien's conclusions ludicrous because the media have led them to believe that women's fight for equality is nearly won. The fact that women represent 50 percent of the work force, have their own credit cards, have laws that protect them, are part of the space program, watch shows like *Roseanne*, and hold two positions on the U.S. Supreme Court leaves the majority thinking that women have enough social equality. But the alien did not get the wrong impression—the general public has become too calloused to see what is right in front of them. To create images that better reflect the needs and desires of half of humanity, our society must turn a critical eye on women's image in advertising.

Ironically, the daily deluge of advertising messages make the advertiser's job more competitive and difficult. People, unable to recall yesterday's images, aren't as easily shocked or sated. According to Susan Sontag (1973), the more images people are fed, the hungrier they become. The number and variety of ads are increasing. Commercial television has invaded public schools, groceries, waiting rooms, airports, and gas stations. Even orbital billboards that will appear the size of the moon may soon become a reality (Reeves, 1993). The advertisers' job of maintaining a light, happy, consumer-friendly, fantasy world is all the more difficult given today's down market. Out of economic necessity advertisers' tactics rely more heavily on "sure sells." Unfortunately, women's sexuality has a long history of aiding the sale of everything from toothpaste and tools to Virtual Reality computer technology.

From the advertising pulpit spews the worship of consumption. Whether we unwittingly deify products and their companies through brand loyalty, or consider ourselves enlightened, objective shoppers, we increasingly define ourselves through what we consume. Corporate values have replaced American values. The "American Way" has been reduced to the freedom to choose which name brands we pledge our allegiance to.

Women are not only allowed into the high ranks of this consumer religion, they choose most products, including 80 percent of car purchases (Fawcett-Ward, 1993). Modern confessionals are infomercials in which a woman is shown repentant over the image of her former fat self, then suddenly reborn through her devotion to the micro-diet. Famous stars offer personal testimony of being "saved" through jars of face grease. Advertising creates a heavenly world where diets always work and makeup transforms average women into goddesses. Advertisers promise eternal love—while their real goal is to hawk sexual dissatisfaction. They want to keep women forever searching in the supermarket of love for *the* dress, *the* perfume, or *that* pair of breasts that will seduce her dream mate.

Products are offered as a panacea for all that ails—while what advertisers are really selling is tickets to addiction. In the ad world, *love* is a gift such as diamonds. *Success* equals a sleek sports car, and *excitement* is the product of liquor. Consumer addicts are soothed with amnesia. The inevitable disillusionment when the product fails to satisfy is soon forgotten and transformed into hunger for another purchase.

Advertising's claims to celebrate woman, to cure her wounded ego, and to improve her sex life are promises more dangerous than the arsenic used in the late 1800s to whiten women's skin. Her negative self-image is magnified by advertised images of models with perfect faces and bodies. John Berger (1972) summed this up by saying, "The publicity image steals her love for herself as she is, and offers it back to her for the price of the product" (p. 134).

It is appropriate to think of advertisers as corporate pimps. Affluent advertisers eagerly employ our country's best and brightest, in such diverse fields as anthropology, psychology, sociology, ethnography (study of cultures), hermeneutics (the science of interpretation), and semiotics (the study of symbols). They do so not to further humanity, but to sell products by preying on human weakness, frailty, and self-doubt. The vice president of J. Walter Thompson's agency admits, "Ads are increasingly being designed to reach consumers at the gut level." Electroencephalograms are used by these agencies to measure people's physical reaction to commercials. Saatchi & Saatchi research director Penelope Queen compares the agency's one-on-one interviews to therapy sessions. "We believe people make choices on a basic primitive level," Queen says. "We use the probe to get down to the unconscious" (Miller & Tsiantar, 1989, pp. 46–47).

The advertisers' intent is not only to exploit peoples' thoughts and emotions, but their collective unconscious. Their endless promotion of insecurity, greed, and envy may have helped create a society where children will kill other children for their name-brand sneakers (Collins & Jacobson, 1990). According to Peter Clibbon (1993) U.S. companies spend $130 billion a year on advertising and are allowed to deduct all ad costs as a business expense. Clibbon estimates that this costs the government $34 billion a year in lost tax revenues.

It is becoming common knowledge that advertisers "run the show" by determining the most favorable context for their ads. Articles and programs are either censored or not considered by editors and producers in favor of material that makes the ads look good. Some television writers work with advertisers to create television characters who need the same products advertised during the show. A female character on an August 1992 episode of *Northern Exposure* had a severe case of dermatitis. The fact that this character worked as a waitress and had her hands in dishwater was thought to be related. This scene was followed by a commercial, in bold type: "Amy's Sensitive Skin," selling Palmolive's Sensitive Skin dish soap. On the same show, a nasal dripping disc jockey with allergies was followed by an ad for allergy medicine. It's no coincidence. The current economic climate intensifies penalties for programmers and editors who fail to lure advertisers with "friendly" story lines. "Team players" keep their jobs, whereas journalists and television producers who refuse to play lose theirs.

Women's magazines, known within the trade as Cash-Cow Catalogs, have become one long advertisement catering to the whims of advertisers. According to Gloria Steinem (1990), the old advertisement-based *Ms.* magazine nearly lost its Revlon cosmetics account when the advertiser thought the Soviet women on a potential cover weren't wearing enough makeup. The Soviet women were scrapped, and the Revlon account saved. Gray-haired writer Mary Kay Blakely was told by the gray-haired editor of a leading women's magazine that her article about the glories of gray hair cost the magazine its Clairol account for six months (Steinem, 1990).

Advertisers regularly censor opposing points of view. Articles that might inspire women to think, act, or rebel are increasingly "inappropriate." Articles about the hazards of smoking are censored by editors and their advertisers, even though each year 140,000 American women die from smoking-related causes. A study from the *New England Journal of Medicine* showed that "cigarette advertising in magazines is associated with diminished coverage of the hazards of smoking"—particularly in magazines directed at women ("Criticism vanishes," 1992, p. 23). *Cosmopolitan* editor Helen Gurley Brown admits the reason she censors articles that criticize smoking is related to the fact that cigarette advertisers paid her magazine $8.6 million in 1991. She said, "Having come from the advertising world myself, I think, 'Who needs somebody you're paying millions of dollars a year to, to come back and bite you on the ankle?'" (ibid).

According to Jean Kilbourne (1992), America's fastest growing group of new smokers is girls under the age of 11. Rather than warn women of the risks to their health, *Cosmopolitan* and *McCall's* actually promoted smoking as a way to lose weight ("Criticism vanishes," 1992). Cigarette ad copy that is directed to women invariably includes words like, "trim," "thinner," and "slim." It's not surprising that one study found that 39 percent of the women who smoke do so to maintain their weight (Wolf, 1992).

Advertisements profoundly affect human behavior. Betsy Sharkey (1993) wrote, "In 1955, when Clairol first asked the question, 'Does she or doesn't she?' most women didn't. Clairol's ads, which always used wholesome, girl-next-door-types, suddenly made dyeing hair socially acceptable, and the number of women dyeing their hair jumped from 7 percent to 50 percent almost overnight" (p. 92). People want to believe that they aren't influenced by ads. They prefer to think that ads work only for someone else, someone inferior. Yet the gut-level sales pitches are successfully luring women and men into accepting irrational sales schemes and encouraging mindless and wasteful shopping binges. Spending habits that put designer clothes above rent and heating bills are causing bankruptcy and untold economic hardship. The 1980s' slogan was "Shop Till You Drop." In the 1990s, the term is *retail* or "shopping therapy" ("Not & Hot," 1993, p. 46).

THE IMAGE OF WOMEN IN ADVERTISING

The advertised woman is a conspicuous, two-dimensional artifice. Her lips are sensually parted. There is a finger in or over her mouth, as if to stop her from speaking. Sometimes her mouth is open wide, sucking and nibbling. She doesn't smile easily. If she does, her grin is her private secret. She appears to be teasing, angry, drugged, or scared.

The advertised woman is male-identified; she often desperately competes with other females for male attention. She schemes and manipulates, forever trying to separate a man from his money, as this Cutex ad warns. "By the time you finish your right hand, your left hand can be up to no good." Long, freshly painted pink nails reach around her man and slip into his pocket to take his wallet. Manipulation and deceit have, throughout history, been techniques used by the less powerful as a means of survival. Promoting this stereotype perpetuates the myth that women are not to be trusted.

The advertised woman is the implied bonus that goes along with the trip to Hawaii, the sofa bed, that six-pack of beer. Her link to products is so common that we fail to notice her or question her purpose. Most children grow up in environments that are filled with images of women as products. Too few parents or educators consider warning children that the young female draped around power tools or stripped in sports magazines portrays a dangerously unrealistic view of women's humanity.

To get an overview, I did a brief content analysis of the fall issue of a typical fashion magazine. *Harper's Bazaar* September 1994 issue contained 314 full-page advertisements, interspersed with 149 full pages of editorial. Fourteen pages contained both editorials and ads. Of the 314 ads, only 16 portrayed active women. Seven ads portrayed a woman or women who were running, working out, or dancing. Six were walking, one sat in a car, one played soccer in heels, and one pedaled a bicycle in high heels. Yet, the majority posed rather than attending to any task. One hundred and ninety-seven of the ads featured a woman or women passively posing for the camera. They stood, leaned, or sat, acutely aware of being watched. Five ads had women appear as body parts, in four ads women had their eyes totally closed, nine women were lying on their backs or bellies in the ads, two were nude, one of which was in bondage, three actually exposed their underclothes, and one was baring her arched neck.

Conspicuously absent in women's magazines are ads of working women. Rather than being associated with their work, women are much more likely to be lounging in a supine position—as if their time were unimportant. According to most ads, to obtain sex appeal one must be rich enough to lie around all day waiting for her mate. This is Victoria's Secret: class distinction. According to a United Nations report in 1980, women do two-thirds of the world's work for only 10 percent of the world's income (French, 1985, p. 259). Women play a vital role in today's economy, yet advertising still prefers to teach women to perfect their packages rather than create, invent, or discover.

When ads *do* portray women working, the majority are still homemakers and caregivers who are somewhat less pathologically preoccupied with the tyranny of dirt. Ads from the 1980s promoted the supermom as corporate wife who had it all and still cleaned the toilet, took care of the kids, and had a home-cooked meal on the table by 6:00 P.M. In the 1990s ads, "having it all" has made way for the exhausted, but smiling, woman in a Virginia Slims ad, "Maybe I can't have it all, but I can have the best of the bunch." She holds her cigarette slumped over her choice of watermelons. That working women's fatigue has found a niche on Madison Avenue does little to encourage the men to get up and help.

Women in advertising are portrayed as being keenly aware of the fact that they are being watched and judged. This hypothetical and highly critical entourage has become a part of women's life.

> From earliest childhood she has been taught and persuaded to survey herself continually. And so she comes to consider the **surveyor** and the **surveyed** within her as the two constituent yet always distinct elements of her identity as a woman. She has to survey everything she is and everything she does because how she appears to others, and ultimately how she appears to men, is of crucial importance for what is normally thought of as the success of her life. Her own sense of being in herself is supplanted by a sense of being appreciated as herself by another. . . . Thus she turns herself into an object—and most particularly an object of vision: a sight" (Berger, 1972, pp. 46–47).

She performs a relentless surveillance—is she having a bad hair day, is there a run in her hose, lipstick bleed, oily nose, chipped nail—is she too fat? Transforming ourselves for another's approval is "almost always affected by the dominant culture which is male supremacist, racist, ageist, heterosexist, anti-Semitic, ableist, and class biased" (Morgan, 1991, p. 38).

The animosity between men and women is being heightened with the trend of "in-your face-ads." A tired woman rejects a neighbor's invitation to join him for supper. Instead, she takes a raincheck and *his* ice cream in a 1994 Blockbuster television ad. Olympic figure skater Nancy Kerrigan, powered by Campbell's soup, shoves an ice-hockey thug as his teammates wince. Eddie Van Bloem's bylines for a Bodyslimmer's ad reads; "While you don't necessarily dress for men, it doesn't hurt, on occasion, to see one drool like the pathetic dog that he is." The copy covers the legs of a headless woman in a bathing suit. Although it is refreshing to see aggressive, independent women in control, the power gained from turning men into sex objects, calling them dogs, stealing their ice cream, and using unrealistic Popeyesque self-defense against men with clubs isn't the kind of power image many women want. Both sexes are desperately in need of images in which men and women together can work, play, and enjoy life cooperatively and respectfully as equals.

Sex and Alcohol

Beer, wine, and alcohol commercials have a history of blatantly equating drinking with available female bodies, yet the days of thirsty men popping open inflatable pools and inflatable women bearing a couple of cold ones may soon be a thing of the past. Old Milwaukee's 1991 Swedish bikini team ads hopefully marked the beginning of the end. They featured women with identical bleached-blond hairstyles, bodies, and skimpy swimsuits and were accused of creating an atmosphere conducive to sexual harassment in the workplace. In a suit filed against Stroh Brewery by female employees, subjection to Stroh's sexist advertising became part of a litany of sexual harassment allegations. Stroh did not immediately cancel the Swedish bikini team ads, but they did pull an ad for their Augsburger beer. It featured a simulated television filled with the bottoms of bikini-clad women and the headline, "Why the average beer commercial has more cans than bottles." The copy continued, "Most brewers feature pretty girls and sex in their TV ads, while Augsburger prefers to spend on quality brewing." De Witt Helm, the president of the Association of National Advertisers, scoffed at the lawsuit's allegations, saying that advertisers are "being wrongly swept into the concerns following the Senate sexual harassment hearing involving Clarence Thomas" (Teinowitz & Geiger, 1991, p. 48).

Findings suggest that alcohol advertising may predispose young people to drinking. To prevent drinking problems among our youth, attention should be given to countering the potential effects of alcohol advertising (Grube, 1994). Consider the effects of a popular print ad for Tanqueray gin of a woman sunning herself in a green bikini. The gin label literally etched on her stomach erases the line between her body and the product. John Kamp, vice president of the American Association of Advertising Agencies, stated, "There's no such thing as an inappropriate idea or image" in American advertising (Williams Walsh, 1991, p. 1). Kamp's quote was in response to Molson Brewery using a woman called "The Rare Long-Haired Fox" to sell beer.

Alcohol consumption is directly related to violence to women. Fifty percent of battered wives reported that their husbands were drinking when they were abusive (Frieze & Noble, 1980). About three-quarters of acquaintance rapes involve alcohol consumption on the part of the victim, the assailant, or both (Norris & Cubbins, 1992). In addition to the direct role alcohol plays in violence against women, many alcohol ads reinforce and trivialize the problem. An ad for Attakiska vodka portrays a frozen, half-nude woman slumped over and holding a huge ice block, which seems to be stuck to her naked chest. This torturous image reaffirms the myth that women enjoy abuse. Not all images are this hateful. In fact, a hopeful change in the climate has caused a few advertisers to switch from common beach scenarios to scenes where men and women drink beer together (Teinowitz, 1993).

Ageism and the Cult of Youth

The typical woman in ads is young. Childlike portrayals play up a woman's innocence, dependence, and powerlessness. Adult women mimic high baby voices. Women strive to be baby soft, to have baby's hair color, to have baby skin, and to baby themselves. For example, an illustrated ad from Cutex features an adult woman's red, painted lips sucking on an adult-sized pacifier. "Lipstick that makes your lips baby soft." Youthful-looking older women have begun to appear more often in ads. Isabella Rossellini, in her 40s, appears in makeup ads behind fuzzy filters to soften the lines. Lauren Hutton, who is in her 50s, appears wrinkle-free and without a hint of gray hair. Women are strongly urged to dye their hair because, as one ad says, "Why be gray when you can be yourself?" Women know men are attracted to women who emulate sweet, wide-eyed, waiflike baby dolls.

Women deny their maturity by shaving their body hair so they appear to be preadolescent—voluminous hair being, of course, restricted to their heads. The most heinous monster to attack the feminist movement is body hair, according to *Time* magazine. "Hairy legs haunt the feminist movement . . ." (Wallis, 1989, p. 81). Although men maintain their option to shave, women don't.

Advertisements sexualize little girls without alluding to the possible consequences of them imitating adult behavior. In one of Revlon's "Most unforgettable women in the world" ads, one of the models, heavily made-up like the adult women, is only seven or eight years old. The same child was used in a perfume editorial in *Harper's Bazaar* three or four years earlier. She was shown heavily made-up with a nude upper torso. Socializing females to be passive and to manipulate with their looks essentially sets them up to be victims. Socializing males to be attracted to this youthful ideal of beauty encourages them to seek the young and powerless to satisfy their sexual appetites. Statistics show that infants are being raped and preschoolers are being diagnosed with gonorrhea and other sexually transmitted diseases of the throat.

That we have all *learned* to worship this youth-crazed beauty standard means we can also *unlearn* it. We can all challenge the beauty ideal that preaches, "You can't be young enough."

Racism

Racism is an implicit part of the advertised image. When women of color do appear, they are often portrayed as animals, savage beasts, or sexual servants.

Native American women wore skintight, see-through cowhide suits, their bodies branded with Will Rogers's initials, to help advertise New York City's Broadway show, *Will Rogers' Follies*. The players of the video game *General Custer's Revenge* must traverse a difficult course to get to the Native American woman who is tied to a pole. The player is led by his saber-like penis, which he forces on the woman, who then "kicks up her legs in dubious delight." The motto: "When you score, you score" (Crenshaw, Matsuda, Lawrence, and Delgado, 1993, p. 119).

Women of color are doubly oppressed through advertised images. They are commonly portrayed through stereotypes and rendered invisible through a lack of representation. When advertisements do portray women of color, they are often urged to remove their ethnicity by straightening their hair, using bleaching agents, or wearing blue contacts. These women are shown "freely choosing" to aspire to this racist ideal. Asians westernize their eyes. Jewish women seek surgery to reduce their noses. African-American women reduce their lips, whereas Caucasian women seek to enlarge their lip size.

The fact that women of color are occasionally portrayed as articulate, intelligent, fully clothed humans may say more about the media executive's awareness of the increasing female audiences than any newfound scruples on their part. What is important to notice is that racially diverse images of women are the exception, not the rule.

Voluntary Slavery

Women voluntarily enslave themselves to dangerous diet regimes in hopes of reaching the advertisers' ideal weight, which is increasingly thin and waiflike. Abnormally tall and thin fashion models exemplify endocrine or genetic abnormalities, not average women. Average women stand approximately 5'4" and weigh 144 pounds (Gilday, 1989). This discrepancy between the "ideal" and the real has increased the diet industry's annual revenue to more than $30 billion (MarketData Enterprises, 1990). The diet industry's advertising and marketing is based on the creation and perpetuation of fear, biases, and stereotypes. Diet ads are famous for misleading claims regarding their safety and long-term effectiveness. Guilt and fear-based strategies make fat women blame themselves if they regain weight. Studies show that crash diets reduce life span, and that nearly all dieters who lose weight regain it within a year. Fat people are portrayed as unhealthy, unattractive, asexual, weak-willed, lazy, and gluttonous. Many women come to accept and expect rejections, mistreatment, and discrimination because of their weight. These messages lower fat women's self-esteem and foster discontent, self-doubt, and self-hatred.

Diet industry ads help fuel anorexic women's hallucinatory belief that they are obese, even as they literally starve themselves to death. According to the Association for Anorexics and Bulimics, 150,000 American women die yearly from anorexia. This is many more deaths than those who die from AIDS (Wolf, 1992).

Cosmetic surgery, like the diet industry, is another lucrative market. The average cosmetic surgeon makes $1 million a year (Wolf, 1992). In a shopping mall in Santa Monica, California, after shopping for shoes you can go next door for a new nose. Cosmetic surgery, which is increasingly accessible, is the fastest growing medical specialty. Elective cosmetic surgery takes healthy women and transforms them into potential victims of side effects. Liposuction, the most popular form of cosmetic surgery, entails full anesthesia while a suctioning device is shoved under the skin and the fat—hopefully just the fat—is vacuumed out. Women trim their ears, lift their faces, enlarge their breasts, reduce their noses, break their jaws, shoot collagen into wrinkles and lips, and remove their ribs. One doctor offered to saw off a patient's bones to reduce her height. The physical dangers are minimized through the use of innocuous terminology. "Snip it, tuck it, exercise it—or learn to love it" (Newman, 1993, p. 364). These serious surgical interventions can result in infection, hemorrhage, numbness, embolism, pulmonary edema, facial nerve injury, unfavorable scar formation, skin loss, blindness, crippling, and death. These "minor complications" are rarely mentioned. Instead, the dissatisfied woman is encouraged to carve herself into the person *she* wants to be. Many women deeply believe that their only access to social and economic success is through surgery. As they see it, their survival depends on it. Already, the social deviants tend to be women who refuse cosmetic surgery. The question is no longer whether women will have "elective" cosmetic surgery, but when.

> For virtually all women, success is defined in terms of interlocking patterns of compulsion: compulsory attractiveness, compulsory motherhood, and compulsory heterosexuality, patterns that determine the legitimate limits of attraction and motherhood. Rather than aspiring to self-determined and woman-centered ideals of health or integrity, women's attractiveness is defined as attractive-to-men; women's eroticism is defined as either nonexistent, pathological, or peripheral when it is not directed to phallic goals; and motherhood is defined in terms of legally sanctioned and constrained reproductive service to particular men and to institutions such as the nation, the race, the owner and the class—institutions that are, more often than not, male-dominated. Biotechnology is now making beauty, fertility, the appearance of heterosexuality through surgery, and the appearance of youthfulness, accessible to virtually all women who can afford that technology—and growing numbers of women are making sacrifices in their lives in order to buy access to the technical expertise (Morgan, 1991, p. 32).

Serious contenders in the beauty game turn to professionals for expert advice on their makeovers. In 1989, GuyRex Associates, the manager duo famous for creating Miss USA queens, helped groom the fifth Miss Texas, Gretchen Polemus, to win the Miss USA title. Gretchen underwent breast implants, hair weaving, dental work, and had her lower ribs removed to win the crown. "There are no more queens," explains GuyRex partner Richard Guy. "Momma doesn't make apple pie anymore, it's all frozen, all corporate-owned" (Chaua-Eoan, 1989, p. 85).

Beautiful women are often both envied and hated. Women are judged and judge one another, rather than acknowledging one another as allies in an oppressed position. Beauty contests are an institutionalized form of judging women and girls. The Miss America "Scholarship" program is one of the most dangerous, given that it is the largest educational scholarship available for women. Women are required to hobble on high heels and parade their bodies in order to earn an education. These contests might be less bothersome if they crowned their queens Miss Chevrolet, Miss Fruit of the Loom, or Miss Procter & Gamble. One needs only to watch a few minutes of these shows to understand they are just another advertiser's gimmick to sell products.

Women in Pieces

Women are dismembered in ads: their bodies are reduced to a pair of breasts, a leg, an object, a rear-end, a crotch. A 1994 television ad for L'eggs flashed headless women "putting on their legs" in cars and on couches that merged with close-ups of their miniskirted rear ends. One of the most menacing results is that most women automatically view themselves in pieces. They may run through their checklist asking, "What do my thighs look like, my rear end, my legs, breasts, hands, ankles, toes and knees?" Women rarely think of themselves as whole and complete human beings. Men partake in this segmented view of women through such compliments as, "Nice legs," or "Nice breasts." Convicted rapists have been known to justify their rapes because their victims didn't seem human to them—they were just objects. Viewing women in pieces creates the objectification. Pieces of women's anatomy are literally strewn throughout our daily environment. A billboard for Epi-products featured a blow-up of a woman's thigh with the slogan, "Treat cellulite like dirt."

Violence to Women

Advertisements help legitimize and normalize violence against women. According to the National Institute for Mental Health (1982), violent images of women in the media reinforce violent behavior toward women. In a Hanes ad, a frightened-looking woman wearing a cocktail dress and heels crouches against a wall, her hands over her ears. She seems to be avoiding a shrill noise or someone who is about to hit her. The copy surrounds her: "The shape you want to be in." In an ad for Kenar clothing, a model lies belly down on a tile floor. Her head is lifted, as if to avoid placing her face on the floor. Her pensive stare suggests she might be asking to get up.

Advertised women look hurt, frightened, dirty, or attacked. They are victimized, running away, humiliated, and slapped. Many women and girls believe that being sexy and feminine means imitating victims. Ads help teach them that their sexuality is enhanced by being powerless, subordinated victims, and that inequality is alluring.

Men not only don't have to take responsibility for their sexually deviant behavior, they can actively blame it all on women. A London Fog ad, for example, showed the back of a man opening his trench coat in flasher fashion with the caption, "London Fog wants to show you something you've never seen before." This blame-the-victim attitude is reinforced by advertisements of women flaunting their sexuality—appearing to invite, if not deserve, male aggression. The women in Guess ads look young, poor, and sexually available. Their legs are open wide, or they wear lacy teddies, unzipped jeans, and unbuttoned blouses in public. In one image the model's hair is dirty and her black bra is held together with safety pins.

These Guess ads were shot by fashion photographer Wayne Maser, who shared his thoughts with writer Susan Faludi.

> The trouble with advertising today is everyone's afraid to take a stand on women. Everything's done to please the feminists because the feminists dominate these advertising positions. They've made women bland. My work is a reaction against feminist blandness," he says. But, he wants to make clear, he isn't trying to restrict women, just endorse their new options. "It's a post-feminist period," he explains. "Women can be women again. All my girls have a choice."
>
> Jeffrey Thrunher, Maser's assistant photographer, explains to Faludi why so many models are reluctant to work with Maser. "I've seen Wayne take a model who isn't cooperating, just standing there not showing any emotion, and push her face against the wall. Or he'll tell her, 'Get undressed'—in front of him—and if she doesn't, he'll say, 'Get the fuck out of here.' He plays with their minds" (Faludi, 1992, p. 199).

Restriction, according to these fellows, looks great on females. The women appear to adore the restriction, smiling as they are tied in bondage in *Harper's Bazaar* or *Vogue*. The implication is that women are out of control, needing to be held down, held back. The media rarely shows the general populace the horrifying results of domestic violence. Instead we are fed a diet of glamorous beauties in lovely outfits, who cope well with being bruised, unconscious, or dead.

Sadomasochistic or S&M fashions help costume a society where pain and violence have become synonymous with love and being sexy. Chains and bondage themes appear in ads, in department store windows, and in major movie releases. What was big in the 1980s is growing even bigger in the 1990s. Helmut Newton's layout in the September 1992 issue of *Vogue* is filled with anorexic women in chains, dirtied, next to anorexic women dressed like men. The controversial S&M styles challenge women to be rebellious. Being different is in style as long as everyone imitates one another. The rebel S&M look is just another marketing ploy being peddled to women. Be liberated—wear chains. Be avant garde—pierce your clitoris. Primitive rituals performed for only $39.95—just sign this waiver. Self-mutilation is touted as self-control. Permanent scarring, brands, and tattoos are temporarily in vogue. S&M trends are sold to women as their chance to rebel, to shock, and even to gain control over their bodies. Some women imagine adornments and constrictive accessories will help them recover what has been taken away (Kauffman, 1993). And they believe it. After all, no two piercings are alike, no two tattoos identical. Is this choosing your own image, or another advertising ploy to preoccupy women with their looks, another angle to brand women with the willing-victim look as beauty theme?

The ad world claims they merely give society what it wants, or that ads are pure fantasy—they aren't real. The reality for women is that domestic violence is the leading cause of injury for women ages 15–44, and every 6 minutes 40 women are beaten badly enough to seek emergency medical attention (Smolowe, 1992). In 1990, 102,555 rapes were reported to the police in the United States. Of those, 18,024—fewer than one in five—resulted in convictions. The average time served was less than three years (Vachss, 1993). Fear of attack is understandably far greater in women than in men. Many women, who jump at every sound, have come to accept large doses of adrenaline continually coursing through their veins. The physiological effects of attack and the fear of attack make women more vulnerable to heart attacks, high blood pressure, and all diseases that stem from compromised immune systems (Kushner-Resnick, 1992). Yet women are continually portrayed as victims, hunted and preyed on as if it were all just an adventure. Gloria Vanderbilt ran a series of ads with women being stalked by ominous male shadows, with the caption, "Let the adventure begin."

Mainstreaming Pornography

The line between what is pornographic and what isn't has become indistinguishable. Pornographic values pervade our lives so completely that they have become normalized, accepted, and anticipated. Pornographic films, which outnumber other films by three to one, gross an average of $1 million a day. Film, television, and magazines are having to compete with the $10-billion-a-year pornography industry (Russell, 1993).

Mainstream advertising imitates many of the values, images, plots, stereotypes, and even the costumes of pornography. *Playboy* pinball machines groan and moan like a woman supposedly having an orgasm each time the ball hits the target. The nationwide Hooters chain of "breasturants" have their all-female wait-staff wearing denim cut-offs and half-top T-shirts that read, "More than a Mouthful." There has been a sharp increase in the popularity of "sophisticated" topless bars and strip clubs. In some strip clubs, men can purchase topless women to give them a shoeshine. In the past few years, topless donut shops, topless car washes, topless hot dog stands, and topless housecleaning services have been made available (Ciriello, Buchwald, Fletcher, and Roth, 1993). *Glamour* and *Cosmopolitan* recently touted topless dancing as a good way for female students to put themselves through college. After all, dancers don't have to have sex with their customers (Silverman, 1993; Haynes, 1993). A Neutrogena ad in the same *Cosmopolitan* issue asks, "Why not spend more time in the nude?" Another ad in the same issue, for Club Carnell's active wear, shows a nude woman's bare back. She hides her breasts and glances over her shoulder. The caption: "We can't wait to show you what we have." An ad in a railway station in Tokyo portrays a young Caucasian teenager naked from the waist up. The caption reads: "Get to know a real live high school girl." It is difficult to know what is for sale until you spot a small can of juice on the right. The word for *know* in Japanese, *shiru*, also has the meaning "to have sex." Here a poster associates the taste of fresh juice with the "taste" of a virgin.

"Even such innocuous products as Liquid Drano and Hebrew National salami are being sold," the *New Republic* recently declared, "with a sexual explicitness once reserved for pay customers of soft-core pornography" (Muro, 1989, p. 77). *Harper's Bazaar* highlights the mainstreaming of pornography in an article touting the wonders of pornography *for women* (Darling, 1994).

In former Yugoslavia, the rape of women is being filmed for use as anti-Muslim and anti-Croatian propaganda and for profit. Serbian soldiers forced Muslim women to pretend to be Serbian for these rape films. "These materials become a potent advertisement for war, a perfect motivator for torturers, who then do what they are ordered to do and enjoy it. Yes, it actually improves their morale," says Catharine MacKinnon, of the University of Michigan (1993, p. 28). There have been reports that a Serbian tank that rolled in to "cleanse" a village was plastered with images from pornography.

In a stark, black-and-white ad for DKNY, from September 1993's *Glamour*, two women appear harried, poor, and hungry. One holds her head in her hand, the other looks wary, bracing for an attack. The two figures seem to lean together for comfort in the harsh light. The women look Slavic, and the image of Bosnian rape survivors is brought to mind.

POLITICAL IMPLICATIONS

The media play a powerful role in depoliticizing violence to women. Advertisements that threaten violence and overt acts of violence to women help maintain male domination. Whenever advertisers reduce women to objects or dehumanize them, they engage in the act of publicly celebrating violence against women. Women's health and dignity have become expendable, secondary to a free market where women are peddled as products.

Many women who have been victims of male violence don't comprehend the political context in which they have been violated. Rather than seeing male terrorism within the context of the millions of women violated, it is viewed as a private problem. This is partly due to the fact that globally, many acts of violence to women aren't criminal; they are entrenched in social custom, and what isn't criminal is blamed on the victims themselves. Advertisers do their part by isolating women and teaching them that *they* are the ones in need of therapeutic help—retail, surgical, or otherwise.

Many women learn early on to vacate their bodies. Learning the let's-get-it-over-with trick helps women endure catcalls, obscene phone calls, the application of makeup, cosmetic surgery and piercing, incest, rape, and the act of prostitution.

Women are taught to be willing to perform anonymous sex—for a price. "A wife. After all, it wouldn't mean anything. It's just my body. It's not my mind. It's not my heart. It's not my soul." This is an excerpt from the ad copy for the movie *Indecent Proposal*. The poster displayed the lower torso of a woman in underwear lying on a bed of money. Brides are for sale and prostitutes are rented (Clarke, 1993). The wholesaling of women in today's marketplace is far from being a victimless crime. Every woman is hurt when women as a class or group are for sale.

Depression is a predictable reaction to being tortured, denigrated, and undervalued. At least 7 million women have diagnosable depression (Avenoso, 1993). One study out of Duke University found that much of women's depression is the product of physical and social oppression. Up to 37 percent of U.S. women have suffered significant physical or sexual abuse before the age of 21, and 25 to 50 percent have been battered by a partner. Up to 71 percent of working women have experienced sexual harassment at work. Women receive inadequate child support, and women are usually the ones who care for aged parents. Women abuse weight-loss drugs, laxatives, amphetamines, and Valium disproportionately. Women make up 70 percent of the lucrative market for antidepressant drugs worldwide (Avenoso, 1993). According to the U.S. Bureau of the Census, American women face the worst gender-based pay gap in the developed world, with more than 80 percent of full-time working women making less that $20,000 a year (Rix, 1989). The pressures on women are tremendous. No wonder they are depressed.

The following ad shows a woman sitting on a bed in her push-up bra, looking into a mirror that reflects an open door. The woman looks slightly startled, as if anticipating someone about to enter. The copy litters the page,

I'm his night light. I'm his heater. I'm his favorite channel. I'm his umbrella. I'm his blanket.
I'm his weapon. I'm his little voice. I'm his painkiller.
I'm his savior. I'm his pillow.
Which I guess could also make me his worst nightmare.
Lilyette Bras and Panties Your underneath.

The advertisers' fantasy of creating the perfect female consumer may quickly be turning into a nightmare. While advertisers encourage women's sense of worthlessness, how will they stop their plummeting self-esteem? Drug abuse and death are not ingredients for ideal shoppers. Of course, advertisers are relentless—women who suffer from immobilizing depression can always tune into the home shopping network.

WHAT CAN BE DONE?

The promotion of sexist imagery, debasing language, and anti-woman biases found in advertising is clearly helping to promote major mental and physical health problems for women. Making the elimination of sexism a priority will entail enormous education. Americans deserve to know every possible risk associated with consuming our daily tonnage of sexist advertising. In-depth studies should be dedicated to understanding the consequences of consuming thousands of "sexy women" commercials. Individuals are also entitled to judge for themselves whether or not they are offended by advertising. A National Advisory Board should provide a consumer hotline with an 800 number that viewers can call to register their complaints. This number should be aired every hour or two on TV and on commercial radio, and should be a mandatory part of magazines and newspapers.

Commercial-Free Zones should be established, starting with schools, books, and museums. Zoning boards can be urged to curb or remove billboards. Congress could be encouraged to investigate the harmful effects of advertising in our society and to eliminate advertisers' tax deductibility of ads for tobacco and alcohol. Sales tax could be placed on advertising. The FTC should be pressured to regulate advertisers' influence of editorial or program content. The government should be pressured to label all ads, including product placements, advertorials and infomercials, as paid advertisements (Collins & Jacobson, 1990).

Ads don't have to draw from sexism and violence to work. Esprit's "What would you do if you could change the world?" ads gave young women a chance to espouse their political views on the world and were both innovative and powerful. This campaign initiated a new portrayal of women standing on their own two feet, fully clothed and speaking out about vitally important issues.

Women's groups and other silenced groups can use marketing strategies to their own ends. One billboard from the women's group, Labrys, proclaimed, "Murdering and Raping Women is unacceptable. We will Fight Back!" (*off our backs*, 1991). Independently created Public Service Announcements can also be effective. Unfortunately, two independent groups, *Direct Effect* and Canada's Media Foundation, have had their spots—on topics such as sexual harassment, sexism, and media addiction—rejected by the three major networks and a number of cable channels.

The Fairness Doctrine, which stipulated that broadcasters should air opposing views on controversial issues, was scuttled by the FCC's deregulatory campaign during the Reagan administration. Media moguls claimed the rule—rarely enforced since its inception in 1959—constituted undue government meddling and had a chilling effect on free speech. This was essentially the same objection raised by the tobacco industry when cigarette commercials were banned from the airwaves. Whenever television is criticized, broadcasters cry foul and plead that their First Amendment right of free expression is threatened (Lee & Solomon, 1990). Many media industries make money at the expense of public welfare by hiding behind these protections. Supporting free speech is imperative, yet free speech remains an ideal that is not equally available to every citizen. Women who are silenced daily through rape, incest, and battery don't have the same access to free speech that advertisers, pimps, and pornographers do.

For the American consumer, freedom of speech is now the freedom to be manipulated by corporate voices. Yet, if the only voices the American consumer hears are corporate voices, how free is speech? It's time people asked, "Free for whom?" Meanwhile, advertisers stand by with their First Amendment lawyers, determined to keep commercial speech free.

The FCC must initiate a mandatory allotment of time for citizens to voice *their* concerns on television. Imagine exposing racial prejudice in a 30-second commercial showing how Guns 'n Roses, Madonna, and Howard Stern become rich and famous by being as nasty as they want to. Yet when African-American rappers like 2 Live Crew are *equally* nasty, they land in jail. It isn't a lack of airtime that keeps controversial messages from reaching the airwaves. Free airtime is clearly available. Groups like the Ad Council, a corporate-sponsored consortium that creates nonprofit commercials, received more than $1 billion worth of free airtime and ad space in 1989 alone. The Media Foundation, working to help people receive their rightful access to the airwaves, established both a petition to the FCC asking for this mandatory airtime and a hotline, at 800-663-1243. The success of their campaign will take the involvement of people like you.

Making sexist images socially reprehensible through public education is not impossible. The Harvard Alcohol Project, in cooperation with dozens of television producers and writers, spearheaded 95 televised episodes delivering negative messages about drunk driving. Messages about the negative effects of sexism could also be similarly conveyed to the viewing public.

Governmental regulation is a possibility, yet in countries like Canada and Australia, drafting and enforcing codes for advertising has proved difficult. Self-regulation is obviously the preferred first step, but self-regulatory systems need a great deal of consumer input. Penalties levied against advertisers must be made public, and the guidelines for advertisers need to be clear and easily understood. In the United States, self-regulation and governmental regulation policies lag far behind other developed countries. According to William Johnson, deputy chief of the Federal Communications Commission, "Basically, there's no federal regulation at all regarding sex in TV ads" (Muro, 1989, p. 77).

Consumers to Stop Sexist Alcohol Advertising, a U.S.-based group that began with members of the medical community and administrators of a battered women's shelter, has initiated The Dangerous Promises Campaign. It proposes that the beer and distilled spirits industry associations amend their advertising guidelines to read: "Alcohol advertising and promotion should not reinforce or trivialize the problem of violence against women. Alcohol advertising and promotion shall not (1) degrade, demean, or objectify the form, image or status of women or any ethnic or minority group; (2) associate alcohol with adversarial, abusive, or violent relationships or situations; or (3) suggest sex as an expected result of or reward for drinking alcohol" (The Trauma Foundation, 1992). The Wine Institute adopted the guidelines in September 1993.

The best defense is public action, consumer awareness, and an understanding that advertisers desperately need the public's money to survive. Products that use sexist, racist, or violent advertising should not be purchased. Boycotts are *very* effective since most corporations respond only when their profit margin is threatened. The *National Boycott News, Boycott Action News,* and *Media Watch* will mail you their boycott lists on request.

The Media Foundation has initiated an annual, international Buy Nothing Day, September 24, for a 24-hour, continent-wide moratorium on consumer spending. Buy Nothing Day is designed to remind both the consumer and retailer of the true power of the buying public.

Letters to advertisers are also effective. They should be clear and concise, and should offer a return address for a response. Letters should be addressed to the president of a corporation or advertising company, rather than the public relations officer. Library reference desks are helpful sources of addresses, phone numbers, and names.

CONCLUSION

The biggest barrier to social equality may be that many women have become unwittingly attached to the woman who is on sale and on display. Without understanding their options, women have become a part of the daily beauty contest vying for the prize look, the winning smile, the ephemeral crown. Unfortunately, most women don't comprehend their power to change the rules to the beauty game, especially if they are in a position in their work where they are both marginally respected and decently paid. Some women, understandably, want to paint their nails in peace. They want to pluck their eyebrows without someone trying to convince them that it hurts. They *know* it hurts. Women often lose their jobs, their identities, and their loves if they don't play the game. They make the most of their price tags, conspicuous as they are.

The beauty game can't be won. No one wins when women are raped and then blame themselves, rather than a political system that openly degrades their humanity. Women's lowered status allows the dominant male community to neglect their health and their financial status, and to neglect to study why they continue to be so neglected. Women are so actively hated that the hatred itself can't be acknowledged publicly.

Each year 150,000 women die from anorexia. Four die each day at the hands of their male sexual partners and an untold number die from complications related to cosmetic surgery (no one knows because accurate medical records are not being kept). If White men were dying at this rate, a medical emergency would be announced, funds would be allotted, research initiated, sweeping changes would be made to national policy—and a possible monument might be erected in their honor. When women die, the stench from their bodies is ignored. They aren't allowed to pile up together. They are slipped out one by one. The enormity of pain, death, abuse, and hate being heaped on females is judged as unfortunate—but generally considered women's fault.

The advertising industry has done more than its share in reinforcing the idea that females are trivial, vile commodities and can, as a group, be easily trashed. Clearly, advertisers didn't invent woman-hating, rape, domestic violence or child abuse, but consumers must hold them accountable each and every time they promote it.

REFERENCES

Avenoso, K. (1993, February). Women's blues: Biology or backlash? *Elle*, 72–76.

Berger, J. (1972). *Ways of seeing*, British Broadcasting Corporation, pp. 46–47 (paragraph breaks omitted).

Boycott Action News/Co-op America. 1850 M St. NW, Suite 700 Washington, DC 20036.

Chaua-Eoan, H. (1989, March 13). No more apple pie. *Time*, 85.

Ciriello, S., Buchwald E., Fletcher P. & Roth M. (Eds.). (1993). Choice? Commodification of women: Morning, noon, and night. In *Transforming a rape culture*, pp. 265–274. Minneapolis, MN: Milkweed Editions.

Clarke, D. & Reti, I. (Ed.). (1993). Consuming passions: Some thoughts on history, sex, and free enterprise. In *Unleashing Feminism*. Santa Cruz, CA: Her Books.

Clibbon, P. (1993) News from the mental environment. *Adbusters Quarterly*, 2, 10.

Collins R. & Jacobson M. (1990, September 19). Commercialism versus culture. *Christian Science Monitor*, p. 19.

Crenshaw, K., Matsuda, M., Lawrence, C., and Delgado, R. (Eds.). (1993). *Words that wound: critical race theory, assaultive speech and the First Amendment*. Boulder, CO: Westview Press.

Criticism vanishes in puff of journalistic smoke. (1992, January 30, Special Issue from Fairness & Accuracy in Reporting). *New England Journal of Medicine*, 23.

Cubbins, L., & Norris, J. (1992, June). Dating, drinking and rape: Effects of victim's and assailant's alcohol consumption on judgments of their behavior and traits. *Psychology of Women Quarterly*, 16, 179–191.

Darling, L. (1994, August). Women who love pornography. *Harper's Bazaar*, 168–171.

Faludi, S. (1992). *Backlash*. New York, NY: Crown Publishing.

Fawcett-Ward, A. (1993, February 8). Narrowcast in past, women earn revised role in advertising. *Advertising Age*, p. S-10.

French, M. (1985). *Beyond power: On women, men and morals.* NY: Ballantine.

Frieze, I. H., & Noble, J. (1980). *The effects of alcohol on marital violence.* Paper presented to the American Psychological Association Convention. Montreal, Canada.

Gilday, K. (1989). *The famine within* [Film]. Toronto Film Board.

Grube, J. (1994, February). Television beer advertising and drinking knowledge, beliefs, and intentions among schoolchildren. *American Journal of Public Health, 84(2),* 254–259.

Haynes, K. (1993, August). The lowdown on topless bars: Can these girls really undress for success? *Cosmopolitan*, 200.

Huston, A., Donnerstein E., Fairchild H., et al., (1992). *Big World, Small Screen: The role of television in American society.* Lincoln: University of Nebraska Press.

Kauffman, L. (1993, June). Beauty knows no pain. *Elle*, 65–67.

Kilbourne, J. (1992, Special Issue from Fairness & Accuracy in Reporting). Smoking as Liberation: The tobacco industry targets women. p. 22.

Kushner-Resnick, S. (March–April 1993). Fear itself. *Utne Reader,* pp. 64–65.

Lee, M., & N. Solomon. (1990). *Unreliable sources: A guide to detecting bias in news media.* New York, NY: Carol Publishing Group, p. 75.

MacKinnon, C. (1993, July–August). Turning rape into pornography: Post-modern genocide. *Ms.*, 24–30.

MarketData Enterprises (1990). Lynbrook, NJ.

Media Watch Boycott List, P.O. Box 618, Santa Cruz, CA 95061.

Miller, A., & Tsiantar, D. (1989, February 27). Psyching out consumers. *Newsweek,* 46–47.

Morgan, K. (1991, Fall). Women and the knife: Cosmetic surgery and the colonization of women's bodies. *Hypatia, 6(3),* 26–53.

Muro, M. (1989, April, 16). A new era of eros in advertising. *Boston Globe,* pp. 77–78.

National Boycott News, 6506 28th Ave., N.E., Seattle, WA 98115.

National Institute for Mental Health. (1982). In *Dangerous Promises: How alcohol advertising reinforces and trivializes violence against women.* The Trauma Foundation, San Francisco, CA, and Los Angeles Commission on Assaults Against Women, Los Angeles, CA, p. 3.

Newman, J. (1993, September). The latest word in body reshaping. *Elle*, 364.

Not & Hot (1993, August). *Allure*, 46.

off our backs. (1991, February).

Reeves, J. (Summer, 1993). Giant billboard to orbit earth. *Adbusters Quarterly, 2,* p. 7.

Rix, S. (Ed.). (1989). *The American Woman 1988–89: A Status Report.*

Russell, D. (Ed.). (1993) *Making violence sexy: Feminist views on pornography.* Athene Series, Columbia University, New York, NY: Teachers College Press.

Sharkey, B. (1993, February). You've come a long way, Madison Avenue. *Lears*, 94.

Silverman, J. (1993, April). Night and day: The double life of a topless dancer. *Glamour*, 243.

Smolowe, J. (1992, June 29). What the doctor should do. *Time*, 57.

Sontag, S. (1973). *On photography*. New York, NY: Farrar, Straus & Giroux.

Steinem, G. (1990, July–August). Sex, lies and advertising. *Ms.*, 22–23.

Teinowitz & Geiger. (1991, November 18). Suits try to link sex harassment, ads. *Advertising Age*, 48.

Teinowitz, I. (1993, February 8). Days of "beer and babes" running out. *Advertising Age*, p. 58.

Trauma Foundation, Bldg. 1, Room #400, San Francisco General Hospital, San Francisco, CA 94110 415-821-8209, FAX 415-282-2563 or LACAAW, Los Angeles Commission on Assaults Against Women, 6043 Hollywood Blvd., Suite 200, Los Angeles, CA 90028 213–462-1281, FAX 213–462-8434.

Vachss, A. (1993, June 27). We need to go to war. *Parade*, cover.

Wallis, C. (1989, December 4). Onward, women! *Time*, 81.

Williams Walsh, M. (1991, April 4). Hopping mad in Canada: Controversy brews as Ontario bans sexist beer ads. *Los Angeles Times*, Part E, p. 1.

Wolf, N. (1992). *The beauty myth: How images of beauty are used against women*. New York, NY: William Morrow, p. 182, 229.

Wyndham, D. (1987, August). Admen, subtract women: Profit without honour. *Media Information Australia, 45*, pp. 52–58. United Nations (1980), cited in *Women in the Media*. Paris: UNESCO.

Contemporary [cartoon] shows are either essentially all-male, like "Garfield," or are organized on what I call the Smurf-ette principle: A group of male buddies will be accentuated by a lone female, stereotypically defined. (Pollitt, 1991, p. 22)

four

PRIME-TIME TELEVISION:
From Lucy to Murphy

HISTORY

A large part of television's early development was based on the programs, stars, and audience of the radio and motion picture industry. Although television was introduced in 1939, World War II held back its growth. In contrast, radio reached its height during the war. By the late 1940s, American commercial television had grown more rapidly than its predecessors (radio or motion pictures), in part due to the programming television borrowed from both. Daytime television programs were copied after radio's talk shows and afternoon game shows. Television drew matinee serial-film audiences because women stayed home to watch soap operas. During evening hours, families viewed variety shows, dramas, and adventure series (many of which were originally heard on radio), watching some of their favorite radio stars who had moved to television (Bob Hope, Jack Benny, Milton Berle, George Burns and Gracie Allen, Perry Como, Bing Cosby, and Dinah Shore).

In addition to television's use of radio stars and radio programs, television networks were patterned after radio networks first established in 1922 (Becker, 1992, p. 278). The networks' function was to provide affiliates (first radio, later television) across the United States with programs in exchange for the right to broadcast national advertisements. Networks were not stations themselves. Although networks owned key stations, most affiliates were not owned by networks. The relationship between networks and affiliates, then, was based on programming and commercial space within the programming. Networks purchased individual programs or full seasons of shows from production companies. The local affiliates were given these purchased programs by the networks, free of charge. In exchange for this programming, affiliates agreed to run the network programming as scheduled and also run specific advertisements between and within the programs. In addition to free network programs, the affiliates were given open advertising slots in which they placed local advertisements. The arrangement between the network and affiliates allowed networks to guarantee to advertisers a certain number of stations across the country broadcasting a specific advertisement at a specific time. In exchange, affiliates received free programs and advertising slots to sell to local advertisers. This same relationship between networks and affiliates continues today.

The first years of television have been called the "Vaudeo" era (1948–57) beginning with NBC's *The Milton Berle Show* (1948), which brought together the broad slapstick of vaudeville and the new video medium (Brooks & Marsh, 1988, p. xiv). Variety shows were joined by situation comedies such as *I Love Lucy* (1951). A few years later, the networks focused on America's interest in the family, with such sitcom-type programs as *The Adventures of Ozzie and Harriet* (1952), *Our Miss Brooks* (1952), and *Amos 'n Andy* (1951) (Jones, 1992, pp. 39–40).

Programs that made the successful switch from radio to television "were those which lent themselves to frequent interruptions, strong personality identifications, mass audience involvement, and a conventional moral view unlikely to ruffle the sponsors" (Rose, 1985, p. 6).

Popular television genres rose and fell throughout television's history. Because television was more expensive than its predecessor, radio, when a specific genre was successful (i.e., had high ratings), the majority of the producers and advertisers did not experiment with the untried or unconventional. For example, "adult westerns" were popular from 1957 to the early 1960s; the "idiot sitcoms" ran from the early 1960s to the late 1960s; "relevant" programs (focusing on political and social issues) were popular from the late 1960s through 1975, and "fantasy" programs took precedence and populated the airwaves until 1980. In the 1980s, nighttime soap operas and "real people" programs became popular (Brooks and Marsh, 1988). Though some theorists (Erik Barnouw and Todd Gitlin) argue these genres are tied to specific historical events or trends, Rose believes genres "more often [are] the result of network programming practices and production techniques than a sudden thematic reaction to new cultural concerns" (1985, p. 8). For example, increased dismay by American consumers and the threat of government intervention is more likely to affect the amount of sex and violence on television in the 1990s than the end of the Cold War. Producers of television content prefer to change the content, continuing to regulate themselves rather than be overseen by governmental regulatory agencies. The 1990s may become the "nonviolent" era.

Minor changes are expected in entertainment television programming while incredible developments simultaneously may occur in their delivery. Cable stations, telephone companies, and broadcast stations are looking into the "superhighway" as a method in which to bring video material combined with data transmission (computer, telephone, information) into your home through the same "wire" and viewed on the same "television" (computer/video terminal). Along with the new delivery, expect new ways of advertisers identifying you as an audience. Although a family may choose exactly what type of programming it will receive, those who distribute the program will also be able to target their messages. You and your neighbor may watch the same sporting event, but your family may receive ads for mountain bikes (because your household watches a lot of "camping" programs) while your neighbor views travel commercials to France (because they belong to the "winery" channel). It might seem laughable, but it's right over the horizon.

Although there were fewer women than men on television in the 1950s, women were not excluded. Sydney Head, broadcast historian, reported in a 1954 study that 32 percent of all television drama characters were female, and women were portrayed in the early situation comedies. Perhaps the most well known was the zany and incompetent Lucille Ball in *I Love Lucy* (1951), who is well described by Gerard Jones as:

> the embodiment of female energy with no valid outlet. She is the mid-century American woman with no job, no power, no reinforcement for her aspirations, no kids, not even much housework (this being the age of the labor saving device), yet with a mind and spirit excited by the possibilities of the twentieth century. She is a comic demon called forth from the boredom and frustration of an entire generation of housewives. She is what happens when a woman is allowed to go to college, tantalized with career possibilities, asked to give her all to war-work, and then told to retreat to the kitchen because that's what good girls are supposed to do (1992, p. 68).

Following the success of *I Love Lucy* (1951–61), producers copied its format, producing shows with ditzy, pretty female characters such as those in *I Married Joan* (1952–1953), *My Little Margie* (1952–55), and *Dear Phoebe* (1954–56). Few of these copies were successful, and producers moved to the family sitcom where women were portrayed as helpful, competent, housewives in *The Adventures of Ozzie and Harriet* (1952–66), *Father Knows Best* (1954–63), and *Leave It to Beaver* (1957–63). The White, middle-class homemaker was an important part of the economic development during the 1950s and 1960s. Women had been taken out of the job market and returned home. A woman's place in the home was "central to the economy in that her function as homemaker was the subject of consumer product design and marketing" (Haralovich, 1992, p. 111). Television households were spotless, smoothly managed, and the women who took care of the homes looked as if they spent the day in the beauty parlor. Problems in the family were easily solved, although usually by men in the family, and women were rarely portrayed outside the home.

Family comedies continued through the 1950s and into the 1960s in *The Patty Duke Show* (1963–66) and *The Andy Griffith Show* (1960–68), but different families such as the Addams family, the Jetsons, and the Stevens (on *Bewitched*) were also popular. Even in these, however, women were still positioned within the family. The portrayal of single women continued to be limited to such roles as Sally in *The Dick Van Dyke Show* (1961–66) or Ann Marie in *That Girl* (1966–71) (Taylor, 1989, p. 85).

One surprise hit was *Julia* (1968–71), a program about an African-American woman who was a nurse and a mother, starring Diahann Carroll. NBC felt they'd accomplish something of social value in programming a show starring a Black woman, but they didn't expect it to succeed because it was programmed against the very successful *Red Skelton Show,* "where it was expected to die a noble, dignified death, having demonstrated the network's desire to break the prime-time color bar" (Bodroghkozy, 1992, p. 143). *Julia* was the first comedy to focus on a Black woman, and although a rating success, was criticized for its unrealistic portrayal of Black families living in the 1960s.

The 1970s saw an increase in the number of programs about women in general, and single women in particular: *The Mary Tyler Moore Show* (1970), *Rhoda* (1974), *Phyllis* (1975), *One Day at a Time* (1975), and *Alice* (1976). Unfortunately, these portrayals were countered with "jiggle shows" such as *Charlie's Angels* (1976), *Three's Company* (1977), and *Flying High* (1978).

By the mid-1970s, women police officers were acceptable on prime time but only if they looked good and weren't too tough. *Police Woman* (1974) starred Angie Dickinson and *Get Christie Love* (1974) starred Teresa Graves. Whereas *Police Woman* lasted four seasons, *Get Christie Love* lasted only one. A representative of the Ted Bates Advertising Agency stated, "The Black woman heroine may be O.K. for urban movie audiences but it won't play in Heartland, U.S.A." (Dreyfuss, 1974, p. K5).

Black female characters in the 1970s and early 1980s were stereotypes: Mammy, Aunt Jemima, Sapphire, and Jezebel (Jewell, 1993, pp. 37–47). The "mammy" stereotype was subtly changed, but it was still apparent in such characters as Florida in *Good Times* (1974), Nel in *Gimme A Break* (1981), and Shirley in *What's Happening!!* (1976) (Jewell, 1993, p. 48). Jewell argues that characters such as Jackie on *227* (1985) perpetuated the Jezebel/bad girl stereotype, and Florence in *The Jeffersons* (1975) combined the "images, that of mammy and Sapphire" and "evoked considerable laughter by constantly putting down and insulting her employer" (1993, p. 48). Louise Jefferson is described as a combination of mammy and Aunt Jemima images, but Helen, "the African-American neighbor whose husband was White" does not "conform to traditional cultural images of African-American women" (1993, p. 49).

Although there was an increase in the number of women characters in the early 1970s, studies analyzing the portrayal of women and men in television found the following:

1 More male than female characters on television programs (Tedesco, 1974), except during daytime television, when the number of male and female characters was the same (Downing, 1974).

2 More diverse and less stereotypical roles assigned to males than females during television programs (Downing, 1974; McNeil, 1975).

3 Younger and more attractive female characters during daytime television (Downing, 1974).

4 Less competent female characters than male characters on television (Seggar, 1975).

5 Predominantly male voice-overs (spoken or sung) in television commercials (Courtney and Whipple, 1974; Screen Actors Guild, 1974).

6 Females in nonspeaking roles as often as males in commercials (Screen Actors Guild, 1974).

7 Males used most often as product representatives during commercials with the exception of daytime programming (Courtney and Whipple, 1974).

8 Two males for every female in the average television commercial (Screen Actors Guild, 1974).

The National Commission on Working Women studied the top 25 programs from 1972 to 1981 and found only 44 percent of the female characters on television worked outside the home, whereas in real life, over 60 percent of women work outside the home (1982).

A program that broke the pattern of the 1970s of few females, mostly younger and more attractive females portrayed in stereotypical roles in prime-time television was *Cagney and Lacey*

(1981–88), a show about two female police officers. Written in script form in 1974, it took seven years, a successful made-for-TV movie, and a loyal "letter-writing" audience to create and keep the series going. Most studios wouldn't look at the script unless actresses like Raquel Welch and Ann-Margret played the leads, and even when CBS accepted the script for a made-for-TV movie, they did so only if "two sexy young actresses" played the leads. Barney Rosenzweig, co-creator of the script, told CBS:

> You don't understand, these policewomen must be mature women. One has a family and kids, the other is a committed career officer. What separates this project from *Charlie's Angels* is that Cagney and Lacey are women; they're not girls and they're certainly not objects (Rosen, 1981, p. 50).

The made-for-TV movie (starring Tyne Daly and Loretta Swit) received a 42 share of the television audience, whereas the other networks pulled in high 20s for the same period (Turner, 1983, p. 52). Television audiences were ready for the realistic portrayal of women and endorsed a program with two female leads (the first of its kind).

Cagney and Lacey was followed by another "new-woman" sitcom called *Kate and Allie* in 1984. Women's reform groups such as National NOW embraced the positive portrayal of women, and even *TV Guide* gave a "cheer" to the networks for upgrading the portrayal of women (1985, p. 22).

Women in the 1980s were portrayed as superwomen, able to work a job, raise a family, and run the home with little difficulty, as portrayed in *Family Ties* (1982) and *The Cosby Show* (1984–1994). Yet women were portrayed in more diverse roles as older women in *Golden Girls* (1985), *Murder, She Wrote* (1984), and *Frank's Place* (1987); as single women in *The Days and Nights of Molly Dodd* (1987) and *Cheers* (1982); and as career women in *Murphy Brown* (1988). Another achievement was the interaction of women with other women. Prior to the late 1980s, men were more likely to interact with other men, whereas women were more likely to interact with men, thus reinforcing the idea that women compete with one another and prefer to be with men. In the mid-1980s, groups of women were shown as friends and family for one another in such programs as *Golden Girls* (1985) and *Designing Women* (1986).

It is not until the 1980s that significant changes in the portrayal of African-American women on television occurred. "Like progress in other areas, the changes that have occurred are in direct response to the demands and initiatives of African Americans. If it had not been for the efforts of Bill Cosby, the introduction of the first positive images of African-American women would not have occurred" (Jewell, 1993, p. 50). In a study by the National Commission on Working Women, the percentage of Black female characters on television programs increased threefold between 1979 and 1989. In addition, their roles were more positive and stronger, but were still found predominantly in comedies ("Black Women on Television," 1989, p. 10).

In the 1990s, a wider variety of female characters are portrayed in prime-time programs such as *Roseanne, Murphy Brown, Evening Shade, Northern Exposure,* and *Home Improvement.* Some of the "new woman" image on television is due to the effort of women writers and producers who fight hard to portray women in more of their diversity. Unfortunately, these programs are more the exception than the rule, and, overall, there are still fewer, younger, more physically attractive White women than men on prime-time programming. Might this pattern finally impact the viewer? A recent Center for Media and Public Affairs (CMPA) study shows that violence is down in the 1992–93 and 1993–94 season. A Gallup Survey for The Family Channel found that "58.4% of women surveyed said they were more frequently offended by television programming than they were a year earlier" ("Believe it or not," 1994, p. 2). A high percentage (93%) stated they watched television less often because of offensive programming and "83.9% believe that television programming contributes to violence in the nation" ("Believe it or not," 1994, p. 2).

EMPLOYMENT

Prior to television, a few women were employed in radio, but most station managers believed women's voices were unsuited for reading the news so women ended up producing or hosting "women's advice" programs on such topics as housekeeping, cooking, and fashion. With a couple of exceptions, few women had their own programs or held management positions. Among these exceptions was Ruth Crane Schaefer. Crane started out in radio in 1929 with a program on homemaking targeting a women's audience (Beasley & Gibbons, 1993, p. 169). Crane made the move into television in 1946, and like many of the pioneers in television, was the producer, the host, the researcher, and anything else that needed doing. Crane worked with a number of programs, most of which were directed toward women: shopping by television, a cooking program, and even a program to promote interest in television to bolster television set sales (Beasley & Gibbons, 1993, p. 173).

Probably the most important study providing figures for the employment of women and minorities in television was *Window Dressing on the Set* (1977, 1979) by the U.S. Commission on Civil Rights. The original document and its update detailed roles assigned to women and minorities in front of the camera as well as behind it. Its findings on the employment of women and minorities in the broadcast industry included the following:

- Women and minorities are not fully utilized at all levels of station management nor at all levels of local stations' operations.

- Women, particularly minority women, are concentrated within the clerical ranks, and the percentage of women and minorities in these positions has increased.

- In comparison to their presence in the work force in general, a relatively high proportion of minority females are employed in visible positions as on-the-air talent. Increased visibility on the screen without comparable representation in decision-making positions suggests that minorities and women serve as window dressing.

- Broadcast stations misrepresent the number of women and minorities in decision-making positions, but through an examination of their job titles and salary, it can be determined that the positions are clearly clerical (1977, pp. 148–49).

In general, *Window Dressing* recommended that the industry make training and placement opportunities in decision-making positions available and that Congress empower the FCC to regulate equal employment opportunity at networks (requiring all broadcast licensees to examine the composition of their work force, and submit a list of employees classified by job category).

In the 1980s, women made up "about one-third of the work force at the network headquarters and at network-owned and -operated stations" (Whetmore, 1987, p. 162). Women controlled less than 2 percent of broadcast properties, and the American Women in Radio and Television (AWRT) offered seminars for women who wanted to get into broadcast ownership. Others in the industry stated that women were moving up the ladder. "In the area of sales, . . . things are booming" and "women with technical expertise can virtually 'write their own ticket,' according to one source, because there are so few of them" (Whetmore, 1987, p. 162).

The 1990s statistics failed to show growth in areas of broadcast employment. "Sixty-one percent of the broadcasting work force is made up of men and 39 percent of women; 80.9 percent of the workers are White, 11.8 are Black, and 5 percent are Hispanics. Other minority groups are represented to a much smaller degree" (Willis & Aldridge, 1992, p. 225). The Equal Employment Opportunities Commission broke this down further. Males "have 68.6 percent of the managerial positions, women 31.4 percent [and] only 6.1 percent of TV station presidents are women" (Willis & Aldridge, 1992, p. 225). These figures are reversed when looking at the clerical positions, where women are 82.1 percent of the clerical staff, with men 17.9 percent. In the technical areas where women "can write their own ticket," 85.5 percent of the technical positions and 90 percent of the craft positions were held by men. Of the 65,000 hours of prime-time drama produced between 1949 and 1986, women directed 115 hours. Of those 115 hours, 35 were directed by Ida Lupino in the 1950s (Lazin, 1986). In general, "men outnumber women in the [broadcast] labor force almost two to one" (Willis & Aldridge, 1992, p. 225). In the area of sales, women have almost equaled men in numbers: 56.3 percent for men, 43.7 percent for women.

Considering the recommendations by the U.S. Commission on Civil Rights (1977, 1979) and the optimism of the 1980s, the final tally 15 years later hasn't changed much. Although women constitute 52 percent of the total population, they play one-fifth of the roles on television, write 17 percent of the scripts, and direct 10 percent of the productions.

REFERENCES

Beasley, M. H., & Gibbons, S.J. (1993). *Taking their place: A documentary history of women and journalism.* Washington, DC: The American University Press in cooperation with the Women's Institute for Freedom of the Press.

Becker, S. L., & Roberts, C.L. (1992). *Discovering mass communication* (3rd ed.). New York: HarperCollins Publishers.

Believe it or not: Serious violence said to be down in prime time. (1994, Winter). *Media Report to Women, 22,* 1–3.

Black women on television triple during the decade. (1989, March 6). *Jet, 74,* 10.

Bodroghkozy, A. (1992). "Is this what you mean by color TV?" Race, gender, and contested meanings in NBC's *Julia*. In Spigel & Mann (Eds.), *Private Screenings: Television and the Female Consumer,* (pp. 143–168), Minneapolis: University of Minnesota Press.

Brooks, T., & Marsh, E. (1988). *The complete directory to prime time network TV shows: 1946–present.* New York: Ballantine Books.

Courtney, A. E., & Whipple, T. W. (1974, Spring). Women in TV commercials. *Journal of Communication, 24,* 110–118.

Downing, M. (1974, Spring). Heroine of the daytime serial. *Journal of Communication, 24,* 130–137.

Dreyfuss, J. (1974, September 1). Blacks and television, part I: Television controversy covering the Black experience. *Washington Post,* p.K5.

Haralovich, M. B. (1992). Sit-coms and suburbs: Positioning the 1950s homemaker. In Spigel & Mann (Eds.) *Private Screenings: Television and the female consumer.* (pp. 111–141), Minneapolis: University of Minnesota Press.

Head, S. (1954). Content analysis of television drama programs, *Quarterly Journal of Film, Radio and Television,* 9, 181.

Jewell, K. S. (1993). *From mammy to Miss America and beyond: Cultural images & the shaping of U.S. social policy.* New York: Routledge.

Jones, G. (1992). *Honey, I'm home! Sitcoms: Selling the American dream.* New York: Grove Weidenfeld.

Lazin, L. (producer) (1986). *The 20th anniversary of the National Organization for Women.* Los Angeles: Peg Yorkin Production.

McNeil, J. C. (1975, Summer). Feminism, femininity, and the television series: A content analysis. *Journal of Broadcasting, 19,* 3, 259–271.

National Commission on Working Women (1982). *What's wrong with this picture? A look at working women on television.* Washington, DC: Sally Steenland.

Pollitt, K. (1991, April 7). The Smurfette principle. *New York Times Magazine,* pp. 22–24.

Rose, B. G. (Ed.) (1985). *TV genres: A handbook and reference guide.* Westport, CT: Greenwood Press.

Rosen, M. (1981, October). *Cagney and Lacey. Ms., 10,* 4, 47–50, 109.

Screen Actors Guild. (1974, November 13). The relative roles of men and women in television commercials. New York: New York Branch Women's Conference Committee.

Seggar, J. F. (1975, Summer). Imagery of women in television drama: 1974. *Journal of Broadcasting, 19,* 273–281.

Spigel, L., & Mann, D. (Eds.). (1992). *Private screenings: Television and the female consumer.* Minneapolis: University of Minnesota Press.

Taylor, E. (1989). *Prime-time families: Television culture in postwar America.* Berkeley, CA: University of California Press.

Tedesco, N. S. (1974, Spring). Patterns in prime time. *Journal of Communication,* 24, 2, 119–124.

Turner, R. (1983, October 8–14). The curious case of the lady cops and the shots that blew them away. *TV Guide,* 52.

TV Guide. (1985, February 2), 22.

U.S. Commission on Civil Rights (1977). *Window dressing on the set: Women and minorities in television.* Washington, DC: U.S. Government Printing Office.

U.S. Commission on Civil Rights (1979). *Window dressing on the set: An update.* Washington, DC: U.S. Government Printing Office.

Whetmore, E. J. (1987). *Mediamerica* (3rd ed.). Belmont, CA: Wadsworth Publishing Co.

Willis, E. E., & Aldridge, H. B. (1992). *Television, cable, and radio: A communications approach.* Englewood Cliffs, NJ: Prentice-Hall, Inc.

PROJECT IDEAS

1   What was your favorite television program ten years ago? If it's available, watch a rerun. What are the roles assigned to women and men? How are those characters similar to the women and men you know? Do the mothers/wives in the program act like mothers/wives you know? Do they have jobs? Are they portrayed at a job in the program or in the home? Do the fathers/husbands in the program have jobs? Are they seen more at home or at the job?

2   Study what you consider to be educational children's shows: *Barney* or *Sesame Street,* for example. Count the number of males and females and the roles each are assigned in the programs. Who are in the lead roles? Who are in the supporting roles? Do they differ from the more "commercial" children's programs?

3   Many content analyses have been conducted on the portrayal of women and men in soap operas. In the Bibliography (in the back of the book) under "Television" is a subsection titled "Soap Operas." Many of the references are studies that focus on the portrayal of women and men in soaps. Select one study, review it, and replicate it by videotaping one week of a soap opera and analyzing its content. Do your results reinforce or refute the original study's results?

4   Look at current prime-time programs. How do shows such as *Roseanne* differ from the program types discussed in the introduction to this section? Do we need to construct a new category? What might you call it?

NAMES

The following list identifies women who have been or are currently part of the television industry. Women who were previously mentioned in this introduction are not duplicated in this list.

Gracie Allen—Co-star of *The George Burns and Gracie Allen Show* (1950–58).

Lucille Ball—Co-star of *I Love Lucy* (1951–61), *The Lucy-Desi Comedy Hour* (1962–67), and *The Lucy Show* (1962–74).

Gertrude Berg—Star of *The Goldbergs* (1949–54), originally on radio.

Linda Bloodworth-Thomason—Television producer, writer (*M*A*S*H, One Day at a Time, Rhoda*). Creator, writer, and producer (*Designing Women* 1986–91) and executive producer (*Evening Shade* (1990–94).

Marcy Carsey—Co-producer with Tom Werner: *The Cosby Show* (1984–92), *Roseanne* (1988–present), and *Grand* (1990–91).

Madelyn Davis—Co-writer of *I Love Lucy* (1950s).

Diane English—Television writer: *My Sister Sam* (1986–88) and *Murphy Brown* (1988–92), *Love and War* (1992–present).

Gail Fisher—First Black woman to win an Emmy award (for *Mannix*) (1970).

Randa Haines—Director of *Knots Landing, Hill Street Blues, Something About Amelia* (1970s–80s).

Susan Harris—Television writer: *Soap* (1977–81), *The Golden Girls* (1985–92), and *Empty Nest* (1988–present).

Patricia Jones—Writer for *The Bob Newhart Show* (1980s).

Brianne Murphy—Cinematographer on programs such as *Highway to Heaven* and *Little House on the Prairie* (1970s–80s).

Agnes Nixon—Writer of soap opera series: *Search for Tomorrow* (1951–86), *As The World Turns* (1964–present), *One Life To Live* (1968–present), and *All My Children* (1983–present).

Irna Phillips—Writer of soap opera series: *The Guiding Light* (1952–present), *The Edge of Night* (1956–84), *Another World* (1956–present), and *Days of Our Lives* (1965–present).

Trera Silverman—Writer for *The Mary Tyler Moore Show* (1970–77).

Marlo Thomas—Star of *That Girl* (1966–71); produced children's programs including *Free to Be Me* (1974).

Mary Tyler Moore—Co-star of *The Dick Van Dyke Show* (1961–66), *The Mary Tyler Moore Show* (1970–77), *Mary* (1978), and *The Mary Tyler Moore Hour* (1979).

Ethel Waters—First Black person nominated for an Emmy award in drama, *Route 66* (1962).

ORGANIZATIONS

Equality Productions
    1304 18th Street, NW
    Washington, DC 20010

Screen Actor's Guild Women's Committee
    7750 Sunset Blvd.
    Hollywood, CA 90046

Women in Cable
    500 North Michigan Avenue
    Suite 1400
    Chicago, IL 60611

Women in Media
    4–8 Donegall Street Place
    Belfast BT1 2FN, IRELAND

Women's Video Collective
    P.O. Box 1609
    Cambridge, MA 02238

These lists were, in part, derived from Hill et al.'s *Black women in television: An illustrated history and bibliography* (1990), New York: Garland; Marc & Thompson's *Prime time, prime movers* (1992), Boston: Little, Brown and Company; and Meehan's *Ladies of the Evening: Women characters of prime time television* (1992), New York: Scarecrow Press.

Even though few of us notice the gender imbalance in television programs, an imprint is made. Girls grow up with fewer role models. Their choices are smaller.

11

CONTENT ANALYSIS
OF THE IMAGE OF WOMEN
ON TELEVISION

SALLY STEENLAND

Sally Steenland writes and consults on issues concerning women and the media. For ten years, she worked at the National Commission on Working Women and Wider Opportunities for Women, where she authored more than a dozen reports on women and television and women's employment. She has written major studies on television's portrayal of children and families, adolescent girls, older women, minorities, and others. She has also published studies on the employment of women in the television and film industry. Most recently she authored "What's Wrong With This Picture?," a comprehensive examination of male and female portrayals and employment patterns in entertainment television. Currently, she writes articles, essays, and columns for magazines, newspapers, and books.

During the 1980s and early 1990s, the National Commission on Working Women, a nonprofit advocacy organization in Washington, D.C., conducted research on the portrayal of women in prime-time entertainment television series.

The commission issued annual studies analyzing the image of women on new fall programs and published reports examining particular groups of women on prime-time TV (older women, teenage girls, children and families, women of color).

Altogether, more than a dozen studies looked at female characters and compared them to women in real life. The commission's studies were a kind of Census Bureau; they examined the TV population by occupational status, race, age, marital status, and economic status.

By taking demographic snapshots of TV's women, the studies were able to make comparisons between female characters and women in real life. By examining patterns of divergence, the reports revealed areas in which television is remarkably different from reality.

It is important to analyze the gaps between television and the real world—and their recurrence season after season—because they help us understand the messages, both intended and unintended, that are transmitted from the world of TV to ours.

This chapter summarizes the findings of the National Commission on Working Women published between 1982 and 1990. Because each study measured a different universe of programs, specific statistical comparisons are, for the most part, not available.

However, general comparisons of trends and themes can reliably be made, and they are emphasized in the chapter. Statistical findings are listed at the end.

THE WORLD OF WORK

Twenty years ago, most women on TV inhabited a domestic world, while the men went off to work. Only a few female characters held jobs; those who did were young and single. However, as the 1970s progressed, television began to catch up with the real world (where record numbers of women, especially mothers, were working outside the home), and to reflect their pressures and conflicts (such as the balancing of family and career).

At the same time, TV distorted these social changes and reflected to viewers images of the workplace and of working women that were idealized and unrealistic. For example, most working women on TV have lucrative professional careers (in the real world, 75 percent of working women are in relatively low-paying, nonprofessional jobs). Also, workplace success for TV women comes quite easily (little experience is required to reach the top, the barriers of bias are virtually nonexistent). In addition, women on TV juggle the difficult responsibilities of home and job with relative ease.

The 1970s

On September 19, 1970, *The Mary Tyler Moore Show* premiered. It was one of the first TV programs to portray a working woman with authenticity and dimension, one whose job was meaningful and integral, rather than a prop. The character, Mary Richards, was feisty, independent, respected, and loved by her colleagues. She was a vast improvement over previous "single girls" on TV, whose main goal was to marry a handsome man.

As the 1970s progressed, additional working women appeared on the screen, most in blue-collar and service-sector jobs. Programs such as *Rhoda* (a department store window-dresser), *Laverne and Shirley* (factory workers), *Alice* (a waitress), and *Charlie's Angels* (detectives) were in the top 20 Nielsen ratings during the decade.

However, these female characters with jobs remained in the minority. In 1976, working women on TV constituted only one-third of all female characters; the other two-thirds didn't have paying jobs. Most of them were full-time homemakers, in suburbs or on the farm, in shows such as *Little House on the Prairie, The Waltons, Happy Days, The Jeffersons*, and *All in the Family*.

The 1980s

In the 1980s, the majority of TV women began going to work, this time in glamorous, high-powered careers. Shows like *Dallas, Dynasty*, and *Falcon Crest* portrayed wealthy female executives who headed multi-million-dollar corporations. On *Hart to Hart*, a rich, beautiful sleuth solved crimes with her handsome husband. On *Hotel*, an affluent aristocrat ran an elegant hotel in San Francisco.

This was a dramatic shift from the working-class characters of the 1970s, such as Alice and Laverne and Shirley. To a certain extent, TV's obsession with wealth and glamour reflected a fascination similar to that going on in the real world during the decade.

Another TV trend during the 1980s was the increased number of working mothers, both single and married. Again, TV was catching up with the real world, where more than half of women with children had jobs outside the home.

Unlike the real world, though, most mothers on TV held professional jobs. For example, Clare on *The Cosby Show* was a lawyer, Elyse on *Family Ties* was an architect, and Maggie on *Growing Pains* was a reporter. On *Kate and Allie*, a buddy show about two single mothers, Kate worked in an office, while Allie agonized over whether to go back to work or remain a homemaker. On *Cagney and Lacey*, a buddy show featuring a single woman and a mother, both were police officers.

The 1990s

With the popularity of programs such as *Roseanne* and *Murphy Brown*, TV's working women in the 1990s have broadened in scope, to encompass both blue-collar and professional women. The ultra-glamorous female executives from the 1980s have disappeared from the screen. In their place are more recognizable women with more conventional jobs, such as secretary and waitress. In fact, during the 1990 season, the most common job for women on TV was clerical work (the same is true in the real world).

By 1990, working women on TV were the rule, not the exception.

What's Missing from the Screen

Although TV has made progress in increasing the number of working women and portraying them with a greater degree of authenticity, significant flaws remain.

First of all, most TV programs focus their attention on working men, rather than women. For example, viewers are more likely to see the male character's office, to see him actually working, to watch plots about his job. The career aspect of male characters is more carefully drawn than women's. Too many women on TV hold jobs that are accessories—details added to their character, rather than an intrinsic part of it.

In addition, TV programs rarely capture, with any degree of authenticity, the struggles and politics of the workplace. Most reduce office dynamics to individual interaction.

The result is an artificial world without bias or prejudice. The great dissatisfactions felt by so many real-life working women—from managers who bump their heads against the glass ceiling to secretaries who can't get promoted—are virtually nonexistent.

Also missing from the TV screen are certain types of workers. In the real world, the work force is becoming increasingly diverse, with greater numbers of Hispanics, Asians, Blacks, women, and immigrants. By the end of the decade, these groups will be the majority of new workers. However, TV has not yet caught up with this trend.

RACE AND WOMEN TV CHARACTERS

In the past 20 years, the number of Black characters on TV has significantly increased. The TV universe has gone from one that is artificially, almost totally White, to one in which Black people are visible in certain types of programs. In 1970, the percentage of Blacks on TV was far less than that in the real world; now it is more.

The emergence of the Black sitcom has accounted for much of this growth. Also, Black characters are now sprinkled among White casts in both comedies and dramas.

However, the number of Hispanic and Asian characters has not significantly grown in two decades. In fact, Hispanic and Asian characters remain virtually invisible on the screen, despite their rapid growth in the real world.

The 1970s, 1980s, and 1990s

As TV began to reflect the civil rights movement, it developed and aired sitcoms featuring mainly Black casts. During the 1970s, sitcoms such as *The Jeffersons*, *Good Times*, *Sanford and Son*, and *What's Happening!!* were popular with viewers.

For the most part, the women on these shows were Black homemakers and mothers, devoted to their families and husbands, ready with wisecracks and wit.

In the 1980s, Black females began to assume center stage and star in all-Black sitcoms. Shows such as *227* and *Amen* were slapstick and silly—similar in style and characterization to shows from the 1970s.

However, a breakthrough program, *The Cosby Show*, premiered in 1984, and within a season became the most popular show on TV. Audiences saw a well-educated, professional Black family, in which a lawyer mother and physician father were raising five sprightly children with authority, common sense, humor, and grace. A spin-off show, *A Different World*, portrayed the diversity of Black life at a fictional college, and also became popular.

In addition to starring in sitcoms, Black women in the 1980s appeared in supporting roles on shows with mostly White casts, such as *Miami Vice*, *Hotel*, *Head of the Class*, and *Dynasty*. Almost every program, however, featured only one token Black female.

In the 1990s, additional Black sitcoms emerged, spawned by the success of *The Cosby Show*, *In Living Color*, and others. Shows such as *Martin*, *Hangin' With Mr. Cooper*, *Roc*, and *Family Matters* portrayed characters less affluent than the Cosbys—most were middle- or working-class.

What's Missing from the Screen

The absence of Hispanic and Asian women (and men) on entertainment TV is a glaring, long-standing omission. Their lack of visibility means they are still suffering token status on TV, where the term *minority* seems to mean Black. Despite their rich cultures and significant presence as a viewing audience, they seem not to have captured the imagination of writers, or to have appealed to the marketing interests of programming executives. As a result, Hispanic and Asian characters simply do not exist on TV in any measurable way.

Also missing from TV are roles for women of color in dramatic programs, which would expand their presence and allow more serious discussion of social issues. Currently, women of color are segregated to sitcoms, which, by their very nature, present an essentially light-hearted, cheery world of manageable problems. In comedies, real evil never intrudes, and negativity can be turned around in 30 minutes.

AGE AND MARITAL STATUS

Unlike the real world, where females slightly outnumber males (and older women greatly outnumber older men), on TV the reverse is true. Men on TV have outnumbered women since the medium began, and they still do (57% to 43% in 1990).

The only exception to this male surplus is childhood, where girls under 13 years old outnumber boys. Beginning in adolescence, though, the numbers shift and boys start to dominate.

Most women on TV are between the ages of 20 and 40. At age 40, the number of female characters drops sharply. For men, the drop begins in their 50s. Very few male or female characters are in their 60s or older.

On TV, men are more likely to be single than women. Nearly three out of four male characters are single, divorced, or widowed, whereas two-thirds of female characters are unmarried. Also, more men on TV are widowers than divorced.

The 1970s, 1980s, 1990s

During the 1970s, most female characters were in their 20s and single. However, as the real-world population began aging, TV characters began to age slightly as well. For example, Murphy Brown, a popular TV character in the 1990s, is about ten years older than Mary Richards, her counterpart from the 1970s. Still, the majority of TV characters are younger than the population at large.

In 1990, the majority of female characters in prime-time shows were in their 30s. During the 1990 season, there were twice as many male as female characters over age 40. Only 5 percent of women characters and 7 percent of men characters were in their 50s. Only 3 percent of women characters and 4 percent of men characters were over age 60.

Prime-time soap operas such as *Dallas, Dynasty,* and *Falcon Crest* provided the majority of roles for older women during the 1980s, although their portrayals tended to fall within two stereotypes: that of devoted matriarch or power-hungry villain.

Also during the 1980s, two prime-time series went on the air that portrayed older women positively and realistically. Both *Murder, She Wrote* and *The Golden Girls* starred women in their 50s and 60s; equally significant was the fact that neither show contained a recurring male character. Both programs defied the

TV industry's conventional wisdom that said a show featuring older women couldn't hold an audience, especially without male characters. Both shows became long-running hits.

Over the decades, female TV characters also became increasingly likely to be married. In the 1970s, most were single or divorced. However, in the 1980s, the nuclear family returned to the air in shows such as *Family Ties, The Cosby Show, Growing Pains, ALF, Mr. Belvedere, The Wonder Years, 227, Married . . . With Children, Roseanne, The Simpsons, Family Matters,* and *Life Goes On.*

A significant difference between these shows and family sitcoms of the 1950s and 1960s, such as *Leave It To Beaver, Ozzie and Harriet,* and *Father Knows Best,* was that in the 1980s, TV mothers went to work.

The 1980s also produced an abundance of comedies starring single dads caring for kids. Unlike the real world, where the overwhelming majority of single parents are mothers, kids on TV are more likely to live with their dads. Programs such as *Gimme A Break, Benson, Who's the Boss, My Two Dads, Full House, The Hogan Family, Punky Brewster,* and *Baywatch* all featured men fully engaged in caring for youngsters, with little hint of fatigue or threat to career and social life.

What's Missing from the Screen

TV has made some progress, in stretching by a decade or so the age at which women become invisible. Female characters used to drop off the screen in their 30s; now they disappear after age 40. It is hard to find women older than that on TV, although in real life, older women who are powerful, vibrant, and passionate come in abundant supply.

Also, although it is heartening to see portrayals of devoted, nurturing fathers on the screen, TV seems to go overboard in portraying them as heroic, while giving scant attention to single mothers who are equally heroic and who, in real life, are the majority of full-time single parents.

ECONOMIC STATUS

Just as TV characters are younger than the real-life population, they also have more money. Conventional wisdom in the entertainment industry says that viewers would be uninterested in, and even repelled by, entertainment programs featuring poor people.

Furthermore, advertisers are seeking attractive surroundings for their 30-second commercials. They want programs featuring affluent characters who can afford to buy their products (and whose TV homes already contain appealing items).

Within this TV world, however, there are seasonal swings of the pendulum. During certain decades, glamorous, glitzy programs reign; in other years, blue-collar shows find a huge audience. Whenever the pendulum swings and a shift occurs, the television industry adjusts its conventional wisdom to explain the phenomenon it previously discredited.

The 1970s

During the 1970s, the TV pendulum swung in the direction of blue-collar characters with whom audiences could identify. Shows such as *All in the Family, Laverne and Shirley, Alice, Good Times, Taxi, Little House on the Prairie, The Waltons,* and *Happy Days* featured women and men who were either middle-class or aiming for it. Homes were comfortable, sometimes a bit shabby; furnishings and wardrobes blended in rather than stood out.

These 1970s programs were in the vein of shows like *The Honeymooners,* starring Jackie Gleason in the 1950s, in which characters aspired to better themselves and had dreams of riches and success. Viewers identified with these characters and could recognize themselves on the screen.

The 1980s

All that changed in the 1980s, as the pendulum swung in the opposite direction and working-class characters became nearly extinct. Even the middle-class on TV was overshadowed by the wealthy.

Female millionaires on popular prime-time soap operas and dramas accounted for most of the affluence and, in fact, created a new occupational category for women little before seen on TV—that of leisure class.

These female millionaires were joined by those in the upper-middle-class, so that by the mid-1980s, affluent women accounted for more than half of all females on the screen. (In the mid-1980s, only 1 percent of real-life women had annual incomes over $50,000.)

Even conventional sitcoms such as *Family Ties, Growing Pains* and *The Cosby Show* contained a sheen of affluence. Missing from any of these programs was ordinary economic struggle.

On dramatic programs such as *Miami Vice* and *Moonlighting,* opulent homes, sports cars, and glamorous, expensive wardrobes were as eye-catching as the fast-moving plots.

The 1990s

By the end of the 1980s, the pendulum had swung back again, toward blue-collar characters (a reflection of recessionary changes in real life). With the immense popularity of working-class shows such as *Roseanne, Married . . . With Children,* and *The Simpsons,* programmers realized that viewers were getting tired of opulence and glitz, and were eager to see characters whose lives more closely matched their own.

And so, shows were spawned featuring characters with tight budgets. On *Roseanne*, the husband Dan was unemployed for long periods; the washing machine broke down; the parents couldn't afford new sneakers for their kids. Once again, home furnishings looked as if they came from K mart or a department store in the mall rather than from a designer showcase.

What's Missing from the Screen

Because television is an advertiser-supported medium, its self-interest lies in airing programs that enhance the accompanying commercials. It would be counterproductive for the industry to produce programs next to which advertised products looked foolish, unnecessary, or wasteful. Therefore, TV will probably never air shows featuring characters who are poor, who can't afford even the most basic items advertised on TV.

Still, within its economic constraints, TV could do a better job of expanding its universe to encompass characters with little or no money—they too have stories worth telling.

THE IMPORTANCE OF TV'S MESSAGES

At its most rudimentary level, television is a storyteller. Its stories, however, are limited. In TV's tales, men are more visible, more important, more varied and interesting. That's because it's mainly men who are telling the stories—they comprise most of the producers, writers, directors, and executives in Hollywood.

Such distorted stories have consequences for viewers. TV sets are on in homes more than seven hours a day. And the bias on the screen compounds the bias experienced in society. It's the norm for men to talk more, give orders, solve problems, and run things. Society's bias is so commonplace, it seems normal. Research in classrooms reveals that when girls talk less frequently than boys, they appear to be speaking as often. When they talk as much as boys do, they appear to be taking over.

Even though few of us notice the gender imbalance in TV programs, an imprint is made. Girls grow up with fewer role models. Their choices are smaller.

One way to improve the picture is to hire more women behind the camera. Enough women over enough time can make a difference, despite industry strictures and constraints. In fact, women working in the industry are already making a difference. They are hiring and promoting other capable women; they are speaking up against exploitive portrayals and titillating camera shots. As more women gain greater influence, they can take bigger risks. They can increase the visibility of older women and expand roles for women of color. They can air programs with themes and messages considered by Hollywood to be unimportant or taboo.

The 1990s presents the television industry with great opportunity: to capture and reflect the vibrant mix of American society. To do that, the industry must expand its pool of storytellers and air more varied tales. It is in TV's self-interest to become a more diverse medium—a more fluent storyteller—one that captures the variety and dimension of us all.

NUMBERS AND PERCENTAGES[1]

For each commission report, prime-time programs were taped off the air and then viewed and coded. The following information was tabulated for each recurring female character: age, race, occupation, marital status, and socio-economic status. At least five randomly selected episodes were monitored for each show. Real-life statistics were obtained from the U.S. Bureau of the Census, Current Population Survey.

Visibility

- Fewer than half of all characters on entertainment television series are women. On prime-time shows, women are 43 percent of the population; in real life, women are 51 percent of the population.
- Men characters outnumber women by almost two to one in dramas.
- Most women characters are clustered in sitcoms (62%). Domestic comedies are the only entertainment programs with more females than males.

Occupation

- Most women characters do "women's work," while men do "men's work." The single most common female occupation on TV is clerical (14%). The most common male occupation is law enforcement (26%).
- More than 40 percent of all TV characters have professional careers. Men are more likely to be doctors, lawyers, and therapists. Women are more likely to be nurses and managers.
- In real life, only 26 percent of employed women and men have professional careers.

1. Excerpted from report, *What's Wrong With This Picture? The Status of Women on Screen and Behind the Camera in Entertainment TV,* 1990.

Race

- Twenty percent of all TV characters are minority women and men: 16 percent are Black, slightly more than 1 percent each are Hispanic and Asian, and less than 1 percent are Native American.

- Most TV minorities are Black. They comprise 84 percent of all minority characters. About 47 percent of Black characters are female; 53 percent are male.

- Eighty-six percent of Black women characters appear in sitcoms.

- In real life, 24 percent of the population belongs to minority groups. Twelve percent are Black, 8 percent are Hispanic, and 3 percent are Asian and Native American.

Age

- Men characters outnumber women in all age groups, except childhood. On TV, girls under 13 outnumber boys.

- The greatest percentage of TV characters are in their 30s (32% women, 26% men). About one-quarter are in their 20s.

- At age 40, the number of women characters drops dramatically. There are over twice as many male as female characters over age 40.

- At age 50, visibility declines for both genders. Only 5 percent of women and 7 percent of men are in their 50s. Only 3 percent of women and 4 percent of men are over age 60.

- In real life, the population is older. Sixteen percent of the population is in its 20s, 17 percent in its 30s, 12 percent in its 40s and 9 percent in its 50s. Fourteen percent of women and 10 percent of men are over age 65.

Marital Status

- Men on TV are more likely to be single than women. Nearly three out of four male characters (73%) are single, divorced, or widowed, whereas two-thirds of female characters (67%) are unmarried.

- More men on TV are widowers than divorced. Unlike real life, there are more widowers than widows on TV.

- In real life, over half of women and men are married (53% women, 58% men).

Chapter 11   Content Analysis

Debbie Allen's contributions to American popular culture have crystallized the fact that women, specifically African-American women, have the ability, skills, and talents to create in all forms of media.

12

THE DEBBIE ALLEN TOUCH

BISHETTA D. MERRITT

Bishetta Merritt, Associate Professor and Chairperson of the Department of Radio, Television, and Film at Howard University, earned her Ph.D. from Ohio State University. Her research interests include the images of African Americans and mass media, television criticism, and political communication. Her most recent publications include "Illusive Reflections: African-American Women on Primetime Television" in Gonzalez, Houston, and Chen (Ed.), *Our Voices: Essays in Culture, Ethnicity, and Communication.*

Debbie Allen made "different" a better world when she became the director of the situation comedy *A Different World* in 1987. This venture, however, was not her first, nor last, challenge in show business. Her career, beginning as a dancer and singer on Broadway, covers appearances as an actress, director, and producer on the large and small screen. Never satisfied to rest on her laurels, Allen has gone from one career peak to another. Her motto, "Be prepared," has served her well in the years since she graduated cum laude from the College of Fine Arts at Howard University (Washington, D.C.), where she majored in dance and classics.

PREPARING TO SUCCEED

Being prepared helped Allen overcome obstacles and rejection as she pursued her interest in dancing. This steadfastness of resolve germinated in part from her strong family background and the experiences that make up her life history. Allen's mother, Vivian Ayers-Allen, exposed her children, Debbie, Phylicia, Andrew, and Hugh, to the arts and African-American culture from birth. They even spent one year in Mexico City for a year of study and exposure to an entirely different lifestyle (Sanders, 1983). Her father, Dr. Andrew Allen, a Houston dentist (now deceased), strongly encouraged her to remain in college when she wished to do otherwise.

As an eight-year-old Allen was refused admittance to the Houston Foundation for Ballet, and as a teen she was rejected by the North Carolina School of the Arts, but these events did not short-circuit her motivation to become a dancer. It is unclear why Allen was initially denied admittance to the Houston Foundation for Ballet. Six years later (after she studied privately), however, she was recruited by Mme. Titiana Semenov and given a full scholarship. A change in the racial climate from 1958, which was four short years after the historic *Brown vs. Board of Education* case, to 1964, the year of the passage of the Civil Rights Bill, may account for the change in attitude. This "new" attitude did not prevail in North Carolina. When she was a senior in high school, she applied for admission to the North Carolina School of the Arts. Allen had the following to say about that rejection. "I traveled all the way from Houston to North Carolina to audition, and it was my first big trip away from home all by myself. I danced for them and was so good that they used me to demonstrate for the other kids. But when we finished, the dance director walked over to me and said that I hadn't made it and that I was 'built wrong'" (Sanders, 1983). Undaunted by this blatant display of racism, Allen reassembled her self-esteem and looked to the future. She was accepted at Howard University; she spent her summers attending dance festivals and her winters dancing with various student groups (Sanders, 1983). Upon graduation, her professional career began in New York. And, as the old cliché goes, the rest is history!

ACHIEVING FAME

When Allen graduated from Howard in 1971 and ventured to New York, she became a dancer for the George Faison Dancers (Gritten and Oulahan, 1982). Broadway was the next stop. Her roles included chorus-line performances in *Purlie* and critically praised roles in such plays as *Raisin in the Sun, West Side Story, Ain't Misbehavin', Sweet Charity, Alice, Sheba, Louis,* and *Guys and Dolls* (St. John, 1978; Sanders, 1983; Gill, 1986). On the small screen, Allen acted, danced, and sang in the miniseries *3 Girls 3*, portrayed comedic roles in *Good Times* and *Love Boat*, and played dramatic roles in *Roots II* as Alex Haley's wife and in *Fame* as Lydia Grant. Even television commercials did not escape the Allen touch—she appeared in ads for Nice 'N Easy, Excedrin, and Final Touch (Simon, 1980, 1981; Ivory, 1982; Dates and Barlow; 1993). In film, she landed parts in *The Fish That Saved Pittsburgh, Ragtime,* and (opposite Richard Pryor) *Jo Jo Dancer, Your Life Is Calling* (St. John, 1978; Kroll, 1986; Edwards, 1992). For her role as Anita in the revival of *West Side Story*, Allen won a Drama Desk Award and a Tony nomination in 1980 (Stark and Alexander, 1988).

From the small role of Lydia Grant in the motion picture *Fame*, a fictionalized drama of the students who attend the New York High School for the Performing Arts, Allen parlayed her talents into a starring role in the television series of the same title. At that point her career made a major shift from being an actress and dancer to that of a choreographer, producer, and director.

When the producers of *Fame* approached Allen for the role of Grant, she agreed to accept if she would be given the opportunity to choreograph some of the dance scenes. Allen quipped, "No need of having the ability, if you can't employ it on a continual basis—that's how you keep growing" (Ivory, 1982). And grow she did. When the series was finally canceled, Allen was the choreographer for all the episodes and had directed 11 shows, in addition to her acting role. When the *Fame* stars toured England, Allen produced, directed, and choreographed the performances (Scott, 1983). From these experiences, Allen learned the power of words and discovered the value of camera movement and good writing (Allen, 1992). As a choreographer, Allen's work also appears in the play *Carrie* and appears in the Academy Award broadcasts.

Allen, known and respected for her professional attitude in the workplace, received words of praise from the producer of *Fame*, Bill Blinn. "I might sound like a public relations person for her, but I'm an idolater for professionalism, and there's no more professional person than Debbie Allen." When Allen wanted the names of the dancers in the show to roll with the credits at the end of each episode, and asked to hire an assistant choreographer, she got it (Sanders, 1983). Allen remarked,

> There's a responsibility that goes along with this [position on *Fame*] for me because there are not many of us [African Americans] where I am. I'm in a situation where I have a certain ability to hire people and make job opportunities. It's a responsibility that goes along with being a positive image, a Black positive image on television. I wear the responsibility well and I'm glad to have it. I just wish I had more company (Oliver, 1984).

Allen's role offered television audiences an opportunity to view a positive, caring, no-nonsense, conscientious African-American woman in a continuous dramatic series, a rarity on television even today. It offered the producers of the show exposure to an organized, hardworking, talented African American who knows her craft and practices it in a professional manner. When the series ended, in addition to winning two Emmys for choreography, Allen had taught many lessons in front of and behind the camera.

MAKING A DIFFERENCE AS DIRECTOR

When Bill Cosby approached Allen to add her touch to the premiere season of *A Different World*, she was just too busy to accept. When her role as leading lady in the Broadway hit *Sweet Charity* ended, and the musical *Carrie*, for which she was choreographer, closed to scathing reviews, Allen accepted the task of revitalizing *A Different World* (Stark and Alexander, 1988). Cosby was aware of her ability as a director and producer and knew that she had life experiences similar to the basic premise of the show, and an artistic eye to develop it (Debbie Allen tells why . . . , 1992). *A Different World*, set in Atlanta at the mythical Hillman College, depicted life at a predominantly Black American institution steeped in tradition.

Improving this series was a major challenge for the hardworking Allen. The program, although number two in the ratings, was plagued by negative criticism and unrest among its cast (Randolph, 1991). Allen applied the concepts of people management she had utilized on the set of *Fame*, where a family atmosphere had existed. She spoke individually with all the stars of the series to learn about their needs and concerns. She also screened each episode with the cast, and they were quick to see the flaws from the first season.

In addition to cast problems, Allen recognized that the series content needed a major overhaul. She remarked, "The stories they did last year—I mean, the show could have been in high school. They did an episode about an egg. The show's about college students—there has to be some social significance. We will not be doing any shows about eggs" (Stark and Alexander, 1988).

Allen also met with the program's writers (four African Americans and four Whites) and communicated to them her concept about how African-American college students should live, act, and appear on a contemporary university campus. To accomplish this goal, Allen relied on her experiences at Howard, where she believes people became politically, socially, economically, and sexually more mature. Allen said, "I grew up there and recommitted myself to goals, to what I wanted to do" (Hill, 1989). She, therefore, grounded the series in the African-American experience.

Film critic Gladstone Yearwood (1982), in his definition of the Black cinema, has said that new paradigms must be established and old paradigms must be broken to create a cinema that is truly based in the African-American cultural tradition. Black filmmakers need not use Hollywood traditional narrative that generally presents the underworld or underside of American Black lives. Black people are a multidimensional people and their lives are full of situations, discussions, and experiences on world events, poetry, drama, South Africa, Russia, and relationships. This same theory should be applied to television and the content of programs that are directed by and star African Americans, and are created to reflect the African-American community.

Bill Cosby, when creating *Fat Albert and the Cosby Kids*, *The Bill Cosby Show*, and *The Cosby Show*, followed this theory. These programs included characters that were multidimensional people involved in realistic situations carved from Cosby's experience, not created through reading the pages of 18th-century race literature or viewing old tapes of *Amos 'n Andy* (Merritt, 1990). Cosby introduced unique elements of Black culture to his audiences through the use of themes based on the Black lifestyle and through subtle, nonverbal ways. This included depicting family members wearing T-shirts from historically Black universities (Howard, Tuskegee, Shaw, for example), displaying anti-apartheid posters in addition to art work and portraits of well-known Black people, discussing the 1963 March on Washington and other historical events relevant to African Americans, playing music by Black jazz and blues artists, and presenting these same artists as guests on the program. He set a standard by which all television portrayals of Black characters and culture should be compared (Merritt, 1990).

Allen followed Cosby's lead and created a series that confirms that the lives of African Americans are symbolically rich. She made *A Different World* Black without trying to explain blackness. Susan Fales, head writer and executive producer of the series, commented, "It's gone from being a completely irrelevant and frivolous show to being a show that attempts to deal with pressing issues of American life today" (Johnson, 1992). Episodes included topics on AIDS, apartheid, date rape, the Gulf War, and the riots in Los Angeles following the announcement of the Rodney King verdict.

Allen's touch was the charm, and when the Nielsen ratings were published in May 1988, only one year after she became the show's director, *A Different World* won first place for most-watched show in prime time (NBC sweeps May sweeps in record style, 1988). African Americans appreciated the series as well, and by 1991, it ranked as the most-watched prime-time program among Black households (Nielsen Media Research, 1991). Her keen sense of Black collegiate life and African-American culture in general appealed to all audiences, and the program remained successful and continuously ranked in the top-20 most-viewed shows by American television audiences until it was canceled in 1993 by the network. Available in syndication, the series is still broadcast in most of the major television markets (Freeman, 1991).

In the midst of directing and producing *A Different World*, Allen also completed the musical *Polly!* for NBC in 1989. Allen was the show's director and choreographer, and her sister Phylicia Rashad starred as Aunt Polly.

Stompin' at the Savoy, the television movie about four African-American women who live, work, and fall in love in New York during the late 1930s and early 1940s, offered Allen an opportunity to direct a feature-length TV drama. During its heyday, the Savoy Ballroom, located in Harlem, earned the title "The Home of Happy Feet." In its first 20 years, 28 million feet stomped on the smooth, block-long waxed floor of the ballroom doing all the current dances of the time, including the jitterbug, Lindy Hop, fox trot, rumba, two-step, and slow drag (*Stompin' at the Savoy* stars . . . , 1992).

Film editor and playwright Beverly Sawyer wrote the script based on stories her mother told her about the Savoy Ballroom. Allen solicited the assistance of Norma Miller and Frank Manning, original dancers from the Savoy Ballroom, to add authenticity to the choreography (*Stompin' at the Savoy* stars . . . , 1992; Allen, 1992). The critics received the movie with mixed reviews because of the shallow plot scripted by Sawyer, but the drama offered a slice of African-American life during this time period not often seen on television (*Stompin' at the Savoy* . . . , 1992).

In addition to the programs already discussed, Allen's directing skills have enhanced episodes of *The Bronx Zoo*, *Family Ties*, *Quantum Leap*, and *The Fresh Prince of Bel-Air* (Hill, 1989; Randolph, 1991).

LOOKING AHEAD

Debbie Allen is married to the former basketball player, Norm Nixon, and the couple has two children, Vivian Nichole and Norman, Jr. Her first marriage to Win Wilford ended in divorce. Family obligations have not hindered her work schedule or her resolve to continue to write, produce, and direct for television and film. Her latest projects include writing a feature-length film script based on the death of her father and a script for a new situation comedy. In May 1993, Allen received an honorary degree in Humane Letters from Howard University for her contributions to the arts.

Allen's contributions to American popular culture have crystallized the fact that women, specifically African-American women, have the ability, skills, and talents to create in all forms of media. She made television's *Fame* a hit with audiences in the United States and England, improved *A Different World* so significantly that it earned a number-one rating for prime-time programs from the general and African-American audiences, choreographed dances for the Academy Awards, won two Emmys for her choreography of *Fame*, received glowing reviews and awards for her stage and small-screen performances, hired African-American technicians and assistants on her production teams, and directed feature-length films, dramas, and situation comedies for television. Her touch has made a difference in the image of women in media professions and in the content of storylines depicting African-American culture. She is a major contributor to the creation of a new paradigm for the treatment of African-American characters and subject matter on television.

REFERENCES

Allen, D. (1992, April 11). Stompin': How the *Fame* choreographer's new TV-movie gives the American musical a swift kick. *TV Guide*, 26–27.

Dates, J., & Barlow, W. (1993). *Split image: African Americans in the mass media*. Washington, DC: Howard University Press.

Debbie Allen tells why "A Different World" is rated tops among Black TV viewers. (1992, April 27). *Jet*, 58–60.

Edwards, A. (1992, May). The fifth Essence awards. *Essence*, 74.

Freeman, M. (1991, September 30). Top of the week. *Broadcasting*, p. 25.

Gill, B. (1986, May 12). *The New Yorker*, p. 95.

Gritten, D., & Oulahan, R. (1982, April 19). For Debbie Allen, the price of fame is time without her husband, CBS exec Win Wilford. *People*, 71–73.

Hill, M. (1989, August 13–19). Debbie Allen: She made "different" a better world. *Washington Post TV Week*, pp. 8–9, 11.

Ivory, S. (1982, July). Hollywood's toughest, hottest actress. *Sepia*, pp. 43–45.

Johnson, P. (1992, November). The difference that makes a different world. *Young Sisters and Brothers*, pp. 48–53.

Kroll, J. (1986, May 12). New fame for Debbie Allen. *Newsweek*, 78.

Merritt, B. (1990). Bill Cosby: TV Auteur? In Harry B. Shaw (Ed.). *Perspectives of black popular culture*. Bowling Green, OH: Bowling Green State University Popular Press.

NBC sweeps May sweeps in record style. (1988 May 30). *Broadcasting*, p. 22.

Nielsen Media Research. (1991).

Oliver, S. (1984, March). Debbie Allen. *Essence*, p. 62.

Randolph, L. (1991, March). Debbie Allen on power, pain, passion and prime time. *Ebony*, 24–30.

St. John, M. (1978, October 2). Debbie Allen swings on a star. *Encore American & World News*, pp. 26–29.

Sanders, C. (1983, March). Debbie Allen. *Ebony*, 74–79, 84.

Scott, V. (1983, March 10). Debbie's a driving force to fame. *The Washington Times Magazine*, p. 7D.

Simon, J. (1980, March 3). The jets and the jetsam. *New York*, p. 13.

Simon, J. (1981, October 5). Theater. *New York*, p. 14.

Stark, J., & Alexander, M. (1988, November 14). It's a different world for dancer and choreographer Debbie Allen: She's moved to prime-time directing. *People*, 105–106.

Stompin' at the Savoy stars return to home of happy feet on new TV film. (1992, March 23). *Jet*, 58–61.

Yearwood, G. (1982). Towards a theory of Black cinema aesthetic. In Gladstone Yearwood (Ed.). *Black Cinema Aesthetics*. Athens: Ohio University Center for Afro-American Studies.

13

PRIME-TIME FEMINISM:

Entertainment Television and Women's Progress

BONNIE J. DOW

Bonnie J. Dow, Assistant Professor of Communication at North Dakota State University, earned her Ph.D. from the University of Minnesota in 1990. Her research interests include rhetorical criticism, women's public address, television criticism, and women and popular culture. She is currently working on a book tentatively titled *Prime-Time Feminism: (Tele)visions of Social Change Since 1970* for the University of Pennsylvania Press.

■ or many years, but especially since the women's liberation movement of the 1960s and 1970s, the status of women in American society has been challenged and debated. Naturally, television has commented on this process in a variety of ways. In this essay, I discuss two programs, *The Mary Tyler Moore Show* (1970–77) and *Murphy Brown* (1988–present), that have been perceived by their creators and popular critics as offering progressive portrayals of women, portrayals that have been linked to the influence of feminism.

Using these two programs as examples, I discuss the limitations of television's representations of feminism, limitations linked to television's economic base as well as to its relationship to its audience and to American culture. *The Mary Tyler Moore Show* and *Murphy Brown* illustrate how television programming uses strategies of representation that, while they acknowledge social change, also work to contain it. In what follows, I first discuss why entertainment television, as an institution, is resistant to the influence of feminism. Second, I begin the discussion of *The Mary Tyler Moore Show* and *Murphy Brown* by explaining how these programs can be viewed as representations of feminism. Third, I analyze how the depictions of feminism in these programs, though they differ, have a common function of reinforcing traditional cultural notions about the "proper" role of women and the negative consequences of women's progress.[1]

TELEVISION AND FEMINISM

Commercial network television entertainment programming is, strictly speaking, a vehicle for advertising. Television programming is supported by the money that advertisers pay for time used to broadcast commercials for their products and services. This relationship between TV programming and advertising has special significance for women because women, specifically women ages 18–49, are the primary target for most television advertising. Sponsors recognize that women do most of the shopping—for themselves and for their families. Indeed, advertisers rely on women's feeling of responsibility as conscientious consumers for themselves and their loved ones (Nightingale, 1990).

One of the reasons why television is resistant to the messages of feminism, then, is that they view those messages as conflicting with women's desire to con-

Portions of this chapter are based on the following:

Bonnie Dow (1990), "Hegemony, feminist criticism, and *The Mary Tyler Moore Show*," in *Critical Studies in Mass Communications*, 7, pp. 261–274. Used with permission by the Speech Communication Association.

Bonnie Dow (1992), "Femininity and feminism in *Murphy Brown*," in *Southern Communication Journal*, 57, pp. 143–155. Used with permission by the Southern States Communication Association.

1. This analysis of *The Mary Tyler Moore Show* and *Murphy Brown* is a synthesis and revision of arguments made in Dow, 1990, and Dow, 1992.

sume. What is the logic here? Women buy products, it is thought, to please their families and to make themselves more attractive. Feminism, which argues that women should not base their self-image on the approval of others, inhibits women's desire to consume. Given this logic, advertisers (and consequently television producers) have more incentive to create female characters who are attractive, warm, maternal, and domestic (good role models for the ideal female consumer) than they do to create female characters who are independent and self-centered (Kaplan, 1987). A blunt appraisal, to be sure, but it captures the essence of the problem.

However, the sexism visible in television programming is not solely due to economic motives. It comes from a variety of cultural sources that reinforce one another. Americans are ambivalent about feminism because it represents significant changes in traditional ways of thinking and acting. Television producers understand this point; they are unlikely to create programming that wholeheartedly endorses ideas that make many viewers uncomfortable. After all, the biggest hits are those shows that make people feel good about coming back week after week, that create the illusion that "everybody knows your name."

Finally, television's representations of feminism are shaped by the nature of television entertainment shows. Such programs depict issues at the level of the individual, through characters and their experiences. Particularly in formats like situation comedy, problems that are social in origin, such as sexism, are packaged by television entertainment as individual difficulties to be solved by the characters in 30-minute episodes (Gray, 1989). Television implicitly supports a worldview that discounts the ways in which cultural norms and values affect people's lives. Television's individualistic worldview implies that most problems can be solved by hard work, good will, and a supportive family (Feuer, 1986). Television does not deal well with complex social issues; it prefers the trials and tribulations of the individual.

All these factors contribute to television's role in the system of cultural hegemony. *Hegemony* is a term that refers to the wide-ranging and subtle ways through which the dominant ideology (a system of meanings, beliefs, and values favored by those in power) is reinforced, reproduced, and maintained through cultural institutions like television. Todd Gitlin (1982) argues that television furthers hegemony, even while seeming to respond to social change, by incorporating or "domesticating" radical ideology. One protects the dominant ideology from radical change by incorporating small amounts of an oppositional ideology (such as feminism) in a process rather similar to being inoculated for a disease. You get a bit of the "virus," but not enough to harm you.

Thus, television adjusts to social change by "absorbing it into forms compatible" with existing ways of seeing the world (Gitlin, 1982, p. 450). So, for instance, the demands made for more minority and female representation result in higher visibility for these groups on television. But the specific ways in which these characters are portrayed may implicitly work to contain the more radical changes such representation implies. In this process, there is limited progress in content, but the general hegemonic values remain intact (Gitlin, 1982). Those who champion the oppositional ideology (such as feminism) may be satisfied that their demands are having an impact on television, whereas those who create the programming have made only cosmetic changes in representations of the disputed group.

However, the hegemonic system is not hermetically sealed; it leaks. When subversive notions are incorporated, some manage to stick. If a woman is portrayed as a lawyer, even if she spends little time in court, the seed has been planted. Women *can* become lawyers. To retain its dominance, the hegemonic system must adapt (Gitlin, 1982, p. 449). It is difficult to argue that television never changes; it clearly does. However, understanding television's hegemonic role allows us to see that TV is less progressive than we think. Although the medium adjusts to social change, it can do so in a manner that simultaneously contradicts or undercuts a progressive premise.

Analyzing TV entertainment's representations of feminism is a useful way to study TV's use of hegemonic strategies to contain oppositional ideology. Feminism challenges many aspects of the dominant ideology. It critiques traditional assumptions about the "natural" roles of women as wives, mothers, and daughters (and generally "other-centered" creatures), and it analyzes the ways in which cultural norms and values work to undermine women's independence, action, and success. The hegemony of the patriarchal system that devalues women is pervasive. It operates through socialization, education, religion, and government, as well as cultural institutions like mass media. Television producers, advertisers, and so on participate in the perpetuation of hegemony, not only because they believe it is in their economic interest, but also because they live in, benefit from, and may not be able to see beyond the norms of the patriarchal culture (Japp, 1991).[2]

Understanding television's role in the hegemonic process is key to understanding television's approach to feminism, and vice versa. *The Mary Tyler Moore Show* and *Murphy Brown* are particularly suitable for this kind of analysis because both programs have been extremely successful and have been hailed as examples of television's positive response to feminist ideology.

Although their debuts are separated by almost 20 years, *The Mary Tyler Moore Show* (*TMTMS*) and *Murphy Brown* are similar in a number of ways. They are examples of what has been television's dominant approach to feminism: the single-working-woman comedy (other examples include *Rhoda*, *Phyllis*, *Alice*, and *One Day at a Time*). Both shows are set in the workplace, where the primary female character is surrounded by a family of sorts made up primarily of coworkers, most of whom are male. When *TMTMS* debuted in 1970, these characteristics were important in signaling its status as a comedy about a "new" kind of woman.

2. Adrienne Rich defines *patriarchy* as "any kind of group organization in which males hold dominant power and determine which part females shall and shall not play, and in which capabilities assigned to women are relegated generally to the mystical and aesthetic and excluded from the practical and political realms" (1979, p. 78).

Indeed, following a television tradition that had stereotyped women as "goodwives," "bitches," "victims," and "courtesans" (Meehan, 1983), the character of Mary Richards as an independent career woman on *TMTMS* was a challenge to the portrayal of women on television. Arriving as it did on the crest of the developing women's liberation movement, *TMTMS* was informed by and commented on the changing role of women in American society. One of the show's creators, James Brooks, observed that, although the show did not explicitly address the issues of the women's movement, "we sought to show someone from Mary Richards' background being in a world where women's rights were being talked about and it was having an impact" (quoted in Bathrick, 1984, pp. 103–104).

Both this remark and the premise of the show itself demonstrate that *TMTMS* was intended to be a departure from the tradition of sexist portrayals of women on television. *TMTMS*'s status as the first serious attempt to address the influence of women's liberation earned it a place in television history. Describing the program as "one of the most believable, lucid, and lovable portrayals of the single woman in American society of the seventies," Arthur Hough has noted that "while there are a thousand sitcoms in television history, 'The Mary Tyler Moore Show' will probably still be among the top ten in terms of historical and social significance" (Hough, 1981, p. 221; see also Alley & Brown, 1989).

Murphy Brown also has been interpreted as a breakthrough in television portrayals of women. From its debut in 1988, press coverage characterized *Murphy Brown* as a challenge to the typical portrayal of women on television and suggested that the series' title character, a successful, 40ish, female television journalist, was "different," an example of the "womanpower" taking hold in prime-time network television (Waters & Huck, 1989, p. 48). Critics highlighted certain qualities: her ambition and competitive drive (O'Reilly, 1989; O'Connor, 1989; Elm, 1989), her often harsh wit and sarcasm (Wisehart, 1989; Cavett, 1989), and her checkered past as an alumna of the Betty Ford Center (Panitt, 1989; Wisehart, 1989). In short, critics claimed that Murphy Brown represented "the very apotheosis of the new video woman" (Waters & Huck, 1989, p. 49). Various adjectives used to describe her—"workaholic," "Amazon," "highly competitive and confident," and "tough"—gave potential viewers clues as to the original slant of the character (Wisehart, 1989, p. 39; Zehme, 1989, p. 1; O'Connor, 1989, p. 17y; Panitt, 1989, p. 40).

These descriptions of the progressive slant of *Murphy Brown* illustrate the changes in television since 1970. When *TMTMS* debuted, it was perceived as different simply because an unmarried, 30-year-old working woman was unusual as a sitcom premise in 1970. By 1988, this premise was no longer innovative, and the difference that reviewers found in *Murphy Brown* was related more to her *character* as a powerful, ambitious, wealthy woman with a "bad attitude" and checkered past, than to her *situation* as a single, working, 40ish woman.

Despite the differences, reactions to *Murphy Brown* often stressed the program's similarity to *TMTMS*. Like Mary Richards, Murphy Brown is a bright, single, attractive woman working in a television newsroom. However, the most important link between the two sitcoms is their perceived status as feminist artifacts. The ABC news magazine show *PrimeTIME LIVE* of July 25, 1991, introduced a feature on *Murphy Brown* by placing the show on a continuum of "liberated woman" sitcoms that included *That Girl* and *The Mary Tyler Moore Show*. Indeed, the producers of *Murphy Brown* claim that they "intend Murphy to be for the 90s what Mary Richards was for the 70s" (Horowitz, 1989, p. 1H), and a headline in *USA Today* described the sitcom as "Mary Tyler Moore Updated for the Eighties" (cited in Alley & Brown, 1990, p. 204).

The perceived progressivism of *Murphy Brown* and *TMTMS* rests in their emphasis on the liberal feminist ideal of increasing women's access to the public sphere (Jaggar, 1983, p. 188). Generally, liberal feminists compare women's economic, legal, and social positions with those of men and argue that women's rights and privileges should be expanded to equal those of men. Programs like *Murphy Brown* and *TMTMS* that feature single, independent, working women who have chosen career over marriage and motherhood promote liberal feminist values by rejecting television's tradition of domestic women and by portraying female characters in roles formerly reserved for men. Indeed, the characteristics that the press claims make Murphy Brown unique ("workaholic," "highly competitive," "tough") seem unusual only when applied to a female character. *TMTMS*'s and *Murphy Brown*'s embrace of the notion that progress for women requires rejection of domesticity (the feminine sphere) and pursuit of a career (the masculine sphere) has long been attached to liberal feminism, reinforced by such things as Betty Friedan's *The Feminine Mystique* and the battle over the Equal Rights Amendment.

In short, *TMTMS* and *Murphy Brown* indicate that television's most visible response to the demands of feminism has been to allow women the opportunity to act like men. Producers place women in traditionally masculine situations (*TMTMS*) or give them traditionally masculine character traits (*Murphy Brown*). However, *TMTMS* and *Murphy Brown* employ hegemonic strategies that work to undermine their progressive, liberal feminist design. Different strategies dominate in each show, but their effect is similar: In each case, these strategies limit or contain the challenge that the program's premise presents to a patriarchal culture.

THE DOMESTICATION OF MARY RICHARDS IN *TMTMS*

Set in a Minneapolis television newsroom (WJM-TV), the regular cast of *TMTMS* included Lou Grant (producer of the news), Mary Richards (associate producer), Murray Slaughter (newswriter), and Ted Baxter (anchorman). For the first four years of the show, Mary Richards' neighbor and best friend, Rhoda

Morgenstern, and their landlady, Phyllis Lindstrom, were also regulars. Although the series included episodes with scenes in Mary's home, the majority of the action took place in the newsroom. In the last four years of the show, the character of Sue Ann Nivens, the hostess of the *Happy Homemaker* show at WJM, was added, and the role of Georgette Franklin Baxter, Ted Baxter's girlfriend and later his wife, was expanded.

These characters behaved in many ways as an extended family. The presentation of a family structure is common to many of the most successful comedies in television history, and, in the 1970s, the family structure was adapted to include groups of people who might not technically be considered "family." Lawrence Mintz has noted, "All sitcom is 'domestic' or family-oriented if we expand the definition to non-blood-related groups that function as families" (Mintz, 1985, p. 116). Audiences are presented with a group of people who care about each other, and who bond together on the basis of living or working relations. *The Mary Tyler Moore Show* was an early example of this trend. However, reliance on a family structure familiar from decades of domestic sitcom can limit the development of progressive roles for women, and *TMTMS* exemplifies this problem. Although it was set in the workplace, its narrative consistently portrayed Mary Richards in the implicit roles of mother, wife, and daughter.

Mary as Daughter

The paternal role that Lou Grant plays toward Mary Richards, and her submission to his authority, illustrate the patriarchal patterns at work in *TMTMS*. Mary seeks Lou's approval and goes to him for advice on personal and professional matters, whereas Lou, in turn, guides and protects her. For example, in one episode, Sue Ann Nivens' boyfriend makes a pass at Mary. Mary becomes upset and takes her problem to Lou, who, with fatherly indignation, offers to "kill him." Mary refuses this offer, but later takes Lou's advice that she should tell Sue Ann. Ultimately, Mary comforts Sue Ann, and the situation is happily resolved. This illustration echoes the pattern of the classic father-and-child problem-solving plot familiar from *Father Knows Best* or *Leave It to Beaver*; the child has a problem and goes to the father, who tells the child to do "the right thing," which the child intuitively knows she should do anyway. With the advice and pressure of the parent, the child overcomes her reluctance, does what is required, and the situation is resolved happily, demonstrating the wisdom of the father.

Lou's patriarchal superiority is underscored by the negative consequences that result when Mary refuses to follow his advice. After being promoted to producer, Mary meets a female swimmer whom she is convinced would make a good sportscaster for WJM. Lou ridicules the idea, and Mary accuses him of sexism. However, Lou tells Mary that, as the producer, she has the authority to hire anyone she likes, and Mary hires the woman. In her first broadcast, the new sportscaster reports on nothing but swimming, ignoring baseball and football. The woman later reveals to Mary that she does not believe in contact sports and will not report them. Mary is forced to fire her. At the conclusion, Mary tells

Lou that she was wrong about the sportscaster, bemoaning her failure to strike a blow for women. Lou assures her that she has indeed proven something—"that a woman has the chance to be just as lousy in a job as a man." Like a good parent, Lou allows Mary to make and learn from her own mistakes (and it is doubly interesting that this lesson involves female "incompetence"). This plotline also implies that Mary needs Lou's paternal guidance in professional matters even though she is supposedly qualified as a television producer.

TMTMS was replete with episodes similar to those described here, in which Mary, the daughter figure, solicits advice from the older and wiser Lou, the father figure.[3] Under Lou's tutelage, Mary copes with her problems. The daughter role can be viewed as a hegemonic device that works to contain Mary's independence. *TMTMS* tells us that Mary cannot really "make it on her own," either personally or professionally, without fatherly guidance. In this fashion, Mary's independence is domesticated.

Mary as Wife and Mother

At the same time that she is Lou's dutiful daughter, Mary also acts as a nurturing wife/mother to Lou and to other characters. It is her responsibility to maintain the interpersonal relations within the group, and she does this through personal advice, support, and mediation of conflict.

For instance, Mary is constantly accessible; her friends, who drop by at any time, are received warmly. When Ted Baxter, the station's anchorman, cannot have a child, he comes to Mary, who reconciles him to the idea of adoption. When Ted has sexual problems, his wife Georgette comes to Mary for advice. When Sue Ann feels threatened by her rival sister, she seeks comfort from Mary. Later in this same episode, Sue Ann becomes so demoralized that she takes to her bed, convinced that she is no longer wanted or needed. Although Sue Ann has always treated Mary unkindly, Mary assumes nurturing responsibility.

Mary's role as nurturer is established in the series' very first episode, when Lou shows up drunk at Mary's apartment the night after he hires her for the job. His wife is out of town, and he decides to write her a letter on Mary's typewriter. Although Lou interrupts a visit from Mary's former boyfriend, she accommodates him, ultimately viewing his behavior as "kind of sweet" rather than intrusive. Later in the series, Lou decides to redecorate the living room as a surprise for his wife. He seeks Mary's advice, who enlists Rhoda, her neighbor, for the job. Following his divorce, he is frequently at Mary's apartment for dinner, seeking the wifely/motherly functions that he misses. Whenever a "woman's touch" is needed, Mary is there.

3. Interestingly, the proscription against incest that would exist in a true father–daughter relationship is implicitly revealed in an episode late in the series in which Mary asks Lou for a date. Lou comes over to Mary's house for dinner, and both are extremely nervous and uncomfortable. They decide to end the suspense and they kiss, during which both begin to giggle. Agreeing that a dating relationship will never work, they settle down to talk about the office. Clearly, the patterns created in their father–daughter relationship prohibit romance.

Mary is the ideal wife/mother surrogate in these situations. Like other sitcom mothers such as Harriet Nelson or June Cleaver, she is other-centered, sublimating her own feelings or needs to those of her "family." The idea that only Mary can adequately fulfill these "womanly" functions is reinforced in the rare instances in which she flatly refuses to perform. Even when she attempts to assert herself, she returns to her accommodating patterns by the end of the episode. For example, when a former WJM staff member returns for a visit, Lou decides a party at Mary's home would be appropriate (most social interaction outside the office takes place in Mary's apartment). Mary refuses this imposition, suggesting Lou's house for the party. On the given night, she arrives early at Lou's to assist with preparations, only to find Lou in a state of total and carefree unreadiness. It is clear that Lou has counted on Mary's last-minute assistance, and when she, recognizing the manipulation, refuses to comply, Lou redirects his manipulation. The guests, he claims, knowing Mary, will *assume* that she helped him, and so she will be blamed for the mess. Mary frantically begins to clean.

Two aspects of this situation are significant. First, Mary is concerned about others' assessments of her traditional "womanly" qualities and would not want to be viewed as an inadequate homemaker or hostess. Second, this example emphasizes Mary's role as social facilitator for the group. Lou's confidence that Mary would take over demonstrates his realization of her role, and Mary's acceptance of it is clear when she gives in and begins to clean. The nurturing aspect of Mary's character is not just an extension of the fact that she is a "nice" person. Certainly Murray Slaughter, her friend and the newswriter at WJM, would be described as a nice person; however, he does not perform the nurturing and interpersonal facilitation that Mary does.

Mary's sensitivity, relationship skills, and willingness to spend her time and energy on the problems of others are symptomatic of her status as mother to the group. Like the traditional mothers of domestic sitcoms, her value as a person comes from what she can do for others. The lyrics of the theme song from *TMTMS* echo this assumption: "Who can turn the world on with her smile? / Who can take a nothing day and suddenly make it all seem worthwhile?" In *TMTMS*, Mary is a woman in a man's world, and her primary function is to enhance the lives of others in ways a male supposedly cannot. As Adrienne Rich notes, "The patriarchy looks to women to embody and impersonate the qualities lacking in its institutions . . . such qualities as intuition, sympathy, and access to feeling" (1979, p. 80).

This analysis illustrates the contradictions that exist within *TMTMS*. Although it took the sitcom from the home to the workplace, it did not alter significantly the traditional male/female roles of the genre. Superficially, *TMTMS* seems progressive, but the interaction of its characters demonstrates the hegemonic patterns that undercut Mary's status as a liberated woman.[4]

---

4. Although I do not deal with Mary's relationship with her female friends here, it is addressed in the larger version of this analysis in Dow, 1990.

TMTMS and *Murphy Brown* both offer troubling representations of feminism, yet they take different approaches to their feminist characters. Whereas Mary Richards' feminist function is limited by her traditional role, *Murphy Brown* caricatures feminism. Murphy Brown can be viewed as a symptom of the 1980s backlash against feminism, a time when discourse about the ill effects of feminism was circulating in American culture (Faludi, 1991). One of the sources of that rhetoric was prime-time television. In *Murphy Brown*, the title character enacts, in many ways, the perceived costs of feminist choices. Although she is professionally successful, much more so than Mary Richards, Murphy Brown pays for that success with a difficult private life. *Murphy Brown*'s interpretation of feminism repeatedly emphasizes two themes: that femininity and feminism are incompatible, and that a woman's professional success limits her chances for personal happiness. In doing so, *Murphy Brown* widens the perceived gap between the public and private spheres, indicating that women, unlike men, cannot successfully inhabit both realms.

MURPHY BROWN: PAYING THE PRICE FOR PROGRESS

The regulars on *Murphy Brown* consist of Murphy's colleagues at "FYI," the weekly prime-time news magazine show of which she is a co-anchor. The other primary anchor on "FYI" is Jim Dial, an older, experienced television newsman. Miles Silverberg, the executive producer of "FYI" and Murphy's boss, is less experienced and younger than Murphy, a situation that Murphy finds irritating. Two other regulars are Frank Fontana and Corky Sherwood, reporters for the program. Frank is an experienced investigative reporter and Murphy's closest friend in the group. In contrast, Corky has little journalistic experience. She is an ex-Miss America who was hired at "FYI" for her beauty queen status. Murphy does not see Corky as her professional equal, and a strong theme in their relationship is Murphy's disdain for Corky's journalistic ability. Two other regulars on *Murphy Brown* are not connected to "FYI." They are Murphy's ever-present housepainter, Eldin Bernecky, who appears in most of the scenes set in Murphy's home, and Phil, the owner of a bar frequented by the "FYI" staff.

This review of characters shows a kinship between *Murphy Brown* and *TMTMS*. Like Mary Richards, Murphy is surrounded by men, reinforcing the liberal feminist orientation of "a woman in a man's world." However, unlike Mary Richards, Murphy does not achieve success by bringing a "woman's touch" to the workplace; rather, she absorbs the characteristics of "a man's world," illustrating the negative "de-feminizing" effects of liberal feminist success. This interpretation can be supported by an examination of her personal and professional characteristics and by the contrast of her "masculinized" character with Corky's enactment of traditional femininity.

Femininity vs. Feminism

Murphy's masculine persona can be discerned on several levels. Her name is not traditionally feminine; culturally, "Murphy" would be more likely to refer to a man than a woman. She is a very attractive woman, but her "look" is not traditionally feminine. Murphy's clothing is severely tailored, and she tends to wear high collars and boxy suits with straight lines. Even her less formal clothes have a masculine aura; when Murphy is relaxed, she often wears a baseball cap, tennis shoes, and baggy, man-tailored slacks. Reinforcing the idea that she and Corky are two extremes on a spectrum, Murphy's black, brown, and strong colors are in contrast to Corky's pastels, soft scarves, and bows. Whereas Murphy often wears flats, Corky always wears high heels. Murphy's subdued makeup and hair are also striking in comparison to Corky's teased, bleached hair and bright lips. Corky's appearance is part of her performance of femininity, whereas Murphy's style reflects the goal of gaining credibility in a male world.

Murphy's physical presence and aggressive style also are significant in defining her character. Her stride is powerful, her gestures strong, and she is supremely confident about her own opinions, often with little regard for others' feelings. For example, in a 1989 episode, Murphy is disgusted by the way the men around her are handling a management/union dispute. She accuses them of being blinded by male pride, and comments, "Just pull down your pants, I'll get a ruler, and we'll settle this once and for all."

A clear message of *Murphy Brown* is that the personality traits alluded to, such as aggression, competitiveness, and insensitivity, are key to Murphy's professional success in a patriarchal world. For example, in another 1989 episode, Murphy is so relentless while interviewing a subject that he has a heart attack and dies on the air. A guilty Murphy vows to be a nicer person, and in subsequent scenes she is uncharacteristically polite and considerate to her colleagues. They are shocked and dismayed at the change in her behavior, concerned that it is affecting the quality of her work.

This episode is instructive because it implies that Murphy's display of traditionally "nice," feminine qualities is not only shocking, but incompatible with her success as a journalist. To compete in a male culture, Murphy becomes an extreme version of it, a caricature of the consequences of liberal feminism. Alison Jaggar notes that a typical liberal feminist argument is that "women are capable of participating in male culture and of living up to male values" (1983, p. 250). Murphy's success proves this argument; however, the negative consequences she suffers illustrate the anti-feminist subtext of *Murphy Brown*.

As the following extended example indicates, a recurring theme in *Murphy Brown* is that Murphy's aggression is excessive, and that her professional success requires a corresponding lack of traditionally feminine qualities. In this episode, the major plot line concerns Murphy's week-long stint as the substitute co-anchor of "Today America," a program much like "Good Morning America." Murphy ridicules the "soft news" orientation of the program, and she is unhappy to discover that Corky is to be her cohost. Corky, excited by the assignment, prepares carefully for the programs. Murphy does no preparation.

On the first morning show, they interview the male author of a popular children's book. While Corky praises the inventiveness and popularity of the book, Murphy asserts that the setting of the book, "the Land of the Woogies," emulates a male-dominated society, and that the story represents the larger culture's "struggle for sexual equality in the workplace." The author protests that his characters do not have a sex, but Murphy is relentless, claiming that the "Fifis," another group in the book, are female and represent "an oppressed minority of sorts." At this point, Corky steps in, soothes the author, and ends the interview.

The contrast between Murphy's feminism and Corky's femininity are clear in this scene. Murphy personifies the intensity and humorlessness of the stereotypical feminist ideologue, refusing to enact the supportive, gracious role required in such a situation. Although her argument that the children's book is sexist may be correct (and some viewers may see it as a good point to make), the audience of the episode is encouraged to view her claim as absurd and her behavior as inappropriate. Corky, in contrast, is at home in the "soft news" format that reflects traditionally female interests.

Corky is praised for her performance, but Murphy is described by colleagues as "acerbic, humorless, inflexible, and unprepared." The next day, Murphy panics when she hears that she must participate in a segment with a bake-off champion, and she moans, "The last time I tried to bake brownies, I had to call in an industrial cleaning service." Corky's baking expertise is manifest, and Murphy tries to compete with her. Predictably, Murphy starts a fight with the bake-off champion and ruins the segment.

By the end of this episode, Murphy is humbled, and she must admit that Corky did the better job. Murphy is humiliated because she is not traditionally feminine enough, in terms of social facilitation or cooking skills, to fulfill the assigned role. Even though her particular traits have led to success in "hard news," when she fails at "soft news," she is punished. Murphy is the victim of dual and conflicting expectations. Corky, whose traditionally feminine skills are appropriate for the situation, shines on the morning show, although she has failed in the past at "hard news" assignments.

This episode reinforces *Murphy Brown's* contention that a woman cannot be professionally successful and traditionally feminine. Murphy is rich and famous, but not a "real" woman in personality or in personal relationships. Corky, in contrast, is more traditionally feminine in appearance and behavior, but she is professionally competent only in the typically female province of lower status "soft news" situations. *Murphy Brown* allows only for polar conceptions of womanhood, refusing to permit integration of bifurcated masculine and feminine qualities attached to the public and private spheres.

Public vs. Private Success

Murphy's lack of domestic and interpersonal skills are a consistent source of humor on *Murphy Brown*. Her interpersonal difficulties extend into her private life, where she enacts the stereotype of a driven career woman with no time or talent for relationships. Unlike Mary Richards, Murphy has no close female friends. Outside the newsroom, her closest relationship is with Eldin, her housepainter. Unmarried, childless for the first four years of the series, and without a satisfying romantic relationship, Murphy's character embodies what many would consider the negative consequences of female independence.

Several episodes of *Murphy Brown* comment on the effect of Murphy's life choices on her personal relations, offering the message that her professional ambition precludes lasting personal relationships. Her most consistent involvement has been with Jerry Gold, an abrasive talk-show host. In their first try at a relationship in a 1990 episode, Murphy eventually called it off, saying, "I'm good at a lot of things, but this isn't one of them. I start saying things I don't normally say, I start doing things I don't normally do. . . . Oh, God, I'm wearing an apron. See what I mean?" This remark comes after a failed dinner party that Murphy concocted to introduce Jerry to her colleagues. It is telling that Murphy equates her failure at the relationship with her unsuitability for a domestic role, reinforcing the dichotomy between the private and public spheres.

In the next season, Murphy and Jerry try once more for a relationship, but it ends when Jerry takes a job in California and Murphy is too busy to pursue a long-distance romance. Again, this episode creates an inverse relationship between Murphy's personal happiness and her professional success. Murphy and Jerry are brought together when a new "FYI" segment requires that they debate political issues each week. Their sharply contrasting political views make this a lively and popular segment. However, after they rekindle their romance, Murphy is no longer aggressive and sharp-witted in the debate segment; instead, she exhibits traditionally feminine qualities. She is supportive, polite, and willing to compromise with Jerry's views. Her colleagues are horrified, concluding that her romance with Jerry has affected her professional performance.

With such plotlines, *Murphy Brown* reiterates that personal happiness and professional success are incompatible for Murphy, arguing that, for women, the qualities the public world requires are radically different from those necessary for success in the private world of relationships. Murphy simply cannot win. *Murphy Brown* implies that she must act one way to be professionally successful and another to be personally fulfilled. For many female viewers, Murphy's difficulties could strike a responsive chord. However, the episodes of *Murphy Brown* that deal with this issue are structured to encourage viewers to perceive such problems as Murphy's fault because she is unwilling to compromise career for relationships. The troublesome assumption that she must make such a choice in the first place is not addressed. Men in her position are accustomed to "having it all," but Murphy's attempts to do so have problematic results.

When Murphy becomes pregnant at the end of the 1990–91 season, her decision to keep the child would seem to provide an opportunity for character development. When she first discovers she is pregnant, it is unclear who the father is—her ex-husband, Jake, with whom she has had a brief fling, or Jerry Gold. When Jake discovers that he is the father, he has little interest in marriage or in fatherhood. After Jake leaves, Murphy and Jerry Gold make a brief attempt to live together, but they cannot get along. Murphy decides that their relationship makes her feel too dependent and "needy." Murphy's most consistent companion throughout her pregnancy is Eldin, her housepainter, who is motivated, he claims, by the realization that Murphy would be a rotten mother, and he would be an excellent one. Indeed, after Murphy has the baby, she hires Eldin to be the child's nanny. Although Eldin's skill at child-rearing could be viewed as a feminist statement (that is, men can be caretakers as well as women), it can also be viewed as underscoring Murphy's maternal incompetence (that is, an itinerant housepainter can be as good a mother as she can).

Murphy seemingly defies feminist stereotypes by reproducing at the age of 42. However, the context in which she decides to have the baby, except for the fact that she is financially well-off, is far from ideal. The father of the child has no interest in her or the baby. She is having the child at an age when complications are more likely. If this is the feminist mode of reproduction, it is fairly unappealing. What is most disturbing is that Murphy, who has been anti-child for three years on the program, suddenly decides that a baby will give meaning to her life. This decision gives credence to the anti-feminist argument that women who make feminist choices eventually "come to their senses" and regret the impact on their personal lives. Given her age, her lifestyle, her attitudes, and her lack of familial support, Murphy makes a rather irrational decision to have this child. It makes sense only as a reflection of the sexist adage that all women have a deep and irrepressible desire to reproduce that is merely waiting to be triggered. Indeed, this interpretation of Murphy's motivation is given support in the "birth" episode from the beginning of the 1992 season. In this episode's final scene, Murphy cradles her new infant in her arms, singing to him, "You make me feel like a natural woman," words from an Aretha Franklin song that take on a powerful meaning in this context. Having given birth, Murphy is miraculously transformed, albeit briefly, from an "unnatural" (professional) to a "natural" (maternal) woman.

Ultimately, Murphy's child, Avery, makes little difference in the patterns of her character or in the narrative of the program. Murphy's personality remains largely unchanged, and the child functions primarily as a comic device to provide plotlines for Murphy's antics. Various episodes center on child-derived plotlines, such as her search for a nanny (she can't get along with any of the candidates) or her attempt to create a perfect, traditional Christmas for Avery (which turns into an exploration of her dysfunctional extended family). In the end, becoming a mother provides little balance for Murphy's character. She has finally done something traditionally female—but in the most unconventional and undesirable fashion possible.

CONCLUSION

TMTMS and *Murphy Brown* exemplify television's guarded approach to feminism. Feminism, by seeking to alter the status of women, poses a threat to the traditional perceptions of women that have provided the artistic grounding for entertainment programming and the economic foundation for the television industry. *TMTMS* and *Murphy Brown* illustrate that television representations of feminism are unlikely to challenge fundamental, traditional assumptions about women. Both programs reinforce the public/private dichotomy that separates the roles and responsibilities of men and women in a patriarchal culture, and both uphold conventional cultural valuations of masculine and feminine behavior. Mary Richards' success in the public sphere is possible because she brings with her stereotypical qualities of womanhood from the private sphere. Viewers are given a great deal of evidence that she is a nice person, but very little that she is professionally competent. Murphy Brown, in contrast, is highly competent, but at the cost of not being a "good" woman.

The comparison of these two programs illustrate how television adapts to social change. In the 1970s, Mary Richards was a comforting example of how women's liberation could be accommodated without really challenging conventional relations between the sexes. By the late 1980s, when Murphy Brown appeared, the cultural mood had changed and so had prime-time feminism. Murphy is as much a symbol of the *costs* of feminism as she is a symbol of the *benefits* of feminism.

However, considering that these programs are viewed by many as symbolic of women's progress, they clearly can be interpreted at more than one level (Fiske, 1986). In *TMTMS*, for example, Mary's *situation* was progressive, but her *behavior* did not threaten ideals of traditional womanhood. These characteristics explain the show's continued success. Mary was threatening to no one. She was "womanly" enough within her surrogate family to quiet the fears of those uneasy with women's liberation. For champions of feminism, Mary was a symbol of the possibilities for women—she was independent and happy.

The same possibility for mixed messages applies to *Murphy Brown*. In *Murphy Brown*, the feminist influence goes beyond the situation, emerging clearly in Murphy's behavior. As a representation of liberal feminism, however, *Murphy Brown* also can be interpreted by viewers on more than one level. For those who search for progressive images of women on television, Murphy is a walking advertisement for what women can achieve. She is successful, belligerent, and rich, qualities Mary Richards never attained. However, such surface characteristics are countered by other messages available in the program. Murphy is, in conventional terms, a dysfunctional woman. She plays into stereotypes about the negative effects of feminism in a variety of ways. As Diane English, the show's creator, put it in an interview, *Murphy Brown* "was a sort of cautionary tale about getting what you wished for" (De Vries, 1993, p. 20). Murphy has little success with men, she is obsessed with her work, and she lacks traditionally feminine skills and interests. In the program's narratives, these characteristics make her an object of humor.

Murphy's problems, as *Murphy Brown* tells it, are a result of her aberrant (for a woman) personality rather than a product of a culture that has conflicting messages and expectations for women. Within television's individualistic focus, it is difficult to interpret Murphy as a victim of patriarchal culture; rather, it is easier to see her as the cause of her own problems. Given that the program appeared at a time when American culture had begun to experience a strong backlash against feminism and its supposed effects, *Murphy Brown* can be interpreted as a *caricature* of feminism as easily as it can be interpreted as an *affirmation* of feminism.

This analysis of *TMTMS* and *Murphy Brown* provides insight into the process through which hegemony is maintained. Just enough difference is introduced to give the appearance of change, yet enough remains the same to avoid upsetting the balance within the dominant ideology. In this way, television entertainment can address feminism, and appear progressive, while still maintaining patriarchal conceptions of womanhood. Thus, the claim is not that television "*manufactures*" ideology, but that it "*relays* and *reproduces* and *processes* and *packages* and *focuses* ideology" [emphasis in original] (Gitlin, 1982, p. 430). However, *TMTMS* and *Murphy Brown* show that this process opens gaps that allow for contrasting evaluations as audiences assign "different values to different portions of the text and hence to the text itself" (Condit, 1989, p. 108).

Just as television advertising packages and sells products, television programming "packages" and "sells" depictions of the meaning of social change. *TMTMS* and *Murphy Brown*, as two important examples of prime-time feminism, illustrate the key role of critical analysis as a tool for understanding the source, the meanings, and the implications of entertainment television's complex relationship to women's progress.

REFERENCES

Alley, R., & Brown, I.B. (1989). *Love is all around: The making of The Mary Tyler Moore Show*. New York: Delta.

Alley, R., & Brown, I.B. (1990). *Murphy Brown: Anatomy of a sitcom*. New York: Delta.

Bathrick, S. (1984). *The Mary Tyler Moore Show:* Women at home and at work. In J. Feuer, P. Kerr, & T. Vahimagi (Eds.), *MTM: 'Quality television'* (pp. 99–131). British Film Institute.

Cavett, D. (1989, December 23). Candice Bergen: She's no dummy. *TV Guide*, pp. 7–9.

Condit, C. (1989). The rhetorical limits of polysemy. *Critical Studies in Mass Communication, 6*, 103–122.

De Vries, H. (1993, January 3). Laughing off the recession all the way to the bank. *New York Times Magazine*, pp. 19–21, 24, 26.

Dow, B. (1990). Hegemony, feminist criticism, and *The Mary Tyler Moore Show. Critical Studies in Mass Communication* 7, 261–274.

Dow, B. (1992). Femininity and feminism in *Murphy Brown. Southern Communication Journal, 57*, 143–155.

Elm, J. (1989, December 23). What TV's real newswomen think of Murphy Brown. *TV Guide*, 4–7.

Faludi, S. (1991). *Backlash: The undeclared war against American women.* New York: Crown Publishers.

Feuer, J. (1986). Narrative form in American network television. In C. McCabe (Ed.), *High theory/low culture: Analysing popular television and film* (pp. 101–114). New York: St. Martin's Press.

Fiske, J. (1986). Television: Polysemy and popularity. *Critical Studies in Mass Communication, 3*, 391–408.

Gitlin, T. (1982). Prime time ideology: The hegemonic process in television entertainment. In H. Newcomb (Ed.), *TV: The critical view* (3rd ed., pp. 426–454). New York: Oxford.

Gray, H. (1989). Television, Black Americans, and the American dream. *Critical Studies in Mass Communication, 6*, 376–386.

Horowitz, J. (1989, April 9). On TV, Ms. Macho and Mr. Wimp. *New York Times*, pp. 1H, 36H.

Hough, A. (1981). Trials and tribulations—Thirty years of sitcom. In R. Adler (Ed.), *Understanding television: Essays on television as a social and cultural force* (pp. 201–224). New York: Praeger.

Jaggar, A. (1983). *Feminist politics and human nature.* Totowa, NJ: Rowman and Allanheld.

Japp. P. (1991). Gender and work in the 1980s: Television's working women as displaced persons. *Women's Studies in Communication, 14*, 49–74.

Kaplan, E. A. (1987). Feminist criticism and television. In R. Allen (Ed.), *Channels of discourse: Television and contemporary criticism* (pp. 211–253). Chapel Hill: University of North Carolina Press.

Meehan, D. (1983). *Ladies of the evening: Women characters of prime-time television.* Metuchen, NJ: Scarecrow.

Mintz, L. (1985). Situation comedy. In B. Rose (Ed.), *TV genres: A handbook and reference guide* (pp. 107–129). Westport, CT: Greenwood.

Nightingale, V. (1990). Women as audiences. In M. E. Brown (Ed.), *Television and women's culture* (pp. 25–36). London: Sage.

O'Connor, J. (1989, November 27). An updated Mary Richards in 'Murphy Brown.' *The New York Times*, p. 17Y.

O'Reilly, J. (1989, May 27). At last! Women worth watching. *TV Guide*, 18–21.

Panitt, M. (1989, February 4). Murphy Brown. *TV Guide*, 40.

Rich, A. (1979). *On lies, secrets, and silence: Selected prose, 1966–1978*. New York: W.W. Norton.

Waters, H. F., & Huck, J. (1989, March 13). Networking women. *Newsweek*, 48–55.

Wisehart, B. (1989, December 24). Murphy and Mary: Similar but so unalike. (Minneapolis) *Star Tribune*, p. 39.

Zehme, B. (1989, November 6). Candice Bergen: Sitcom queen cracks the mold. *Chicago Tribune*, pp. 2:1–2.

When I was a teenager, a career in broadcasting meant being an actress on a popular radio soap opera or in a nighttime drama. Women sang, sold products, and were entertainers, not serious news correspondents [according to Marlene Sanders].

(Sanders & Rock, 1988, p. 15)

five

TELEVISION NEWS:

Women on the Front Line

HISTORY

The first television network newscast, *Douglas Edwards with the News,* aired in 1948. This 15-minute program was the standard for network news shows until 1963, when news programs were lengthened to 30 minutes. By the 1950s, "television news moved to the center of the political process," changing it "from top to bottom" (Donovan & Scherer, 1992, p. ix). Network news brought mega-events into people's living rooms: presidential addresses, Congressional hearings, wars, assassinations, political and civil unrest, social movements, and foreign policy. In the 1960s, almost 80 percent of television viewers watched the network news. Audiences' favorite anchors (determined by ratings) were Huntley and Brinkley (NBC) in the 1960s and Walter Cronkite (CBS) in the 1970s.

In the mid-1970s, Thornton Bradshaw, chairman of RCA, brought together a panel of experts to examine how network news might fare in the future. "Looking into their crystal balls, his panel of Cassandras came up with the gloomy news that by the end of the 1980s, the networks' audience was due for a plunge. Unfortunately for the networks, Bradshaw's group of experts turned out to be right" (Goldberg & Goldberg, 1990, p. 30).

By the early 1980s, network news audiences dropped to 70 percent. Covering the anchor desks at the time were NBC's Tom Brokaw (1981), ABC's Peter Jennings (1983), and CBS's Dan Rather (1980). As forecasted, by 1989 only 57 percent of those watching television were watching the network news. Goldberg and Goldberg argue that the decline occurred because there were more viewing options available: more broadcast channels, more cable channels, and more news channels. In addition, network affiliates found they could make more money selling local advertisements during reruns of *Jeopardy* than they could running the network news (1990, p. 31).

Although the network news rarely broke even in terms of costs, most people in the network news business believed the news was a public service, one that brought respect and credibility to the networks. By the mid-1980s, all three network news divisions were purchased by new owners—corporations that believed in the bottom line . . . ratings. "The watchwords were 'lean and mean'" in the news divisions (Goldberg & Goldberg, 1990, p. 104). The new owners considered the network news to be no different than entertainment programs like *The Cosby Show.*

At the beginning of 1990, only NBC was making a profit, whereas the other two networks broke even (Lichty & Gomery, 1992, p. 3). With the increase in sensationalized "news-style" programs such as *A Current Affair* or *Entertainment Tonight,* the network news programs moved to "include more entertainment and arts coverage in their own broadcasts" (Lichty & Gomery, 1992, p. 4). On the local scene, the approach to news shows varied from straight reporting (1950s), to "happy talk" shows (1970s), finally settling into the "Live Eye," action-packed news of the 1980s. This new format includes on-location reports, high-tech weather paraphernalia, interspersed with snappy repartee between anchors. With cheaper equipment and more accessibility, large local stations no longer have to rely on network news programs for coverage.

So what's the future for network news? Lawrence Lichty and Douglas Gomery discuss some conclusions. Among those are:

- There will continue to be several national newscasts.
- Each of the traditional networks will air one newscast.
- Total news time throughout the day will expand.
- Expansion will come from outside prime time.
- Growth will be seen in specialized magazine or news/information formats.
- News-gathering organizations will make cooperative deals, and form alliances with one another.
- Networks will find other ways in which to earn income (selling footage, producing specials, selling news to local stations) (1992, p. 11).

Network news programs continue, but the ways of the 1960s and 1970s have passed: "Predictable formats, epitomized by the authoritarian closing words of Walter Cronkite every evening ('And that's the way it is'), have given way to a cacophony of voices and images" (Lichty & Gomery, 1992, p. 3).

PORTRAYAL

How are women in the news portrayed? How many news stories highlight women on the network news? When experts are sought, are they women?

Until the 1970s, no systematic studies analyzed women's portrayal in television news. A 1977 report, *Window Dressing on the Set: Women and Minorities on Television,* conducted by the U.S. Commission on Civil Rights, studied network news programming from March 1974 to February 1975. The commission found the following:

- Of the 230 news stories reported by the three networks, 9 stories dealt with issues relating to minorities and 3 stories focused on concerns of women (totaling 5.2 percent of all stories).

- Of the 141 newsmakers (people who were identified by the anchor or the reporter and appearing in the news), 9.9 percent were White females, 7.8 percent were minority males, and 3.5 percent were minority females. White males accounted for 78.7 percent of all newsmakers the audience saw on television.

- Of all newsmakers, there were zero to 12 women in each category (government officials, public figure, criminal, or private individual). Most women newsmakers were wives of presidents, or experts in areas that were considered to be "women's topics" (abortion or birth control). (*Window Dressing,* 1977, pp. 49–53).

In general, few stories on the nightly news related to women, "none [focused] on their achievements or accomplishments and, furthermore, [women] rarely served as correspondents" (1977, p. 54).

In a follow-up study based on 1977 data, the figures changed little.

- Of 330 stories, only 2.4 percent (8) related to women or minorities compared to 5.2 percent in the 1974 study.

- Of the 248 newsmakers, 88.4 percent were White male, 6.8 percent were White female, 4.4 percent were minority male, and 0.4 percent were minority female.

- In the category of government officials, 2 women appeared. Of the 34 public figures, 3 women appeared (all in the role of a wife). Under the category of "private citizens," women were most often presented as the victim (of murder, flood, or disease). One woman appeared as an expert. As was the case in the previous study, no minority females appeared as experts (1979, pp. 24–25).

In general, the 1977 data indicated that women and minorities appeared as often or less often than in the 1974 study.

A *Women, Men, and Media* study of network newscasts in 1989 found that the number of stories in which women were the focus included the following: 13.7 percent of ABC's news stories, 10.2 percent of CBS's stories, and 8.9 percent of NBC's stories. In general, "women were rarely the subject or focus of interviews on the nightly news" (Women in Communications, Inc., 1990, p. 8). Although women are still not seen as often on network news as men, the figures are on the increase. A 1994 *Women, Men and Media* annual report found men reported 79 percent of the network news and were "76 percent of those interviewed" in the network news (1994, p. 1).

EMPLOYMENT

Television news, much like radio news, was closed to most women. Some exceptions were Pauline Frederick, the first newswoman to work full-time for a television network; Alice Weel Bigart, one of the first women news producers to work on the *Douglas Edwards with the News* program; and Dorothy Fuldheim, television's first news anchorwoman on a local affiliate (Cleveland, Ohio).

In the 1950s and 1960s, most television news reporters were male. By the 1970s, not only was there a steady growth in the employment of news personnel in general, but the FCC categorized women as a minority, thus allowing television stations to include them under equal employment opportunities guidelines. Both events increased the number of women in television news, until by 1982, the number of women in the field had grown to 33 percent (Weaver & Wilhoit, 1986, p. 21).

Several firsts occurred during these years. In 1976, Barbara Walters became the first woman news anchor on a commercial network. That same year, Casse Mackin and Linda Ellerbee were the first women to co-anchor a network news show; it was aired on Sunday morning at dawn (Lazin, 1986).

As news became less profitable and deregulation took some of the power out of the hands of the FCC, the upward swing in the employment of women leveled off. Although some studies reinforce this leveling off (Stone, 1988; Women directing, 1993), Chapter 14 on women in network news demonstrates that the percentage of women in network news may be increasing, even though the number of network news jobs are not.

As women entered network news, they were assigned stories considered most appropriate for women: health, education, welfare, and reproductive issues. Few women or minorities were assigned choice beats: Washington, D.C., foreign affairs or the economy (*Window Dressing,* 1977; Singleton & Cook, 1982).

Although women have gained more jobs in network news, the amount of money they make in general is less. In some cases, the inequality has to do with experience and age; men have been in the field longer than most women. The few women who do break into upper management demand and receive the same salaries as their male counterparts (Reed, 1989). It is the entry-level positions where the real disparity occurs. In a 1986 survey of 200 network-affiliated television stations, Smith, Fredin, and Ferguson Nardone found male reporters made an average $470 a week, whereas female reporters made $385 a week. "This amounts to about 82 cents for women against each male dollar" (1989, p. 229). The average age for male reporters in this sample was 30 years with seven years of experience, compared to female reporters who were 27 years old and had five years of experience. Therefore, the pay gap could be due to years of experience and age, as discussed earlier.

Another difference in the hiring of male versus female correspondents in network news is appearance. One scholar suggests that male reporters are hired based on their experience, whereas female reporters are hired based on their appearance (Fung, 1988). One of the most publicized court cases against a news station concerned just this issue. When Christine Craft accepted a position as anchor for KMBC (Kansas City), she stressed to the management she was to be hired based on her journalistic experience (of which there was a great deal) and not based on her appearance, which was not what she called "band-box perfection" (Sanders & Rock, 1988, p. 144). Nine months later, KMBC management decided to move her to a reporter position because she was "too old, too unattractive, and not deferential enough to men" (Craft, 1986, p. 68). After many court battles, Craft lost her case;

however her experience with network management and the court system alerted women that appearance continued to be a factor in network news.

When Diane Sawyer left CBS for ABC and a co-anchor spot on *PrimeTIME LIVE* in 1989, she started a round of musical chairs. Networks immediately strengthened their ties with women newscasters through salary increases to keep the women newscasters they currently employed (such as Maria Shriver) or by luring other women newscasters away from competing networks with salary increases or promotions (Mary Alice Williams from CNN and Connie Chung from NBC) (Nash, 1989, p. 242).

Soon after (June 1, 1993), Connie Chung joined Dan Rather as co-anchor on *CBS Evening News*. Some argue that Chung was hired to attract Americans under 35 to the news, because barely 1 out of 13 watch any network television news (Andersen, 1993, p. 71), but CBS denies the decision is ratings driven, stating co-anchoring allows both Chung and Rather to cover big stories in the field at a moment's notice (McClellan, 1993, p. 7). Others believe the "torch is being passed from age to youth, from male to female, and from White to Asian-American" (Marin, 1993, p. 8). Network affiliates have urged CBS to bring Chung on board for several years. *CBS Evening News with Dan Rather and Connie Chung* becomes the second network evening news program with male and female co-anchors. Seventeen years earlier (1976–78) Barbara Walters and Harry Reasoner co-anchored the ABC network news. The years between Walters/Reasoner and Chung/Rather reinforce the slow pace of network news progress for women.

In 1994, Diane Sawyer received a new contract from ABC to co-anchor a weekly news magazine program, *Turning Point*. Her co-anchors include Barbara Walters and Peter Jennings. Although Sawyer's yearly salary is $7 million, it is the stature, not the money, that kept her at ABC (Marin, 1994, p. 10). She is now one of the most influential and powerful people in the news business.

In general, there are still fewer women than men in high-powered positions in television news, but a few are breaking through the "glass ceiling." In a recent study of the top TV reporters by The Center for Media and Public Affairs, women reported 23 percent of the network news stories on television. Of the top ten reporters in 1993, three were women: Andrea Mitchell (NBC), Rita Braver (CBS), and Lisa Myers (NBC). Although women reporters are outnumbered by male reporters by almost 4 to 1, the number-one reporter in terms of number of stories was Andrea Mitchell, reporting 175 stories (Women Reporters Make Gains on TV News, 1994, p. 3). Brit Hume followed with 139 stories. These figures signify the influence women are having on the television news field.

REFERENCES

Andersen, K. (1993, May 31). Does Connie Chung matter? *Time*, 141, 71.

Craft, C. (1986). *Christine Craft: An anchorwoman's story.* Santa Barbara, CA: Rhodora/Capra Press.

Donovan, R. J., & Scherer, R. (1992). *Unsilent revolution: Television news and American public life.* New York: Woodrow Wilson International Center for Scholars and Cambridge University Press.

Fung, V. M. (1988, October). Sexism at the networks: Anchor jobs go to young women and experienced men, *Washington Journalism Review,* 20–24.

Goldberg, R., & Goldberg, G. J. (1990). *Anchors: Brokaw, Jennings, Rather and the Evening News.* New York: A Birch Lane Press Book, published by Carol Publishing Group.

Lazin, L. (producer) (1986). *The 20th anniversary of the National Organization for Women.* Los Angeles: Peg Yorkin Production.

Lichty, L. W., & Gomery, D. (1992). More is less. In Cook, P.S., Gomery, D., & Lichty, L. W. (Eds.), *The future of news: Television-newspapers-wire services-newsmagazines.* Washington, DC: Woodrow Wilson Center Press; Baltimore, MD: Johns Hopkins University Press.

McClellan, S. (1993, May 24). Affils look at Rather/Chung boost, *Broadcasting & Cable, 123,* 7.

Marin, R. (1993, June 5–11). Make room for Connie. *TV Guide, 41,* 8–14.

Marin, R. (1994, March 26–April 1). Diane and the art of the deal. *TV Guide,* 8–14.

Nash, A. (1989, October). Will women change prime-time TV news? *Glamour, 87,* 242–245.

Reed, B. (1989). Women and the media. In Emery and Smythe (Eds.), *Readings in mass communication: Concepts and issues in the mass media* (7th ed., pp. 199–217). Dubuque, IA: Wm. C. Brown Publishers.

Sanders, M., & Rock, M. (1988). *Waiting for prime time: The women of television news.* New York: Harper & Row.

Singleton, L. A., & Cook, S. L. (1982, winter). Television network news reporting by female correspondents: An update. *Journal of Broadcasting, 26* (1), 487–491.

Smith, C., Fredin, E. S., & Ferguson Nardone, C.A. (1989). Television: Sex discrimination in the TV newsroom—Perception and reality. In P. J. Creedon (Ed.), *Women in mass communication: Challenging gender values* (pp. 227–246). Beverly Hills, CA: Sage

Stone, V. A. (1988). Minority men shoot ENG, women take advancement tracks. *Radio-Television News Directors Association Communicator,* pp. 10–14.

U.S. Commission on Civil Rights. (1977). *Window dressing on the set: Women and minorities in television.* Washington, DC: U.S. Government Printing Office.

U.S. Commission on Civil Rights. (1979). *Window dressing on the set: Women and minorities in television: An update.* Washington, DC: U.S. Government Printing Office.

Weaver, D. H., & Wilhoit, G. C. (1986). *The American journalist: A portrait of U.S. news people and their work.* Bloomington: Indiana University Press.

Women directing radio news reach pay parity with men, lag in TV (1993, Spring). *Media Report to Women, 21* (2), 1.

Women in Communications, Inc. (1989). *Women, men and media: A women in communications resource kit.* Arlington, VA: Author.

Women, Men and Media (1994). Arriving on the scene: Women's gaining presence in the news. Press release.

Women reporters make gains on TV news; minorities struggle, annual study finds. (1994, Spring). *Media Report to Women, 22* (2), 3.

PROJECT IDEAS

1   In network news, there are many examples of men as co-anchors, a few examples of male/female co-anchors and only one example of women co-anchors. What might be the rationale behind the absence of women co-anchors of the nightly news?

2   More and more women are employed by the non-network news sources such as CNN. Review 30 minutes of a network newscast and its CNN counterpart. How many women are on-screen? How many stories relate to women? How many women as experts are within the stories?

3   Check out the credits on a network news staff and compare them to the CNN news staff credits. What positions do women and men hold?

4   There are a few all-women news programs. For example, *To the Contrary* is a program similar to The McLaughlin Group on PBS in Washington, D.C. Typical news programs have one woman and/or one minority among White men. In what ways might a program consisting of all-women journalists differ from a program consisting of all-men journalists? Consider the ways women newspaper columnists differ from their male counterparts as described by Schulman in Chapter 4.

NAMES

The following list identifies some of the women who have been or are currently part of the television news industry. Women who were previously mentioned in this introduction are not duplicated in this list.

Christine Amanpour—Cable News Network (CNN) reporter covering the Persian Gulf (1991).

Ruth Ashton—One of the few women news broadcasters during the 1950s.

Hilary Brown—Foreign correspondent for ABC (1970s); anchor for Canadian Broadcasting Corporation in Toronto (late 1980s).

Frances Buss—First woman television director of news (1950s).

Katie Couric—Joined NBC *Network News* (1989). Co-anchor of *Today* (1991–present).

Faith Daniels—Broadcast journalist (1980s–present).

Pauline Frederick—First newswoman to work full-time for a U.S. television network (1953).

Charlayne Hunter-Gault—First Black woman to be a regular correspondent on a daily network news program, *The MacNeil/Lehrer Report* (1978), now known as the *MacNeil/Lehrer NewsHour.*

Cheryl Gould—Senior producer of "NBC Nightly News" (1988).

Shirley Lubowitz (Wershba)—Newswriter for radio and television (1940–1980s).

Jane Pauley—Cohost of *Today* (1976–89). Sole anchor *NBC Nightly News* (1980).

Renee Poussaint—Washington, D.C. anchor (1970s–present).

Cokie Roberts—Cohost of NBC's *Today* (1991).

Martha Rountree—Originator of *Meet the Press* (1950s).

Jessica Savitch—Principal reporter and writer for Saturday Edition of *NBC Nightly News* (1977–83).

Leslie Stahl—Washington-based reporter for CBS News (1970s); White House reporter for eight years; Host for *Face the Nation* (1983).

Joan Snyder—One of the first female field producers in network TV news (1960s).

Bree Walker—KCBS-TV news anchor (1980s–present).

Judy Woodruff—Network television White House correspondent (1977–82) and chief Washington correspondent for *MacNeil/Lehrer NewsHour* (1983).

Paula Zahn—Co-anchor *World News Now* (1987–90) and co-anchor *CBS This Morning* (1990–present).

ORGANIZATIONS

American Women in Radio and Television, Inc.
    1101 Connecticut Avenue, N.W.
    Washington, DC 20036

Black Women-Talk
    P.O. Box 14695
    Cleveland, OH 44114

Hersay
    P.O. Box 11010
    San Francisco, CA 94101

WINGS: Women's International News Gathering Service
    University of Texas at Austin
    Center for American History
    Austin, TX 78712

Women Make News, Inc.
    51 Turtle Bay Drive
    Branford, CT 06405

These lists were, in part, derived from Sanders and Rock's *Waiting for prime time: The women of television news* (1988), New York: Harper and Row; and Beasley and Gibbons' *Taking their place: A documentary history of women and journalism* (1993), Washington, DC: The American University Press in cooperation with the Women's Institute for Freedom of the Press.

Pioneers such as Pauline Frederick, Nancy Dickerson, Lisa Howard, Marlene Sanders, Marya McLaughlin, Liz Trotta, and Barbara Walters established themselves during the 1950s and 1960s in network news, but it was not until the 1970s that women made significant entry into the profession. (Hosley & Yamada, 1987)

14

WOMEN CORRESPONDENTS
AND THE EVENING NEWS

JOE S. FOOTE

Joe S. Foote, Dean of the College of Mass Communication and Media Arts at Southern Illinois University at Carbondale, earned his Ph.D. from the University of Texas. His research interests are broadcast journalism, international media, and political communication. His publications include an earlier version of "Women Correspondents' Visibility on the Network Evening News" in *Mass Comm Review* and a book titled *Television Access and Political Power: The Networks, the President, and the "Loyal Opposition."*

Since the Federal Communications Commission adopted rules in the late 1960s to encourage broadcasters to hire women and minorities, the role of women in television news has become a challenging issue, especially at the networks, which have symbolized the pinnacle of the broadcasting profession (Memorandum Opinion and Order, 1968). Various groups have tracked the hiring practices of organizations and the visibility they give women and minorities. There has been considerable interest in the upward mobility of women who entered the work force in the 1970s and 1980s.

BACKGROUND AND PREVIOUS RESEARCH

Pioneers such as Pauline Frederick, Nancy Dickerson, Lisa Howard, Marlene Sanders, Marya McLaughlin, Liz Trotta, and Barbara Walters established themselves during the 1950s and 1960s in network news, but it was not until the 1970s that women made significant entry into the profession (Hosley & Yamada, 1987). Flander (1985) describes three distinct waves of women entering television news: (1) the small group of women listed who preceded the 1968 FCC ruling; (2) correspondents like Connie Chung, Lesley Stahl, Carole Simpson, Catherine Mackin, Jane Pauley, Sylvia Chase, and Jessica Savitch, who were hired during the late 1960s and early 1970s just as an emphasis was being placed on recruitment of women; and (3) correspondents hired by the networks during the late 1970s and early 1980s who had come to expect expanded opportunities in television news and whose role models were women in the first wave of correspondents. This group includes correspondents like Diane Sawyer, Lynn Sherr, Martha Teichner, Andrea Mitchell, Judy Woodruff, Ann Compton, Ann Garrels, and a larger group of lesser-known names.

Although women were increasingly being hired as correspondents, their overall visibility on the evening news—the flagship broadcast—was low. Marlene Sanders, one of the first women network correspondents and the first woman network news vice president, believed that women correspondents were relegated to the second string:

> Air time is the broadcast equivalent of column space at a newspaper. If you are on the evening news regularly, the anchorman or executive producer is in your corner and you've made page one. If you are relegated to the early morning or weekends, fringe broadcasts or radio, then you are on the back pages. The favored correspondents, part of the so-called "A-team," get the major beats, while the workhorse correspondents, part of the "B-team," get the rest (Sanders & Rock, 1988).

A portion of the analysis within this chapter was previously published in *Mass Comm Review*, Vol. 19, Nos. 1/2, pp. 36–40 by Joe S. Foote titled "Women Correspondents' Visibility on the Network Evening News."

More and more women correspondents became concerned that their visibility was far lower than it should be and that their paths to advancement were blocked. In 1985, a group of women correspondents at ABC used a luncheon honoring Barbara Walters to protest to News President Roone Arledge their lack of airtime on the evening news. Subsequently, the National Organization for Women (NOW) branded ABC as the "most sexist" of the three major networks (Alter & Weathers, 1985).

During the 1980s, research began to support the women correspondents' claims that they were being given second-class status. Foote (1985) found that during 1983 and 1984 the majority of women correspondents were clustered in a "women's ghetto" where they comprised 30 percent of the bottom 30 correspondents but only 10 percent of the top 30. In 1986, NOW in a two-month study of network news broadcasts found that women reported only 10.5 percent of the stories on the three network evening news shows (Sanders & Rock, 1988).

Ziegler and White (1990), in a three-week sample of network evening newscasts, found that only 12 percent of the stories were reported by female correspondents. Sanders and Rock's (1988) survey of network news content in November 1986 showed that women reported only 13 percent of news stories. A study by DWJ Associates in 1987 (Zacks, 1988) found that no women were among the top ten in terms of total airtime. My (1992) seven-year content analysis of network news found almost no upward mobility for female evening news correspondents from 1983–89 in terms of increased visibility.

This chapter follows up on my 1992 study with a census of all correspondent reports aired on network news for a ten-year period from 1983 through 1992. It provides a comprehensive, longitudinal picture of women correspondents' visibility on the evening news. The research questions are as follow:

1 What differences exist in the exposure patterns of men and women correspondents on the network evening news?

2 Are there differences between the networks in the visibility of women?

3 How did women correspondents' exposure patterns change over the ten years of the study?

4 Does geographic assignment appear to influence the visibility of women on the evening news?

METHOD AND DESIGN

The Vanderbilt *Television News Index and Abstracts* were used to compile the visibility of correspondents on the evening news from January 1983 to December 1992. The unit of analysis was the network news correspondent report. Names of correspondents were obtained from the television networks and from the index of correspondents found at the beginning of each monthly index. Coders used the Vanderbilt index's listing of correspondents to calculate the monthly visibility of each individual. Full-time anchors, correspondents when serving as substitute anchors, and network commentators were not included in the study.

Correspondent visibility totals were grouped by month, quarter, and year. The sex of the correspondent, assignment, and the network for which he or she worked were also recorded. When a correspondent changed networks or assignment over the course of the study, the most recent assignment and place of employment were recorded.

Because none of the coding involved subjective decisions, only one coder worked on a particular phase of the study. At several intervals over the ten-year study, a separate coder randomly double-checked the original coders' accuracy. The figures for the top 100 correspondents were double-checked for accuracy for all ten years. In order to eliminate affiliate station reporters, temporary reporters, correspondents assigned to the evening news, consultants, or others who were not considered full-time network correspondents, a threshold of five reports per year was set for inclusion in the study.

Setting the visibility threshold at five reports per year risked excluding full-time correspondents with very low visibility. Yet, it would be difficult to imagine the networks retaining full-time personnel in these difficult budgeting times who contribute so little to the news product. The five-report cutoff was a reasonable way to exclude those who appeared occasionally on the evening news but were not full-time correspondents assigned primarily to that program.

RESULTS

Over the ten-year period, 83 percent of the correspondents were men and 17 percent were women. The figures for the first nine years were remarkably consistent, providing a static environment for women correspondents (1983, 16.7%; 1984, 16.7%; 1985, 16.7%; 1986, 16%; 1987, 16.3%; 1988, 15.3%; 1989, 17.1%; 1990, 17.7%; 1991, 17.1%). It was not until 1992 that the percentage of women increased significantly to 23 percent of correspondents. Although the relative percentages between men and women remained constant each year until 1992, there was an overall decrease of 39 network correspondents in the study (25%)—a net decrease of 43 males and a net increase of 4 females. The number of women decreased in proportion to men during the late 1980s, but the number of women increased in 1992 while the number of men continued to decline. Thus, reductions in force at the networks over the whole ten years affected men in the end far worse than women.

Table 14.1 compares the exposure of men and women correspondents during each of the ten years of the study. In every year, women registered higher than men in the lowest exposure category. Likewise, men clearly dominated the highest exposure category except during the later years, when women narrowed the gap. The year 1988 appears to be an aberration because of the temporary high visibility given a few women during the presidential campaign. Thirty-nine percent were in the highest exposure category, almost as high a percentage as that of men (49%). In real numbers, there were more than twice as many female correspondents in the highest exposure category in 1992 than ten years earlier in 1983.

Table 14.1
Correspondents' Visibility by Sex 1983–1992*

Number of Exposures	1983		1984		1985		1986		1987	
	M	F	M	F	M	F	M	F	M	F
5–15	21	15	35	15	43	13	43	15	31	8
	12%	42%	18%	39%	22%	33%	23%	42%	19%	25%
16–24	35	9	41	8	28	9	38	7	22	10
	20%	25%	21%	20%	14%	23%	20%	19%	13%	31%
25–39	63	6	58	13	63	13	57	7	54	8
	35%	17%	30%	33%	32%	33%	30%	19%	33%	25%
40+	60	6	61	3	61	4	51	7	57	6
	33%	17%	31%	8%	31%	10%	27%	19%	35%	19%
Total Number	179	36	195	39	195	39	189	36	164	32
Total Percent	83%	17%	83%	17%	83%	17%	84%	16%	84%	16%

Number of Exposures	1988		1989		1990		1991		1992	
	M	F	M	F	M	F	M	F	M	F
5–15	29	7	26	12	32	11	32	7	21	15
	19%	25%	17%	38%	20%	32%	21%	23%	16%	37%
16–24	15	4	21	8	22	10	21	7	16	4
	10%	14%	14%	25%	14%	29%	14%	23%	12%	10%
25–39	48	6	45	5	41	6	30	5	29	7
	31%	21%	29%	16%	26%	18%	20%	16%	21%	18%
40+	63	11	63	7	63	7	67	12	70	14
	41%	39%	41%	22%	40%	21%	46%	38%	51%	35%
Total Number	155	28	155	32	158	34	150	31	136	40
Total Percent	85%	15%	83%	17%	82%	18%	83%	17%	77%	23%

*Correspondents who had less than five reports during each year were not included in the study.

When compared to earlier years, both 1991 and 1992 seem to represent significant exposure gains. There were approximately the same number of female correspondents in 1985 (39) and 1992 (40), but the distribution was far different; in eight years, the number of women in the highest exposure category had increased nearly 500 percent. Interestingly, the numbers in the lowest exposure category (15) had not changed, but the mid-level people from 1985 had migrated upward to the top category by 1992.

Table 14.2 lists the correspondents in terms of their competitive rank. In seven out of the ten years, no more than one woman was among the ten most visible correspondents. In 1991 and 1992, however, 30 percent and 40 percent of the top ten correspondents, respectively, were women. In 1992, 11 of the top 50 correspondents were women, a huge improvement over the previous high year (1988), when 7 women were among the top 50. Comparing the two years of the study when the raw numbers of women were roughly equal (1986 and 1992), only 27 percent of women were in the lowest exposure category in 1992 compared to nearly half in 1986. Less than one-quarter of the women were in the top 100 correspondents in 1983, but nearly half were in 1992 (48%). Thus, by 1992, women for the first time were beginning to achieve visibility beyond their overall percentage of the correspondent corps.

Table 14.2

Rank of Women Correspondents 1983–1992*

Rank	1983		1984		1985		1986		1987	
0–10	0	0%	0	0%	1	3%	0	0%	0	0%
11–50	4	11%	4	10%	3	8%	5	13%	4	12%
51–100	5	13%	5	12%	6	16%	7	18%	8	24%
101–150	7	19%	11	26%	12	32%	8	21%	10	29%
150+	21	57%	22	52%	15	41%	19	48%	12	35%
Total	37	100%	42	100%	37	100%	39	100%	34	100%

Rank	1988		1989		1990		1991		1992		TOTAL	
0–10	0	0%	3	9%	1	3%	3	10%	4	10%	12	3%
11–50	7	22%	3	9%	5	14%	2	6%	7	18%	44	12%
51–100	8	25%	2	6%	3	9%	11	36%	8	20%	63	17%
101–150	8	25%	13	38%	14	40%	9	29%	10	25%	102	29%
150+	9	28%	13	38%	12	34%	6	19%	11	27%	140	39%
Total	32	100%	34	100%	35	100%	31	100%	40	100%	361	100%

* Correspondents who had less than five reports during the year(s) were not included in the study.

In each individual year, there was no more than one woman among the top ten correspondents until 1989, when there were three: Lesley Stahl (CBS), Andrea Mitchell (NBC), and Rita Braver (CBS). The top ranks of women correspondents were dominated by CBS. In 1992, for example, six of the top eight women correspondents came from CBS. During most of the decade, no ABC correspondent was among the top 10 and, in some years, not in the top 50. By 1992, each network had roughly the same number of female correspondents in the study (ABC, 14; CBS, 12; NBC, 14), but CBS clearly provided higher visibility for its women. Women were reporting 20 percent of all network stories in 1992 but 27 percent of the stories on CBS.

Assignment location influenced visibility for both male and female correspondents. The majority of the highly rated correspondents over the ten-year period were assigned to Washington. The White House provided an automatic entry to the evening news regardless of sex. The assignment of three women at the White House over the last decade (Lesley Stahl, Susan Spencer, and Andrea Mitchell) gave them automatic top-ten exposure. When no woman was listed in the top ten, no woman was assigned to the White House full time.

DISCUSSION

The earlier version of this study, covering the years 1983–89, painted a grim picture of women's visibility on the network evening news. According to the data, women correspondents "were locked into a static underclass, going neither up nor down. Some correspondents gained high visibility each year, but usually these were substitutions, not expansions." These results were surprising because one would have presumed at least some upward mobility in one of the most visible professions in an industry that was presumed to have a good record of inclusion.

Women were making gains as anchors of high-profile prime-time magazine programs, but these were token gains compared to the correspondent corps, where most of the network women worked. Except for an assignment on a prime-time news program, correspondents gained status within the organization by their ability to gain access to the flagship evening newscast. Most women correspondents did not receive the quality, permanent assignments that guaranteed regular visibility. Many were left dangling in low-visibility general-assignment positions while men got the favored Washington beats where exposure was guaranteed. If a "B" team of less-favored correspondents who received marginal assignments and little airtime existed in network news, women were clearly overrepresented. The majority of women correspondents got on the air less than twice a month.

The addition of three more years to the database has changed the portrait of women's visibility on network news. A trend of upward mobility began in

1991 that continued in 1992. Not only were there more women reporting, but the majority of women by 1992 had moved into the ranks of the top 100 correspondents. At CBS, women were reporting one out of every four stories on the evening news, a percentage never approached in the early years of the study.

To a significant degree, the women were helped by the misfortune of the male correspondents, whose ranks were devastated by the upheaval of the networks beginning in 1985. In seven years, nearly 30 percent of the men were gone, creating greater opportunities for women. Because fewer correspondents were left to fill the requisite 22 minutes of airtime, the networks no longer had the luxury of having reporters who never got on the air. Therefore, many women moved up the exposure ladder.

Another factor helping women's visibility was the growing sensitization of the networks to the plight of women. After several reports documented the lack of visibility of women correspondents on the network evening news in the late 1980s, management seemed to make a conscious effort to provide women with higher quality assignments. During this period, there were ongoing discussions between management and women correspondents concerning their visibility.

The earlier study reported that discouraged younger women were leaving the networks, but better conditions seem to have stopped that trend. Most women entering the correspondent corps now have a better chance of exposure than their predecessors. Questions still remain, however, concerning the life span of high seniority women correspondents. Veteran women correspondents worry about aging in an insecure environment where a woman's appearance might mean the difference between getting an assignment or even keeping their job. It is too early to ascertain whether the aging of women correspondents is as serious a problem as it appears. Certainly first-wave women like Marlene Sanders and Marya McLaughlin found the networks no longer interested in their services. The real test will come when the second, larger wave of women move past their 50s. The inclusion of age as a variable in future studies of this type would help in following this trend. In this study, the women with moderate to high visibility at the beginning of the study continued to sustain exposure at the end.

A significant factor in women gaining higher visibility on the evening news during the 1990s will be the quality of assignments they can draw. Women remain badly underrepresented at the prestige beats, but the assignment of two women simultaneously to the White House recently was a major step forward. General assignment reporters may have surges in exposure from covering elections, natural disasters, riots, and so forth, but this exposure often does not have long-term impact on their careers. If upward mobility is to continue for women, assignments to the Pentagon, State Department, Capitol, and similar power beats must follow.

Executives at the networks and local stations should have no shortage of women to choose from in future years. With more women than men graduating from mass-communication programs, the prospect of a "pink ghetto" effect with lower pay scales and lower professional status may pose a larger problem in the long run to women journalists than the visibility inequalities described in this chapter. Educators fear that depressed pay and stunted upward mobility may discourage outstanding students, female and male, from pursuing careers in broadcast journalism.

The contrast in results between an earlier version of this study and the current one demonstrates the importance of having an ongoing census of correspondents' visibility to provide a definitive portrait of dynamic trends in the workplace; it can be misleading to rely on a single snapshot. Further longitudinal research should document women's exposure on other network news programs and on other networks, such as CNN, National Public Radio, and local television news. Employment trends for those behind the camera in production, bureaus, and executive positions should especially be examined. There is also a need to evaluate the quality and quantity of exposure to determine how well each does and if women are given assignments and stories comparable to men.

REFERENCES

Alter, J. & Weather, D. (1985, July 22). TV women: Give us some air. *Newsweek*, 70.

Flander, J. (1985, March). Women in network news: Have they arrived or is their prime time past. *Washington Journalism Review*, pp. 39–43.

Foote, J. (1992). Women correspondents' visibility on the network evening news. *Mass Comm Review*, 19, 36–40.

Foote, J. (1985). Too many female TV correspondents stuck in "woman's ghetto." News release, Cornell University.

Fung, V. M. (1988, October). Anchor jobs go to young women and experienced men. *Washington Journalism Review*, pp. 20–24.

Hosley, D. H., & Yamada, G. K. (1987). *Hard news: Women in broadcast journalism*. New York: Greenwood Press.

Memorandum opinion and order and notice of proposed rulemaking to require broadcasters to show nondiscrimination in their employment practices, 13. (1968). Washington, DC: FCC, 2d 770; Report and order in the matter of petition for rulemaking to require broadcast licensees to show nondiscrimination in their employment practices, 23. (1970). Washington, DC: FCC, 2d 240.

Sanders, M. & Rock, M. (1988). *Waiting for prime time: The women of television news*. Urbana: University of Illinois Press.

Stone, V. A. (1988). Trends in the status of minorities and women in network news. *Journalism Quarterly, 65,* 290.

Stone, V. A. (1991, May). RTNDA Research. *Communicator,* 20–21.

Too many female TV correspondents stuck in "woman's ghetto." (1985, July 25). News release, Cornell University.

Zacks, R. (1988, February 13). *TV Guide,* A-5.

Ziegler, D., & White, A. (1990, Spring). Women and minorities on network television news: An examination of correspondents and newsmakers. *Journal of Broadcasting & Electronic Media, 34,* 215–23.

15

Career

JENNIFER SCHULZE:

*From Window Dressing on the Set
to WGN-TV News Director
—a 15-Year Odyssey*

SUSAN J. KAUFMAN

Susan J. Kaufman is an Associate Professor of Journalism at Eastern Illinois University, where she is also the director of Education and Outreach for the Radio Television Center and WEIU-TV. Her doctorate in educational administration was earned at Indiana State University. Her research interests include women and media, management, and leadership. She is currently co-editing a book on women's media and communications issues with Ramona Rush and Donna Allen with the working title: *Women Transforming Communications: Global Intersections for the 21st Century.*

Jennifer Schulze

I count myself among those who believe strongly that it is important for women to speak for themselves (Allen, 1989; 1991; Heilbrun, 1988), so it seemed that the best way to tell Jennifer Schulze's story was to have the news director do it herself. What follows are selected parts of an afternoon conversation with Schulze, videotaped in the loft apartment she and her husband, Chicago Alderman Edwin Eisendrath, share on Chicago's near north side.

Schulze is the oldest of six children. Her mother was a teacher until she had children. Her father was a dentist. He still pursues his long-time hobby of photography. Schulze grew up in Elk Grove Village, a northwest Chicago suburb.

Kaufman: What about those early years of grade school, friends? What were you into as a kid?

Schulze: As a little girl I used to write books about my siblings. (I'd) write them on pieces of paper, give them titles, staple them together, and have books and stories about the family. I was always trying to organize the neighborhood kids. I was the oldest of this tremendous group of children in this neighborhood by a couple of years and the only female. I used to put on plays, based on the popular movies of the time like *Oliver* and *The Sound of Music.* I used to put on circuses and carnivals. I was very active. They tell amazing stories about the things I used to do, and they're not necessarily happy about the things I used to do. At a recent wedding—my sister got married—and one of the old neighbor boys came up to my fiancé [Eisendrath] and said, "Did you know that your soon-to-be wife used to tie ropes around me and my brothers and her brothers and make us be the horsies and she would be like in the wagon train and she

In preparing an edited version of the transcribed videotape for use here, it was necessary to cut substantial portions of the interview. It also became necessary to reorganize some of the interview so that cohesive parts came together within the printed context. Similarly, there were times when conversational repeats of phrases and thoughts were edited out, in an effort to preserve the flow of the message. Jennifer Schulze has read and approved this edited version for publication.

would make us run around the neighborhood?" And that gives you an idea how things worked.

Kaufman: So in growing up, did you have a sense of who or what you wanted to be?

Schulze: When I was a little kid I wanted to be a dancer, some sort of performer. I wanted to be an actress, a dancer, a singer. And then suddenly I wanted to be an artist. I took all the lessons: dance lessons, gymnastics. I was in the school plays, but I wasn't very talented. As I started to grow taller, become more awkward, it became readily apparent I wouldn't be able to do any of those performance things, because I was totally uncoordinated and, frankly, quite unattractive in that puberty stage. So then I decided I wanted to be an artist. I wanted to be creative. So, junior highish into high school, I thought, "I want to be an artist!" In fact my junior high yearbook, where it says your name and what you want to be when you grow up? Mine says "artist." I was, again, not very good at that, either. I could go to a point and that was it. But I had all the things. I took art lessons, I had all the supplies. My mother made sure that I had all these things so that if there was some ability there it would be nurtured.

(Schulze's dad taught her to use his Leica when she was in junior high school. Pictures of friends and family came first, then she moved into more serious work.)

Schulze: Well, then I said, "If I'm not going to be an artist, because I'm not creative enough, maybe I'll be a photographer! But I don't want to be an artsy photographer, I want it to have a little bit of an edge, so photojournalism seemed to be the right thing for me. I can be creative but also make a statement about something." And so I did that for a while.

(She did it through high school, working on the school yearbook and eventually becoming its photo editor. In addition to photography, she took courses in writing, editing, and layout and design. And in high school, she found her first mentor.)

Schulze: I had a high school teacher, Laverne Holt. She was the high school yearbook editor [adviser] and English teacher at Elk Grove Village High School. She was the one who counseled me about what to do next. She spent a lot of time with me, paid a lot of attention to me, and was a really great role model for me. I had determined by that point that I wanted to go into journalism and take pictures for *Newsweek* magazine or the *New York Times.* She counseled me to learn how to write as well as take pictures because then I would be more valuable. She said, "A lot of people just take pictures. You have an opportunity, you have some skills here to learn to write too, so that when you go into Afghanistan or wherever, you can tell the story completely." She was the one who counseled me to go to the University of Illinois. I didn't get in because I muffed my application form, and then I was depressed.

My father had a mid-life crisis when I was about 16. It took him about a year to figure out where he wanted to move and what kind of a job he wanted to take. That was between my junior and senior year of high school. They moved to east central Illinois and I stayed here and lived at my girlfriend's. The deal was I had to graduate early, then move home with my parents and figure out where I was going to go to college. I was so traumatized by the whole thing and not getting accepted at the college of my choice, because I screwed up the application, that I neglected to find another college to go to until the very last minute. . . .

(A relative saw to it that Schulze entered Eastern Illinois University, in Charleston.)

My parents didn't want me to go out of state. I was a party gal. So, I ran around a lot. Went to a lot of parties. Drank a lot of beer in high school, stayed out late. Got grounded all the time. My parents were very concerned. "When is this girl going to settle down?" I wanted to go to a school with a good photojournalism program and have a good time, skiing . . . maybe Vermont . . . Colorado.

My parents said, "No, way! You're not going to get out of our sight."

(At Eastern Illinois, Schulze pursued photography, working on the student newspaper and becoming its photo editor, but that wasn't enough.)

Schulze: Somewhere along the line, I can't remember what happened, but I know that I felt like it got to a point where, first of all, I didn't think there were many opportunities in photojournalism, for me, for women, for anybody. I didn't know that I necessarily had great ability at it. I knew the basics. Professional photography types told me I had a great eye. I just started to think that that wasn't enough, and people started to talk to me and ask if I'd ever thought about television. And a woman from a television station in Decatur, I don't remember her position, but she came to talk to us in my sophomore or junior year at Eastern. She said, "Why don't you consider taking video for television?" Eastern didn't have that kind of thing. I had no exposure to that kind of thing. I thought, "I love television!" People would say when I was growing up, "Why don't you be Barbara Walters?" because Barbara Walters was the only woman on television, really, when I was growing up. While I was growing up she was the only person that people generally recognized in news.

(The summer between her junior and senior year, Schulze got an internship at WTWO-TV, the NBC affiliate in Terre Haute, Indiana, about 50 miles east of Charleston. She recalls going into the internship thinking this was just another way of taking pictures, and then was shocked when station news managers wanted to put her on the air as a reporter.)

Schulze: I had no idea, no exposure, no nothing. No classes in school. I was clueless. I'd barely figured out how to hoist the big camera up on my shoulders. That was the time you still had that big audiocassette thing, so you're lugging around this 30-pound recorder. I remember my first time out in the field with this thing, and they're training me, and it's a story about a road and I'm down there taking pictures of gravel and I'm falling. It was awful. Then they said, "Why don't you go to the Special Olympics and do this story?" and I said, "What? What do you mean? How do you do that?" Nobody told me how to do that. Nobody told me how to be on TV. Now that I look back on it, it was really frustrating and awful. And the story was awful. I did it. I didn't know what I was doing. I followed some of the training I had in journalism school and I asked the right questions. I didn't understand the medium at all. I didn't know what to say. Didn't know how to look. I had the wrong hair, wrong makeup, I had on a T-shirt. So it was a disaster. They didn't think it was, so they had me do it the next day and the next day and the next day and the next day.

(Schulze wasn't paid to do her internship. In fact, most television internships are still unpaid positions. To pay for gas from her parent's home to Terre Haute she'd taken on a second job with a newspaper in Paris, Illinois.)

Schulze: At the same time I'm working in the morning at the *Paris Beacon News* as a reporter/photographer. I'd get in at 8 and work until noon, drive from Paris to Terre Haute (a half-hour to 45-minute drive), and work in Terre Haute from, like, 2 until 10, and I did that all summer long. That was a hell of a summer. I learned a lot from that experience. I never had a soul in my first couple years who said, "This is how this is done." I never had classes where people said, "This is how you write copy for television." I never had anyone talk to me about putting together a television story at any level, or the performance aspect of it. I had no help. I was out there winging it. So I'd watch the network news, or I'd watch the local news.

(Schulze says these early experiences are why she goes out of her way to help young people today, working with college students, returning to her own alma mater and other campuses to talk with young journalists.)

Schulze: I like to be like someone's big sister. I'm doing that with my own sister right now. She wants to be a TV reporter. People were always willing to tell you what button to push, but they probably didn't know enough themselves to give advice about what direction to take or to say, "Why don't you stand this way? Why don't you fix your hair like this? Why don't you do your makeup this way?" I remember the first time I went on TV on the set and did a story. No one knew what to tell me about how I should do my hair, what makeup to wear. They were all men. The men didn't know. They just slapped orange makeup on their faces and they didn't really worry about it. I spent about an hour in the bathroom before the 10 o'clock news on Saturday putting on makeup. I figured, "Television and bright lights: just put on more of the same." So I come out of there and I have a clown face. I go on television. I have tons of hair spray, too much makeup. My family's watching at home. They said it was awful. And it *was* awful. Bright lipstick, blush, makeup. No one at that television station knew enough to tell me what I should be doing. There was only one other woman on the air there. Her name was Debbie Reynolds. I'd say Debbie, "What should I do?" She'd say, "I don't know. They haven't told me either!"

(Whatever Schulze was doing, she was impressing the managers at WTWO. Her senior year of college she was hired to work weekends as an assignment editor, producer, and reporter.)

Schulze: Someone else would go out and take pictures of a story. What I didn't understand then and I understand now was that they wanted another woman on TV on the set. We had a female weathercaster. We had a female anchor and a male anchor and a male sportscaster, and then I would show up as window dressing on the set at 5 and 10 o'clock every night on a story that I hadn't reported. I would just do what they told me to. I didn't know anything about television. And so I would sit there and I would deliver a story about a traffic accident in Terre Haute, or sometimes I would take the network video and say, "A thousand people died in Bangladesh." But I hadn't done any of the reporting on any of this stuff. But I was there delivering it as another female on television. Every Saturday and Sunday night, there I was. And I would work these really long shifts, 12 hours a day, and then I'd drive back to college (at least an hour's drive) on Sunday nights at midnight. It was an interesting year.

(During her senior year in college, Schulze wrote a paper on women in broadcasting. She consulted with Paul Davis, the news director at WCIA-TV, the CBS affiliate in Champaign, Illinois. Davis's mother, Zona B. Davis, of Effingham, Illinois, was the first woman to work as a radio news director in the United States. Paul Davis gave Schulze her next job; ironically, when she took over the helm at WGN-TV in 1993, it was Paul Davis she replaced.)

Schulze: I was hired [*pause*] . . . I know the reason I was hired. I was hired because of the way I looked. The news director thought I was attractive, and he liked my legs. And to this day he tells people that. I'm not happy about that. I'd like to think that I was hired because I had previous television experience, I was smart, I had a good resumè, I knew the area, and all those good reasons. And he continually tells people that I was hired because when I walked into his office I had a dress on and he liked my legs.

There weren't very many women there, and they certainly didn't work as a group. There wasn't any mentoring going on there or even colleague-to-colleague kind of stuff. It was pretty much every person for themselves [*sic*]. In Champaign the level of news was a little bit higher, but it wasn't a lot of enterprise reporting. It was event stuff, it was stuff that somebody else had set up: the opening of a mall, a press conference, a dead body. It wasn't stuff we were usually going out and developing. The news was a little bit better, but not much.

(Schulze spent two years trying to move out of Champaign. She started work on a master's degree at the University of Illinois and found her way to WLS-TV in Chicago as vacation relief.)

Schulze: The networks were fat. They brought in folks to fill in for union employees taking vacation. I was hired as a vacation relief news writer. At the time, I was hired into a newsroom that was dominated by men. There was a male news director. Every management job was filled by a man, and every show producer job was held by a man. I knew it was going to be a struggle. All the guys hung around together. Most of the managers had worked at two or three television stations together prior to landing in Chicago. They were a group. They weren't going to let anyone into that inner circle, no way! And they hired men just like them to produce the news. It was interesting. They were all White males of a certain physical build, and they would all dress alike. There was no breaking into this circle. I was hired with three or four other people. Of course the day you walk in you're very excited, it's a big step. And for me, to be back in my hometown working at a big television station, it was a wonderful thing. I was making a ton more money than I was making in Champaign, and I was very excited to be there and a little bit overwhelmed, because it was a totally different scene. There were 160 people in the newsroom and I'd come from a place where maybe there were 30?

(Schulze had produced a couple of noon newscasts in Champaign, and she'd liked it. She set her sights on being a producer at WLS-TV).

Schulze: The minute you walk in the door, aside from being thrilled that you're there, you start to figure out how you're going to get them to give you a full-time job. This was a six-month job. It was a full-time job with no benefits, no permanence. You had to join the union, but you had no security. Immediately you start figuring out who you have to impress to give you a job. It became pretty clear, pretty early, that I was going to have trouble with that because there was not much penetrating this male group here. The two male news writers who came into the group got jobs before the women did. And within a year, one of those men was producing the news. And I knew that he was producing the news because he was drinking buddies with these guys. You were stuck. You'd say to yourself, "I know that I'm at least as talented as this person. I'm not even going to get a shot here. I'm not buddies with these guys, they're not going to give me the time of day. They think that I'm exactly where I need to be and they're not going to pay any attention to me. They're not going to try and nurture me in any way. They've got their team, that's it."

Eventually, though, I finally got recognized by these guys, and they started to say things like, "Wow, she can really do this well. She can really turn out these stories quickly." They started to assign me to more high-profile things. Eventually, they put me on as news writer for the late news and made me part of what they called the A-team. There were three guys, one woman—me. We were the main writers for the 10 o'clock news, which was the big news.

"And then, much to my delight, they hired a woman to come in and produce the 10 o'clock news. Thank God! There was a woman in there who had the moxie to kind of break into the boy's group, and she then became a mentor to me—Phyllis Schwartz, now the news director at WLS-TV. Phyllis and I became good friends right away. Phyllis was doing the job I wanted to do. And she helped me do that. She would talk to me about the work. There was a dialogue where there had not been one before.

I pressed to become a show producer, because the road to success behind the scenes to management was news writer, producer, manager. I knew that to get ahead I needed to produce, and the managers just wouldn't give me the time of day. They would say, "You're one of five people who want to do this, and what makes you think that you'd be better than anyone else?" And I'd say, "I know I can do this, just give me a chance," and they wouldn't.

Then suddenly, two people quit to go on to other jobs in the same week, and they were desperate. They came to me and asked me if I could produce the early weekend news. "Yeah, this is great! I really want to do it. You should have trained me, because now you're throwing me into something I do not know how to do."

I knew I could do it, but I thought I was at a great disadvantage. This is a very high-pressure job, I'd never even been given the opportunity to parallel somebody and watch them while they did it. They threw me in there cold. They had the other weekend producer help me, but I was doing the job. There was no training. They were short. They had not done any long-range planning. They had no contingency plan, they just said, "Boom, you're in there!"

So there I am producing the news at WLS. I don't have a clue what I'm doing. They seemed to think I was doing an okay job. They left me there. Frankly, I didn't do it for very long. It got to a point where there was some more movement. Phyllis became executive producer of the 10 o'clock news. Then, the person who was producing the 10 o'clock news left. She went to management and told them she wanted me to do it. They said, "but she's only been producing for a couple months." She said, "I don't care, I know she can do it. We think alike and I want her to do this job!" So there I was producing the 10 o'clock news, which was the number one newscast in Chicago. I'd been a show producer for all of four months. We figured it out. We worked real well together. Had Phyllis not done that for me, who knows what would have happened to me. That was a very significant move in my career. Huge! Huge!

(Schulze did extremely well producing the 10 o'clock news at WLS. She was the kind of producer a news director wanted in the control room when all hell broke loose, as it often did in the Windy City. After two years, she knew she'd hit the wall. Her first marriage was in a shambles, and she wanted a personal life.)

Schulze: My personal life was lousy. I had done it. I had done it well and I had enough. We'd get off after late news and party. I wanted a personal life. I'd worked weekends. I was never home. I asked them (management) if I could be a regular person for once in my life. I'd had Thanksgiving off twice in 14 or 15 years. I'd worked Christmas . . . you just don't have a life. I've worked with people who have let television ruin their personal lives. People in TV news who've been married, divorced, married, divorced. Lots of drinking, drugs, short fuses.

People whose lives are a little lopsided. Now I have a practice where I don't socialize much with the people I work with. I think you should remain a little detached. You block out a good part of the community if you don't.

(Those were rough years. In 1989, she received a terrible blow. Her sister Ellen, just graduated from the University of Illinois engineering school and working her first job with the Illinois Department of Transportation, was killed at a construction site in Champaign. Ellen's death had a profound effect on the entire family. To Schulze, the message was clear: "If you want to do something, do it. Take a couple chances, but don't wait around for things, because you don't necessarily have time on your side." With her life stabilizing a bit as producer of the 5 o'clock news, Schulze began to look seriously at moving into management.)

Schulze: The people whom I was working with, except for Phyllis Schwartz, weren't doing a very good job. A lot of people above me didn't have the experience I had in television and were bad managers. I think people in television tend to be bad managers because we get ahead because we're good at journalism, good at writing. But we have no management training along the way. Suddenly, we're thrust into this job and you've gotten there because you produced really good newscasts, but not because you manage people really well. And suddenly there you are. Most of the managers I had knew little or nothing of feedback, team building, motivation. I decided I would be pretty good at this. My news management didn't agree with me. They thought I should go to a smaller market. They thought I wasn't ready.

(The folks at KING-TV in Seattle, Washington, thought differently. They hired Schulze as executive producer, part of a team brought in to rebuild a once-mighty station gone wrong.)

Schulze: We were in a rebuild situation. They had hired a new news director and me to fix it. I learned a whole lot about managing people. I had a lot to learn. I had had particularly bad news managers along the way. I remembered the things I didn't like as an employee and did the opposite. I also asked the employees, "What do you think?" People want to know what's going on. They want to be in the loop. This is what I'm doing. I ask them, "What do you think?" Or, I'll say, "Help me solve this problem." People don't like to be kept in the dark. I had the ability to hire a bunch of people in Seattle: 18 people. Diversity was very important. Bob Jordan (the news director) believed that a television station at every level should reflect the community. Seattle had a large Asian population and smaller Black community. We were underrepresented by women. I actively recruited women producers, reporters, and anchors. I didn't hire too many White males when I was there. There were enough of them. There're always enough of them. They're already there, they've already had the job. I went out of my way to hire women and minorities. And I was looking for women who wanted to move into management. I try to encourage women— especially college students—to consider other jobs behind the scenes, and those are the jobs that lead to power and influence and money. You don't have to be an anchorwoman. They see Barbara Walters on TV, but they don't see her producer. There are three female news directors in Chicago at this point in time. I know that I was hired in Seattle because I was a woman. I like to think I was also hired because I had big market experience, because I was good at what I did. But I know I wasn't hired because I had good legs. In fact, I made a point of wearing pants when I went to the interview.

(In her two-and-a-half years in Seattle, Schulze made quite a splash. She had numerous job offers. But her heart, and Edwin Eisendrath, were still in Chicago. She came back to Chicago without a job, but quickly got one as executive producer of WMAQ. She talked about her career with her advisers: Bob Jordan, Phyllis Schwartz, and "a couple other women friends in television: anchorwomen, and producers, who all said, 'It's better to have a job than not have a job.'" Five months later, WGN-TV called and asked if she'd be their news director.)

Schulze: And I said, "When do I start?" I've always wanted to be a news director.

(We took the Emmy off Schulze's bookshelf and placed it on the table to her right. She'd won the Emmy in 1986 as part of a WLS-TV group responsible for live, continuous news coverage of flooding in suburban Chicago. As the tape rolled and she started to talk in the last segment of our interview, Schulze traced her finger lightly along the statuette's base and grasped the feet of the woman holding the globe in her outstretched arms. "You shouldn't judge your success on awards and things like that. You never win when you really deserve it, when you really did great work.")

Schulze: This is a big deal to win one, but I have since learned that your best work doesn't always get acknowledged by awards. But it's fun to have one. Now I have one, I don't have to have another one.

Kaufman: What do you consider your best work?

Schulze: To date my best work is the rebuilding of KING-TV. That's the thing I'm most proud of. Soon I hope to be able to say that about WGN, but I'm not there yet. That will take me a while. A year from now I would like to be able to say my best work was rebuilding WGN news.

(Schulze's workday at WGN, with more than 36 million viewers, usually runs 11 hours, and she still brings work home. She says she doesn't see herself as a risk-taker. She strategizes. "Things don't happen by chance. I'm always taking steps for the next step. I'm always trying to take a step ahead in my mind." As for potential conflicts of interest between her alderman husband's job and her own . . .)

Schulze: It's never been a problem for us. It has been a concern of prospective employers, colleagues. They'll ask, "Well, how do we handle this?" I tell them, "If my husband is in the news I will not participate in any of the editorial decisions involving that particular story." And then, I tell them, "You should, in turn, not come to me for insider information." I've had that happen in previous jobs. Edwin is so busy and involved with his job and I am with mine that we frequently don't know a lot of what the other one is doing. We know big-picture things. It's not a problem for my employer. It certainly doesn't seem to hurt anything, but I don't know that it helps.

REFERENCES

Allen, D. (1989). *Directory of women's media.* Washington, DC: Women's Institute for Freedom of the Press.

Allen, D. (1991). *Media without democracy and what to do about it.* Washington, DC: Women's Institute for Freedom of the Press.

Heilbrun, C. G. (1988). *Writing a woman's life.* New York: W. W. Norton.

In 1982, Barbara Walters pointed out that she was generally considered to be the "Grande Dame" or the old broad—depending on your bias—of television news. She was fifty. Dan Rather was considered the brash young kid when he replaced Walter Cronkite. He was also fifty. (Ellerbee, 1986, p. 100)

16

Criticism

WOMEN IN BROADCAST NEWS:

More than Window Dressing on the Set, Less than Equal with Men

SUE A. LAFKY

Sue Lafky, Assistant Professor of Journalism and Mass Communication at the University of Iowa, earned her Ph.D. from Indiana University. Her publications include "The Progress of Women and People of Color in the U.S. Journalistic Work Force," "A Long, Slow Journey" in Creedon's (ed.) *Women in Mass Communication* (2nd Ed.), and "Women Journalists" in Weaver and Wilhoit's *The American Journalist.* Lafky is a founding member of the Feminist Teacher Editorial Collective and has worked on newspapers in Oregon and Indiana.

In the beginning, there was Edward R. Murrow. He gained the respect and admiration of millions of Americans, first during World War II with his live radio broadcasts from London rooftops as Germans bombed the city, and then in the postwar years with his hard-hitting television documentaries and his challenge to the excesses of an anti-communist senator from Wisconsin named Joseph R. McCarthy (Sperber, 1986).

The men who worked at CBS with this "founding father" of television news, and who followed in his footsteps, were known as Murrow's boys. Edward R. Murrow's name and heroism were invoked in the news department of CBS for many years to come, and his legacy is still invoked when broadcast journalists gather together and remember past days of glory.

"There was in Murrow a quality that moved people," Barbara Matusow wrote in her book *The Evening Stars*. "As a broadcaster he made a deep impact with his rich, resonant voice and his elegant but restrained prose" (1983, p. 52).

Murrow's most famous successor at CBS was Walter Cronkite, who became a national icon in his own right. Cronkite's authority as an anchor was so uncontested that he could, without arousing protest, end each evening's broadcast with the reassuring and fatherly words, "And that's the way it is."

Indeed, Cronkite was so popular and revered that CBS executives began to worry years before his retirement about who would replace him to carry on the Murrow legacy.

Cronkite's retirement on March 9, 1981, marked a changing of the guard. Yet one thing that did not change was the perception on the part of the CBS management that someone with a rich, resonant voice—a male—should read the news to America each evening. Cronkite's replacement was Dan Rather.

The other networks followed a similar model in hiring individuals to fill the evening anchor slot, and little had changed by 1988, when veteran broadcaster Marlene Sanders, in her book *Waiting for Prime Time*, observed, "It is still being debated whether a woman's voice could hold the nation's attention in the anchor position on the main news broadcasts" (Sanders and Rock, 1988, p. 13). An anchor position on the CBS Evening News was coveted by women seeking equality with men in journalism:

> The Rather broadcast counted for everything, and if you didn't meet its producers' standard of charisma, looks or age, no matter how good you were, you were not part of the group that mattered (Sanders & Rock, 1988, pp. 1–2).

On June 1, 1993, the physical qualifications of those on the list of who mattered changed when the network added a seat at Rather's anchor desk for veteran journalist Connie Chung. With that change, *The CBS Evening News with Dan Rather* became *The CBS Evening News with Dan Rather and Connie Chung*. "It's the 1990s," Rather told reporters during a celebratory news conference announcing the new partnership (Marin, 1993, p. 8).

Chung's promotion to Rather's side clearly marks progress for women in broadcast news, just as Diane Sawyer's success in landing a $7-million-a-year contract with ABC is an important landmark for women in broadcast journalism (Marin, 1994, pp. 8–14). However, such accomplishments are the exception rather than the rule. The contributions of most women in broadcast journalism remain undervalued in comparison to the value placed on the contributions of their male colleagues. This chapter examines the participation of women in the broadcast news industry and the types of barriers women face in broadcast journalism, as well as standards of femininity that have historically limited the ways women have presented and covered television news. As the title of this chapter suggests—borrowing from the title of a 1977 report by the U.S. Commission on Civil Rights—women and people of color still too often serve as little more than *Window Dressing on the Set*.

So while it is important to celebrate the rise of a Chinese-American woman to the position of permanent co-anchor on a major evening news show, or the successes of famous female journalists such as Diane Sawyer or Barbara Walters, it is also important to acknowledge that women and people of color are still far from achieving equal footing with White men in the broadcast industry. As of 1992, people of color made up only 11.8 percent of the television newsroom work force, and Asian Americans made up only 1 percent of U.S. newsrooms as a whole (Weaver & Wilhoit, 1992, p. 6). Furthermore, both statistical and anecdotal evidence suggest that women face more barriers in television newsrooms than they do in other segments of the mass media work force.

HISTORICAL CONTEXT

Like many journalists in the early years of television, Pauline Frederick gained her start in radio, making her debut in 1939 with an interview for NBC radio with the wife of a Czechoslovakian foreign minister after Hitler invaded her country. Frederick later undertook radio freelancing work from overseas, but despite her tenacity, vast knowledge, and well-honed skills, she found it difficult to land a regular job in broadcast journalism.

While seeking out a full-time position with a network, Frederick worked as a stringer for ABC and found herself relegated to stories involving so-called women's issues. Thus, the astute political observer found herself assigned to covering a forum on "How to Get a Husband" and a market rush on nylon hosiery (Hosley & Yamada, 1987, pp. 62–66). However, she also became well known for her exclusive and perceptive radio reports from the United Nations.

Frederick's entrance into television came in 1948, when she was asked to help cover the first televised Democratic National Convention, held in Philadelphia. TV news departments were not nearly as sophisticated in show business practices as they are today, so she found herself in charge of her own makeup for the cameras as well as the makeup for the women she was assigned to interview, including First Lady Bess Truman and actress-turned-New-Deal-politician Helen Gahagan Douglas.

After the convention, Frederick divided her time between radio and television broadcasts at ABC, with six regular radio broadcasts each day and three television programs every week, including a non-news television show on Saturdays.

Frederick was hired by NBC in 1953, where she covered the United Nations and the 1956 political conventions. Her United Nations coverage included the Cuban missile crisis as well as China's admission into the United Nations. After retiring from NBC in 1974, Frederick worked as an international analyst for National Public Radio. When she died in 1990, at the age of 84, Frederick was remembered as someone who opened doors for women's acceptance in television and radio journalism (Associated Press, 1990).

By 1960, things had improved a bit for women. Each of the television networks employed one woman correspondent (Marzolf, 1993, p. 36). Marlene Sanders broke a barrier for women when she became the first woman to anchor a network evening news program in 1964 when the regular anchorman, Ron Cochran, lost his voice. Her access to the anchor seat at ABC was short-lived and confined to weekends, however, and she quit broadcasting after she was relegated to an off-hours shift usually reserved for entry-level journalists. During these years, just about the only work women could get on television involved working for programs aimed at homemakers or serving as on-air decorations while reading the weather report. For women, the prestigious anchor position seemed to be an endless revolving door that turned only on weekends and during non–prime-time hours.

Thus, it was seen as a victory for the women's movement when ABC paired Barbara Walters at the evening news anchor desk with Harry Reasoner in 1976. But even though ABC had a more permanent position in mind for Walters, the anchor position also turned out to be a revolving door for her. During her brief tenure in the anchor seat, Walters faced personality conflicts with Reasoner as well as sniping from fellow journalists about the details of her $1 million contract and lack of "hard" journalistic experience. There was much "sputtering and harrumphing in the press about whether a 'celebrity interviewer' like Walters was fit to share an anchor desk with a 'real journalist' like Harry Reasoner" (Holston, 1993, p. 1E). Walters also endured negative reactions from some audience members not accustomed to seeing women in the anchor seat. The prejudice perpetuated by colleagues in the newsroom is not the only type of prejudice that women TV journalists face.[1] Matusow described the pairing of Walters and Reasoner as a "fiasco" (1983, p. 199).

1. See also Vernon Stone's article (1973–74) in which he describes the results of a survey dealing with attitudes toward TV newswomen. Stone's research indicated that television news directors overestimated the audience resistance to women on-air reporters. In fact, although most of the news directors said they thought their viewers would prefer to see a man in the anchor seat, the most frequent response in all the audience groups surveyed (university students, university professors, fourth and fifth graders, and parents in a small town) said that it made no difference to them whether the newscaster was a man or a woman.

Yet even before the "fiasco," Walters had discovered that television news was a man's world and that discrimination against women in the work force existed in subtle as well as not-so-subtle forms (Benokraitis & Feagin, 1986). For example, after Walters was hired as the first woman writer for *The Today Show* in 1961, producer Fred Freed assigned another staff member to take Walters to lunch and make sure she wasn't "difficult"—a label that many women who have sought equality with men have found themselves wearing. "The prevailing feeling among men in the business at the time was that the few women in television were 'bitches' who were impossible to work with," wrote Jerry Oppenheimer in his biography of Walters (1990, p. 110).

In an interview years later, Walters recalled: "I was not allowed to write anything for men. I couldn't write anything that supposedly was hard news, or that had to do with science, or that had to do with economics" (Remington, 1992, p. F2). Furthermore, as co-host of *The Today Show*, Walters was not allowed to ask questions of political guests until after her male colleagues had asked three questions first.

CURRENT STATUS OF WOMEN IN TOP POSTS

Women, as well as people of color, have endured what scholars Jannette Dates and William Barlow have called a split image, meaning that they are considered good enough to be seen up front and on camera, but not to be trusted with the reins of power (Dates & Barlow, 1990; Thornton, 1990, p. 390). A 1992 survey of U.S. television stations found that women made up only 17 percent of the news directors (Stone, 1993, p. 68).[2]

In an article for a special issue of the *Media Studies Journal* (1993), 18 deans and directors of university journalism and mass communication programs rated various media industries on their treatment of women employees. These academic leaders have firsthand knowledge about where the women who make up 60 percent of their enrollments go after graduation. This survey graded nine media industries for their efforts in hiring, developing, and promoting women.

Overall, the electronic media—made up of television, cable, and radio— were graded lower than other media industries, with both the radio and cable industries earning grades of C+ and television earning a B-. In contrast, public relations earned an A- in the survey, advertising earned a B+, and newspapers and magazines both earned B's. Meanwhile, the field of media research earned a B-, and the wire services earned a C. The results of the survey suggest that discrimination does not end after the hiring is completed.

---

2. Carole Simpson became the first African-American woman to anchor a network evening newscast in 1989. Her tenure? Two consecutive nights when she sat in for ABC's Peter Jennings (Noble, 1981).

LOOKS AND TV NEWS

CBS's teaming of Connie Chung with Dan Rather conforms to a formula that television news has used for many years, particularly in local markets—the mature, seasoned newsman and his younger, pretty TV "wife" (Holsten, 1993, p. 5B).

In this case, the mature, seasoned newsman was in his early 60s, and the younger, pretty TV "wife" was in her late 40s, making them both older than the typical on-camera person in local television news. As *TV Guide* writer Rick Marin observed: "It's a crude, sexist formula, but a proven ratings getter" (1993, p. 4).

In fact, the news conference announcing that Connie Chung was being paired with Dan Rather was treated by CBS as well as the rest of the news media like the announcement of the engagement of a royal couple, a perception not lost on *CBS Evening News* producer Erik Sorenson. "For better or worse, the Connies and Dans and Peter Jennings of the world are the kings and queens of the TV news world," he noted.

Even before the Rather/Chung news conference began, Sorenson saw too much distance between his celebrity co-anchors. "Shouldn't we be sitting closer together, you guys?" he cracked (Pergament, 1993, p. 6). The duo obliged by not only sitting closer together, but also by embracing and kissing as the announcement of the pending union was blessed in front of the assembled media guests.

Not everyone found such a spectacle appropriate for serious journalism. *New York Times* writer Frank Rich called the embrace of Chung and Rather "the most embarrassing photograph so far this year" (1993, section 6, p. 70). He added:

> Rather's clinch reduced the professional breakthrough of a journalist to the frivolous crowning of a prom queen. And his words about their future roles didn't exactly bail him out. Rather explained that he would now more often "get out to report on stories" while Chung minded the desk back home. He proudly referred to his new partner as "Miss Congeniality."
>
> Couldn't he have at least settled for Ms. Congeniality?

Meanwhile, a Gannett News Service columnist jokingly compared the first couple of network news to Princess Di and Prince Charles:

> Everyone said the union couldn't last.
>
> Yet the heir to Cronkite's kingdom and the energetic, younger newswoman gathered their peers and announced their intentions. And since their news conference, the world has been watching Connie Chung and Dan Rather "honeymoon" on the *CBS Evening News*.
>
> The Connie–Dan partnership has been the most talked about pairing since Charles and Diana (Van Valkenburg, 1993).

And just as great attention is placed on the sartorial finery of coronations and weddings, much attention was paid to what Rather and Chung wore during their first night as co-anchors. But in a sign that at least some aspects of the women's movement had affected their thinking, television critics strained themselves to achieve gender equity in their coverage of the fashion angle of the Chung/Rather story, with one reporter noting without irony that Rather "chose a charcoal gray suit and light gray tie" (Bark, 1993, p. 33A).

Patrick MacDonald, a television critic for the *Seattle Times*, also spent a substantial part of his review of the first night by taking note of how the news people looked.

> Chung, in a bright red collarless jacket accented by a black scarf, was her usual professional self, articulate and animated without being self-conscious. Her eyebrows were painted too high, giving her a look of perpetual surprise, but she wisely toned down her eye shadow with a subtle charcoal shade, rather than the purple stuff she used to cake on.
>
> While on the subject of the show's dress and makeup—television news is as much show business as it is journalism—Dan was dressed down, perhaps in deference to his new co-star. He wore a gray business suit with a white shirt and conservative silver tie with dots, and his hair was plastered down like a schoolboy ready for church (1993, p. E6).

Because television is a visual medium, it is not surprising that a high premium is placed on looks for both women and men. Rather made news years ago by wearing a sweater rather than a suit on the air. Then, while broadcasting from Des Moines, Iowa, during the summer 1993 floods, Rather made news again by wearing a shirt open at the collar that revealed his chest hair.

Indeed, many men have been told to part their hair on another side, shave a mustache, grow a mustache, or find a new suit to wear on the air. Furthermore, as Linda Ellerbee has observed with her sharp trademark humor: "There's no shortage of bubble-headed, bleached blonds who happen to have penises, and happen to be anchormen" (1986, p. 111).

Yet, as is true for society as a whole, the standards of beauty are not applied equally to the men and women of television news. For women, in particular, the emphasis on looking good is closely tied to an emphasis on looking young (Fung, 1988). Why else would older men in television news be described as having "credibility," while older women are seen as "washed up?" Observers such as Ellerbee have commented on the double standard for men and women in the TV news business.

> In 1982, Barbara Walters pointed out that she was generally considered to be the "Grande Dame" or the old broad—depending on your bias—of television news. She was fifty. Dan Rather was considered the brash young kid who had replaced Walter Cronkite. He was also fifty. It raises questions. (Ellerbee, 1986, p. 100)

Although Ellerbee's observation provided insights into perceptions of women on television and in society as a whole, Barbara Walters, like Rather (who has a contract with CBS News that runs until the year 2000), remains employed in television journalism more than a decade later, and celebrated her 15th anniversary with ABC in 1992. But Walters is an exception to the rule, and she still looks terrific.

Marlene Sanders is among the many who have observed that "younger women who hold positions as anchors seem to wash out in their forties," and not by their own choice (Sanders, 1988, pp. 147–148). This means that women in the field are out of their positions at precisely the moment when they have the most experience and are building up their authority. Meanwhile, their years of experience are not welcomed in management, where men make most of the decisions (Stone, 1993).

In a study of a television news operation in a mid-sized, midwestern community, Pamela Carstens found that men as well as women were frustrated with the emphasis on looks. Members of both groups have experienced being held back in television because of appearance. But besides not having the right look, women continue to find stereotypes about femininity limiting their story assignments, and women complained about being pigeon-holed into reporting on events that have a "human" angle that could benefit from a so-called feminine touch. Reporters described what might be called a cult of masculinity in the newsroom. Noted one reporter:

> Newsrooms often have one or two tough males who dominate the reporter staff. These males will get the tough stories—all the hard news. The fires, the murders (Carstens, 1993, p. 149).

Yet other journalists offered their opinion that gender stereotypes were breaking down, and almost all of the newsworkers said that they resented the overemphasis of form over substance that too often characterizes local television news. The newsworkers in Carstens's study agreed that "news directors have a responsibility to educate the audience" and to stress journalistic skills over visual appeal (1993, p. 237). However, the tyranny of trying to attract a large audience with appealing on-air personalities rather than quality reporting continues to limit the possibilities for reform of the current system. Carstens said:

> News directors seem much more willing to work on the skills or accept the poor skills of a person who has the looks, than to work on or accept the looks (p. 237).

CONCLUSION

Unfortunately, women continue to face barriers on the job that cannot be eliminated simply by signing legislation that calls for equal opportunity in hiring. In order to be successful, the struggle for equal opportunity in the broadcast work force must also draw from a broader movement for gender equity. This broader movement is one that, among other things, fights against unreasonable standards of physical attractiveness for women television journalists, "a male-dominated buddy system" that affects job referrals and leads to the promotion of more men than women into management positions, and negative attitudes toward the competency and effectiveness of women broadcast journalists (Ferri, 1988, p. 667). Until all people have equal opportunity in society as a whole, unequal treatment in the broadcast news industry will continue.

REFERENCES

Associated Press. (1990, May 14). Broadcaster Frederick dies.

Bark, Ed. (1993, June 2). Rather and Chung debut smoothly as co-anchors of CBS Evening News, *The Dallas Morning News*, p. 33A.

Beasley, M. H., & Gibbons, S. J. (1993). *Taking their place: A documentary history of women and journalism.* Washington, DC: The American University Press.

Benokraitis, N. V., & Feagin, J. R. (1986). *Modern sexism: blatant, subtle, and covert discrimination.* Englewood Cliffs, NJ: Prentice-Hall.

Carstens, P. J. (1993). *Selling the "show": A study of the impact of market pressures on a local television news department and its newsworkers.* Unpublished doctoral dissertation, University of Iowa, Iowa City.

Craft, C. (1988). *Too old, too ugly, and not deferential to men.* Rocklin, CA: Prima Pub. and Communications.

Dates, J. L., & Barlow, W. (Eds.). (1990). *Split image: African Americans in the mass media.* Washington, DC: Howard University Press.

Eddings, B. M. (1980). Women in broadcasting (U.S.) De Jure, De Facto. *Women's Studies International Quarterly 3*, 1–13.

Ellerbee, L. (1986). *"And so it goes": Adventures in television.* New York: G.P. Putnam's Sons.

Ferri, A. J. (1988). Perceived career barriers of men and women television news anchors. *Journalism Quarterly 65* (3), 661–667, 732.

A field guide for women in media industries. (1993, Winter/Spring). *Media Studies Journal*, 81–98.

Fields, B. (1993, August 9). TV weathermen forecast, but they don't tell all. *The Houston Chronicle*, p. A-11.

Fung, V. M. (1988, October). Sexism at the networks: Anchorjobs go to young women and experienced men. *Washington Journalism Review*, 20–24.

Gelfman, J. S. (1976). *Women in television news.* New York: Columbia University Press.

Holsten, C. (1993, January 15). Anchorwomen hope to come of age. *St. Petersburg (Fla.) Times*, p. 5B.

Holston, N. (1993, June 5). Chung and Rather? It's show biz, folks. *(Minneapolis) Star Tribune*, p. 1E.

Hosley, D. H., & Yamada, G. K. (1987). *Hard news: Women in broadcast journalism.* New York: Greenwood Press.

MacDonald, P. (1993, June 2). Dan and Connie show displays balance and potential. *Seattle Times,* p. E6.

Marin, R. (1993, June 5–11). Make room for Connie. *TV Guide,* 8–14.

Marin, R. (1994, March 26–April 1). Diane and the Art of the Deal. *TV Guide,* 8–14.

Marzolf, M. T. (1993, Winter/Spring). Deciding what's "women's news." *Media Studies Journal,* 33–47.

Matusow, B. (1983). *The evening stars: The making of the network news anchor.* New York: Ballantine.

Noble, G. (1981). *Black is the color of my TV tube.* Secaucus, NJ: Lyle Stuart.

Oppenheimer, J. (1990). *Barbara Walters: An unauthorized biography.* New York: St. Martin's Press.

Pergament, A. (1993, July 20). Team of Rather and Chung is window dressing for CBS. *The Buffalo (N.Y.) News,* p. 6.

Remington, B. (1992, February 9). "Baba Wawa" gets last laugh. *(Montreal) Gazette,* p. F2.

Rich, F. (1993, June 13). Endpaper/public stages; Whose Hillary? *New York Times,* section 6, p. 70.

Sanders, M., & Rock, M. (1988). *Waiting for prime time: The women of television news.* Urbana: University of Illinois Press.

Sperber, A. M. (1986). *Murrow: His life and times.* New York: Freundlich Books.

Stone, V. A. (1973–74). Attitudes toward television newswomen. *Journal of Broadcasting 18* (1), 49–62.

Stone V. A. (1993, August). Good news, bad news. *RTNDF Communicator,* pp. 68–69.

Study charges bias in TV industry. (1977, August, 20). *Facts on File World News Digest.* p. 642 G2.

Thornton, L. (1990). Broadcast news. In J. L. Dates and W. Barlow (Eds.), *Split image: African Americans in the mass media* (pp. 389–418). Washington, DC: Howard University Press.

U.S. Commission on Civil Rights. (1977, August). *Window dressing on the set: Women and minorities in television.* Washington, DC: Author.

Van Valkenburg, N. (1993, June 9). Valk: Advice from the Wales to Chung and Rather. *Gannett News Service.*

Weaver, D., & Wilhoit, G. C. (1992). *The American journalist in the 1990s: A preliminary report of key findings from a 1992 survey of U.S. journalists.* Arlington, VA: The Freedom Forum.

Women with roles in feature films earned just 40 to 60 percent of what [male] actors make—a pay gap that begins at the age of 10. "From birth through age 9," Meryl Streep noted tartly [in a Screen Actors Guild meeting], "a girl can make a pretty fair living." (Lacayo, 1991, p. 36)

six

FILM:

The Celluloid Female

HISTORY

In 1895, the first film projection system was unveiled, amazing an audience who watched this silent motion picture, consisting of short clips of a train speeding toward the audience and waves breaking on the beach. Years later, silent films were replaced by "talkies." *The Jazz Singer* (1927), starring Al Jolson, was the first feature-length narrative sound film. Talking movies prompted a shift in the attention away from the silent stars who looked good on film to actors with stage experience who could speak as well as move.

In response to growing doubts about the moral character of Hollywood stars (Fatty Arbuckle, a film comedian, was charged with the rape and murder of a young star), Hollywood producers formed the Motion Picture Producers and Distributors Association of America. Will Hays, a conservative, was hired in 1922 to head the organization and put together a code of ethics for films. Hays set up the Office of Production Code Administration to review scripts, scenes, and films. Historian David Cook explains, the Production Code forbade "scenes of passion" and "required that the sanctity of the institution of marriage and the home be upheld at all times" (1981, p. 266). In general, the code eliminated "vile and unwholesome" material, especially material that was sexual in nature. Women's roles were especially affected by the code. Roles such as those played by Mae West were considered unacceptable. Acceptable roles forced women into more traditional, down-to-earth roles (Cook, 1981, p. 267).

With the onset of the World War II, many Hollywood stars enlisted; the men to serve at the front, the women to work in hospitals, and both women and men performed in USO shows. Those left behind in Hollywood were asked to play a significant role in helping America win the war.

> Addressing Congress, Roosevelt had outlined the six areas around which films and propaganda generally might be usefully constructed: the war itself; the nature of the enemy; the United Nations and their people; increased production; the home front; and the fighting forces. Hollywood dutifully complied despite its problems, of which the drafting of its work force was only one (Norman, 1987, p. 114).

Concern over increased film costs and a shortage of ammunition for filming battle sequences didn't stop Hollywood from making what some critics believe were among their finest dramatic films.

By 1948, movie attendance had peaked. With the help of Senator Joseph McCarthy and the hearings before the House Un-American Activities Committee (HUAC) in the 1950s, Hollywood production declined. Many talented actors, producers, and directors were blacklisted, banned from working in the film industry. Classic studio-produced films were in decline.

The 1950s were conservative times, and therefore many of the films of the 1960s were reactions to that conservatism. In addition, the audience shifted from a general audience to a younger audience who went to the movies to see films like The Beatles' *A Hard Day's Night* (1963). The inclusion of socially relevant themes and stars is seen in such films as *In the Heat of the Night* (1967), starring Sidney Poitier, and *Easy Rider* (1969), starring Peter Fonda and Dennis Hopper.

The 1970s brought mega-films and those featuring disasters—*The Towering Inferno* (1974), *Jaws* (1974), *Star Wars* (1977)—and sequel films: *Rocky* (1976) and *Superman* (1978). Reliance on sequels continued through the 1980s, until even Hollywood mocked the trend (*Naked Gun 33 1/3*). The late 1970s also focused on the Vietnam War in such films as *Coming Home* (1978), *The Deer Hunter* (1978), and *Apocalypse Now* (1979). In addition, *All the President's Men* (1976), *The Parallax View* (1974), and *Three Days of the Condor* (1975) reflected growing suspicion of the government. "On the whole the seventies represented the decade in which the liberals struck back or, at least, came out of hiding. Once more 'the system' was being questioned in films as it had not been since the end of the 1930s" (Norman, 1987, p. 225).

Although some big movies, such as *The Godfather* (1972), *Chinatown* (1974), and *Shampoo* (1975), brought adults back to theaters, spurring an economically healthy movie industry, another kind of film and audience was developing. In 1974, a little film titled *Jaws* was made.

> And it was the end of the grown-ups. From that moment on the seven major grossing pictures in the history of the industry were made by two guys—George Lucas and Steven Spielberg. What we hadn't realized, of course, was that there was this enormous audience out there, these kids (Norman, 1987, p. 307).

"Juvenilization," as coined by Peter Bogdanovich, a pre-Brats (Steven Spielberg, George Lucas, Francis Coppola, Martin Scorsese, John Milius, Brian de Palma, Gary Kurtz) film director, meant movies were less complex in structure and subject matter. They focused on special effects and aimed to please young audiences. Films such as *Top Gun* (1986), *E.T.* (1982), *Raiders of the Lost Ark* (1981), *Indiana Jones and the Temple of Doom* (1984), *Ghostbusters* (1984), and *Back to the Future* (1985) had few meaningful messages but targeted young moviegoers. Producers with scripts aimed at older audiences found trouble obtaining financial backing (Norman, 1987).

However, by the late 1980s and into the 1990s, "women's" films, produced by major movie studios, gained a large audience. These included *Hannah and Her Sisters* (1986), *Steel Magnolias* (1989), *Fried Green Tomatoes* (1991), *Thelma and Louise* (1991), and *The Joy Luck Club* (1993). Although "women's" films were produced as early as the 1940s—the "decade of great female stars," (Acker, 1993, p. xix)—and the 1970s promised that "women would finally (and of course, independently) see their real lives on the screen" (Acker, 1993, p. xx), only recently have women's films been given some of the same marketing support as some of the blockbusters.

PORTRAYAL

"In 1990, Julia Roberts was the only actress to make the list of top-ten box-office attractions. The year before only Kathleen Turner made it" (Lacayo, 1991, p. 35). One year later, Meryl Streep, addressing the Screen Actors Guild (SAG), stated:

> Three years ago, women were down to performing only one-third of all the roles in feature films. In 1989, that number slipped to 29 percent. Of course, that was before the figures for this year (1990) were tabulated. Just wait till they factor in our contributions to *Total Recall, Robocop II, Days of Thunder, Die Hard 2, The Hunt for Red October, The Abyss, Young Guns II, Miami Blues, Last Exit to Brooklyn, Dick Tracy,* and *The Adventures of Ford Fairlane.* We snagged a good six or seven major roles in those movies. If the trend continues, by the year 2000 women will represent 13 percent of all roles. And in 20 years, we will have been eliminated from movies entirely ("Screen Actors Guild," 1991, p. 7).

The roles portrayed by women in film have changed with the times, but, in general, the number of roles open to women has never equaled those available to men.

In the 1920s, films stereotyped both women and men. Women were flappers, working girls, virgins, or vamps. Men were gallant and macho in such roles as pioneers, western heroes, thieves, pirates, and war heroes.

In the early 1930s, women in the cinema played more liberated characters. Greta Garbo, Jean Harlow, and Marlene Dietrich portrayed women who initiated sexual encounters, pursued men, and embodied some male characteristics without seeming masculine or predatory. Unfortunately, these roles didn't last.

During World War II, films for women and about women were popular. The reasons were practical ones: Few male stars were available (most were serving in the Armed Forces), and film audiences were predominantly women. MGM musicals, for example, dealt with the "the good old days" prior to the war, or with home and family. Other movies highlighted female characters awaiting their male relatives who were at war.

The 1950s introduced the ultimate male fantasy, Marilyn Monroe, but movie audiences were changing and getting younger. Such films as *Rebel Without a Cause* and *On the Waterfront* were popular with younger moviegoers, neither of which had strong women characters. In fact, the heroines of the 1930s and 1940s were more active, assertive, and independent than their 1950s and 1960s sisters. Stars like Katharine Hepburn and Rosalind Russell often played women with serious careers who went toe to toe with their male counterparts and in some cases . . . were socially and professionally above their male suitors (Rapping, 1994, pp. 27–28).

The popular male heroes of the 1960s, James Bond and Clint Eastwood characters, treated women as sex objects or not at all. For women, the 1960s reinforced stereotypes. Intelligent women weren't seen. In fact, the late 1960s "mark the gradual decline in the importance of women on the screen" (Gamble & Gamble, 1986, p. 269). "Whereas women make up 50 percent of the top stars of the 1930s, for example, they comprise little over 10 percent during the 70s, and this 10 percent stems from the dominant presence of Barbra Streisand" (Steinberg, 1982).

Women's film roles in the early 1970s, "according to some feminist critics, were worse than reactionary" on screen and nonexistent behind the camera (McCreadie, 1990, p. 146). Yet 1977, proclaimed the year of the "woman's film" by newsmagazines, showed some advances for women in film. In 1978, Jill Clayburgh portrayed *An Unmarried Woman.* Jane Fonda moved from her role as a hooker in *Klute* (1971) to Lillian Hellman in *Julia* (1977) to a television newscaster in *The China Syndrome* (1979). Some women's roles were more progressive (more diverse and more real) in response to the women's movement. Working-class women were portrayed in *Norma Rae* (1979). Roles for younger women opened up in *Taxi Driver* (1976) and *Manhattan* (1979), and older women were allowed to be sexually aggressive in *Moment by Moment* (1978).

By the early 1980s, women in films (*The Big Chill,* 1983) were portrayed as "superwomen," those who manage "to reach for and get it all: men, careers, and families" (McCreadie, 1990, p. 153). Men were often portrayed as supportive of women's choices (*Flashdance,* 1983) or mentors (*Educating Rita,* 1983). Although many films continued to portray Cinderella and her prince (*An Officer and a Gentleman,* 1982), at least there was a wider range of portrayals. Although women did not receive equal screen time by the 1980s, McCreadie argues that "the signs of progress are unmistakable" (1990, p. 148).

African-American women in motion pictures continued to be stereotyped through the mid-1980s. Considerable debate occurred over *The Color Purple* (1986), which depicted African-American women and men in a series of stereotypes. States Jewell, "The theme of the bad-Black-girl was portrayed by Shug Avery, while the African-American male was portrayed as a brute in his conflict-ridden relationships with the characters portrayed by African-American women" (1993, p. 51).

By 1987, the Best Actress nominee list included Meryl Streep in *Ironweed,* Glenn Close in *Fatal Attraction,* Holly Hunter in *Broadcast News,* Cher in *Moonstruck,* and Sally Kirkland in *Anna.* So why, Elayne Rapping asked, "am I so depressed?"

It's easy to see the continuity. Marriage, men, and babies—to the exclusion of meaningful work—were being pushed down our throats in movie after movie. . . . In each film, the nuclear family and old-fashioned romantic love of the kind that leads to "happily ever after" were presented as more or less unproblematic ideals. Independent women, for their part, were portrayed as seriously in trouble, in one way or another, for reasons that ranged from

garden-variety Freudian female neurosis to downright psychopathic ev
p. 24).

The late 1980s and early 1990s saw the new female buddy films (Out
Beaches, Thelma and Louise, and A League of Their Own). Other top films
with a strong supporting role by Whoopi Goldberg, an African-American v
(1989), which reverted to the search for Prince Charming. Films by the gr
American male film producers in the 1990s continued to perpetuate the bad
movies as Eddie Murphy's Harlem Nights and Spike Lee's School Daze. On the other hand, Lee's
Jungle Fever reflected "varied images but includes some positive images of African American
women" (Jewell, 1993, p. 51).

Although 1992 has been called "The Year of the Woman" and the Academy of Motion Picture
Arts and Sciences focused their program on "Oscar Celebrates Women and the Movies," the practical
matter is that in 1992 few women were seen on the screen or behind the camera. The five Best Picture
nominees were The Crying Game, A Few Good Men, Howard's End, Scent of a Woman, and Unforgiven, three of which "were old-fashioned, macho genre pieces produced by, for, and about the most
traditional male audiences and heroines" (Rapping, 1994, p. 58). In fact, of the five nominees for
leading actress, two were in foreign films (Indochine and Howard's End), whereas the other three were
from small films with small budgets (Passion Fish, Love Field, and Lorenzo's Oil).

In addition to the small number of "women's films," few women work in the film industry; only
34 percent of the positions in the film industry (from the lowest-paid assistant to the biggest star) in
1993 were held by women, and they earned 33 percent less than their male counterparts (Rapping,
1994, p. 58).

EMPLOYMENT

We most often recognize the names of actresses rather than directors, editors, or producers in film.
Richard Lacayo stated, "Hollywood is always ready to make some woman a goddess. But just let her
try to become a director. Or a producer. Or a studio chief" (1991, p. 35).

In the early days of film, few women were known other than actresses. Recognizable names
included Edith Head, a well-known costume designer, and Hedda Hopper, gossip columnist, both of
whom held fairly traditional roles for women. Rarely did audiences know women directors such as
Lillian Gish (remembered for her acting), or Mary Pickford, known as "America's sweetheart" of the
silent screen, but co-founder of United Artists studio in 1919 with Charlie Chaplin, D. W. Griffith, and
Douglas Fairbanks. Lacayo (1991) describes Pickford "beneath her curls and petticoats," as "one of
the shrewdest business minds in Hollywood history and the first star to control all aspects of her
films" (p. 36).

Other women found their niche in Hollywood as writers, such as Anita Loos, who wrote Gentlemen Prefer Blondes, but in general, the ratio of men to women writers in Hollywood dropped from 52
out of 238 (in 1928) to 64 out of 608 (in 1940) (Rosen, 1973).

omen directed in the early years. "One statistic has it that between 1949 and 1979 . . . of 1 percent of all films released by American major studios were directed by women" (Quart, , p. 1). Two of the better known early women film directors were Dorothy Arzner (1930s, 1940s) nd Ida Lupino (1950s). The absence of women is truly amazing when one considers that though many major films stars during this time were women, apparently the industry believed they must be told how to act (that is, be directed) by men. Besides acting, the only film roles women played were in support positions: editors and clerical. One of the most well-known editors of the 1960s was Dede Allen of *Bonnie and Clyde* (1967) and *Dog Day Afternoon* (1975) fame.

In the late 1970s and early 1980s, more women directors succeeded with major motion pictures at the box office in films such as Susan Seidelman's *Desperately Seeking Susan* (1985) and Amy Heckerling's *National Lampoon's European Vacation* (1985).

The 1980s also brought change in the boardroom. Sherry Lansing became president of Twentieth Century-Fox. Dawn Steel, chief of production at Paramount for three years (*Footloose,* 1979, and *Top Gun,* 1986), became president of Columbia Pictures—a first for a woman. More women directed films, usually through their power as actresses (Barbra Streisand, Goldie Hawn, and Jodie Foster) or through their connection to powerful men in the film industry (Penny Marshall). Even though few received recognition from the Academy for their films, the audiences enthusiastically accepted their work.

A 1992 Directors Guild of America study showed that work by women and minorities (not to mention minority women) is only a small amount of the filmmaking in the United States and has increased only slightly since 1983. Women directors work on average 8 percent of the total days worked by male directors. Of 9,759 total members of the Directors Guild, 1,875 are women, 260 are Black, and 167 are Latino. Martha Cooleridge, director of *Rambling Rose,* stated in the *Los Angeles Times,* "Did we think it was getting enormously better over the last few years? It just sounds like business as usual to me. There is an enormous resistance to women (directors)" ("Director's Guild Study," 1992, p. 7).

Yet, there are many reasons for Hollywood to take note of women directors. On average, a film directed by a woman brought in $46.7 million (box office gross) in 1992 compared to $32 million for an average man-directed film. Not only do women's films earn more money, on average they cost less to produce. Women-directed films cost on average $18.5 million to produce, whereas men-directed films cost $28 million (Reel Women, 1993). An even stronger argument for the hiring of women is the 1994 Academy Award for Best Director presented to Jane Campion, director of *The Piano.* Hollywood's admission of talented women in film may secure future positions for women behind the camera.

REFERENCES

Acker, A. (1993). *Reel women: Pioneers of the cinema 1896 to the present.* New York: The Continuum Publishing Company.

Cook, D. A. (1981). *A history of narrative film.* New York: W. W. Norton & Company.

Directors Guild study: Action limited for women, minority directors. (1992, Summer). *Media Report to Women*, 7.

Gamble, M. W., & Gamble, T. K. (1986). *Introducing mass communication.* New York: McGraw-Hill.

Jewell, K. S. (1993). *From mammy to Miss America and beyond: Cultural images & the shaping of U.S. social policy.* New York: Routledge.

Lacayo, R. (1991, Spring). Women in Hollywood. *People Magazine Extra,* pp. 35–89.

McCreadie. M. (1990). *The casting couch and other front row seats: Women in films of the 1970s and 1980s.* New York: Praeger.

Norman, B. (1987). *The Story of Hollywood.* New York: New American Library.

Quart, B. K. (1988). *Women directors: The emergence of a new cinema.* New York: Praeger.

Rapping, E. (1994). *Media-tions: Forays into the culture and gender wars.* Boston: South End Press.

Reel Women. (1993, Winter). *The Creative Woman.*

Rosen, M. (1973). *Popcorn Venus: Women, movies, and the American dream.* New York: Coward, McCann & Geoghegan.

Screen Actors' Guild women's committee documents gender gap; Streep speaks. (1991, January/ February), *Media Report to Women,* 7.

Steinberg, C. (Ed). (1982). *Reel facts: The movie book of records.* New York: Vintage.

PROJECT IDEAS

1   List last year's top films (in terms of box-office success). Who directed, produced, and wrote them? What films received Academy Awards? Were they the same as the box-office successes? Who wrote, produced, and directed the award-winning films?

2   Identify two films marketed as "women's films" and two films marketed as "men's films." Who directed, produced, and starred in these films? Explain in detail why these films were placed into "women's films" or "men's films" categories.

3   Few film roles over the past 30 years have been available for Latina women. Identify and describe the portrayal of Latina women in film. Look at *West Side Story, White Men Can't Jump,* and *Peter's Friends,* as well as artists such as Rita Moreno in the book *Reel Women* (see Bibliography).

4   Lesbians in films have been portrayed both positively and negatively. Choose three films from the following list, and analyze lesbian roles in them. In what ways are they positive characters? In what ways are they negative characters? How do the times in which they were produced impact the portrayal?

Morocco (1930)

Touch of Evil (1958)

The Children's Hour (1962)

Lilith (1964)

Rachel Rachel (1968)

Windows (1980)

Personal Best (1982)

Silkwood (1983)

Lianna (1983)

Desert Hearts (1986)

Basic Instinct (1992)

Claire of the Moon (1992)

NAMES

The following list identifies some of the women who have been or are currently part of the film industry. Women who were previously mentioned in this introduction are not duplicated in this list.

Gilliam Armstrong—Australian director. *My Brilliant Career* (1980), *Mrs. Soffel* (1985).

Margaret Booth—Pioneering editor in Hollywood. *Mutiny on the Bounty* (1935), *The Owl and the Pussycat* (1970), *The Way We Were* (1973), *Annie* (1982).

Christine Choy—Well known as a documentary filmmaker. *Who Killed Vincent Chin?* (1988), *China Today* (1989).

Julie Dash—Independent Black filmmaker. *Four Women* (1978), *Illusions* (1982).

Lee Grant—Actress and director of documentaries, made-for-TV movies, and feature films. *Nobody's Child* (1987), *Stay Together* (1989).

Alice Guy-Blache—First woman film director. Directed, produced, and supervised nearly 300 films. *The Cabbage Fairy* (1896), *In the Year 2000* (1912).

Lillian Hellman—Writer of films known for their controversial topics. *Little Foxes* (1941), *Julia* (1977).

Viola Lawrence—One of Hollywood's first female editors. *O'Henry* (1916), *Anything Goes* (1936), *Pepe* (1960).

Frances Marion—"The Dean of the Hollywood Screenwriters" in the 1920s and 1930s. *Camille* (1915), *Anne of Green Gables* (1919), *The Clown* (1953).

Brianne Murphy—First woman director of photography to gain entry into the film union. *Man Beast* (1955), *Pocket Filled with Dreams* (1973), *Cheech and Chong's Nice Dreams* (1981).

Euzhan Palcy—First Black woman filmmaker to direct a feature-length Hollywood film: *A Dry White Season* (1989).

Lotte Reiniger—German filmmaker and animator credited with creating and producing the first full-length animated film: *The Adventures of Prince Achmed* (1923–26).

Patricia Rozema—Canadian film director of *I've Heard the Mermaids Sing* (1987).

Joan Tewkesbury—Screenwriter and director. Wrote *Nashville* (1975) and *The Accused* (1987).

Virginia Van Upp—Executive Producer for Columbia Pictures in 1945. *Pursuit of Happiness* (1934), *Gilda* (1946).

Margarethe von Trotta—Known as the world's leading feminist filmmaker. *Marianne and Julianne* (1982), *Sheer Madness* (1987).

Agnes Varda—Film pioneer and known as the figurehead of the 1970s women's movement in France. *La Pointe-Courte* (1954), *One Sings, the Other Doesn't* (1977), *Kung Fu Master* (1989).

Lina Wertmuller—Among the first women to win international acclaim as a female director. *The Lizards* (1963), *Swept Away* (1975).

Pearl White—Known as "Poor Pauline" in *The Perils of Pauline* (1914). She did most of her own stuntwork.

Mai Zetterling—Actress and director of films dealing with women's oppression. *The Truth About Women* (1958), *Loving Couples* (1964), *Van Gogh* (1971).

ORGANIZATIONS

Ishtar Films
6253 Hollywood Boulevard
Suite 623
Hollywood, CA 90028

New Day Films
121 West 27th Street
Suite 902
New York, NY 10001

Women in Film
6464 Sunset Boulevard
Suite 900
Hollywood, CA 90028

Women in Film, Atlanta
P.O. Box 52726
Atlanta, GA 30355

Women Make Movies
225 Lafayette Street
Suite 207
New York, NY 10012

These lists were, in part, derived from Acker's *Reel women: Pioneers of the cinema 1896 to the present* (1991), New York: Continuum and Griffin, and McCann's *The book of women* (1992), Holbrook, MA: Bob Adams, Inc.

17

AFRICAN-AMERICAN WOMEN
AND THE OSCARS

MARY FRANCES STUBBS

Mary Frances Stubbs has a Ph.D. in English with a minor in Film Studies. Her interests are Black films, the film adaptation of literary works, and script writing. She recently completed a film script titled *The Boy From Georgia,* and another is in progress. Her publications include "Black Women in American Films: A Thematic Approach" with Elizabeth Hadley Freydberg, in D. Carson, L. Dittmar, and J. R. Welsch (Eds.), *Multiple Voices in Feminist Film Criticism.* Stubbs currently works at Howard University in Institutional Advancement. Her responsibilities include acting as liaison and fund developer for the Arts Visitation Program and the Department of Radio, TV, and Film.

On March 29, 1991, Whoopi Goldberg stepped forward to receive the Oscar for Best Actress in a Supporting Role for playing the part of Oda Mae Brown, the charlatan spiritual medium in Jerry Zucker's film *Ghost*, and became only the second African-American woman in the 67-year history of the Academy of Motion Picture Arts and Sciences to ever receive the coveted award. More than 50 years had passed since Hattie McDaniel had been honored with an Oscar for her role as the maid in the legendary movie *Gone With the Wind*. In that 50-year span, the social fabric of the American landscape had changed. Broad technological advances, affirmative-action policies and social and political movements such as the civil rights and women's movements had transformed the lives of all American women, including the lives of African-American women.

BACKGROUND

Observers of American culture, reflecting on the image of African Americans in the media, have argued that very few substantive changes have occurred in the 50 years between the time the Oscar was awarded to an African-American woman for the role of maid, and the time it was awarded for the role of spiritual medium. Although the lives of African-American women have changed, becoming more varied economically and professionally and more dynamic politically, these observers argue, their representation in films has often been negative.

Certainly, American movies historically, as Pearl Bowser and other have asserted, "have not been a humanistic medium for Blacks. As a powerful tool for propaganda and the maintenance of the status quo, movies have defined Black Americans in White terms, reinforcing the totem-pole structure of American racial arrangement" (Bowser, 1982, p. 42). The Black woman's place in the racial/sexual totem pole has been documented by such critics as Liz Gant, bell hooks, Edward Mapp, Margaret Sloan, and Donald Bogle. Mapp argues, "The sexual dimension of American racism is reflected in the motion picture portrayal of the Black woman. Her film image has been defined by others rather than by herself. When she is not a figment of White male fantasy, she is a product of White female thinking. Few Black female writers have gained employment in the film industry. The result is a tragic history of stereotyping and a steady procession of mammies, maids, and miscegenists, matriarchs, madams, and assorted 'make-it-for-money' types" (Mapp, 1982, p. 6). Other equally damaging stereotypes appearing in the film medium have included whores and seducers, Amazons and tragic mulattos, exotics and long-suffering spouses. Critics argue that these stereotypes serve the film industry's purpose of pandering to the prejudices and racial attitudes of the majority culture.

The concerns that these critics and others have voiced about the repetition of stereotypes and the visual representation of African-American women are grounded in a belief that motion pictures are not only an agent of socialization, but also powerful tools that both shape and reflect society's values. Motion pictures can, in short, influence society's perception and treatment of people, including women and ethnic and racial groups.

Over the years, the movie industry has rarely produced films in numbers reflective of the racial composition of the American population or the racial makeup of the movie audience, even during periods of relative prolificacy of Black films. The number of portrayals of African Americans in movies are so limited as to suggest a racial bias. And within these numbers, the portrayals of American women have been even fewer.

The number of African Americans who have received Oscar nominations over the years further supports the idea of racial bias against African Americans in mainstream movie production. Figure 17.1 shows a timeline of all the Oscar nominations and awards made to African Americans. In the history of the Academy of Motion Picture Arts and Sciences, the organization that evaluates films and gives the awards based on merit and achievement as well as honorary awards, only 26 of the 838 performers nominated for Oscars in the four acting categories have been African Americans, representing 3 percent of the total. Of these 26 nominations, only 4 have won Oscars: Hattie McDaniel, Sidney Poitier, Whoopi Goldberg, and Denzel Washington.

The ratio of African-American Oscar nominations to White nominations cannot serve as a scientific indicator of the number of African Americans in films in any given year because of the status that both the movie industry and society accord the Academy and because of the complex interplay between films and their social, political, and cultural settings. However, statistics on Oscar nominations of African Americans are instructive about the industry's relationship with this racial group.

Obviously, African Americans have a far greater nomination rate than a rate of winning the Oscar (Figure 17.1). Three percent of the nominations in the acting categories are African-American nominations, whereas only .48 percent have won Oscars. The category breakdown tends to bear out the totem-pole structure in that, overall, more nominations for African Americans are in the supporting role category. However, as would be expected in the race–gender arrangement, more African-American men than African-American women receive nominations for leading roles. Thus, the category breakdowns are as follows: Of the 172 nominations made by the Academy in the Best Actor category, 5 are African-American men (with 1 Oscar); in the Best Actress category, 5 of 164 nominations went to African-American women (no Oscar winners). Of the 206 nominations in the Supporting Actor category, 8 are African-American men (1 Oscar winner); and in the Supporting Actress category, 8 of the 206 nominations are African-American women (2 Oscar winners).

Figure 17.1
African-American Oscar Nominations and Awards
■ = Received Award

1927	**Oscars First Awarded**		
1939	**Hattie McDaniel** ■	*Gone With the Wind*	Supporting Actress
1949	**Ethel Waters**	*Pinky*	Supporting Actress
1954	**Dorothy Dandridge**	*Carmen Jones*	Leading Actress
1959	**Juanita Moore**	*Imitation of Life*	Supporting Actress
1963	**Sidney Poitier** ■	*Lilies of the Field*	Leading Actor

1967	**Beah Richards**	*Guess Who's Coming to Dinner*	Supporting Actress
1969	**Rupert Cross**	*The Reivers*	Supporting Actor
1970	**James Earl Jones**	*The Great White Hope*	Supporting Actor
1972	**Diana Ross**	*Lady Sings the Blues*	Leading Actress
	Cicely Tyson	*Sounder*	Leading Actress
1974	**Diahann Carroll**	*Claudine*	Leading Actress
1981	**Howard Rollins**	*Ragtime*	Leading Actor
1982	**Louis Gossett, Jr.**	*An Officer and a Gentleman*	Supporting Actor
1983	**Alfre Woodard**	*Cross Creek*	Supporting Actress
1984	**Adolph Caesar**	*A Soldier's Story*	Supporting Actor
1985	**Margaret Avery**	*The Color Purple*	Supporting Actress
	Oprah Winfrey	*The Color Purple*	Supporting Actress
	Whoopi Goldberg	*The Color Purple*	Leading Actress
1986	**Dexter Gordon**	*Round Midnight*	Leading Actor
1987	**Morgan Freeman**	*Street Smart*	Supporting Actor
	Denzel Washington	*Cry Freedom*	Supporting Actor
1989	**Morgan Freeman**	*Driving Miss Daisy*	Leading Actor
	Denzel Washington ■	*Glory*	Supporting Actor
1990	**Whoopi Goldberg ■**	*Ghost*	Supporting Actress

An examination of Oscar nominations received by African-American actresses offers a valid approach to the discussion of the portrayal of African-American women in mainstream Hollywood films. Although these nominations were made for roles in films that are only a small fraction of the vast number of films produced by the industry, the Oscar nomination and awards process have come to symbolize mainstream Hollywood. The Oscar nomination has been accepted as a validation device, and films receiving nominations reflect the image that the film industry wants to convey of itself, or as Levy points out, "The films and performers honored by the Academy tend to be those reflecting the celluloid American dream invented and nurtured by Hollywood" (Levy, 1987, p. 191). An examination of all Oscar-nominated roles of African-American women will offer insights into the representation of Black characters in contemporary mainstream Hollywood films.

METHOD

The current research focuses on the portrayal of African-American women in those roles nominated to receive awards by the Academy of Motion Picture Arts and Sciences. Although the Academy makes merit awards in 23 categories, as well as other honorary awards, this research involves only 2 categories—Best Actress in a Leading Role, and Best Actress in a Supporting Role. The results are based on analysis of 13 roles (see column 2 in Tables 17.1 and 17.2) in 11 films—every film containing a nomination for an African-American actress. *The Color Purple* received three nominations in these two categories.

In an effort to provide comprehensive, detailed data on mainstream Hollywood's portrayal of African-American women, a content analysis of African-American women's roles nominated for awards by the Academy of Motion Picture Arts and Sciences was conducted. Specifically, this research sought to determine to what extent the movie industry perpetuates racist stereotypes or negative representation of African-American women and, similarly, to determine in what ways these roles conform to the norm (majority) nominated roles and Oscar-winning roles.

The results reported in this analysis are based on acting roles in the following films: *Gone With the Wind* (1939), *Pinky* (1949), *Carmen Jones* (1954), *Imitation of Life* (1959), *Guess Who's Coming to Dinner* (1967), *Lady Sings the Blues* (1972), *Sounder* (1972), *Claudine* (1974), *Cross Creek* (1983), *The Color Purple* (1985) (three roles), and *Ghost* (1990). Because most prior research on the representation of African Americans in motion pictures has been theoretical and critical rather than empirical, this research utilized category definitions primarily employed in the content analysis of television portrayals of African Americans. These include those variables used by Bradley Greenberg and associates; John Seggar and associates; and Stroman, Merritt, and Matabane. The two sources most utilized for research on the Oscar awards were Anthony Holden's *Behind the Oscar*, which provides statistical, historical, and other data, and Emanuel Levy's *And the Winner is: The History and Politics of the Oscar Awards*, a text that gives an excellent sociopolitical and cultural interpretation of the Oscar phenomena.

Variables coded included two types of information: (1) characteristics of individual movies and (2) characteristics of individual characters. Character attributes include occupation, marital status, childless/number of children, family membership, socioeconomic status based on signs of affluence within the movie, including occupation, and physical depiction of the characters, including dress style and attractiveness.

Characteristics of individual movies covered in this research include the variables of film genre, geographic setting or location, racial composition of cast, race and gender of director, and race and gender of scriptwriter.

A comparative method was also utilized as a way to clarify distinction between racial and sexual stereotypes, and to ascertain the degree to which African-American women's roles conform to typical Oscar roles played by other women. Reference is made to Oscar roles in general, as well as to those roles that won the Oscar award in the year in which an African-American woman was nominated.

Table 17.1
Oscar nominations for best actress in a leading role

Year	African-American Nominees/Movie	White and Other Nominees/Movie
1954	Dorothy Dandridge *Carmen Jones*	*Grace Kelly *The Country Girl* Judy Garland *A Star Is Born* Audrey Hepburn *Sabrina* Jane Wyman *Magnificent Obsession*
1972	Diana Ross *Lady Sings the Blues* Cicely Tyson *Sounder*	*Liza Minnelli *Cabaret* Maggie Smith *Travels with My Aunt* Liv Ullmann *The Emigrants*
1974	Diahann Carroll *Claudine*	*Ellen Burstyn *Alice Doesn't Live Here Anymore* Faye Dunaway *Chinatown* Valerie Perrine *Lenny* Gena Rowlands *A Woman Under the Influence*
1985	Whoopi Goldberg *The Color Purple*	*Geraldine Page *The Trip to Bountiful* Anne Bancroft *Agnes of God* Jessica Lange *Sweet Dreams* Meryl Streep *Out of Africa*

* Oscar winner

Table 17.2
Oscar nominations for best actress in a supporting role

Year	African-American Nominees/Movie	White and Other Nominees/Movie
1939	*Hattie McDaniel *Gone With the Wind*	Olivia de Havilland *Gone With the Wind* Geraldine Fitzgerald *Wuthering Heights* Edna May Oliver *Drums Along the Mohawk* Maria Ouspenskaya *Love Affair*
1949	Ethel Waters *Pinky*	*Mercedes McCambridge *All the King's Men* Ethel Barrymore *Pinky* Celeste Holm *Come to the Stable* Elsa Lanchester *Come to the Stable*
1959	Juanita Moore *Imitation of Life*	*Shelley Winters *The Diary of Anne Frank* Hermione Baddeley *Room at the Top* Susan Kohner *Imitation of Life* Thelma Ritter *Pillow Talk*

This analysis recognizes the notions that the American movie industry *thrives* on formula, patterns, and repetition, and that roles for all women in mainstream films exist along a continuum from the fully realized, well-rounded character to the stereotype. Levy has shown that there are not only consistent or typical Oscar roles for women, but that women's roles in general are stereotypical. These stereotypical roles are "reflected and reinforced by the Oscar awards" and have persisted in the American cinema for half a century—with few or minor alterations, most female roles up to the 1970s have been a variation or reworking of these formulaic conventions (Levy, 1987, p. 197). This being the case, how then do African-American women's roles differ or conform to the typical Oscar roles of other women? In approaching these questions, one can expect to find that along the continuum, roles for African-American women may be at once racist *and* sexist.

Year	African-American Nominees/Movie	White and Other Nominees/Movie
1967	Beah Richards *Guess Who's Coming to Dinner*	*Estelle Parsons *Bonnie and Clyde* Carol Channing *Thoroughly Modern Millie* Mildred Natwick *Barefoot in the Park* Katharine Ross *The Graduate*
1983	Alfre Woodard *Cross Creek*	*Linda Hunt *The Year of Living Dangerously* Cher *Silkwood* Glenn Close *The Big Chill* Amy Irving *Yentl*
1985	Oprah Winfrey *The Color Purple* Margaret Avery *The Color Purple*	*Anjelica Huston *Prizzi's Honor* Amy Madigan *Twice in a Lifetime* Meg Tilly *Agnes of God*
1990	*Whoopi Goldberg *Ghost*	Annette Bening *The Grifters* Lorraine Bracco *Goodfellas* Diane Ladd *Wild at Heart* Mary McDonnell *Dances With Wolves*

* Oscar winner

RESULTS AND DISCUSSION

Table 17.3 provides an overview of the attributes of movies with Oscar-nominated African-American actresses. Levy has demonstrated that the Academy of Motion Picture Arts and Sciences tends to favor dramas, and within that broad category, "biopictures" over fictional films. Roles inspired by real-life personalities have received 21 percent of all Oscar nominations made over the history of the Academy. The number of biographical Oscar roles has been twice as large among men (27%) as among women (14%), particularly in the lead categories: 35 percent of all Oscars awarded have been in the Best Actor category for men playing real-life personalities, compared with only 15 percent of Oscar nominations going to the Best Actress category for roles of women playing real-life personalities (Levy, 1987, p. 182). A clear gender-related bias exists. But is there also a racial-related bias? Do the Oscar nominations of African-American actresses follow these same trends?

Roles in Biographies

Of the 11 films under discussion, all are dramas; 2, or 18 percent, are bio-pictures: *Lady Sings the Blues*, a film based on the life of legendary blues singer

Table 17.3
Attributes of movies with Oscar-nominated African-American actresses

Attributes	Number	Percentage
Film Genre		
Comedy	0	0
Musical	0	0
Drama	11	100
Romantic Comedy	0	0
Setting/Location		
Urban/North	5	45
Rural/Southern	5	45
Urban/West	1	9
Director—Race and Gender		
Black Female	0	0
Black Male	0	0
White Female	0	0
White Male	11	100
Screenwriter—Race and Gender		
Black Female	0	0
Black Male	1	9
White Female	2	18
White Male	6	55
Collaboration	2	18
Cast—Racial Composition		
Predominantly Black	5	45
Predominantly White	5	45
Black/White	1	9

* Due to rounding, total percentages may not add to 100%.

Billie Holiday, and *Cross Creek*, an adaptation of the memoir of Marjorie Kinnan Rawlings, author of *The Yearling*. Levy shows that most of the biopictures that win Oscars and Oscar nominations are about women who were performing artists or women in show business. Although Diana Ross lost to Liza Minnelli (Best Actress in *Cabaret*), *Lady Sings the Blues* conforms to this pattern.

The Oscar-nominated roles for African-American women in biopictures are 50 percent of each acting category, such as Diana Ross, nominated for Best Actress, and Alfre Woodard, nominated for Best Supporting Actress, for her performance as a maid in *Cross Creek*. A comparison of these roles with roles of African-American men will further reveal whether a racial or gender bias exists in reference to the attribute of movie genre. Of the 13 films in which African-American men have received Oscar nominations, 4, or 31 percent, are biopictures (compared to 18 percent of the 11 films with women nominees). These include James Earl Jones for *The Great White Hope*. For his role in *Cry Freedom*, the story of South African freedom-fighter Steven Biko, Denzel Washington received a Best Supporting Actor nomination, and he won Best Supporting Actor Oscar for his performance in *Glory*, a fact-based film about a White Massachusetts aristocrat and his all-Black regiment in the Civil War. Dexter Gordon won a leading-role nomination for *Round Midnight*, a film based on the life of jazz musician Bud Powell. There are fewer biopictures featuring African-American women than there are such films featuring African-American men.

In his discussion of the underrepresentation of women in biographical films, Levy states that on the one hand, the underrepresentation "suggests perhaps there have not been as many prominent women in science, politics and literature for the movies to draw upon; thus, films have not had a large pool of 'important' women as sources for their narratives." On the other hand, this phenomenon may be a function of the fact "that movies have been reluctant to use the real-life heroines who were appropriate for screen biographies, thus functioning as agencies of social control, keeping women in their place, by confining them to the domestic arena or to show business, both traditional female domains" (Levy, 1987, p. 182).

Occupational Patterns

Similarly, African Americans in general, and African-American women in particular, are victims of the movies as agents of social control. This accounts for both their underrepresentation and the repeated negative images. Thus African-American women are "kept in their place," relegated to one status because of their race and to a still lower status because of their gender. Race–gender-determined status is demonstrated in the attributes of occupation and economic status of the African-American Oscar-nominated roles: Of the 14, 5 of the characters work as maids, and a sixth, Oprah Winfrey in *The Color Purple*, is unjustly convicted for defending herself against racial insults and is forced as a prisoner to become the maid to the sheriff's family.

The lack of Oscar-quality roles for women in Hollywood films might account for some discrepancies between the roles of White and African-American women. Still, whatever the limitations for other women, they are greater for African-American women, suggesting again a racial bias. A cursory glance at the list of most-nominated actresses (actresses receiving five or more nominations) is revealing. There are no African-American women in the group. The list is headed by Katharine Hepburn (12 nominations, 4 wins), followed by Bette Davis (10 nominations, 2 wins), Meryl Streep (9 nominations, 2 wins), Geraldine Page (8 nominations, 1 win), Jane Fonda (7 nominations 2 wins), Deborah Kerr and Thelma Ritter (6 nominations each), and about 15 actresses with 5 nominations each (Holden, 1991, pp. 608–609). Whoopi Goldberg remains the one and only African-American woman to have been nominated more than once for an Academy Award. She was first nominated in the Best Actress category for her role as Miss Ceily in *The Color Purple* and then in the Supporting Role category for her part in *Ghost*, for which she won the Oscar.

Not only have there been fewer roles for African-American women, the roles available to them have been more confined and stereotypical. This is reflected in the number of maid roles nominated for Oscar awards (Table 17.4). Of all the stereotypes of African-American women, none have provoked as much discussion as the mammy, and the maid roles are perceived by many critics to be just one or another version of the mammy.

In an effort to more accurately examine the representation of African-American women, an attempt is made to quantify an image, to break apart the whole into attributes. An analysis of the maid/mammy image serves this purpose. This image has been melded into American culture through such symbols as the Aunt Jemima of pancake mix fame, a creature who "satisfies a need in the White psyche to believe that their loyal, devoted servant not only recognizes and accepts the superiority of the Whites but who also supports the maintenance of such hierarchy" (Stubbs & Freydberg, 1994, p. 483). Hattie McDaniel, large and big-bosomed, with her head wrapped in a scarf Aunt-Jemima style, is the epitome of the mammy. Through the trials of the Civil War and after, she is a loyal pillar of strength, devoted to Miss Scarlett and the White family with whom she lives. She is a familiar figure to the other Blacks on the plantation and, because of her position in the big house, occupies a certain status among them. But she appears to have no children or family of her own.

In *Pinky*, Ethel Waters plays Aunt Dicey, the washerwoman grandmother to the mulatto child, Pinky (played by White actress Jeanne Crain), whom she harshly chastises for "passing" for White up North. Aunt Dicey attempts to persuade Pinky to accept the substandard status accorded to Blacks. Aunt Dicey, having accepted her oppressed status, "moves about with an Uncle-Tom loyalty to the 'good' White folks, fulfills the old-style 'mammy' cliche, notwithstanding Ethel Waters' brave attempt to invest the part with some dignity" (Jerome, 1950, p. 42). Aunt Dicey lives apart from the White family, and it is clear that

Table 17.4

Attributes of characters played by Oscar-nominated African-American actresses

Year	Actress/ Film	Category	Actress Age	Socio-economic Status	Occupation	Marital Status	Family	No. of Children
1939	Hattie McDaniel *Gone With the Wind*	Supporting	44	Working	Maid	Unknown	Unknown	None
1949	Ethel Waters *Pinky*	Supporting	49	Working	Maid	Unknown	Family Community ties	Grand-daughter
1954	Dorothy Dandridge *Carmen Jones*	Leading	43	Working	Factory Worker	Single/ Unknown	None	None
1959	Juanita Moore *Imitation of Life*	Supporting	?	Working	Maid	Formerly married	Family Community ties	One daughter
1967	Beah Richards *Guess Who's Coming to Dinner*	Supporting	34	Middle	None	Married	Family Community ties	One son
1972	Diana Ross *Lady Sings the Blues*	Leading	28	Working	Night Club Blues Singer	Single/ Mistress		None
	Cicely Tyson *Sounder*	Leading	?	Working	Sharecropper farmer	Marries	Family Community ties	One
1974	Diahann Carroll *Claudine*	Leading	39	Lower/ Working	Maid	Twice married; divorced	Family Community ties	Seven
1983	Alfre Woodard *Cross Creek*	Supporting	30	Working	Maid	Single; has lover	Family not visible	None
1985	Whoopi Goldberg *The Color Purple*	Supporting	31	Working	Farmer; Nonpaid	Married	Family	None of own; step-children
	Margaret Avery *The Color Purple*	Supporting	34	Working	Blues Singer	Single/ Mistress	None	None
	Oprah Winfrey *The Color Purple*	Supporting	31	Working	Farmer; Nonpaid	Married	Family Community ties	Several
1990	Whoopi Goldberg *Ghost*	Supporting	35	Lower/ Working	Spiritual medium	Unknown	None	None

she is centered in her own family and community—factors that enabled her to some extent to dignify her role as mammy.

In the 1959 version of *Imitation of Life*, Juanita Moore played Annie Johnson, a more refined mammy who must raise her own troubled mulatto child while caring for the White woman and child with whom they live. Annie Johnson is not overweight; she is rather attractive in plain and simple day dresses in contemporary styles. But she is self-sacrificing toward the White family and displays the subservient behavior and devotion of maids in earlier films. To Annie Johnson's credit, it is clear that her own child is the center of her life, not the White child. This is a subversion of the film's intent, for in all other ways, the focus is on her relationship with her employers. The audience is not allowed to see Annie's life outside the White household; her mistress (played by Lana Turner) is surprised to find that she has strong ties to church and community and has many close friends.

Diahann Carroll brings a glamorous quality and unique beauty to her performance in *Claudine*. Her role as maid is important, but her primary role is as welfare mother of six children. Being determined that they will live above mere subsistence, she cheats the welfare system by being a maid. The portrayal of her relationships with her children and her courtship with Rupp (James Earl Jones) adds emotional depth and places this character in a realm above the mammy.

In *Cross Creek*, a film set in a small hamlet in Florida in 1928, Alfre Woodard brings a charming freshness to the role of Geechee that is almost anachronistic. Geechee is still the devoted servant who lives in Miss Rawlings's (Mary Steenburgen) household, but she has a life of her own and "use for my wages," as she tells Miss Rawlings. Gone are both the subservience and the asexuality of earlier mammies and maids. Geechee has a lover who shares her bed until he has to leave because of his laziness, and the script makes a point of showing that Geechee learns from Marjorie's independence so that she is able to break away from her frequently abusive lover. There is an attractive rapport between this maid and her White mistress.

Oprah Winfrey as Sophia offers a replay in physical appearance of the mammy in *The Color Purple*. However, although she is decent toward the White child in her charge, there is no great love; Sophia longs for her own children and her own home—characteristics that Alice Walker created in the novel on which the film script was based. As part of the punishment for an unfair conviction, Sophia must become the sheriff's maid.

The image of African-American woman as maid in films fits neatly America's race gender hierarchy. There have been two major lines of work for screen women, both reflected in the Oscar roles—in service and in entertainment (Levy, 1987, p. 191). Maids are considered service positions. Unlike White actresses, no African-American actress has ever received a nomination for roles in those highly stereotypical semiprofessional positions considered to be "appropriate" for women—service roles such as teachers, nurses, and secretaries (Levy, 1987, p. 191).

In the occupation of entertainment, two Oscar nominations are represented: Margaret Avery as Shug in *The Color Purple* earns a living as a popular blues singer, as does Diana Ross in the role of Billie Holiday. Dorothy Dandridge does plenty of singing (the film is based on Bizet's opera *Carmen*) in the lead role of *Carmen Jones*, but her occupation is assembly-line worker in a parachute factory until she seduces Joe, a student air-force pilot, and convinces him to go AWOL and take her away from it all. When she tires of him, her next occupation is as kept woman to Husky Miller, a prizefighter.

In *Guess Who's Coming to Dinner*, Beah Richards plays a genteel member of the Black middle class who apparently has never worked outside the home. Her character is a wife to a retired postal worker (considered middle class), and a concerned but understanding mother to the Nobel Prize winner, Dr. John Prentice (Sidney Poitier), who is engaged to marry a White woman. In *Sounder*, a film set on a small farm during the Depression era, Cicely Tyson does not have a paid occupation. She is the wife of a sharecropper; after her husband is jailed for stealing a ham, "the film follows her through each hot, sweaty day of work and frustration and each night of loneliness as she tries to make ends meet and keep her family fed, clothed, and schooled" (Null, 1975, p. 231).

Whoopi Goldberg as Oda Mae Brown has the most unusual occupation— that of spiritual medium in *Ghost*. She is portrayed as having been a successful trickster, running bogus seances in a small shabby room in the ghetto until she becomes, to her surprise, the medium between ghost Sam Wheat (Patrick Swayze) and his endangered lover, Molly Jensen (Demi Moore). Oda Mae "helps" the lovers have a last dance together and helps Sam solve a crime, get revenge for his own death, and prevent the murder of Molly Jensen.

Location of Movies

In portraying African Americans, contemporary Hollywood favors movies with settings in the urban north, with time periods in the present or the recent past. If set in the South, the movie is likely to be a period piece. The production of the movies *Driving Miss Daisy, Cross Creek*, and *The Long Walk Home*, all set in the South of the past, suggests that society finds such films reassuring because they reflect a time when racial arrangements were different, more "comfortable" for the majority population. Of the 11 films, 5 have locations in the urban North (*Carmen Jones, Claudine, Ghost, Imitation of Life*, and *Lady Sings the Blues*) and 5 are rural or Southern (*The Color Purple, Cross Creek, Gone With the Wind, Pinky* and *Sounder*). *Guess Who's Coming to Dinner* presents an anomaly in this attribute, as it does in other attributes, for it is set in San Francisco, the Urban West, where Dr. John Prentice (Poitier) and his White fiancee, Joanna Drayton (Katherine Houghton) arrive from Hawaii, where they met while both were vacationing.

Work Behind the Scenes

Mapp and others have asserted that the negative representation of African-American women is due in part to the absence of African-American women employed in the mainstream film industry. Filmmaking is a collaborative process requiring expertise in a range of fields. Based on their effect on the final product, including the representation of women, two of the most important behind-the-camera jobs are screenwriter and director. Of the 11 films in this study (Table 17.4) none are directed by African-American women, nor are any directed by African-American men.

As for screenwriters, playwright Lonne Elder III is an African-American male who wrote the screenplay for *Sounder*. The screenplay for *The Color Purple* is based on the novel by African-American writer Alice Walker, and although Walker reportedly consulted on the script, Menno Meyjes's name appears in the film's credits. The screenplay for *Lady Sings the Blues* represents collaboration across race and gender lines because it was written by the team of Terrance McCloy, Chris Clark, and Suzanne de Passe, an African-American woman. White women wrote the screenplays for 2 of the 11 films as follows: Fannie Hurst based the screenplay for *Imitation of Life* on her novel of the same name, and for *Cross Creek*, Darlene Young adapted the autobiography of Marjorie Kinnan Rawlings's memoirs.

The racial composition of the cast (Table 17.4) and the nomination categories (Tables 17.1 and 17.2) show that African-American women have received Oscar nominations in the leading role category (five nominations) only in predominately Black films. There have been no winners in this category. This reflects Hollywood's persistent exclusion of African-American women from lead roles in mainstream films where casting is not color-blind. Moreover, this exclusionary practice thus presents within the film a racial hierarchy (White women as leads, Black women as supporting cast) that exists external to the film as well.

A more complex analysis than is possible within the parameters of this chapter is needed to determine the scope of race–gender influence (of director and screenwriter) on the representation of African-American women. However, one can speculate that in the aggregate, the more African-American women are employed in the movie industry, the greater their numbers on the screen, and the greater the range of portrayals.

Marital and Economic Status

Although occupation is a significant attribute in determining the value of the representation of African-American women, an examination of other attributes such as marital and socioeconomic status (Stroman, Merritt, & Matabane, 1989) can assist in the interpretation of an image. Of the 14 roles examined, 13 present working-class situations for the African-American characters. Only Beah Richards in *Guess Who's Coming to Dinner* is presented as clearly middle class. Carmen Jones is the only character who is overtly an "exotic sexual fantasy," a role well played by Dorothy Dandridge, an actress often described as the Negro soldiers' pin-up girl. Carmen was one of the three characters, the blues singers Billie Holiday and Shug Avery being the other two, who were portrayed as single and mistress. All others were either single, formerly married, or formerly common-law married. Three of the films, *Guess Who's Coming to Dinner*, *Sounder*, and *The Color Purple* (Sophia and Ceily are both married), depict the African-American woman with a husband. The maid/mammy role strips many of the characters of their sense of sexuality and femininity, and the more stereotypical the character, the weaker the ties to a lover, family, and community, and the less likely she is to have children of her own. Thus, Geechee, Claudine, and even Annie Johnson seem to many critics to carry less of the baggage of the stereotypical mammy.

CONCLUSION

The films examined in this chapter are but a sample of the films produced by the mainstream film industry, but the portrayal of African-American women in them is indicative of both the paucity of roles for Black actresses and the types of roles available. What is also revealed through this study is the film industry's reluctance to expand the repertoire of roles for Black women, and to cast African-American women in substantive leading roles of films where the cast is largely White. Moreover, films such as *The Trip to Bountiful* or *Cross Creek*, where a Black woman's story is featured, are not likely to appear in movie theaters. African-American actresses are mostly viewed as appropriate for supporting roles of a certain type, and for leading roles only in films where the cast is largely Black. And even the popular fare, the run-of-the-mill films such as *Made in America* with Whoopi Goldberg and Ted Danson, an interracial couple, are rare. Where are the Black woman/White woman buddy films of the *Thelma and Louise* type or the interracial type we see with Mel Gibson and Danny Glover (the *Lethal Weapon* series)? The interracial friendship of the women in *Grand Canyon* was refreshing because Hollywood has primarily depicted the maid/mistress relationship as the only one possible between White and Black women.

Although a limited discussion of this topic was undertaken in this chapter, the findings of this research support the theoretical work that posits that race and gender of the screenwriter and director can influence image and representation in films. The absence of African-American women from the silver screens of America's theaters has been profound, but their exclusion from positions behind the camera has been extraordinary. The movie industry is competitive and hierarchical, but as African-American women make inroads, one can expect to see films whose representations of this group reflect the range and complexity of the lives of African-American women, films that are of such quality that they win Oscar awards.

REFERENCES

Bowser, P. (1982). The sexual imagery and the Black woman in American cinema. In G. L. Yearwood (Ed.), *Black Cinema Aesthetics: Issues in Independent Black Filmmaking* (pp. 42–51). Athens: Ohio University Center for Afro-American Studies.

DelGaudio, S. (1983). The mammy in Hollywood film: I'd walk a million miles for one of her smiles. *Jump Cut, 28,* 23–25.

Giddings, P. (1984). *When and where I enter: The impact of Black women on race and sex in America.* New York: William Morrow.

Greenberg, B. S., Simmons, K. W., Hogan, L., & Atkin, C. K. (1978). *A three-season analysis of the demographic characteristics of fictional television characters.* Project Castle Report No. 9. East Lansing: Michigan State University, Department of Communication.

Harris, T. (1982). *From mammies to militants: Domestics in Black American literature.* Philadelphia: Temple University Press.

Holden, A. (1991). *Behind the Oscar: The secret history of the Academy Awards.* New York: Simon & Schuster.

Jerome, V. J. (1950). The new stereotype. In *The Negro in Hollywood Films* (pp. 22–29). New York: Masses and Mainstream.

Klotman, P. R. (1982). *Frame by frame: A Black filmograph.* Bloomington: Indiana University Press.

Klotman, P. R., (Ed.) (1991). *Screenplays of the African-American experience.* Bloomington: Indiana University Press.

Levy, E. (1987). *And the winner is: The history and politics of the Oscar awards.* New York: The Ungar Publishing Company.

Mapp, E. (1982, summer). Black women in films. *The Black Scholar, 4,* 36–40.

Nesteby, J. R. (1982). *Black images in American films, 1896–1954: The interplay between civil rights and film culture.* Maryland: University Press of America.

Null, G. (1975). *Black Hollywood: The Black performer in motion pictures.* Secaucus, NJ: The Citadel Press.

Seggar, J. F., Hafen, J., & Hannonen-Gladden, H. (1981). Television's portrayal of minorities and women in drama and comedy drama, 1971–80. *Journal of Broadcasting, 25,* 277–288.

Selig, M. E. (1988). Contradictions and reading: Social class and sex class in *Imitation of Life. Wide Angle, 10,* 13–23.

Sloan, M. (1974, January). Film: Keeping the Black woman in her place. *Ms.*, 30–31.

Stroman, C. A., Merritt, B. D., & Matabane, P. (1989, Winter). *Twenty years after Kerner: The portrayal of African Americans on prime-time television* (Vol. 2, pp. 44–56). Washington, DC: The Howard Journal of Communications: Howard School of Communications.

Stroman, C. A. (1986). *Black families and the mass media.* Occasional Paper No. 23, Washington, DC: Howard University, Institute for Urban Affairs and Research.

Stubbs, F., & Freydberg, E. H. (1994). *Black women in American films: A thematic approach in multiple voices in feminist film criticism.* In D. Carson, L. Dittmar, & J. R. Welsch (Eds.), *Multiple voices in feminist film criticism.* (pp. 481–491) Minneapolis: University of Minnesota Press.

Women's voices gain authority as they become part of the historical record and, whether as an overt focus or in a less conscious way, the films of Studio D visually record women's history.

18

THE NATIONAL FILM BOARD
OF CANADA'S STUDIO D:

Feminist Filmmakers

ANITA TAYLOR

Anita Taylor, Professor of Communication at George Mason University, earned an M.S. at Kansas State University and a Ph.D. at University of Missouri–Columbia. Her interests are public and interpersonal communication with emphasis (since 1980) in women as communicators and the influence of gender in both public and private communication. She has edited *Women and Language* since 1989. Her book, *Women Communicating*, co-edited with Barbara Bate, led to her discovery of the National Film Board of Canada's Studio D and feminist filmmaking, about which she has written in a number of venues. Taylor's most recent book is *Gender and Conflict*, co-edited with Judi Beinstein Miller.

Some women of Studio D, 1987.

Ron Levine Photography

An unadorned beige box-shaped building squats aside a noisy highway on the outer edge of Montreal. Only a modest sign identifies this as home to one of the world's unique institutions, the National Film Board of Canada (NFB). Within these walls in 1974, three people organized a new studio, Studio D, at that time the only government-funded filmmaking group with a mandate to make films by, for, and about women. From that modest beginning, Studio D grew to the status of icon in women's documentary film history. It has produced or co-produced more than 200 films, including three Academy Award winners. Almost all are intended as more than art—intended as well to change the status of women, and not just the women of Canada. Because of the excellence and uniqueness of Studio D, a brief story of its accomplishments fits especially well the goals of this book.

THE NATIONAL FILM BOARD OF CANADA

In 1938, concerned that U.S. films dominated Canadian movie houses, Canada's Parliament commissioned a study for the development of Canadian government film production. The National Film Act of May 2, 1939, followed, creating a National Film Board (NFB) and the appointment of Englishman John Grierson as its first commissioner. Grierson, one of the world's first producers of documentary films, started the NFB just as World War II threatened North America, which influenced how the new institution developed. Grierson enunciated two goals for the Board: To make films to cover the historical aspects of the war and to "secure the future" by making films about the "everyday things of life, the values, the ideals which make life worth living." Grierson wanted NFB films to show Canadians (and others) that there was "something worth fighting for, worth going back to" (Nash, 1982). He also wanted the NFB to be more than a means to maintain morale in a nation at war. He wanted information flow in the opposite direction, for NFB films to communicate the needs of the Canadian public to government. Knowing how government regulations could stifle creativity, Grierson worked to keep the NFB free from government restraints.

The mix worked. NFB studios took their place among the world's leading documentary film houses, pioneering *cinéma vérité* and other film techniques including animation. Several NFB studios received recognition by garnering U.S. Academy Awards and hundreds of other national and international film awards. What began with Grierson, one assistant, two secretaries, and a supervisor of production grew by 1945, when he left the Board, to a staff of 787 in 12 production units that had created more than 500 films being shown throughout Canada and the United States (Evans, 1984, 1977).[1]

National Film Board of Canada studios still operate under a legal mandate to "produce and distribute, and to promote the production and distribution of films in the public interest." Specifically, NFB films are to interpret Canada to Canadians and to other nations, and the staff are to advise the government in matters pertaining to film and to conduct film research. Canadians can borrow NFB films without charge through libraries, with extensive video rentals and inexpensive sales also available.

CREATION OF STUDIO D

In its early years, NFB filmmakers traveled to local churches, schools, and libraries to discuss their films with those who came to see them, creating a strong synergy between filmmakers and those who "consumed" the work. This practice has largely disappeared in most Board studios, but a similar kind of direct interaction between filmmakers and women audiences has reemerged with creation of a feminist filmmaking unit that grew from the ferment of the 1960s.

Even though it was (and is) a unique environment, the NFB reflects many influences of the artistic environment of the larger society, and its filmmaking was male-dominated. Until recently, virtually all directors and producers have been men; women, when present in filmmaking, played support roles.[2] Women in the NFB, as in outside filmmaking units, were always present, but in small

1. Descriptions and other information relative to all NFB films described in this paper can be seen in the catalog, *Beyond the Image*, which may be obtained from The Women's Forum, or Studio D at The National Film Board of Canada at P.O. Box 6100, Station A, Montreal, QUEBEC H3C 3H5. Studio D's telephone number is (514) 283–9533 or FAX at (514) 283–5487, attn. Studio D.

Identification of distributors for rental or purchase of the films in the United States may be obtained from the National Film Board of Canada, 1251 Avenue of the Americas 16th Floor, New York, NY 10020–1173. Tel.: (212) 586–5131; FAX: (212) 575–2382.

2. For a brief overview of women's early roles in film, see Quart, B. K. (1988). *Women Directors: The Emergence of a New Cinema*. New York: Praeger.

numbers and in supporting roles. But in the late 1960s, as elsewhere in the United States and Canada, the few women in the NFB began to agitate for change. One of these was Kathleen Shannon, who joined the Board in 1956. Working as a sound and picture editor, she contributed to more than 200 films before being permitted to direct or produce. Then, in the early 1970s she began creating "Working Mothers," a series of short films introducing women whose lives involved the difficult juxtaposition of motherhood with paid work outside the home.

While the women in the NFB's French Division chose to work within existing studios, Shannon urged the Board to respond to the excitement about International Women's Year, set for 1975, by creating a new studio. In 1974, that became Studio D.[3] The NFB charged its new "women's studio" to meet the "particular needs of women filmmakers and audiences." In so doing, the NFB acknowledged both a need to improve the status of women within the NFB (a need documented a few years later by the Board's own Equal Opportunity Report) and the absence of films in the NFB catalog that suitably addressed the women's audience (Brassard, Nash, St.-Arnaud, and Tremblay, 1978).

The creation of Studio D typified mainstream responses to feminist agitation in the 1970s. Two women, including Shannon, and one man currently on staff were reassigned to establish the new unit. They received no new budget or new positions. Over the next decade, however, creative budgeting and careful planning attracted others. The budget slowly increased, and the work matured. What began with so tiny a nucleus became a major force, producing some of the NFB's most widely circulated and widely recognized films. Two Studio D films have been awarded U.S. Academy Awards and from 1987–93, the NFB Marketing Division had a major women's promotions program.[4]

TRAINING WOMEN FILMMAKERS

Studio D's first major initiative was to provide technical support and filmmaking opportunities to a large number of inexperienced women though an imaginative series called "Just a Minute." Shannon reasoned that making any film, regardless of length, requires all filmmaking skills, so the Studio published a call for proposals for one-minute films. From the 87 proposals received, 27 were selected, and the women received support in producing these short pieces.

To celebrate its 15th anniversary, Studio D created a similar program. Women throughout Canada were invited to submit proposals for five-minute

---

3. The name, Studio D, has no symbolic significance. Studios in the English Division of the Board were designated by letters.
4. *If You Love This Planet* (1982) and *I'll Find a Way* (1977). *Flamenco at 5:15* (1983) was made by a Studio D director working in another studio.

films. They received a small amount of production support from the NFB and assurance that their work would be widely distributed through the NFB and Studio D marketing system. From more than 200 proposals, 17, almost all from novice filmmakers, were selected for support. Studio D created a feature-length compilation of the completed films, *Five Feminist Minutes*. Launched in 1990, *Five Feminist Minutes* was among the most popular NFB productions marketed that year (Hubert, 1991). The films addressed topics ranging from police harassment of prostitutes to sex education and aging. Each filmmaker retained ownership and distribution rights for her piece, while being widely promoted through Studio D and the NFB.

The Studio has undertaken a number of other direct training programs during its existence (Shannon, et al., 1991). It has sponsored apprentice programs, craft and writing workshops, a contest for drama script writing, and a film production workshop. A project undertaken with the International Youth Year Secretariat in 1986 provided support and in-house training for 26 novice filmmakers, one-third of whom were women of color and Native women. Project director Gerry Rogers achieved this high ratio—a percentage of Native women or women of color found in no film school enrollment at the time—through targeted recruiting. Participants received intensive training in sound and camera, and together produced six films.

During 1991, Studio D launched New Initiatives in Film, a program focused on providing training to women of color and Native women. The program includes development of a computerized listing of women of color and Native women across Canada involved in filmmaking; a summer institute providing intensive workshops in specific areas of documentary filmmaking; and an internship program that provides annual one-year internships at the NFB.

The work of Studio D has provided training in less direct ways as well. By the end of 1993, the Studio had produced, sponsored, co-produced, or otherwise supported well over two hundred films. To the extent possible within budget and Board limitations, the films were made by all-female crews. Thus, the work of Studio D gave experience not otherwise available to women cinematographers, grips, and sound and other technicians. In addition, it has offered directing and producing opportunities.

Prior to the second wave feminist movement, few people in the film industry saw women as suited to directing, producing, or many of the technical tasks. Studio D rejected such views. From its earliest days, Studio D recognized that women who play support roles in filmmaking can direct or produce and should not be bypassed for opportunities to do so. Thus, it has supported many novice directors and producers, and many of its films are a director's earliest work.[5]

Studio D has also provided informal training through the Federal Women's Film Program (FWFP). Conceived and nurtured by Studio D, the FWFP com-

5. Academy-Award-winning director Terri Nash (*If You Love This Planet*) made her first film in the *Just a Minute* series, for instance.

bines resources from various federal agencies to make films for women that help the agencies involved to carry out their various missions. For example, social services agencies make use of a series of films about services for battered women and education agencies supported a number of films about women in nontraditional work roles.[6] With these "outside" resources, Studio D can do many things that would not otherwise be possible. In the FWFP, Shannon noted, they can partially recreate a situation used in earlier years when most editors worked with assistants who, practically speaking, were apprentices (Shannon, October 1991). By the time Studio D was created, the NFB (for a number of unrelated reasons) no longer continued (or could continue) such a practice. In the FWFP, because its resources came from outside the Board, budgets could include assistants, positions in which inexperienced women could then learn filmmaking in a kind of "on-the-job" training experience. A similar kind of professional development activity is included in the 1993–94 New Initiatives in Film plan (NFB, 1993; Stikeman, 1993).

MAKING FILMS FOR AND ABOUT WOMEN

Another important commitment in Studio D's mandate was to make films that meet the needs of women audiences. From the beginning, almost all films it has produced, co-produced, or supported fill some void in the availability of films on topics of concern to women. The first Studio D effort was to complete the "Working Mothers" series, to which the women of Canada responded with unprecedented enthusiasm. The series, a still-popular collection of 11 short films, has "remained unfortunately current" (Shannon, 1986).

Another early major in-house production effort was the Children of Canada Series. In these ten films, director Beverly Shaffer introduced a wide variety of Canadian children. The series includes an Academy Award winner, *I'll Find a Way*, the story of a girl disabled by spina bifida who struggles with strength and good cheer against the restrictions of her disability. Other films in the series present Leonard, son of a lighthouse keeper; Veronica, daughter of Polish

---

6. The first FWFP film was *Attention: Women at Work!* (1983) showing Canadian women active in construction, architecture, and the Coast Guard. Other such films are *Head Start: Meeting the Computer Challenge* (1984), *Doctor, Lawyer, Indian Chief* (1986), and *The Impossible Takes a Little Longer* (1986), which shows how disabled women can work in and outside the home. In the early years, Studio D itself also made a number of films about women in nontraditional careers: *Laila* (1980) shows a Polish-born Canadian who established her own drywall business because contractors refused to hire her when she completed a training course; *Too Dirty for a Woman* (1983) introduces a group of women who work for the Iron Ore Company as truck drivers, engineers, laborers, geologists, warehouse workers, machinists, and mechanics; *Louise Drouin, Veterinarian* (1981) relates the life of a veterinarian; and *I Want to Be an Engineer* (1983) presents three attractive young women who are successful in three different engineering specialties.

A third phase of the FWFP focus on women and work also included the NFB's French Division women's program, Regards de Femmes, in creating a wide-ranging group of films made by many independent directors and craftwomen. All these films help parents and educators expose students to the variety of work opportunities for women outside the home, occupations that generally pay much better than traditional women's work.

immigrants who works in her parents' bakery; Susan, who with her Chinese parents and neighbors was displaced during construction of high-rise office buildings in downtown Montreal; Gurdeep, who works a British Columbia dairy farm with his Sikh parents; and Benoit, a young Quebecois who plays his violin with the Orchestre symphonique des jeunes de Joliette.

All films in this series are sensitively photographed, and unlike most documentary produced at the time, none include a male narrator. Virtually all the voices in each film are those of the children themselves. In this way, the series reflects what has become a Studio D tradition: no male authoritative voice-over narrating.

Another group of Studio D films introduced and historicized a variety of individual women, some exceptional, some not.[7] Many concentrate on artists or focus on professional women or women who played some role in the public arena. This group of films, in its recording of artists and exceptional people, fits solidly within Film Board tradition. Many such films have been made throughout the NFB; Studio D's films are unusual only in that all focus on women. Some of Studio D's films that describe women's lives, however, are relatively unusual in that they focus on "ordinary" women. In so doing, these films do more than record the lives of women; they make a feminist statement. In focusing on "women's" work generally ignored by historians, the films highlight the importance of these roles and give voice to such previously invisible women. The films make women visible in a larger sense than just making a picture of them. They reclaim the value of such work and the women who do it.

STUDIO D'S FEMINIST CHALLENGE

During its first decade, the studio refined its goals. It never abandoned the initial concept embodied in its mandate (to make films by, for, and about women), but the feminist goals became more explicit. A 1989 brochure describing Studio D cited the goals of their films as "to engage audiences, spark discussion and raise

---

7. These include *Eve Lambart* (1978); *Portrait of the Artist—As an Old Lady* (1982); *Maud Lewis: A World Without Shadows* (1976); *The Legacy of Mary McEwan* (1987); *The Lady from Grey County* (1977); *A Love Affair with Politics: A Portrait of Marion Dewar* (1987); *Worth Every Minute* (1987); and *The Right Candidate for Rosedale* (1979).

Among the earliest of these films was *Great Grand Mother* (1975). It paid tribute to women pioneers of the Canadian prairies as well as to their efforts to win suffrage for women. Another such early film is *Patricia's Moving Picture* (1978). It details the mid-life changes of a woman who had raised seven children but battled depression as they matured and no longer needed her mothering.

Others of the films that focus on less extraordinary women record nondomestic work by women. *Adele and the Ponies of Ardmore* (1984) tells of a woman sharing the work of a horsebreeding and training farm with her husband. *The Best Times of Our Lives: Portraits of Women in Mid-Life* (1985) introduces ten different women dealing with menopause and mid-life. Three films about African market women detail their efforts to establish an entrepreneurial niche within East Africa: *Fair Trade* (1991), *From the Shore* (1990), and *Where Credit is Due* (1990). These present, respectively, women who participate in open markets, manage a fishing enterprise in a Muslim community where women cannot go to sea themselves, and who turn small loans into thriving businesses even if, in some cases, they must mortgage their homes to do so.

consciousness," and described the films as "tools for social change and empowerment" (NFB, n.d.). To meet these goals, the Studio made a number of issue-oriented films explicitly challenging the patriarchy. Many of these works exhibit one of two themes: Women can, through individual and shared strength, survive the common and uncommon blows delivered by a patriarchal system; and women can and do explicitly challenge the existing institutions of that system.

The "survivors" films range from more to less hopeful; almost all are deeply moving. The subjects range from incest to nuclear armaments. Many also involve a search theme. One of the earliest such films was *Dark Lullabies* (1985), in which the daughter of a couple who survived imprisonment in German concentration camps relates her search to understand the Holocaust. Another survivor/search theme film is the 1992 co-production, *Women in the Shadows*, in which a Metis woman traces her Indian heritage. Other exceptional examples of this group of films include *The Impossible Takes a Little Longer* (1986), which shows how disabled women can live independent lives or move into the workplace; *Toward Intimacy* (1992), a film in which disabled women discuss the previously taboo subject of their sexuality; and *To a Safer Place* (1987), the experiences of an adult survivor of childhood sexual abuse as she returns to see the people and places of her childhood horrors.

Among the "challenge" films are some of Studio D's most controversial works. Probably the best known of these are *Not a Love Story* (1981), *Abortion: Stories from North and South* (1984), and the Academy-Award-winning film, *If You Love This Planet* (1982). *Not a Love Story* graphically examines the pornography business; it fueled, if it did not spark, the anti-pornography movement that spanned Canada and the United States during the 1980s. A controversial film accused by some of reflecting the phenomenon it deplored, *Not a Love Story* may have had the longest run of any NFB film in commercial theaters both in Canada and the United States. *Abortion: Stories from North and South* uses pictures and conversations from six countries to demonstrate that, whether legal or not, abortions occur with regularity. This film has been shown a number of times on U.S. public television. *If You Love This Planet*, an insistent statement against nuclear armaments that gained a major publicity boost when it was declared propaganda by the U.S. State Department, also helped to fuel a popular movement.

Several other Studio D films made beginning in the 1980s raise provocative questions and challenges to established institutions and practices. These include a look at the women of the Nicaraguan revolution and their role within it (*Dream of a Free Country: A Message from Nicaraguan Women*, 1983); an examination of sexism in the Catholic church (*Behind the Veil: Nuns*, 1984); a record of conversations with Jewish women confronting Judaism and its roles for women (*Half the Kingdom*, 1989); an examination of how Western religions have treated earlier Goddess-based religions (*Goddess Remembered*, 1989); a review of the witch craze in Europe and an argument that the church and the state sanctioned violence against women (*The Burning Times*, 1990); and an English version of an earlier French Division film that questions the role of the toy industry in preparing children to play stereotyped adult roles (*Toying with Their Future*, 1990). A 1992 release, *Forbidden Love*, contrasts the lives of eight lesbian women in the 1950s with popular fiction's stereotyped depiction of lesbians.

Although most of these issue-oriented films focus primarily on Canadian women, few are limited exclusively to Canadians. Almost all emphasize that the connections among women and the problems confronting women transcend national boundaries. *Some American Feminists* (1977), one of few Studio D films to focus on primarily U.S. subjects, is illustrative of the nearly universal nature of the issues the Studio examines. This film, one of Studio D's earliest, features New York leaders of the 20th-century women's movement. Little in that film, however, seems dated today, as it highlights issues of concern within the modern women's movement. Similarly, *Sisters in the Struggle* (1991) features Black Canadian feminists as they discuss the complex barriers to their freedom they encounter from Black men and White women as well as from the White males usually considered to be privileged by a patriarchal system. *Sisters* more explicitly raises issues of class in patriarchal domination than do most Studio D films.

ACCOMPLISHMENTS AND CHALLENGES

In many ways, recent Studio D films epitomize the current struggles of feminists in self-definition. The films raise issues of feminism and reflect aspects of differences among women. *Sisters in the Struggle* addresses continuing racial bias; *Women in the Shadows* (1992) highlights how the European invasion has impacted Native women. *After the Montreal Massacre* (1990) raises the question of what role men should/must play in creating a feminist world. *Faithful Women*, a series created from an interfaith conference of women sponsored by the World Council of Churches, identifies differences among Muslim, Jewish, Christian, Buddhist, Hindu, North American Native, and NeoPagan women.

In many ways Studio D itself reflects the changes among women and within North American feminist movements since 1970. The Studio has become more competent, more overtly feminist, and more widely known. It has also come to be more explicitly seen as involving a wider variety of women as filmmakers. Thus, Studio D's films are, arguably, becoming more important as well. As many feminist theorists have pointed out, because women and their voices have been isolated, women understandably often doubt or undervalue their own experiences (see, for example, hooks, 1989; Kramarae, 1981). Hence the public media can validate what one is thinking or feeling or they can verify what has happened.

But such increase in Studio D's influence has not come without internal struggle. Its efforts to expand beyond a small group of largely White women have been at times problematic.[8] In previous work (1988), I noted that being embedded within patriarchal and bureaucratic structures (the film industry, a government agency) created conflict among the women of Studio D. As a unit created with few resources, not surprisingly Studio D films did not reflect the diversity of women's experiences. During its first decade or so, Studio D tended to submerge (though never completely) the specific concerns of non-White women and to a lesser extent the concerns of working- and lower-class women. Then, just as its feminism and filmmaking seemed to mesh with increasing maturity in a number of films with great impact, the Studio shared the problems of growing economic conservatism within all but a few U.S. and Canadian government agencies.

Like the larger women's and feminist movements of which the filmmakers are a part, members of Studio D have taken and are continuing to take a variety of steps to confront and deal with these issues. Their filmmaking reflects these steps. Inclusion of women of color within a group facing tight budget restrictions is difficult, though it is occurring.

In 1989, Studio D reorganized, moving all staff directors to other NFB studies. Studio D now has no full-time staff directors, freeing Studio D production funds to support the work of a wider diversity of filmmakers, usually employed on a freelance or contract basis. This move enhanced the Studio's ability to support minority filmmakers and to make films that serve the needs of minority audiences. One result is a series, *Women at the Well*, that focuses on Black women in Canada. Included are historical films *Older, Stronger, Wiser* (1989), *Sisters in the Struggle* (1991), and *Long Time Coming* (1993) that introduce the work of Black artists and musicians. These films will be marketed in a group with a production of the NFB Atlantic Region Studio, *Black Mother, Black Daughter* (1990). All will be attractive and useful to an audience long underserved by both documentary and feature film.

This change in the Studio structure doubtless increases the total number of women supported in filmmaking. At the same time, it may do relatively little to improve economic conditions for many women given only short-term work. And the moves were painful to some of the women moved from Studio D to other NFB units. Studio D's struggles exemplify the continuing difficulties of any group in accomplishing feminist goals within a patriarchal culture.

8. Shannon chose a woman of color as one of the three original members of Studio D. Thereafter, for many years the only new staff hire permitted by restrictions imposed on the NFB was that of a secretary. Thus, to a very large extent, new staff members in Studio D came from other places inside the Board, and were people originally hired in male-dominated studios. In 1978, four formerly freelance contract filmmakers for the studio became staff as a result of a labor action brought by the NFB employees union on their behalf. Among these four women (a percentage of women not duplicated in any other NFB studio where other contract filmmakers became staff) were two Jewish women and one woman of color.

Overall, the Studio receives little funding, and exists within an agency that is itself facing funding limitations. At the same time, annually it receives about 200 proposals for film projects (Studio D, n.d.). Thus, Studio members recognize that the steps toward accomplishing their goals have not been huge ones. They agonize at having too few resources to satisfy needs that are too large. They continue, however, in the words of current executive producer Ginny Stikeman, to seek to give women information they need "that's not available in the malestream media" and to try to see "that different filmmakers get opportunity within what is still a small funding pie" (1992).

Overall, Studio D has opened doors for women and provided opportunities not previously available. One merely needs to compare the credits of films produced by Studio D, largely consisting of names of women, with those produced by any other Studio within the NFB to see that women have had more and more influential roles in making films in Studio D than elsewhere within the NFB. A count of every film listed on every 20th page in the 1992 catalog, for instance, shows that of NFB films not made by Studio D, just over 10 percent had women as producers or directors. In contrast, women have produced or directed virtually all Studio D films.

GIVING VOICE TO WOMEN

Studio D's success is also apparent when one looks at its work. The continuing popularity of Studio D films demonstrates that they help reinforce the commonalities among women's experiences, even as the individual films often celebrate diversity. In helping women identify with each other and recognize their common needs, the films of Studio D serve as feminist rhetoric.

Studio D's ambitions are exemplified in the words of a former producer, now a high-level administrator within the Board, who said they sought nothing less than "to change the status of women" (Janes, 1986). Studio D seeks restructuring in how women live their lives, knowing that it requires restructuring the world in which women live. Films with such ambitious goals, at least those with any degree of success, cannot avoid controversy. Whereas most feminist documentary is known and commented on only in women's circles or by film critics, several Studio D films have provoked mainstream protest. Most notable among these controversial works are *Not a Love Story, If You Love This Planet, Speaking Our Peace, Behind the Veil: Nuns,* and *The Burning Times.*

Studio D films have at a minimum participated in a dialogue through which women can learn to seek changes. In so doing, they meet a major Studio goal and contribute directly to helping women's voices be heard. Most of the films frame issues and evoke viewer responses in ways that lead women to confront views different from their own and to uncover issues previously submerged in their own lives. The shared experience of viewing a film and discussing their reactions with each other has helped many women frame and clarify issues of similarity and difference.

If recording and presenting the stories of women who have resisted traditional roles for women helps other women change how they deal with expectations for women, the films of Studio D have made major contributions to achieving the goals of the filmmakers. Studio D has made many such films. A more difficult question is whether those films do more than present the lives of women. Do the films reflect a woman's perspective? They do, I believe, in several ways.

The films of Studio D give women voice. The films have moved from one early film narrated by an authoritative male voice, to women narrators, to using less and less narration by filmmaker, to recent efforts totally devoid of narration. Always the films present women speaking for themselves, whether it is to relate the details of their lives or to demonstrate how long odds have been overcome to achieve goals.

In addition, in addressing a wide variety of issues not previously openly addressed—incest, patriarchal hegemony in medicine (DES, elimination of midwifery, menopause, and midlife), sexuality of the disabled—women's voices are given weight. The films also give voice to previously marginalized women. Among these are older women, women of color, the disabled, lesbians, nuns speaking outside the control of the church, Jewish feminists, and women working in nonprofessional positions. Among these are young women: the Children of Canada series highlights children respectfully as perhaps only a woman filmmaker would do.

Women's voices gain weight as they become part of the historical record, and whether as an overt focus or in a less conscious way, the films of Studio D visually record women's history. They put women and women's concern on record as never before, permanently and visually. They provide models of how to redefine issues previously framed largely in patriarchal ways.

It is, of course, always possible to point out how specific films fail to accomplish their goals, or do so in a less than ideal way. Many films contain flaws, some large, some small. Some critics argue that the Studio D film attacking pornography, *Not a Love Story*, itself uses a voyeuristic gaze. The same argument could be made about *Forbidden Love*. Similarly, some voyeurism, or at the least romanticism, is built into *To a Safer Place*, the incest survivor film. *Goddess Remembered* is properly criticized for its unacknowledged Western bias. Some films reveal the inexperience of a novice director; others have inadequate camera work. I could cite other examples. But such criticisms are beside the point. To expect a body of work such as that of Studio D to be unerringly executed would be to expect what is impossible even in a filmmaking group that did not place training and giving opportunities to newcomers among its highest values.

More striking is that Studio D films give voice to women who would not likely be heard in any other way, that many are visually stunning and emotionally powerful, and that most challenge barriers to women's empowerment. Most of the work of Studio D lets women participate in demanding attention for universal concerns of women; much is timeless and will have utility for years even without considering its historical value. The feminist visions of Studio D films, though not always unerring and appropriately not all the same, pervade the body of work. Most of us would be happy to have the same said of our lives.

REFERENCES

Brassard, C., Nash, M. T., St-Arnaud, M., & Tremblay, M. (1978). *Women at the National Film Board: An equal opportunity study.* Montreal: National Film Board of Canada.

Campbell, K. K. (1989). *No man shall speak for her.* New York: Praeger.

Campbell, K. K. (1989a). The sound of women's voices. *Quarterly Journal of Speech, 75,* 212–258.

Clarke, A. (1991, April). Interview.

Evans, G. (1984). *John Grierson and the National Film Board: The politics of wartime propaganda.* Toronto: University of Toronto Press.

hooks, b. (1989). *Talking back: Thinking feminist thinking Black.* Boston: South End Press.

Hubert, N. (1991, April). Interview.

Hughes, P. H. (1991, May). Interview.

Janes, B. (1986, June). Interview.

Kramarae C. (1981). *Women and men speaking.* Rowley, MA: Newbury House.

Nash, M. T. (1982). *Images of women in National Film Board of Canada films during World War II and the post-war years (1939–1949).* Unpublished doctoral dissertation, McGill University, Montreal, Quebec.

National Film Board of Canada. (n.d.) *Studio D.* Descriptive brochure available from National Film Board of Canada, Montreal, Quebec.

National Film Board of Canada. (1993, Spring). *New Initiatives in Film* newsletter.

Quart, B. K. (1988). *Women directors: The emergence of a new cinema.* New York: Praeger.

Rogers, G. (1991, April). Interview.

Shannon, K. (1985, March). *This is about objectivity, objections, and some objectives.* Address to conference of the Centre for Investigative Journalism, Toronto, Ontario.

Shannon, K. (1986, June). Interview.

Shannon, K. (1991, October). Interview.

Shannon, K. et. al. (1991, February). Submission to the Task Force on Professional Training for the Cultural Sector in Canada from Studio D, National Film Board of Canada. Unpublished Manuscript.

Stikeman, G. (1992). Personal communication.

Stikeman, G. (1993). Personal communication.

Studio D. (n.d.). *Guidelines for proposals made to Studio D.* Unpublished document.

Taylor, A. (1987, November). *The National Film Board's Studio D: Feminists making films for peace.* Paper presented at the annual convention of the Speech Communication Association, Boston, MA.

Taylor, A. (1988). Implementing feminist principles in a bureaucracy. In B. B. Bate & A. Taylor (Eds.), *Women Communicating* (pp. 277–302). Norwood, NJ: Ablex Publishing.

Taylor, A. (1991, November). *Studio D The National Film Board of Canada: Feminist film-makers and women's community.* Paper presented at the annual convention of the Speech Communication Association, Atlanta, GA.

Taylor, A. (1992, April). *Using film to confront violence against women:* After the Montreal Massacre *and* To a Safer Place. Paper presented at the annual convention of the Eastern Communication Association, Portland, ME.

If the paper seems preoccupied with the diaspora experience and its narratives of displacement, it is worth remembering that all discourse is "placed," and the heart has its reasons.
(Hall, 1991, p. 223)

One of these roles given to Asian women by their families and communities is to be the upholders and preservers of "our culture." So what happens if a woman wishes to have her own identity and wear clothes which she alone has chosen? . . .
It is obvious that more than modesty is at stake.
(Wilson, 1989, p. 110)

19

NOT "KNOWING HER PLACE":

The Negotiation of Cultural Identity in Films by Asian/Pacific American Women[1]

LYNDA GOLDSTEIN

Linda Goldstein, Assistant Professor of English at Pennsylvania State University, Wilkes-Barre, received her Ph.D. from Temple University. Her research interests include women's video and film production, women's performance art and the relationships among popular culture forms, and queer theory. She is currently finishing an article on *Northern Exposure* and its theorizations of cultural differences.

1. Part of this title is borrowed from Indu Krishnan's *Knowing Her Place* (1990), a videotape exploring what Vasu, the subject of this documentary, calls "cultural schizophrenia." Krishnan suggests that this feeling of being pulled between two very different cultures is particularly keen for women.

In a recent writing class concerned with issues of multiculturalism and popular culture, students were asked to begin responding to bell hooks's essay "Straightening Our Hair" by writing a short journal entry on the first time they had thought about the relationship between racial identity and beauty. Most of my students (17 Caucasians, 3 African Americans, and 1 Latina)[2] immediately thought about race in terms of Blackness, in part, perhaps, because of the focus of hooks' essay, but in part, too, because we tend to think of race in the United States as a "Black and White" issue, attributing race to Blacks and forgetting that Whites are raced too. Most students penned a "beauty is color-blind" sentiment in their responses, neatly ducking the issues, so it was with particular attention that I read one written by a young Caucasian woman with the blond "girl-next-door" good looks of her Irish heritage. She wrote of having been in second grade when she met a new classmate with whom she fell immediately in love. It was the first time she'd ever seen someone of Asian/Pacific descent, and she was enthralled by her diminutive stature, her "exotic" hair, and what she called the "perfect porcelain cast of her skin." She looked like a "china doll," the student wrote, "and I wished I could have skin like that."

This student's reaction to her new classmate is hardly unusual in a culture that still tries to maintain the "melting pot" ideal of unified "American-ness," as the other students indicated in their writing. The body of the new second-grade student was visibly marked for the writer as racially different, the beauty of which she had been taught to find "exotic."

The images of the Asian girl or woman as "china doll," "Dragon Lady," "Suzie Wong," or virginal "Lotus Blossom" are familiar to all of us from Hollywood films, music videos, or network television. Indeed, the conflicting representations of Asian/Pacific girls and women as exotic, sinister, docile, yet equipped with an extraordinary repertoire of sexual tricks to please men should be recognizable to us from any number of popular films.[3] Just think of the good-hearted prostitutes in *The World of Suzie Wong* (1960), the docile geisha girls in *Sayonara* (1957), or the diabolical "Eurasian" wife in *The Letter* (1940), who blackmails, then murders, her deceased husband's lover to avenge his murder by the lover's hand.[4]

---

2. My campus is located in northeastern Pennsylvania, an area that is predominately Caucasian though ethnically diverse. Few of my White students had thought about issues of race or interacted with those of different races before attending my class.
3. See D. Gee, *Slaying the Dragon*, 1989.
4. In *The Letter*, the "Eurasian" character of Mrs. Hammond is played by Caucasian actress Gale Sondergaard in keeping with the Motion Picture Production Code regulations against depicting miscegenation in a positive manner: It was taboo to have an Asian (descended) actress play an Asian/Pacific woman kissing a Caucasian man. It was acceptable however for a Caucasian actress to play an Asian/Pacific romantic interest. After MPPC's repeal in the late 1940s, a number of films, such as *Sayonara*, foregrounded interracial romantic relations with Asian/Pacific actresses in the roles (often without regard to cultural or national differences), though the women they portrayed were generally of the docile "Lotus Blossom" type.

Asian/Pacific American women filmmakers have recently worked to combat these often cartoonish and contradictory representations of Asian/Pacific women.

THE ISSUE OF TERMINOLOGY

Before turning to the kinds of work that these filmmakers have produced, we should consider what is meant by the terms *Asian, Asian/Pacific,* and *Asian-Pacific American* as categories of cultural identity. The terms generally refer to a vast geographical area encompassing a variety of cultures. In its largest sense, the designation *Asian/Pacific* includes the people of the Pacific Rim collection of archipelagos—including Hawaii and the Philippines—all of which have distinct cultural identities. It stretches west across the Asian continent to include the Indian subcontinent. This geographical mapping of "Asian/Pacific" is one sense of what Stuart Hall means by *place* in the quote at the beginning of this chapter.

But *place*—in terms of a unified cultural identity—is not easily determined and thus may result in an attendant sense of dislocation.[5] Given the array of cultures grouped under "Asian/Pacific" (or any similar term, such as "Hispanic"), we must recognize how complicated and disunified its construction is and carefully consider its usefulness as a catch-all category for thinking about cultural identity. The very designation *Asian/Pacific,* with its slashing bar, indicates to us that this is an identity that is already multilayered and not limited to a single cultural heritage.

Creation of Cultural Identity

The construction of our identities is never simply a matter of popular media, such as Hollywood films, determining who we are. Identities are formed by the interactions of ourselves and those who create representations of our selves. In other words, the sense of (dis)placement felt by some Asian/Pacific Americans is not only determined by Hollywood representations but by the films and other media made by Asian/Pacific Americans, with the most interesting effect coming from a dialogue between these multiple sources of representation. As Hall, following Antonio Gramsci, has argued, these filmmakers evidence the ways in which the subject is composed of a "'plurality' of selves or identities." Indeed,

> This multi-faceted nature of consciousness is not an individual but a collective phenomenon, a consequence of the relationship between "the self" and the ideological discourses which compose the cultural terrain of a society (1986, p. 22).

5. The documentary videotape *Japanese American Women,* by Alfaro and Hagemann, indicates in its very title the importance of trying to negotiate a sense of place, a position for one's identity, when one feels split between at least two cultural heritages.

Thus we may not even be able to speak of "the subject" or of "Asian Americans" without oversimplifying.

THREE FILMMAKERS

This chapter will consider how three Asian/Pacific American women filmmakers have chosen to articulate for themselves what the history, experience, and interpretation—the construction, in short—of such an identity is.[6] And it should be clear that such articulations are not fixed couplings of Asian and American. Indeed, perhaps the only generalization that can be made about the work of independent Asian/Pacific American women filmmakers is that cultural identities experienced as hyphenated are very fluid, blurring what Asian and American mean.[7]

Further, these filmmakers persistently foreground gender as an operative category in the formation and negotiation of cultural identity.[8] As we shall see in the work of Rea Tajiri, Thi Thanh Nga, and Christine Chang, identity is always conceived in relation to others and most often in relation to family—not as something individual. The "collective phenomenon" to which Gramsci refers, then, means not only discourses working together but also bodies in social formations (such as the family) negotiating identity. As Amrit Wilson (1989) indicates, an Asian/Pacific woman's "place" as cultural watchdog necessarily gives her the responsibility of maintaining ties to other places and other times, and all three filmmakers demonstrate the extent to which this is the case for their subjects.

History and Memory

We should think of displacement as not only a spatial phenomenon but a temporal one as well. This is particularly highlighted in Rea Tajiri's *History and Memory*, in which she constructs "history and memory" as always separate and incapable of any representation that unifies the two temporally situated concepts. Like many other Japanese American artists, Tajiri turns to the post–Pearl-

6. The double bind of essentialism—that "natural" racial or gender identity is both confining and a means of identifying with others to effect social change—has been discussed by theorists Judith Butler, Diana Fuss, bell hooks, and Cornel West, among others.
7. I mention video here and in the footnotes because much of the work in this area has not been on film stock but on video. There are obvious financial reasons for this as it is considerably less expensive to produce a video than a film; other reasons include forms of address, consumption, syntactic logic, and image manipulation. All these differ significantly from those of film and should be taken into account when considering the ways they narrativize the dislocations of cultural identity.
8. Gay male Asian and Pacific Rim film and video makers similarly consider the ways in which cultural identity is not a simple, though never simply negotiated, bifurcation between "Asian/Pacific" and "American." See R. Fung (1985), *Orientations* and M. S. Ma (1993), *Toc Storee*.

Harbor internment camps as a defining moment of cultural identity.[9] Required by the U.S. government to sell their property and move to temporary relocation camps in the deserts and mountains east of the Pacific coast (to prevent alleged espionage activities for Japan), Japanese immigrants (*issei*) and their American-born descendants (*nisei*) had to come to terms with what visible racial difference from the dominant White population means in the United States, even when one is an American citizen.[10]

Tajiri's sense of her self as a Japanese American woman is intimately linked to her family's history, yet she discovered that their memories are obscured, missing, or incapable of articulation. Dissatisfied with her mother's refusal to discuss her internment, Tajiri imagined it for her. Her autobiographical quest for knowledge about the camps—personal, familial, and cultural—begins with a textual narrative between two parents discussing their child's nightmares about the Internment, an experience that the child could never have had. On film, her search is condensed into the slow-motion image of a woman drinking and bathing her face from a pump under the hot sun, an image that lyrically punctuates Tajiri's reconstructed history, as does her voice-over narration. She journeys to the camp that relocated her mother's sense of cultural identity as a *nisei*, but it is barren of life (its structures dismantled or in disrepair, its vegetable gardens replaced by tumbleweeds). Its barbed wire hems in a seemingly blank history. This history must be replaced by the constructed memories Tajiri gathers from interviews with relatives and by the history embedded in photographs, newspaper clippings, outtakes from government propaganda newsreels, and Hollywood films representing the Japanese American experience during World War II.

In her juxtapositions of materials, Tajiri demonstrates that history and memory are incommensurable categories of time and of knowledge production. How do we construct a history of experience, asks Tajiri, that does not include the memories of experience? And what happens when those memories are so painful that we erase them or allow them to be consumed by our experience of the present? What happens when the locations of those memories are themselves eradicated? Finally, what happens when those memories never existed? What, then, is one's cultural history? Her *nisei* father, drafted prior to the bombing of Pearl Harbor, served honorably in the military to protect his country—to which he is related by culture—from aggression by a nation to which he is related by ancestry. Like others of his generation, he had literally bought into the American dream, buying property as a means of ensuring economic prosperity as well as

---

9. See, for example, M. Yamada (1976), *Camp Notes and Other Poems;* J. Houston (1973), *Farewell to Manzanar;* and T. Kaneshiro (1976), *Internees: War Relocation Center Memoirs and Diaries.* For other films/videos, see M. Onodera (1988), *The Displaced View* and J. Tanaka (1989), *Memories from the Department of Amnesia.*

10. During the same period, it must be remembered, the United States was waging war in Europe against Germany and Italy (until the latter joined the Allied forces). Although anti-German and Italian feelings ran high against Americans of German and Italian heritage during World War II, neither ethnic group was threatened with communal internment without due process.

rooting his and his family's identification as American. Yet, he returned to find not only his family interned but his house removed from its very foundations. The racist justifications for internment become a history that is inevitably uncontainable by the physical boundaries of the camp. They leak into the small-town dreams of Washington apple farmers and suburban dwellers from the multiple sources that Tajiri's cut-and-paste (bricolage) structure foregrounds.

Technique as the Message

All three directors deploy these bricolage techniques in their films as a way of exploring issues of identity construction and displacement and of *articulating* (in Hall's double sense of the term as "voicing" and "enjoining") the multidimensionality of identity formation. For each, the cut-and-paste strategy of bricolage enables them to envision and voice the contested dislocations of identity marked by a multiplicity of racial/cultural/sexual/gender differences. In their work, the dislocations of the subject are conceived spatially, temporally, metaphorically, and metaphysically. They are most often posed as split between dual terms— past and present, history and memory, body and mind. More often however, the split exists along multiple lines of race, gender, and class fissures—what we might call the constellations of representational practice.[11] As we will see, Christine Chang's deployment of the Mae East, Snow White, Lady Dragon, Madame Butterfly, Cherry Blossom stereotypes of Asian/Pacific women in *Be Good My Children* are especially indicative of the latter.

Although examining these issues for different heritages—Tajiri for Japanese Americans, Chang for Korean Americans, and Nga for Vietnamese Americans, all three directors explore the intersections of gender, race, and sexuality in the formation of cultural identity through representational practices. Their films represent the complicated discursive formation of cultural identity through practices that could be labeled post-modernist. That is, for all their differences, these directors all construct films that are pastiche combinations of documentary talking-head interviews with family photographs with fictionalized recreations with archival footage with indigenous and contemporary music with voice-over narration with lyrical slow motion with visual and aural distortions with computer graphics with campy acting and so on.[12]

From Hollywood to Hanoi

For example, in *From Hollywood to Hanoi*, Tiana Alexander/Nga turns to the construction of the Vietnam War as the moment and place of her dislocation.

11. See Janice Tanaka's video, *Who's Going to Pay for These Donuts, Anyway?* (broadcast on PBS as part of its POV series) for another example of this technique.
12. For a video that does not use these techniques, see Krishnan's *Knowing Her Place*, which relies primarily on a *vérité* documentary style.

The film chronicles her literal return to Vietnam after emigrating as a child in 1966, combining footage from Nga's B-movie career as a karate-babe (and student of Bruce Lee) and aerobics instructor with home movies, newsreel footage, army training films, the red shoes shot from *The Wizard of Oz* (her favorite movie)—"There's no place like home (click), there's no place like home (click)"—with contemporary interviews with Vietnamese Americans, Vietnamese relatives, and documentation of the culturally impossible situation for AmerAsians in Vietnam. In a move to force American men to take responsibility, Nga insists on naming the fathers on camera.

Telling us she "tried to be everybody from Judy Garland to Jane Fonda to Tina Turner," Nga returns to Vietnam as a camera-wielding tourist in an ethnographic twist of "discovering the other" to uncover herself, a self she explicitly positions at the beginning of the film in an address at the University of California, Santa Barbara, as torn between two identities. Indeed, she returns despite the protests of her father and uncle, both of whom served in high South Vietnam government posts before the fall of Saigon, just prior to which her family had fled to the United States. Returned from her trip, Nga distributes presents among her relatives, and shows her father and uncle reacting ambivalently to their gifts: Yet her grandmother expresses an overwhelming desire to be able to return. She, too, feels the fragmentation of her identity (whereas her male relatives simply feel betrayed by the "fatherland" and assume a mythical unified relation to their new country).

The gender difference between their relations to Vietnam are an effect, perhaps, of the closer proximity between the national and cultural identities attached to her male relatives than to herself and grandmother. Such a proximity is literalized in the documentation of the plight of Viet and Duc (representing the North and South), twins joined at the abdomen and sharing a leg, the grotesque result of indiscriminate Agent Orange usage. (She intercuts these shots with Army propaganda film footage intoning that with "the proper delivery of chemicals, no special handling is required, and no harm can be caused to animal or human life.") Following the surgical separation, ironically enabled by the Vietnamese doctor's medical training in Texas, Duc comments that "it was strange being alone for the first time," a singularity of subjectivity that Nga knows is impossible to sustain without grave loss, even death, of one's self, of one's sense of place.

A veritable kaleidoscopic journey down "the yellow brick road" (the GI nickname for the Ho Chi Minh Trail), the film articulates the incoherence and decenteredness of any cultural subjectivity, but particularly for that formed in the specific moment of civil war, of internalized aggression within the national/individual subject. For women, who are keepers of the home culture, as Wilson's epigram indicates, there is always the sense of history and memory simultaneous with one's current notion of the self. No wonder that her grandmother and Nga would feel compelled to "commute between America and Vietnam" as one of the last titles informs us she does.

Be Good My Children

No less complexly organized, though it uses a fictionalized narrative strategy to dramatize the negotiations of identity for an immigrant, single-parent Korean family, is Christine Chang's *Be Good My Children*. The film irreverently combines narrative and musical conventions (destabilizing each) with intercut dream sequences of Mae East, Judy Lee's alter ego, vamping as the "exotic" object of Orientalist desire. This is juxtaposed with the ill-informed prejudices of European-descended Americans, represented by her boyfriend Paul's parents: "If we worked as hard as them [Koreans, referring to the numerous fruit and vegetable stores in New York City]" intones his father, "we would have knocked out the Japanese a long time ago." Clearly, for Paul's father, "Asian/Pacific" identities are constructed by their economic contributions. Yet his distinction between Koreans and Japanese is not based on anything more substantial than one stereotype—"hard-working, model minority"—against another—"inscrutable, sneaky" economic enemy. The heritage of the Pearl Harbor bombing by the Japanese is that any economic or cultural success is viewed by some Euro-Americans as a martial triumph not gained during World War II.

Mae East, obviously an "Asian" version of the vamping Mae West, often disrupts the realistic narrative of Lee family life. Dressed in a blue, glittering crown and blue boa, Mae East sings:

I'm free and easy
I come and go as I choose
. . . So beware of these eyes
I'm a devil in disguise
And they call me sister Honky Tonk

She enters to comment on the narrative and, more important, to highlight the discrepancies between representations and experience. Her eyes, signifying her racial otherness, betray the negative repercussions of "exotic" beauty. Her identity as an object of sexual desire for Euro-American men always mitigates her self-proclaimed identity of independence. Appropriated from American popular culture, Mae East is the quintessential figure of cultural schizophrenia for Judy, who is not alone in her search of popular images for a vision of identity. Asked why she came to the United States, her mother, Mrs. Lee, responds: "I used to watch a lot of American movies, but it sure is different here." What is different is not simply that the images of American life do not match the realities. Rather, "different" also refers to America as a land of splittings and double-edged cultural identities, especially for women.

Not only does Chang deconstruct Hollywood musical conventions in a humorous way (in contrast to the sexy and subservient Suzie Wong stereotype[13]) to articulate the multiple fields of identity formation, but she also points

13. See the documentaries *Slaying the Dragon* or *Japanese American Women* for contrast.

to the difficult negotiations that the process of cultural assimilation presents for the hyphenated subject. The character of Judy Lee, who is studying to be an actress, suggests the performative schizophrenia of cultural identity for some Asian/Pacific Americans, and particularly for women. Indeed her performances suggest that identity is ever constituted inside of representational practices: as an Asian/Pacific American woman, Judy is always bound to already-circulating yet limited images that ignore the realities and complexities of people's lives. During the dinner scene, for instance, Judy's contributions to the conversation are always polite, yet are betrayed by her imagined visions of herself in Mae East vamp outfits. These two aspects of her character indicate how she assumes she is being thought of by Paul's parents and offer a culturally acceptable role for a woman to sass back at the racist and sexist remarks of his parents.

What Chang (as well as Tajiri and Nga) illustrates is the difficulty of negotiating the modern (post-eighteenth-century) concept of the unified subject in a postmodern (mid-twentieth-century) world that is marked by fragmentation and incoherence.[14] Further, Chang's film foregrounds the extent to which the notion of cultural assimilation is problematic for Asian/Pacific American women and men who do not "blend in" as do Euro-Americans, whose physical attributes serve as the standard. In retelling her dreams to her psychotherapist—who ignores the cultural foundations of Judy's anxieties to intone: "I'm certain your neurosis can be centered in psycho-sexual responses"—Judy replays the performance anxieties of Asian/Pacific women. She describes a dressing room in which caricatures—Cherry Blossom, Miss Butterfly, Lady Dragon, Snow White—are introduced by a Picture Bride Agent to a Euro-American man shopping for a wife. All yell, "That's not my name!" breaking momentarily the hold these characters have on Judy's cultural identity as a constellation of representations. Yet, when they burst into a song rife with sexual innuendo, they indicate the extent to which Judy cannot escape from them.

ASSIMILATION ON FILM

All these films indicate the difficulties of negotiating cultural identity, but there are further implications as well. Located on film, these contested identities gain a certain spectacular currency in an American culture that not only values but reifies and commodifies the spectacular. Representations become the *thing itself,* which is why underrepresented populations are often so concerned with how they are represented. The fewer kinds of representations available, the more weight they carry, so much so that they operate not simply as images *of,* say, Korean American women, but *are* Korean American women that circulate in our

14. MTV's editing strategies are a perfect example of this facet of postmodernist artistic practice. For an accessible discussion of postmodernism, see E. Kaplan (1988), *Postmodernism and its Discontents.*

culture as the "real thing," which all of us buy into, literally and ideologically. How these films negotiate assimilation—at the level of the cultural identities they articulate and at the level of their bricolage technique of film construction—ultimately indicates that for these filmmakers, the dislocations and splittings of Asian/Pacific American cultural identity are complicated operations. The process of cultural assimilation, then, is not a matter of matching already circulating images or of blandly blending into a mythological unified identity but is, instead, a sometimes poignant, sometimes celebratory, and always deconstructing attempt to negotiate the multiple mappings of the self through a variety of found and newly made media sources.

REFERENCES

Alfaro, R., & Hagemann, L. (Directors). (1992). *Japanese American women: A sense of place*. Women Make Movies.

Butler, J. (1990). *Gender trouble: Feminism and the subversion of identity*. New York: Routledge.

Chang, C. (Director). (1992). *Be good my children*. Women make movies.

Ching, Y. (Director). (1990). *Is there anything specific you want me to tell you about?* Women Make Movies.

Fung, R. (Director). (1985). *Orientations*. Third World Newsreel.

Fuss, D. (1989). *Essentially speaking: Feminism, nature, & difference*. New York: Routledge.

Gee. D. (Director). (1989). *Slaying the dragon*. Crosscurrent Media.

Hall, S. (1986). Gramsci's relevance for the study of race and ethnicity. *Journal of Communication Inquiry, 10*(2).

Hall, S. (1991). Cultural identity and diaspora. In J. Rutherford (Ed.), *Identity, community, culture, difference*. London: Lawrence & Wishart:

hooks, b. (1992). *Black looks: Race and representation*. Boston: South End Press.

Houston, J. W. (1973). *Farewell to Manzanar*. Boston: Houghton.

Kaneshiro, T. (1976). *Internees: War relocation center memoirs and diaries*. New York: Vantage.

Kaplan, E. A. (1988). *Postmodernism and its discontents: Theories, practices*. New York: Verso.

Krishnan, I. (Director). (1990). *Knowing her place*. Women Make Movies.

Ma, M. S. (Director). (1993). *Toc Storee*. Third World Newsreel.

Nga, T. (Director). (1992). *From Hollywood to Hanoi*. Thi Thanh Nga.

Onodera, M. (Director). (1988). *The displaced view*. Women Make Movies.

Tajiri, R. (Director). (1991). *History and memory*. Women Make Movies.

Tanaka, J. (Director). (1989). *Memories from the department of amnesia*. Women Make Movies.

Tanaka, J. (Director). (1992). *Who's going to pay for these donuts, anyway?* Crosscurrent Media.

West, C. (1993). *Race matters*. Boston: Beacon Press.

Wilson, A. Quoted in Minh-ha, T. (Director) (1989). (film in progress). *India-China*. Quoted in Minh-ha, T. *Woman, Native, Other: Writing Postcoloniality and Feminism*. Bloomington: Indiana University Press.

Yamada, M. (1976). *Camp notes and other poems*. San Lorenzo, CA: Shameless Hussy Press.

An all chick rock group? Not interested. Too temperamental. You can't put any money on it. If they break up, who do you replace them with? (Shapiro, 1975, p. 139)

seven

ROCK MUSIC
AND MUSIC TELEVISION

HISTORY

In the 1950s, a new music market resulted from the postwar baby boom. Teenagers, identifying little with adults, sought their own "youth culture." By the 1960s, amplified guitars, percussion, and saxophones characterized a music form that was "less sentimental, not as abstract or conformist, and less myopically focused on the travails of love" than the music of the previous generation (Denisoff & Peterson, 1972, p. 289).

A few women in the 1950s (Etta James, Peggy Jones, Bonnie Buckingham, Janis Martin, and Wanda Jackson) were part of the transition from rhythm and blues (R&B) to rock music. The 1960s, on the other hand, saw a "recognized trend in rock 'n' roll for the first time, as the 'girl groups,' almost exclusively black women, began to hit the top of the charts" (Garofalo, 1994, p. 86). Garofalo argues:

> With their roots in gospel and rhythm and blues, and with historical ties to the 'a cappella' style of the fifties vocal harmony groups, these women demonstrated considerable talent. Still, they were marketed as much for their sexual appeal as for their musical abilities (1994, p. 87).

Songs performed by girl groups were written by a stable of writers, predominantly adult males, who used a fairy-tale-type story line in most songs. Cinderella met her Prince Charming; they'd marry even though the parents forbade it; and, once out of parental control, they would live happily ever after.

In general, male musicians backed up the girl singers; male producers promoted the image; and all the "girls" had to do was sound dumb and believable. The Shirelles, one of the most popular girl groups, were unlike most girl groups in that they controlled their music and their careers. A bit older than other girl-group members, the Shirelles wrote their own material and were handled by one of the few women in the business, Florence Greenberg. Their hit single, "Will You Still Love Me Tomorrow?" was the first girl group song to reach the top ten.

By the mid-1960s, the "girl singer" replaced the girl group. British singers (such as Petula Clark and Dusty Springfield) were joined by American singers (such as Leslie Gore and Lulu). With the acceptance of Black girl groups came the acceptance of solo singers such as Aretha Franklin and Tina Turner. While girl singers appeared more hip and independent than the girl group singers, they were less popular with the teen audience due to the invasion of British all-male bands (such as the Beatles and Dave Clark Five).

Between 1965 and 1966, White female vocalists lost their audience. American performers, in general, were replaced by British talent. The only American sound that continued to grow was Motown. Based on a faster pulse than R&B, Motown's successes included the Marvelettes, Martha and the Vandellas, and the Supremes.

During this era, a resurrection of political folk music brought with it the emergence of the folk madonna, characterized as a long-haired, slender woman who played a natural, nonelectric instrument such as an acoustic guitar, dulcimer, autoharp, or piano. Most folk madonnas came from a political movement (antiwar, civil rights), and were generally a positive role model for women (active, politically outspoken, and controversial). Yet the political movements within which they sang focused primarily on issues of importance to men (the draft), and when the movements did include women (civil rights, antiwar, and so on) women's positions within the movements were discounted or absent. Folk madonna songs were similar to other genres in their focus on women's relationships to men. Rarely were independent women portrayed in folk madonna songs.

By the 1970s, rock was an enormous part of the cultural revolution—the male cultural revolution. Most rock bands were teams of males: tough, rebellious, lonely, indifferent to the future and to women. This was reinforced by the absence of women on stage and their portrayal in early rock music. Women's duties in "revolutionary" rock music were the same as they had always been: offstage, supporting men, and at home. Men were active, the pursuer. Women were passive, the pursued. Women in rock were left with little to do but fight an uphill battle for recognition.

There were always exceptions. Janis Joplin and Tina Turner performed rock music in these early years. Turner, of course, was controlled off-stage by her abusive husband, and Joplin came across larger than life, strong—part Medusa and part Mae West. Both of their performances revolved around fierce pain and loud, emotional songs, delivered with reckless abandon.

Few women were front singers, fewer still played instruments, and all-women bands were almost nonexistent. The most well known of the all-women bands were Goldie and the Gingerbreads, Fanny, and, in the mid-1970s, Deadly Nightshade (Gaar, 1992).

In the 1970s, the situation shifted as women moved from in front of the microphone to behind electric instruments (The Carpenters, Fleetwood Mac, and Heart). Women playing electric rock guitars (Bonnie Raitt, Joan Armatrading, Nancy Wilson, and Joan Jett), not just acoustic guitars as was the norm for previous women musicians, received recognition from mainstream audiences. Even then, few women were visible. In a study of popular music artists between 1970 and 1979, fewer than 12 of more than 260 acts in rock consisted of individual women or had women in the band (Denisoff & Bridges, 1982).

By the 1980s, the number of female band members increased. In 1989, Stewart split female rock performers into two major categories: younger women who have no problem being female rock stars and for whom "performing rock music seems normal and natural" and women who were part of the late 1970s, as front singers for groups (for example, Tina Turner), as back-up singers for men (such as Ellen Foley), or who had worked hard for many years to break into rock music (such as Chrissie Hynde) (p. 286).

In 1981, Warner Amex Satellite Entertainment Company (WASEC) started Music Television, commonly called MTV, as a new cable program service. Their target audience was ages 12–34 but age was not the MTV audience's commonality. MTV was aimed at "television babies who grew up on Rock and Roll" (Levy, 1983, p. 33).

Following the format of radio, MTV hired veejays who introduced music videos and discussed the artists. MTV videos boosted record sales at a time when recording industry sales were declining. The music culture of MTV differed little from that of rock and roll; in the first few years, many argued that the "M" in MTV stood for *male* (Lewis, 1990, p. 38)

PORTRAYAL

Music is perhaps one of the most powerful tools for the conveyance of ideas and emotions. It is also a great vehicle for propaganda. Lyrics in music reinforce a culture's values. Rock music, as part of the youth culture, always sent out strong messages, picked up by listeners, consciously or unconsciously. Embedded within the messages are female and male portrayals.

Early on, lyrics portrayed females as single-minded. Girl groups' music, for example, portrayed females as existing for one reason—to find their true love (Pavletich, 1980). The songs of the Butterflies, the Crystals, the Ronettes, the Shangri-Las, the Bluebelles, and many others portrayed teenage girls as creatures with a heart but rarely a brain, guided by passion (for love, not sex). Their songs were often sung in childlike voices, taking on the characteristics of "baby talk." Girl groups and their almost exclusively female audience "did not have role models who existed independent of relationships with men. The music of the girl groups did not talk about the women themselves but rather about those who were 'Rebels' and 'Leader(s) of the Pack'" (Garofalo, 1994, p. 88).

With an increase in rock bands, music lyrics reflected values from males' point(s) of view. Lyrics confined women to certain roles: sexual playthings, experienced women, property, or clingers. Rock lyrics portrayed women as dependent, frivolous, and far from ambitious except in obtaining a man.

Although this general trend should be noted, some exceptions occurred. In folk music, folk madonnas wrote songs that were a little more complex and subtle. By the mid-1960s, even some men voiced concern with women who demanded to be unconditionally dependent ("It Ain't Me Babe") while women's discontent became more pronounced (Joplin's "Move Over" and Franklin's "Respect"). Still much of the music from the British invasion reinforced images of women as goddess or the girl next door.

Some rock groups became known for their narrow depictions of women. The most blatant group recorded songs about a "Stupid Girl" who should be kept "Under My Thumb" or a "Honky Tonk Woman" who should give "Satisfaction" (Denisoff & Peterson, 1972, p. 174). Rolling Stones music, at the time, was called "Porn Rock" for its violent and derogatory portrayal of women.

Females growing up in the 1960s and 1970s were offered narrow roles to emulate. As teenagers, they listened to chirpies, love-crazed girl groups, folk madonnas, or sexy Black singers. When rock became popular, teenage girls could be "groovy chicks" or "uptight." In general, women's roles in rock music were prescribed by men and handed to women to fulfill. Real problems (being different, peer pressure, abuse, homosexuality) were rarely discussed. There was little room for growth or diversity.

The Top-40 songs from 1972 through 1982 reflected women as emotional, dependent, loving, seductive, childlike, faithful, attractive, powerful, dangerous, and passive (in rank order). Men for the same time period were characterized as emotional, dependent, independent, competent, loving, faithful, adventurous, lonely, self-assured, and gentle. "While men are pictured as possessing both masculine and feminine characteristics, women largely conform to traditional stereotypic feminine attributes" (Hyden and McCandless, 1983, p. 23).

In many ways, music videos modeled rock and roll's male adolescent culture, excluding, devaluing, and deriding females. Although women were portrayed stereotypically in many music videos, MTV also gave female artists their first opportunity to be seen by millions of viewers (Lewis, 1980, p. 68). From 1980 to 1986, new videos Lewis calls "female-addressed videos [were] designed to speak to and resonate with female cultural experiences of adolescence and gender" (Lewis, 1990, p. 109). MTV exposed millions of potential fans to women who had never been heard before. Millions of female fans skyrocketed female musicians such as Pat Benatar ("Love is a Battlefield"), Madonna ("Like a Virgin"), Cyndi Lauper ("Girls Just Want to Have Fun") and Tina Turner ("What's Love Got to Do With it?") into star status. Female bands like the Go-Gos and the Bangles also gave female audiences an opportunity to participate in a culture that had previously excluded them.

MTV's impact increased record sales of female artists as seen in the 1986 Billboard Hot 10 Chart. Pat Benatar's "Sex as a Weapon" demanded that her lover stop "using sex as a weapon." Tina Turner used her normal rough style in "Typical Male" and "It's Only Love" with Bryan Adams. Annie Lennox's (Eurythmics) "Missionary Man" demonstrated a similar rawness in style and lyrics. Janet Jackson's style moved toward a harder edge with "Nasty" and "What Have You Done for Me Lately?" (Stewart, 1987). Other Top 100 hits of the year included songs by Aretha Franklin ("Jumpin' Jack Flash"), Katrina and the Waves ("Is That It?"), The Pretenders ("Don't Get Me Wrong"), The Bangles ("Walk Like an Egyptian"), and Sheila E ("A Love Bizarre").

In 1987, Suzanne Vega's hit "Luka" helped spotlight women in rock. Mainstream recording companies searched for their "Vega." Women musicians who'd been performing for years now found doors open to them (Tracy Chapman, Indigo Girls, Michelle Shocked, and Melissa Etheridge). Around the same time (mid-1980s), Salt-N-Pepa recorded "Bang Zoom," the first female rappers song to hit the Top 40 charts. Women rappers' success paralleled that of women in rock. Women rappers always existed, but it took the commercial success of Salt-N-Pepa's "Hot, Cool & Vicious" to convince "some rap labels to start promoting female rappers, many of whom had been part of the hip hop underground for years" (Garofalo, 1994, p. 116). Salt-N-Pepa were followed by Queen Latifah in 1989.

By 1990, the focus on women and rock music in both the media and the charts leveled off. "This made little difference to the artists themselves, who had grown tired of being depicted as women first and musicians second" (Gaar, 1992, p. 377). Meanwhile from within the women's music industry (a small independent network of labels, artists, distributors, and retailers), alternative artists became popular: Ferron from Canada, Two Nice Girls out of Texas, and Phranc, a self-proclaimed "all-American Jewish lesbian folksinger." Although these performers came from a women's music perspective, they signed with non-women's-music independent labels to broaden their audience.

One of the most successful and provocative performers, both on MTV and in the charts, was and continues to be Madonna, who bases her career on challenging "conventional perceptions of sex and sexuality" (Gaar, 1992, p. 332). "Like a Virgin" established Madonna as a "full-fledged pop star" (Gaar, 1992, p. 334). Her unconventional approach to music, performance, and life has half the population hating her and the other half loving her. What is so interesting is those halves often change with her newest release. For example, in 1985 Parents Music Resource Center (PRMC), a group concerned with music lyrics, accused Madonna of "teaching her fans 'how to be a porn queen,'" whereas the following year, Tipper Gore (co-founder of PRMC) "praised Madonna's 'Papa Don't Preach' video (in which Madonna plays an unwed mother-to-be who decides to keep her child) for its 'sensitivity'" (Gaar, 1992, p. 428). Planned Parenthood, meanwhile, was concerned this same song taught teens it was cool to get pregnant (Gaar, 1992, p. 428). Madonna challenges society's status quo in every ad, book, concert, film, record, and video with which she is associated. Her videos, interviews, and style changes are infamous, and she continues to be noncategorical.

Although progress has been made for women performing rock music, one need only look at industry magazines to be reminded of how few women are considered great talents in rock and roll. In the February 1993 copy of *Musician Magazine,* the editors chose the "Top 100 Greatest Guitarists." Of the 100, only 3 were women, 2 of whom were described by their identification with men: Maybelle Carter, "And she was Johnny Cash's mother-in-law" (p. 45), and Emily Remler, who is quoted as saying, "I may look like a nice Jewish girl from New Jersey but inside I'm a 50-year-old, heavyset Black man with a big thumb, like Wes Montgomery" (p. 48).

EMPLOYMENT

A great deal of cultural and social conditioning had to be overcome before women as musicians were accepted by mainstream music culture. In the 1960s and 1970s, female artists were promoted if they had a "proper image" (looked sexy, wore tight clothing, and didn't come on too strong). Holly Near, pursuing a major label in the early 1970s, was told she would never make it in mainstream music because her voice didn't have any element of submission to it. Since a career in the industry depended on acceptance by major labels, few female performers spoke out against the popular music industry. Most played it safe and avoided controversy. Others, such as Holly Near, formed their own record companies and became a part of a nonmainstream music culture.

To get women into the business side of music, women needed to reach positions where they were more than support players for men. They needed to learn production, engineering, management, and gain experience. In the 1960s and 1970s, the few women who learned these trades were unwelcome in the music industry. Those who wanted to the learn the business found few places willing to train them.

In these early years, a group of women musicians and women engineers unable to get work in the mainstream music industry joined political activists in the lesbian-feminist movement to form a "women's music" independent recording industry. The industry included women's music recording labels (Olivia), performers and musicians (Meg Christian, Cris Williamson, and Margie Adam), engineers (Joan Lowe, Leslie Ann Jones), producers (June Millington), album designers (Kate Winter), and photographers (JEB). The albums were distributed via mail order or through women's bookstores to thousands of women who wanted music that realistically portrayed their lives. Its success was staggering. With a minimal distribution system, few recording labels, word-of-mouth promotion, and little money for the manufacturing of albums, women's music concerts were standing-room only, and albums sold out. The women's music industry, begun in the early 1970s, continues today as a successful alternative form of music in the United States.

However, during the 1970s, major recording companies kept women out of the business end of the industry. A woman who wanted to work in the "business" was most often placed as a secretary or in publicity. Although more women worked in the music industry in the late 1980s, a panel on sexism at the 1989 New Music Seminar found, "Although more women were receiving promotions at record labels (comprising thirty-two percent of all promotions in the '80s compared with ten percent in the '70s), the percentage of women in vice-president positions at major labels had dropped from fifteen percent to eleven percent during the previous two years" (Gaar, 1992, p. 404).

The 1990s has seen an increase in women on the front of the record cover (the artists) and on the credits of the record cover (producers, engineers, photographers). However, this doesn't mean the playing field is level. It means only that more women have scored on an uneven playing field.

> Women in all areas of the music industry have consistently faced opposition from both the outside world and the music industry itself as they have questioned and challenged assumptions regarding a woman's "proper" position within the industry. But women who have dared to stand up and persevered to maintain a career in their chosen field, have managed to change some of the negatives into positives. While sexism remains an intrinsic part of the music industry, as it is in society, it is also being continually challenged by an increasing number of women in every level of the industry, from the practice room to the board room. The gains may be slow, but they are constant, and as women continue to challenge sexist attitudes in the industry, the resulting changes will be felt in society (Gaar, 1992, p. 435).

REFERENCES

Dates, J. L. & Barlow, W. (Eds.) (1993). *Split image: African Americans in the mass media.* (2nd Ed.), Washington, DC: Howard University Press.

Denisoff, R. S., & Bridges, J. (1982). Popular music: Who are the recording artists? *Journal of Communication, 32,* 132–142.

Denisoff, R. S., & Peterson, R. A. (1972). *The sounds of social change.* Chicago: Rand McNally.

Garofalo, R. (1994). Crossing over. In J. L. Dates & W. Barlow (Eds.) *Split image: African Americans in the mass media* (2nd Ed.). Washington DC: Howard University Press.

Gaar, G. G. (1992). *She's a rebel: The history of women in rock & roll.* Seattle, WA: Seal Press.

Hyden, C., & McCandless, N. J. (1983). Men and women as portrayed in the lyrics of contemporary music. *Popular Music,* 19–26.

Levy, S. (1983, December). Ad nauseam: How MTV sells out rock and roll. *Rolling Stone,* 30–37, 74–79.

Lewis, L. A. (1990). *Gender politics and MTV: Voicing the differences.* Philadelphia: Temple University Press.

The 100 greatest guitarists: You wanna fight about it? (1993, February). *Musician Magazine,* 40–55.

Pavletich, A. (1980). *Rock-a-bye, baby.* Garden City, NY: Doubleday & Company.

Shapiro, S. (1975, May). Rock around the crotch. *Crawdaddy, 48,* pp. 68–69.

Stewart, A. D. (1987). *Declarations of independence or traditional sex roles: The communicative roles of female artists on the 1986 Billboard hot 100.* A paper presented at the Tenth Annual Communication, Language and Gender Conference, Milwaukee, WI.

Stewart, A. D. (1989). Declarations of independence: The female rock and roller comes of age. In C. M. Lont and S. F. Friedley (Eds.), *Beyond boundaries: Sex and gender diversity in communication,* (pp. 283–297). Fairfax, VA: George Mason University Press.

PROJECT IDEAS

1   One could argue that having "girl groups," no matter what their portrayal, was better than no female artists. Which do you think is better? A negative portrayal (dependent, interested only in boys) or no portrayal?

2   The early 1960s have been called the depression of popular music, the barren stretch between early rock and Beatlemania. In fact, teen angels, girl groups, and female vocalists were popular and dominant. Many call the British invasion, which replaced teen music, a revolution. Yet one hardly recognizes it as a revolution when music turned away from the tough, sexy sound of the Shirelles to the whitewashed simplicity of Herman's Hermits and the Dave Clark Five. If the sex of the performers were reversed, would this have been designated a revolution?

3   Examine the roles portrayed by African-American women in the music industry. Start with some of the early artists in the 1950s (Lady Bo—guitarist who played with Bo Diddley), girl groups, female solo singers, women in rock, and women in rap. How have these roles progressed or regressed?

Looking at the lyrics sung by African-American females, do they positively or negatively portray women and men?

4   Use *Billboard* magazine or check with your local record store to locate the top ten hits for one week. Identify the sex of each artist. What's the percentage of men artists versus women artists? If possible, listen to the lyrics of each of the top ten songs. How are women and men characterized within the songs? Are they the same as or different from the Hyden and McCandless study discussed in the chapter on rock music? Do you see any new trends in the portrayal of males and females in popular music?

NAMES

The following list identifies some of the women who have been or are currently part of the rock music industry. Women who were previously mentioned in this introduction are not duplicated in this list.

Laurie Anderson—Performance artist (1981–present).

Michele Anthony—Lawyer and senior vice president for Sony Music/CBS Records (1990s).

LaVern Baker—Rhythm and Blues and Pop recording artist (1953–1980s).

Ruth Brown—Rhythm and Blues recording artist (1949–1957).

Pamela Brandt—Guitarist in all-woman band Deadly Nightshade (mid-1970s).

Exene Cervenka—Lead singer in the band X (1978–present).

Susanne DePasse—Motown Productions president (1981).

Judy Dlugacz—Head of Olivia Records (1970–present).

Marianne Faithfull—Songwriter and recording artist (1960s–present).

Ellie Greenwich—Staff songwriter for Trio music and songwriter of "girl group" songs (1960s).

Debbie Harry—lead singer of Blondie (1970s–1980s).

Darlene Love—Recording artist working under Phil Spector (1950–1960s).

Monica Lynch—President of Tommy Boy Records, a part of Time Warner, Inc. (1985–present).

Martha Quinn—MTV veejay (1980s–present).

Yoko Ono—Singer/songwriter across genres (1970s–present).

Roberta Peterson—Vice president and general manager of A&R at Warner Brothers Records (1975–present).

Tabitha Soren—MTV veejay and reporter (1989–present).

Alison Steele—First female deejay at a major radio station (1966–1979).

Maureen Tucker—Drummer for the band, The Velvet Underground (1965–1972).

Mary Wells—Motown's first solo star (1961–1970s).

American Women Composers, Inc.
    1690 36th Street, NW
    Suite 409
    Washington, DC 20007

Ladyslipper Distributors
    P.O. Box 3124
    Durham, NC 27715

Pleiades Records
    P.O. Box 7217
    Berkeley, CA 94707

Roadwork Inc.
    1475 Harvard Street, NW
    Washington, DC 20009

WHYS Crack Records
    P.O. Box 41
    Provincetown, MA 02657

With respect to the depiction of women in music videos, the criticism raised in the popular press generally condemned music videos as "sexist" across the board.

20

MUSICAL GENRE, "GIRL CULTURE," AND THE FEMALE PERFORMER:

The Root of Variation Between Music Videos

JOHN TAPPER AND DAVID S. BLACK

John Tapper is a doctoral student at the University of Wisconsin–Madison School of Journalism and Mass Communication. He earned his M.A. in 1993. His most recent publication is "The Ecology of Cultivation: A Conceptual Model of the Cultivation Process" in *Communication Theory*. He also published (with Esther Thorson and David Black) "Variations in Music Videos as a Function of Musical Genre" in *Journal of Broadcasting and Electronic Media* and (with David Black) "Beyond Madonna: The Gamut of Music Videos" in B. Winfield and E. Thorson (Eds.), *Proceedings of On the Beat: The First International Conference on Rock 'n Roll, Rap, Mass Media, and Society*. Tapper's research interests revolve around the intersection of television and its audience.

David S. Black is a doctoral student in the University of Wisconsin–Madison School of Journalism and Mass Communication. He earned his M.A. (1991) in Radio and Television from San Francisco State University. His B.S. (1984) is in Speech Communication from Portland State University. His most recent publication (with John Tapper and Esther Thorson) is "Variations in Music Videos as a Function of Musical Genre" in *Journal of Broadcasting and Electronic Media*. He also co-authored (with John Tapper) "Beyond Madonna: The Gamut of Music Videos" in B. Winfield and E. Thorson (Eds.), *Proceedings of On the Beat: The First International Conference on Rock 'n Roll, Rap, Mass Media, and Society*. He is a veteran of radio news and sports reporting, and teaches radio news. Research interests include television and radio production and their effects, music videos, and critical studies in mass media.

Music videos first appeared on the American mass media scene in 1981 with the July 1 introduction of MTV. Critics from both the academic and popular press charged that these single-song visual adventures were harmful to adolescents on a range of fronts. They were said to inhibit the imagination of adolescents (Aufderheide, 1986; Abt, 1986), to present the world as dreamlike and disconnected from reality (Aufderheide, 1986; Kinder, 1984; Tetzlaff, 1986), and to promote violence (Bauder, 1992) and a view of women that robs them of the status of full human beings (Jhally, 1990; Kaplan, 1987).

With respect to the depiction of women in music videos, the criticism raised in the popular press generally condemned music videos as "sexist" across the board. Scholarly criticism was generally more sophisticated. It originated within the general field of critical studies. This field's study of music videos is based primarily on the methodology of textual analysis. This type of analysis involves examining the entirety of a stimulus, in this case a music video, and interpreting it based on the ideas the stimulus implies or expresses outright. This form of analysis cannot reliably be said to faithfully represent a class of stimuli because scientifically acceptable samples are not chosen and because the scientific ideal of intersubjectivity[1] is not satisfied, but critical analyses are valuable to empirical scholars because they often provide carefully considered interpretations and fresh ideas on which to base empirical investigation.

In the case of music videos, the interpretations forwarded by critical scholars rested primarily on two axes. The first concerned the physical depiction of women in music videos. Scholars concerned with the content of music videos, such as Kaplan (1987) and Jhally (1990), generally asserted that few women lead performers could be found and that when they appeared in music videos they were depicted as band members, back-up singers, dancers, or other ancillary actors whose roles as performers could not be distinguished from their roles as beautiful objects to be looked at and desired by an adolescent male audience (Jhally, 1990).

The second axis on which much early scholarly criticism focused was commonly referred to as the form and function of the male gaze. Academic writers such as Kaplan (1987) suggested that the women in music videos seemed to want to be objects of voyeurism. They are said to pose for the camera, even to set themselves up as objects of male desire. This extends to the point at which cameras are often seen in the video, following the female object of desire.

In fact, these writers claim that women in music videos seem to define themselves by their relationship to the male gaze. This is even true in the few

We would like to extend special thanks to Professor Esther Thorson, who aided in the planning of this study and the analysis of the data. Without her contributions, this chapter would not have been possible.
1. Intersubjectivity refers to the scientific ideal of agreement between scientists. In this case, it refers to the ideal situation in which social scientists agree on definitions of sexism and related variables to such an extent to allow agreement on the interpretation of results.

cases in which females are given control of the camera within a camera. Jhally (1990) suggests that when women are placed in the role of photographer, they use the camera as a prop, glorifying the superficial, sexist treatment of themselves and the other women in the video, often filming other women.

This tone of criticism came from grass-roots movements as well as the mass media and scholars. For example, the Parents' Music Resource Center (PMRC) created a sufficient public outcry in 1985 to convince the Subcommittee on Communication of the U.S. Senate Committee on Commerce, Science, and Transportation to hold hearings examining the "pornographic" content of rock music lyrics, album covers, and videos (Lewis, 1988). This organization was headed by the wives of government officials, including Tipper Gore. Although this movement succeeded in placing music videos and, among other things, their representation of women, in the public eye, the congressional hearings did little to alter the face of music videos.

This is likely because the issue of the harmful nature of the content of music videos was, at the time, premature. When the PMRC began to raise its voice in opposition to the content of music videos, little had been done to establish empirically exactly what that content was. The evidence the PMRC brought to bear was essentially anecdotal and tended to mirror the interpretations forwarded by scholars committed to the critical studies approach. This evidence is made considerably more suspect when one considers the breadth of their concerns. Through an examination of the evidence offered by the PMRC, McDonald (1988) was able to show that the examples chosen to represent the general depravity of rock music actually represented only .00214 percent of the total output (in terms of records produced) of the rock music industry.

However, this public outcry did serve to light a fire under previously reluctant empirical investigators. Much of the early work, most of which was published around 1986, was exploratory and designed to subject the assertions of critical scholars to scientific verification. Although this research generally supported the accusations made by critics of music videos, especially those related to the depiction of sexuality and gender in music videos, recent work suggests that these investigations may have been flawed in that they tended to treat all music videos as if they were identical (Tapper, Thorson, and Black, in press). This work suggests that instead of examining music videos as simple entertainment units aimed at an essentially homogenous youth culture, they should be considered as advertisements aimed at specific target audiences that vary by musical genre.

Another way of thinking about the differences between types of music videos was suggested by at least one scholar from the critical studies tradition (Lewis, 1987; Lewis, 1988). Lewis suggests that musical genre may not be the most important source of variation between music videos. She asserts that on MTV in the early 1980s, female artists began an attempt to reframe the discourse of music videos. This new frame was, she argues, more favorable toward women in general. Lewis (1988) suggests that "female-address videos reclaim style for girls and richly articulate style as a symbolic vehicle for female expression." Male-address videos, in contrast, position "girls and women as objects of male voyeurism." Female-address videos "challenge assumptions about boundaries which gender, as a social construct, draws around men and women." These videos are said to depict idiosyncratically female activities, and thus to celebrate female "cultural expression and experience." Further, her reading of the music videos of a few female performers supports her general hypothesis.

This may be an important finding. If female-address videos compose a sizable portion of the videos produced by women artists, then it might be sensible to think of two different music video worlds—one male and one female. This would have important implications for the possible meanings constructed (see Livingstone, 1993) by viewers of male- and female-address videos, respectively. However, Lewis' research does not allow us to gauge the prevalence of female-address videos or their distribution among genres. Further, because Lewis' work rests on the methodology of textual analysis, we cannot know for sure if the differences she found are characteristic of music videos in general or if they are idiosyncratic to the videos that she chose to analyze. Therefore, analyzing the past empirical literature with an eye toward examining Lewis' assertions may be helpful.

REVIEW OF EMPIRICAL LITERATURE

Brown and Campbell (1986) examined the differences between videos on MTV and on BET's "Video Soul." They found that males dominated on both video channels. However, this dominance was much higher on MTV (White males especially). Twenty-five percent of all performers on "Video Soul" were female compared to only 12 percent on MTV.

They also examined the occurrence of themes in the videos on these two channels. This included examining only concept videos. These are videos that consist of a central story line or organizing motif other than performance. Videos were coded as being about domestic, professional, social, solitary, or song and dance themes. Results showed very few differences attributable to race or gender. In general, however, women were shown less often in videos with professional themes and slightly more often in videos with social themes.

The examination of concept videos also found significant differences between races in the occurrence of pro- and antisocial behaviors. Specifically, White characters were much more likely than Black characters to behave in antisocial ways. This difference appears to be caused by racial differences rather than gender differences. These results, taken together, suggest that in 1985 women as a group were not treated much differently from men. However, race was an important differentiating factor.

Vincent, Davis, and Boruszkowski (1987), using a 1985 sample from MTV, examined the level of sexism in music videos. Sexism was measured using a scale designed by Pingree, Hawkins, Butler, and Paisley (1976). This four-item scale, which took into account both occupational and sexual roles, ranked how women were portrayed. Their results indicated that sexism was fairly widespread in music videos, with 57 percent classified as condescending to women. However, there were no significant differences in the level of sexism between videos of all-male groups and videos of all-female or mixed-gender groups. This finding reaffirms the Brown and Campbell findings, and argues against Lewis' 1987 argument.

Vincent reexamined the issue of sexism on MTV in 1989 using a sample recorded in the winter of 1986–87. He used the same scale of sexism that he employed in his earlier study. He found that videos rated as the most sexist (as condescending) decreased in frequency to 35 percent, a 22 percent decline. Additionally, he found that by the winter of 1986–87 the presence of women as lead performers in music videos had begun to make a difference. In fact, he found that the level of sexism varied by the gender of the performer(s). Most interestingly, 63 percent of videos of all-female or partially female groups treated women as fully equal to men. This was only the case for 30 percent of the videos of all-male groups. Interestingly, the occurrence of fully equal treatment nearly tripled for all-male groups between 1985 and the winter of 1986–87. For all-female or partially female groups the increase was twofold.

Finally, Seidman (1992) examined sex-role stereotyping on MTV. He used a 1987 sample and found that sex-role stereotyping was rampant. Ninety-four percent of males were found to be portrayed in traditionally male roles, and 88 percent of women were portrayed in traditionally female roles. Further, he found that males were more likely to display aggressive, violent, or dominant behaviors. Females were similarly more likely to wear revealing clothing, show affection, and both pursue and be pursued sexually.

Given these findings, it seems possible that Lewis is correct in asserting that music videos made by female performers reflect a female sensibility that is discernible from the male fantasy world so often identified as "the music video world." However, with the exception of Brown and Campbell's (1986) investigation, all the literature in this area has focused exclusively on MTV. This music video channel is clearly the most widely received channel, but it by no means constitutes the breadth of the music video universe. Country music videos reach millions of fans through the cable networks CMT (Country Music Television) and TNN (The Nashville Network). An older, baby-boomer audience is sought by the nationally-sold cable network VH-1 (Video Hits-1), and music aimed at an African-American audience is cablecast nationally via BET (Black Entertainment Television). The presence of this variety of musical genres and audiences raises the question of whether the findings just recounted are generalizable to all music videos, or whether they apply only to the musical genres shown on MTV.

Content Analysis

This chapter will present the results of an attempt to verify Lewis' theoretical statements empirically. The investigation will attempt to identify genre differences present in our sample. We will also examine the differences between the videos of musical groups of different races and genders. Finally, the strength and overall pattern of differences will be examined in an attempt to elucidate the interaction of genre and gender effects across a range of variables.

Because the data presented here were designed to identify source of variation between music videos, specifically variations caused by musical genre (see Tapper et al., in press), a variety of content variables were examined. The variables address a range of content variables that have been at the core of much criticism of music videos, and it will be instructive to examine how these variables appear differentially in the videos of differently gendered lead performers and across musical genres.

METHOD

Selecting Videos

Because we wanted a representative sample of the music videos available on MTV, VH-1, TNN, and BET, we stratified our sample by music-video channel. Ten percent of what was identified by program guides as the total number of hours of music videos aired on the four channels (as opposed to news, games, or interviews) in the sampled weeks was recorded off cable systems in two midwestern cities. This was accomplished by recording eight half-hour segments on each of four days from each channel during a two-week period (April 20 to May 2, 1992). Two days were chosen from each week for each channel using a random number table. Segments within the selected days were also chosen randomly.

Because of the differing lengths of the videos and the amount of commercial programming and veejay patter, the sample yielded a slightly different number of videos for each of the four channels, ranging from 45 to 56. To match the samples in number, videos were randomly eliminated until approximately 40 videos from each music video channel were left in the sample ($n = 161$).

Coders

Two coders (one White female, age 19, and one White male, age 25) received 20 hours of training in the use of the coding form. The coders watched each music video three times, each time coding one-third of the variables.

Coded Variables

A total of 15 variables were measured. Musical genre was measured in accord with a definition of each of the seven musical types considered in this investigation (see Definitions and Examples of Musical Types, pp. 344–345). These definitions were accompanied by examples judged by the researchers to be prototypic. The use of examples was suggested by Christenson and Peterson (1988) in their investigation of musical genre preferences of college students.

Lead gender and race were operationalized as the race and gender of the primary performer in the video. When the music in the video was performed by a group of musicians, the lead vocalist's race and gender were coded. Race was operationalized as Black, White, Hispanic, or other. Minority presence was initially coded as presence of African American(s), Hispanic(s), or Asian(s) but was later collapsed into a dichotomous measure.

Sexual appeal was coded as present if coders detected sexual innuendo, symbolism, explicit sexual references, or nudity. It is noteworthy that objectification of women and men was not coded as sexual appeal unless coders perceived it as a sexual innuendo. Audience presence was a measure of whether or not an audience appeared anywhere in the video.

Objectification of women was coded as present if women were presented purely as ornaments to be watched by men. This variable was difficult to code because during training coders occasionally were unable to agree on whether a woman was presented as a legitimate plot device or simply as a sex object. To clarify this difficulty, coders were instructed to gauge the necessity of the woman, and her appearance, to the plot or story line of the video. If a woman's appearance or behavior was judged to be completely extraneous to the plot of the video, then objectification of women was judged to be present. This presented problems of its own because often plot devices seem to be designed to put women into the role of sex object. This was dealt with by asking coders to also code objectification of women as present when it appeared that the plot could have been adequately developed without presenting women as "ornaments." Although this did not completely solve the problem of identifying when women were presented as sex objects, it did improve the agreement between coders. Readers should bear in mind that the rather narrow definition of this variable does not completely correspond to the dimensions of objectification identified in critical analyses or previous empirical investigations.

Violence was defined as physically aggressive behavior toward specific people or objects, verbal aggression toward people, or presence of weapons.

Opposition to authority was coded as present if videos contained a story or presented imagery that took a stance contrary to (1) the police, (2) parents, (3) school, or (4) societal norms.

Videos were coded as having logically ordered scenes if coders sensed that the scenes in the video were logically integrated (that is, one scene flowed logically to the next). An atmosphere of ambiguity was reported if coders felt that they were not intended to comprehend the message of the video. As suggested by Zettl (1991), presence of digital video effects (DVEs) was operationalized as the presence of split screen, nested images, overlay fades/dissolves (overlays), or animation. Two of these post-production effects need further explanation. A nested image was present when one or more images was superimposed on a portion of the primary image or relegated to a small section of the viewing area. Overlays were coded as present when one image was superimposed on another of equal prominence. This effect was not considered present when an overlay/fade was used purely as a transitional device between scenes.

An idea-associative montage is a type of meaning pattern in which "two seemingly disassociated images are juxtaposed to create a third principal idea or concept" (Zettl, 1991, p. 324). Idea-associative montages can be used as forms of either analogy (comparison) or irony (collision) to make a comment on social issues. For example, in a comparative montage, a faded and decaying church may be shown, followed by a scene of a junkyard. This would portray degenerating social morals. In a collision montage, a rich man may be shown emerging from his Mercedes, followed by a scene showing a tattered man digging through a garbage can. This might portray social inequity. Idea-associative montage was collapsed into one I-A montage (present/absent) scale because so few videos contained either type.

RESULTS

Four analyses were performed on the data. The first was an analysis of the representation of women in music videos in general. This analysis focused only on those variables that related specifically to the representation of women. The second analysis concerned only videos that featured female lead performers. The third analysis was an examination of the videos that featured African-American and White female lead performers, respectively. The final analysis treated musical genre as the independent variable. The purpose of this analysis was to examine the strength of the differences attributable to musical genre so that they might be contrasted with the differences due to gender. Each analysis is presented as a separate section.

The numbers referred to in the analysis are percentages of videos containing the relevant characteristics. A simple form of statistical analysis, the chi-square, was used. This was done in an attempt to discern whether the differ-

ences that seem to appear between videos of the various types are in fact du
properties of different types of music videos or whether they could reasor
be attributed to chance. The discussions that follow will indicate when chance
explanations can reasonably be ruled out.

In the first analysis, we wanted to get a clear understanding of the differences between musical genres. Each sampled video was included only once so as
to represent the character of each musical genre. Videos that could not be
clearly identified (either because they were hybrids of two subgenres or because
they did not fit the coding scheme) were coded as "other," and were eliminated
from the analysis because other, in this case, is clearly not a meaningful category.
This eliminated only 7 videos, leaving 154 videos for analysis. In the second
analysis, the excluded videos were included to allow an understanding of how
gender influences manifest content ($n = 161$).

Women in Music Videos

With the current data it was not possible to gain an understanding of the roles
played by women in the story lines of music videos. However, the frequency
with which women appear as lead performers in music videos is of crucial
importance. Because music videos have been shown to differ by musical genre,
the distribution of the gender of lead performers across musical genres was
investigated. This distribution was further broken down by race. As can be seen
in Table 20.1, males dominate in all musical genres. The highest concentration
of female lead performers was in the soul (44% of lead performers were female)

Table 20.1

Distribution of Race and Gender Variables Across Musical Genres

	Musical Genre (by percentage)								
	Rap (n = 24)	Soul (n = 16)	Cntry (n = 42)	H.Met (n = 12)	Pop (n = 40)	Cl. Rk (n = 7)	Alt.Rk (n = 13)	Other (n = 7)	Mean (n = 161)
Race and gender of lead performer									
White male**	0	0	79	92	50	100	69	28	51
White female*	0	6	21	0	10	0	15	14	11
Black male**	88	56	0	8	18	0	8	43	26
Black female**	13	38	0	0	18	0	0	14	11
Hispanic female	0	0	0	0	3	0	0	0	1
Other	0	0	0	0	2	0	8	0	1

$*p < .10$

$**p < .01$

Note: Totals may not add to 100% because of rounding error.

and pop (38%) genres. Not surprisingly classic rock, the genre generally filled with the oldest songs, was exclusively male. Further, heavy metal, which has the reputation of being male dominated, was 92 percent male. In this genre there were relatively few videos ($n = 12$), and it should be noted that the 8 percent reported as having Black male lead performers represent only one video. Generally, the differences observed can reasonably be attributed to musical genre, with the exception of Hispanic females (appearing in only one video).

Table 20.2 shows the distribution of each variable except the race and gender of lead performers across musical genres. DVE, atmosphere of ambiguity, and I-A montage varied significantly as a function of musical genre ($p < .05$). Minority presence, sexual appeal, and illogical scene ordering varied significantly as a function of musical genre ($p < .01$). Slow motion varied marginally as

Table 20.2

Distribution of Variables Across Musical Genres

	Musical Genre (by percentage)							
	Rap (n = 24)	Soul (n = 16)	Country (n = 42)	Heavy Metal (n = 12)	Pop (n = 40)	Classic Rock (n = 7)	Alternative Rock (n = 13)	Mean (n = 154)
Variables present								
Slow motion*	58	50	29	50	48	0	38	42
Digital video effects**	29	25	10	10	23	14	61	24
Minority presence***	100	100	14	33	73	0	23	53
Idea-associative montage**	8	6	5	17	3	0	31	8
Illogical scene order***	25	6	2	17	8	0	92	16
Objectification of women	38	31	21	42	28	0	8	14
Sexual appeal***	46	50	14	8	45	14	23	31
Ambiguity**	13	6	0	8	8	14	62	11
Violence	29	6	14	17	15	0	8	15

*$p < .10$

**$p < .05$

***$p < .01$

a function of musical genre. Although violence seemed to show variation across musical genres, a chi-square test showed no statistically significant differences between musical genres. The mean percentage of videos containing violence or weapons was surprisingly low. As Table 20.2 shows, there were significant differences in the appearance of sexual appeal attributable to musical genre. It is important to point out here, however, that this variable refers to the number of videos containing any sexual appeal, not to the amount of sexual appeal appearing in those videos. Here the soul (50% of videos contained sexual appeal), rap (46%), and pop (45%) genres were the most heavily sexualized. Interestingly, heavy metal contained the least sexual appeal.

Table 20.2 shows that slow motion likely varied as a function of musical genre because it was completely absent in classic rock. DVEs appeared more often than the mean in rap, soul, and alternative rock. A clear concentration was seen in alternative rock.

The objectification of women also appears to differ by musical genre (see Table 20.2). However, a statistical test revealed that chance could not be ruled out as a source of variation for this variable. This is likely caused by the absence of videos that objectify women in the country genre and to the very small number of these videos (one) in the alternative rock genre. Small numbers of observations in particular categories tend to invalidate the chi-square procedure. The reader is invited to make her or his own decision as to the reliability of this finding.

The Videos of Female Musicians

Cross-tabulations similar to those in the first analysis were computed. This time, however, the independent variable was considered to be the gender of the lead performer. As can be seen in Table 20.3, videos in which women were the lead performers were less likely to contain violence or weapons, sexual appeal, or take a stance in opposition to authority than the videos of male performers. They were also more likely to contain minorities ($p < .10$)[2]. Interestingly, there was no statistical difference between the videos of male and female lead performers on the variable "objectification of women" although a higher percentage of the videos of male lead performers did contain objectification of women. Of these variables, only the presence of minority, which seems to be attributable to the racial breakdown of musical genres, is easily explained by variables other than the gender of the lead performer.

2. In the notation $p < x$, x indicates a value representing the degree of certainty a researcher has about his or her results. The smaller the value of x, the more certain the researcher is that his or her results are not due to chance alone. As a matter of routine, social scientists use $x = .05$ or $x = .01$ as what they call the level of significance. For this particular analysis $x = .10$ was used, and the reader should be aware that we cannot be as confident as is usually the case that these differences are not caused by chance occurrences.

In this analysis, the videos with lead performers who were women were partialed by race. The results are far less fruitful than one would expect given the stark contrasts between music video genres (Tapper, Thorson, & Black, in press) and the differential representation of women of different races across musical genres. Only sexual appeal varied significantly by race within the population, defined as all videos of female performers.

African-American women were more likely to include sexual appeal in their videos than were White women. In fact, almost twice as many of the videos in which African-American women were the lead performers contained sexual appeal as did not. This is in sharp contrast to the videos of White-female lead performers, in which those without sexual appeal were more than three times more common than those containing sexual appeal. However, when one realizes that African-American women were clustered in the soul genre (see Table 20.1), which contained more sexual appeal than any other genre, while White women were scattered across genres, the difference that was attributed to race seems far more likely to be caused by genre.

DISCUSSION

This investigation revealed that female lead performers are still heavily outnumbered by males. The only exception to this rule was found in the soul genre. Here, 44 percent of lead performers were women. This finding indicates that there has been a significant increase in the number of female performers in the

Table 20.3
Distribution of Variables Across Lead-Performer Genders

	Gender of Lead Performer	
	Female (n = 37)	Male (n = 124)
Variables present		
Violence*	5	17
Sexual appeal*	29	43
Opposition to authority*	6	0
Minority lead*	68	51
Objectification of women	14	24

$*p < .10$

soul genre since Brown and Campbell (1985) found that 24 percent of lead performers on Black Entertainment Television's "Video Soul" were female. However, overall 20 percent of videos feature female lead performers. This is remarkably similar to the 21 percent Vincent found in 1985 and the 25 percent he found in 1987. It should be noted that the current study included 42 videos from the country music genre, 79 percent of which had male lead performers; previous studies did not include videos from this heavily male genre.

The results of the current investigation do not, however, lend support to Lewis' theorizing that suggests that female performers are the mass culture representatives of "girl culture." In this view, female performers constitute a fifth column within the ranks of the media of the dominant youth culture, the same media referred to as "the fantasy-world of the adolescent boy" (Jhally, 1990 videotape). However, the differences attributable to musical genre are statistically much more stable than the differences attributable to gender. It is important to point out that based on traditional social-scientific standards, we cannot be certain that the differences we attributed to the gender of the lead performer were not caused by chance alone. This is not the case with the majority of differences attributed to musical genre. Further, the differences caused by lead-performer's gender, if real, are not nearly as striking as those caused by musical genre. Although the interaction between musical genre and the gender of the performer could not be examined using the current data because several of the genres contained very few female performers, these findings suggest that the gender differences reported earlier may be artifacts of genre differences. However, it is important to point out that a failure to find support for a hypothesis cannot be equated to a rejection of that hypothesis (Lakatos, 1978). It may be that had other variables been measured, possibly using different methods, Lewis' ideas would have been supported.

It should be noted, however, that the variables violence and opposition to authority that were related to the gender of the lead performer were not related to musical genre at all. Although these two variables are striking in their isolation, they may be interesting for other reasons. It may be that certain variables are related to gender and others to musical genre. Further, it is possible that gender-defined attributes within one musical genre may not be gender defined within another. Finally, it may be useful to catalog gender and genre differences into a typology of music video types. This typology might be important from an interpretive perspective.

Research attention might next fall to the music video audience. It is not at all clear that the a priori categories established to capture latent meaning,[3] such as those used by Vincent, do an adequate job of identifying when sexism is perceived by audiences. As Brown (1990) found when analyzing the meanings that

---

3. Latent content is the meaning of a stimulus. It cannot simply be counted, as can manifest meaning, but must be quantified using a reliable procedure for converting subjective meaning into objective meaning using context clues within the content of stimulus.

different groups of adolescents assigned to Madonna's "Papa Don't Preach," American adolescents who mature in different subcultural environments generally interpret at least some music videos differently. In fact, it may be that subcultural background, defined by either youth or society, is a key variable in predicting variant interpretations. If this is the case, it is possible that the sexist videos of male lead performers are not universally interpreted as sexist by their intended and unintended audiences. Further, the pro-social, nonsexist videos of female performers may be completely misunderstood by male adolescents or by fans of another musical genre. Interestingly, music videos may be an especially fruitful stimulus with which to investigate the effects of sociological factors on message interpretation given that the latent content of music videos is notoriously vague; the current study found that, outside the country genre, 15 percent of all videos seemed to be purposefully ambiguous, and 20 percent had illogically ordered scenes.

The current study, combined with the results of Vincent's investigation (1989), suggests that as the music video industry has matured, female musicians have begun to produce videos that differ, on a handful of dimensions, from those of male performers. These videos may be, as Lewis suggests, created by "girl culture" for "girl culture," but only on a few content variables. They may, therefore, be differentially understood by audiences of different genders or by differentially gendered fans of different musical genres. We would know nothing of these differences if we listened only to critical scholars and the popular press bemoan the plethora of violence and sexual content in music videos. But now, given an empirical place to stand, researchers in this area should begin to examine how patterns of content are manifested in audience interpretation and involvement (both cognitive and affective) in music videos.

DEFINITIONS AND EXAMPLES OF MUSICAL TYPES

Rap—A rhythmic music characterized by prominent, rhyming lyrics (for example, Dr. Dre, Fresh Prince, Snoop Doggy Dog, Salt N' Pepa, Finesse). Hip hop is a version of rap music that includes a melodic component, and often singing (for example, P.M. Dawn, Keith Sweat).

Soul—A musical type of African-American origin combining elements of jazz and rhythm and blues (for example, James Brown, Aretha Franklin).

Country—The straightforward melodic music of rural America. It is characterized by a "twangy" guitar sound and a down-home vocal style (for example, Kenny Rogers, Wynonna, Travis Tritt).

Heavy Metal—Hard-driving, guitar-oriented music. This musical type is characterized by distorted guitars, and flashy guitar solos; lyrics are de-emphasized (for example, Metallica, Pantera).

Pop—This is the general label for mainstream popular music. It is characterized by generally soft musical sounds and a fast beat (for example, Paula Abdul, Madonna, Phil Collins).

Classic Rock—Music in the style of the popular music of the 1960s and 1970s. It is characterized by a general emphasis on musical virtuosity (for example, Led Zeppelin, Jimi Hendrix, the Eagles).

Alternative/College Rock—Music popular among today's college students. It is generally escapist, surrealistic in lyrical content, and characterized by a variety of musical sounds, all of which are to some extent dissonant (for example, The Cure, REM).

REFERENCES

Abt, D. (1986). Music video: Impact of the visual dimension. In J. Lull (Ed.), *Popular music and communication* (pp. 96–111). Newbury Park, CA: Sage.

Aufderheide, P. (1986). Music videos: The look of the sound. *Journal of Communication, 36*(1), 57–78.

Bauder, D. (1992). Policing rap music. Associated Press.

Brown, J., & Campbell, K. (1986). Race and gender in music videos: The same beat but a different drummer. *Journal of Communication, 36*(1), 94–106.

Brown, J. (1990, Spring). The effects of race, gender, and fandom on audience interpretations of Madonna's music videos. *Journal of Communication, 40*(2), 88–102.

Christenson, P. G., & Peterson, J. B. (1988). Genre and gender in the structure of music preferences. *Communication Theory, 15*, 282–301.

Jhally, S. (1990). Dreamworlds: Desire/sex/power in rock video.

Kaplan, E. A. (1987). *Rocking around the clock: Music television, postmodernism, and consumer culture.* New York: Methuen.

Kinder, M. (1984). Music video and the spectator: Television, ideology, and dream. *Film Quarterly, 53*, 2–15.

Lakatos, I. (1978). The problem of appraising scientific theories: Three approaches. In I. Lakatos (Ed.), *Mathematics, science, and epistemology* (pp. 107–127). Cambridge: Cambridge University Press.

Lewis, L. A. (1987, Winter). Female address in music video. *Journal of Communication Inquiry, 11*(1), 73–84.

Lewis, L. A. (1988). Female address on music television: Being discovered. *Jump Cut, 35*, 2–14.

Livingstone, S. (1993). The rise and fall of audience research: An old story with a new ending. *Journal of Communication, 43*(4), 5–12.

McDonald, J. R. (1988). Censoring rock lyrics: A historical analysis of the debate. *Youth & Society, 19*(3), 294–313.

Pingree, S., Hawkins, R., Butler, M., & Paisley, W. (1976, Autumn). A scale for sexism. *Journal of Communication*, 193–200.

Seidman, S. A. (1992). An investigation of sex role stereotyping in music videos. *Journal of Broadcasting and Electronic Media, 36*(2), 209–215.

Tapper, J., Thorson, E., & Black, D. (in press). Variations in music videos as a function of their musical genre. *Journal of Broadcasting and Electronic Media.*

Tetzlaff, D. (1986). Positively MTV: The ideology of simulated spectacle. Paper presented to the International Communication Association, Chicago, IL.

Vincent, R. C., Davis, D. K., & Boruszkowski, L. A. (1987). Sexism on MTV: The portrayal of women in rock videos. *Journalism Quarterly, 64*, 750–755.

Vincent, R. C. (1989). Clio's consciousness raised? Portrayal of women in rock videos, re-examined. *Journalism Quarterly, 66*(1), 155–160.

Zettl, H. (1990). *Sight, sound, motion: Applied media aesthetics.* Belmont, CA: Wadsworth.

This is a real world;
I really want to be a girl.
Bangles song, 1982

We just happen to be chicks, man,
what can we do?
Susanna Hoffs, 1987

21

Career

"THE HERO TAKES A FALL":
The Bangles and '80s Pop

SHARI ZECK

Shari Zeck teaches film in the Theater department at Illinois State University. Portions of her work on women in popular music have been presented at the Midwest Modern Language Association (1987) and at Drake University (1990). Zeck writes on film, popular culture, and feminist theory and plans on being a folk singer in her next incarnation.

Promotional photo for the Bangles album *Different Light*. Unlike the videos, photos on the album and the sleeves of the singles do not show the band with their instruments.

Photo by Larry Williams. © 1986 CBS, Inc.

In the five years that intervened between the celebration of being female in the song "Real World" and the annoyance exhibited by Susanna Hoffs in 1987 when she told MTV viewers that she and her bandmates just happen to be chicks, the Bangles went from L.A. garage band to internationally acclaimed musicians. A little over a year later they broke up, claiming "irreconcilable differences" as the reason for their disbanding. Susanna Hoffs, Debbi and Vicki Peterson, and Michael Steele found their way into the record books by having *Billboard's* longest-lasting number-one single by an all-female group, the catchy "Walk Like an Egyptian." This distinction tells us as much about women's place in the recording industry as it does about this particular tune, as there have been few all-female rock groups to compete with the Bangles for that honor. Hoffs's remarks are typical of the exasperation the group expressed repeatedly with interviewers' inquiries into their feelings about being in an all-female band, an irritation echoed by the current crop of all- (or nearly all-) female bands such as L7 and the Breeders. Frequently the Bangles are compared to the also L.A.-based, also all-female, also defunct Go-Gos. One could assume the comparison has as much to do with geography as gender, if other L.A. groups such as Concrete Blonde or Redd Kross also were brought in to discuss the "L.A. sound," but they are not. It is the media's attempt to find a comfortable context for the Bangles as gendered performers that forces endless comparisons to the Go-Gos—the only other female rock/pop group in the 1980s to have had success similar to that of the Bangles.

Certainly there are other women who topped *Billboard's* charts in the 1980s, some with much greater overall success than the Bangles. Madonna made more money in 1989 than any other woman in the United States, except for Oprah Winfrey. It has been argued by scholars such as Lisa Lewis (1990) and by the writers of *Rolling Stone*, though in somewhat different terms, that the advent of

MTV and the prominent place videos now have in the marketing of new recording artists to the public has been a particular boost to female singers from Madonna (obviously) to Sinead O'Connor. After all, images of women have been perhaps the greatest obsessions of representational forms from oil painting to Hollywood melodramas. When the emphasis in rock and roll shifted from records and live performances to the "commercials" for the performers and songs that we call music videos, woman-as-image became as prominent an object for consumption as the records themselves. There's no doubt that Madonna's videos are what brought her out of the clubs of New York and made her a major force in today's music (at least in terms of popularity and recognizability), but one could also argue that Suzanne Vega's "Luka," a song about child abuse that went to number one, also gained its popular momentum more from the striking rotoscoped video that promoted it than from radio play.

Female solo artists, whether video-promoted or not, however, have been part of mainstream pop and rock since its earliest days. So have all-female groups, though most of them did not play their own instruments (the marginally successful 1970s group Fanny being one exception) or write their own songs as did the Go-Gos and the Bangles. Taking up instruments marks an intervention into the world of music-*making* that has tended to be the province of men. Even very successful female solo artists rarely have women musicians backing them. It was clear in their videos and stage performances that the Bangles understood the male-dominated conventions of rock performance that they were imitating, invariably exaggerating a guitar-herolike gesture with a giggle or a wink at each other. It was the possibility and pleasure of observing these tiny moments of mockery and shared laughter between women that the Bangles uniquely gave to rock audiences in the 1980s.

What intrigues me about the Bangles is that they celebrated femaleness and femininity (the latter being the cultural accoutrements of being female) in their music, their videos, and their stage performances, while being openly weary of discussing the role gender plays in their work. This contradiction, though boldly evident in the discourses that intersect this popular group, is by no means particular to them. From Julia Kristeva to the pages of popular magazines, current eagerness to proclaim "postfeminism" as the appropriate understanding of theoretical inquiry and of current popular culture to my mind exhibits a similar weariness with debates about gender and "strident" politics although clearly gender divisions are still primary cultural determiners of success, of opportunity, and of value. Current female-dominated groups such as L7, Belly, Hole, and the Breeders hesitate to call themselves feminist or admit to facing any sexism in the music industry per se even though they actively participate in abortion-rights activities and clearly don't want to be pushed around by anyone. Kim Deal, formerly of the Pixies and now leading the Breeders, recently complained in *Rolling Stone* that the only people who seem preoccupied with the fact that they are women are journalists (Azerrad, 1993). This is a complaint the Bangles made repeatedly in TV interviews.

It may be true that playful theory and playful femininity are political interventions that are much more palatable in the "Girls Just Wanna Have Fun" 1980s and the 1990s than the "I am woman/hear me roar" politics of a couple of decades ago. Nevertheless, it seems that the tension between proclaiming a fabulously fun femininity on the one hand, and, on the other hand, wanting to pretend gender is no longer an issue is not simply a bit of irritated anti-feminist posturing or a sign of the death of feminism. Rather, these contradictory positions mark how unstable our experience of gender continues to be—how much an area of struggle and debate.

And it is precisely the Bangles' "posturing" that requires discussion. The way the members of this group took up supposedly gender-neutral positions in various scenarios that were abandoned in favor of (or at least in the context of) their identity as a female group challenged the ideology of male-dominated rock and roll—an ideology of guitar heroes and female groupies, not female groups, and that distinguished the Bangles from successful solo artists or female-singer bands like 10,000 Maniacs or Edie Brickell and the new Bohemians, who were popular around the same time and who are now also defunct. Whether they wish to admit to it or not, today's all-female bands have inherited this legacy of female bonding and are continuing to write the history of women together.

"Hero Takes a Fall," the Bangles' first release from their major-label debut album *All Over the Place*, earned the group a substantial amount of TV exposure in the United States and in Europe although it was not the breakthrough hit that "Manic Monday," their first single from their second CBS LP, was. The band had gotten together three years earlier through an ad in a local L.A. musician's paper, and were soon signed to Miles Copeland's short-lived Faulty Products label. On being signed to CBS, the band's original bassist, Annette Zilinskas, left the band, and Michael Steele, veteran of many L.A. bands including the infamous Runaways (for a brief period), joined. "Hero" was written by Hoffs and Vicki Peterson. Most of the Bangles' material was written by the four band members, a fact that was often missed in the popular press, since three of the four hits from the LP *Different Light* were cover songs. "Manic Monday," which reached number two on *Billboard*'s chart, was penned by Prince under the pseudonym "Christopher." That fact rarely escaped mention by commentators on the band's activities in 1986, such as the headline in the April 28, 1986, *People*, "With a little help from friend Prince, the Bangles have become the queens of post-psychedelic pop"—which borders on establishing the Bangles as one of Prince's protégées like Appolonia and Vanity. The most obvious ideological consequence of constantly referring to male collaborators such as Prince or producer David Kahne is that it reduces the Bangles to the status of "mere" performers or interpreters—not real producers or creators of music. This is not surprising, given that the music industry has profited greatly from following the lead of capitalism in general by positing women as consumers and "products" (images for consumption), but rarely allowing their existence as producers.

The first thing that separated the Bangles from the so-called "girl groups" of the past is that they wrote most of their own material and, except for an occasional drum machine on *Different Light*, played their own instruments. Not until 1989's hit, "Eternal Flame," from their final album *Everything*, did they release a video that did not include performance footage. Clearly, they were marketed to the public not just as cute L.A. gals who sang well but as musicians. This emphasis on their roles as the producers of music, not just singers of the songs otherwise controlled by men, obviously also distinguished them from other popular female groups that year, such as Bananarama and The Cover Girls, who sang, danced, and giggled, but did not play any instruments. "Hero Takes a Fall" intercuts shots of the band playing on a street corner in San Francisco with scenes in store windows featuring each band member in an overdetermined bit of sexual role-playing with various male mannequins. In each of these scenes, the mannequin either topples, crumbles, or is decapitated in sync with the refrain, "And I won't feel bad at all/if the hero takes a fall." Each of these scenes implies a conventional narrative of gendered role-playing, with the twist on convention being that the *male* in each scenario is the mannequin and the crumbling figure, not the female. And after each scene we are returned to the Bangles playing, singing, and laughing in the street, together. Though it hardly qualifies as a markedly strident feminist position, the "Hero Takes a Fall" video suggests rather a playful, winking understanding of the threat a group of women together can pose to conventional gendered interactions.

This is no small point. I contend that these moments of group identity, of bonding, in the Bangles' performances and in their performance videos are subtle, but nevertheless powerful, moments of resistance to the control of the camera's (or the audience's) gaze. I base this contention on two fundamental presumptions. First, in order for patriarchy to sustain itself as a patriarchy, it must deny or at least contain the possibility of women bonding together without men. Second, American consumer capitalism continues to promote the myth of individual accomplishment over collective activity, particularly with regard to groups (such as women) that are subordinate to more economically powerful groups (such as men), lest the less powerful groups form alliances to upset the socioeconomic order from which capitalists profit. Therefore, when moments of female bonding find their way into popular culture, they are markers of a double resistance, both to patriarchy's positioning of women in the service of men and to the continuing myth of bourgeois individualism.

It is a commonplace in the music industry and its attendant video and print industries that a leader, usually the lead singer, is established within each band. Witness the many *and* bands: Huey Lewis and the News, Gloria Estefan and Miami Sound Machine (formerly simply Miami Sound Machine even though Estefan has always sung lead), Lisa Lisa and Cult Jam. The average MTV viewer may not know the name of the drummer in Pearl Jam, but can probably name the lead singer, Eddie Vedder. The Bangles are no exception. Of the seven singles released from their two Columbia albums, Susanna Hoffs sings lead on five of them. This prompted many people to think of her as the lead singer of the Bangles even though all four women actually sing lead on their albums. Writing for *Rolling Stone*, Susan Orlean explains the Hoffs phenomenon this way:

> But no one counted on Susanna's very natural, coquettish, camera-ready poise attracting so much attention. No one considered that, poise aside, Susanna is almost a foot shorter than the other Bangles and would consequently appear in the foreground of nearly every photograph of the band. And no one, certainly, could have anticipated Prince's much-publicized affection for her or calculated that its effect would be to vault Susanna into beyond-Bangles celebrity status and alter the equal-party nature of the band. (1987)

Hoffs further established her "beyond-Bangles celebrity" by starring in her first feature film, *The Allnighter*, in 1987. Yet, the Bangles' stage performances contradicted this status in that Hoffs rarely addressed the audience; Michael Steele and Vicki Peterson did most of the talking and introduction of songs. The "Hoffs phenomenon" indeed "alter[ed] the equal-party nature of the band," and did so by playing into the ideology of individual achievement. Therefore, the construction of Hoffs as the visual focus of the group, which was common in their television appearances while they were popular, mitigated the threat that their bonding as an all-female group poses to the status quo. Not surprisingly, then, Hoffs has been the only Bangle at this point to release a solo record, the rather poorly received *When You're a Boy* in 1990.

In the videos for "Hero Takes a Fall" or "Going Down to Liverpool" (from the same album), the woman singing lead (Hoffs in the former, Debbi Peterson in the latter) does not have more than her share of close-ups or individual shots. However, in the three videos from the more commercially successful *Different Light*, Hoffs as lead singer has more screen time than the other Bangles. But the American version of the second single off the album, "If She Knew What She Wants," uses the singling out of Hoffs to good advantage by using Hoffs' visual separation from the group to direct an interpretation of the song that is perhaps more sympathetic to the "she" of the song's title. This gives the song a decidedly different feeling and meaning than when it is sung by its writer, Jules Shear, who performs the song rather plaintively. In a brief MTV introduction to the clip, Michael Steele called the American version of "If She Knew What She Wants" "pretty straight-ahead performance video," but it is hardly "straight-ahead." The Bangles render the song in a dialogic fashion, as when Hoffs sings, "If she knew what she wants," and the rest of the band responds, "he'd be giving it to her." The American video reinforces this dialogic structure by intercutting close-ups of Hoffs singing with group shots and one-shots of the others singing and playing. Multiple close-ups of guitars and drums being played are superimposed over the images of the band members. Moments of narrativity in which black-and-white medium shots of D. Peterson, V. Peterson, or Steele are juxtaposed with a color shot of each of them in a different relationship to a man—kissing, hugging but looking away, moving away from his touch—reinforce the story implied by the song—a man in love with a woman who keeps changing her mind about what she wants, and a narrator (the singer) who has some kind of emotional tie to this relationship.

The conjunction of image and song invites us to understand each band member as an embodiment of one aspect of the indecisive "she" of the song, as well as single players in these individuated situations. The visual presentation of the song breaks up the narrative perspective on the relationship being sung about; the lines of the song do not issue from a single, unified perspective. Instead they are a combination of negative remarks about the woman and approving remarks about the man countered by a more sympathetic reading of the woman's position:

> if she knew what she wants, *he'd be giving it to her*
> (. . .)
> if she knew what she wants *but he can't see through her*
> (. . .)
> but she wants everything *he can pretend to give her everything*
> or there's nothing she wants *she don't want to sort it out*
> he's crazy for this girl *but she don't know what she's looking for*

Separating the lines of the song into two perspectives (one of which is shared by three singers) instead of a single, waffling perspective makes the song less of an indictment of the woman in the relationship, and more of a statement of her position, one in which "not wanting to sort it out" and not knowing "what she's looking for" do not necessarily lead to sympathy for the man who's "crazy for this girl." Rather, he can only "pretend to give her everything" because her needs are shifting and therefore exceed what he can offer. The ideological separation of the main voice and the harmonizing voices leaves the figure who is more identified with the man's unhappiness out of the "fun" at the end of the video. The difference in instrumentation and visual style of this final sequence and the pronounced difference in affect between Hoffs and the others mark this final sequence as having heightened importance. The last verse of "If She Knew What She Wants," which starts out with little instrumentation behind the then stark-sounding voices, begins with a long take of a superimposition of a black-and-white close-up of Hoffs and a color long shot of the other Bangles on a revolving platform playing, singing, and laughing. With the group's laughter, full instrumentation returns, and Hoffs fades out of the image completely. Her serious expression and obsessive lyric is obliterated by the image of female bonding in play. When Hoffs appears alone in the next shot, which fades into a shot of the full group, her reintegration into the pleasure of female bonding comes with her joining the group in laughter. The video ends with a crane with a snorkel lens, which pulls back from behind drummer Debbi Peterson's head until the full group is revealed in long shot as they sing/play the final note, at which point the key light is cut so the video ends with the group posed in silhouette.

I have taken pains to describe these last images of separation and reintegration because in them I believe we have the keys to another narrative trajectory at work, one that connects the video to the trajectory of the career of the Bangles, of the all-female bands currently rising up the alternative charts and peeking over into the Top 40, and to the girls and women who respond to the pleasure in their work. Separated by ideological differences, slotted into roles in a narrative that is not their own, singled out from the group, these women take up the poses convention offers them—and laugh.

REFERENCES

Azzerad, M. (1993, October 28). The real new deal. *Rolling Stone*, p. 18.

Lewis, L. (1990). *Gender politics and MTV: Voicing the difference*. Philadelphia: Temple University Press.

Orlean, S. (1987, March 26). The Bangles. *Rolling Stone*, p. 64.

"I keep thinking about those old black guys, the bluesmen who taught me, the ones who ended up in pine boxes with nothing."

"They were black," I said. "That had something to do with it."

"Yeah," Dee said. "And I'm a woman in a business where not many women front bands, write songs, choose their own arrangements, and play their own guitar."

Linda Barnes—*Steel Guitar* (1991)

22

Criticism

"YOU'RE NOT RID OF ME":

Riot Grrrl Bands and New Roles and Old Roles in the Work of Female Performers

ALAN D. STEWART

Alan D. Stewart is Assistant Professor of Communication at Rutgers University. His publications include "Declarations of Independence: The Female Rock and Roller Comes of Age" in Lont and Friedley's *Beyond Boundaries: Sex and Gender Diversity in Communication.* Stewart's research interests include popular culture theory, subcultural theory, comics, and popular music, especially gender roles in popular music.

Dee Willis, the blues-influenced female rocker in Linda Barnes's Carlotta Carlyle mystery *Steel Guitar,* both identifies troublesome characteristics of the traditional, second-class position of female performers in popular music and embodies central characteristics of a new, more positive role for women.

As Dee Willis implies, women have been and continue to be underrepresented in general in the music business despite such highly visible performers as Janet Jackson, Whitney Houston, and Madonna. More important, female performers have rarely had the control over their recordings or their careers that comes from having their own bands, writing their own songs, choosing their own arrangements, playing their own instruments, or producing their own recordings. As a result, women have stereotypically suffered from a limited range of musical styles, characteristics of vocal performance, emotional complexity, and subject conventions.

The character of Dee Willis, on the other hand, suggests a newer, more open role for women representative of a slowly growing number of performers across many rock styles and closely related musical genres. Like Dee Willis, these new role performers have greater control over their careers and their recordings—they lead their own bands, write their own songs, do their own arrangements or production, or play their own instruments.

In Dee's anthemic signature song "For Tonight," she sings with "a tough-gal sexy edge" that she does not "need anybody to cry out my name/don't need anybody to care/Don't need anybody to tug at my skirt/Don't need anybody to share/For tonight, for a while, I want you." Although milder than the more extreme work of some contemporary female performers, "For Tonight" suggests central characteristics of the new role: lyrical and musical rawness, greater emotional complexity with anger, bitterness, and irony, and a viewpoint that links power and love and sex. In addition, typical of the new role, "For Tonight" makes a declaration of Dee's independence not only from traditional emotional attachments but also from past stereotypes and limitations; this declaration of independence empowers Dee and her audience to enter into new and deeper experiential territory.

Aspects of the underlying pattern that marks this new role have become widespread enough so that even the work of some mainly traditional-role female performers exhibits some characteristics of the new role. Many traditional-role mainstream pop performers now sing songs with direct declarations of independence inside personal relationships (often written for them by male composers). Mariah Carey, on the other hand, may sing about wanting a "dream lover" to "belong" to, but she maintains control over her records and career atypical of the traditional-role performer.

Still, many contemporary female performers provide clear examples of the extremes and the empowering benefits of the new role. Mainstream rock and hard rock performers such as Chrissie Hynde, Bonnie Raitt, Sinead O'Connor, and Joan Jett embody important characteristics of the new role. Madonna, the most complex and controversial mainstream performer of the last decade, exhibits over her career a fascinating mix of traditional- and new-role characteristics that highlight the complex presence and empowering character of the new role, especially in her more recent work. Some milder, "nice girl" performers find ways to embody the underlying new-role pattern although they work in musical styles that might seem more typical of the traditional role such as softer, often alternative, rock, sometimes with echoes of 1960s girl group sound (for example, Two Nice Girls, Juliana Hatfield, and Liz Phair), pop or dance music (for example, Sade, En Vogue, and Neneh Cherry) or the acoustic singer-songwriter genre (for example, Lucinda Williams, the Roches, k.d. lang, Michelle Shocked, and the Indigo Girls). Hardcore female rappers such as Queen Latifah, Yo Yo, and MC Lyte provide even more clear-cut and extreme examples. The best contemporary examples of the new role, though, are the so-called riot grrrl bands and closely related hardcore and alternative performers such as Bikini Kill, Hole, Babes in Toyland, L7, and PJ Harvey.

HISTORICAL BACKGROUND

Historically, most women in rock music (that is, most American popular music forms since 1955, including soul music, dance and disco music, folk rock, singer-songwriter-oriented soft rock, contemporary Top 40 and pop rock music, as well as album-oriented or classic rock) fit into one of four highly limited roles. The first role, singer-songwriters, who usually perform relatively simple, pleasant, polite, acoustic, or pop-based music, is arguably a positive role. These women have some control over their music and their careers because they write their material and often play acoustic guitar or piano. As a result, female performers in this category sometimes speak to women-centered themes and a deeper, more varied sense of experience, especially in the work of some contemporary "nice girls" who find subtle ways to undercut the traditional limitations of the genre. Typically, though, the range of musical styles is limited by an emphasis on melody and softer sounds. The subject matter and treatment deal mainly with romance and introspection as central themes presented in moderate terms. The performance characteristics emphasize prettiness of sound over extremes. All of these limitations implicitly suggest traditional, limited, and, at least in that sense, often negative, female gender roles.

The second role, fronts for male creators and manipulators, is more limited. Musical styles and performance characteristics may be a little more varied than in the singer-songwriter genre, but the female performers have little control over the recorded music. Male writers and producers essentially use these women as the instruments by which they make records. The many girl-group records made by Phil Spector in the early and mid-1960s with performers such as the Ronettes, the Crystals, and even Darlene Love are essentially Phil Spector records. The Motown recordings of female performers are essentially records made by the mostly male Motown writer–producer teams such as the Holland, Dozier, Holland team, which produced many of the Supremes' most important recordings. For example, Diana Ross has both mocked the nasal singing on those recordings and complained that the group was kept in the studio singing until their voices were hoarse—that is, until they sounded less pretty than they would have preferred (see Hirshey, 1984). Almost all records are the result of a collaborative process, but there is a substantive difference between receiving help and feedback from others and getting told what and how to sing.

The third and fourth roles are even more limited and negative but, given women's underrepresentation in the music industry, are much more likely roles. Probably the most available visible (or audible) role for women over the last 40 years has been as backup singers—that is, as helpers and enablers with clearly defined second-class status. Note that women in this category are backup singers, *not* instrumentalists. As limited as the backup singer role may seem, undoubtedly the most prevalent roles for women in rock music are such nonproductive offstage (or off-record) roles as rock writers and critics, girlfriends, groupies, and audience members.

Traditionally, few if any women consistently worked in the harder rock areas of popular music, sang with the harshness typical of rock vocal aesthetics, wrote their own material, led their own bands, played their own instruments, or performed rough, aggressive material with the emotional depth and complexity of important male artists like Bob Dylan, John Lennon, the Rolling Stones, Neil Young, or the Who.

The underrepresentation and second-class position of women in rock music can be demonstrated quickly in terms of both the numbers and nature of women artists on various *Billboard* charts. Stewart (1987) finds that between 1955 and 1986 female artists accounted for only between 12 and 38 of the Top 100 records of the year on the *Billboard* Top One Hundred Charts, even counting male–female duets as records by female performers. The Top One Hundred Charts report popular singles, the area in which one is most likely to find larger numbers of female performers. In time periods such as the late 1950s and mid-1960s, when harder rock and rock and roll forms were more popular, the number of female performers goes down, whereas in time periods in which softer or more pop-oriented musical forms are more popular, such as the post-payola pre-Beatles early 1960s and the disco-oriented late 1970s, the number of female performers goes up. This pattern suggests not only the underrepresentation of women but also the restricted musical roles available to them.

Even contemporary data reveal only slight improvement in either the underrepresentation or the limited roles from a statistical point of view. Over half of the number-one songs on the 1991 *Billboard* Hot 100 Chart were by female artists (1991 was the last full year available for analysis). This number would seem to be an improvement indicating the beginning of equal status for women. However, only about one-third of the top 100 records of the year were by women, and less than one-third of the total charted records were by female artists. Other charts from 1991 show continued restricted roles for women. Seven out of the Top 15 Album Artists on the Top Albums Chart were women, but only 7 out of the Top 30 Albums were by women, and less than 20 percent of the total charted albums were by women. None of the Top 20 Artists of the year on the Album Rock Tracks chart were women, and none of the Top 40 Album Rock Tracks of 1991 were by women. Only around 5 percent of the total charted recordings on the Album Rock Tracks for 1991 were by women. Female artists performed slightly better (indicating the influence of the new role) on the Modern Rock Tracks Chart, which monitors commercial alternative rock, with 2 of the Top 21 Artists, 3 of the Top 40 Modern Rock Tracks, and around 10 percent of the total charted recordings of the year. Even the country music singles charts, with a stereotypically higher presence of women, have only about 25 percent of the Top Country Artists, the Top 40 Country Singles, and the total charted singles of the year by female performers (all 1991 chart information from Whitburn, 1992).

Despite the only gradual change in the statistical position of women in rock music, the basic situation in which female performers had either a limited, secondary status, or no status at all started to change in the early to mid-1970s with the emergence of two very different sets of responses.

First, women's music emerged as a separate cultural genre. In terms of control, some kinds of cultural messages, and marketing, women's music represents a significant break with past, limiting norms. In terms of musical style and performance characteristics, however, most women's music remains firmly rooted in traditional characteristics. Most women's music is stylistically acoustic, folk or pop-influenced music with an emphasis on traditional, beautiful voices and pretty melodies.

The second major response by female performers to the limited, traditional roles for women in rock music is the emergence in the mid-1970s of women performing rock and hard rock music atypical of the traditional role. This trend was marked by the emergence in 1975 of important mainstream performers such as Heart, led by the Wilson sisters, and Fleetwood Mac, featuring Stevie Nicks and Christine McVie, and influential, more extreme performers such as Patti Smith and, later in the 1970s, Chrissie Hynde (of the Pretenders). Since the early 1980s, the numbers of important female rock performers has gradually increased to the point that such performers no longer seem to be an anomaly. In addition, a number of important female artists in a variety of formerly male-oriented musical forms now rival their male counterparts in producing significant records with a rough sound and emotional depth and complexity that represents a new, significant communicative role that breaks traditional stereotypes. The biting, aggressive, emotionally intense and complex, if often unpleasant, music made by these artists represents a declaration of independence from the limited, stereotyped art and lives that women were previously expected to live. Contemporary riot grrrl bands and hardcore rappers are the most clear-cut current results of this second response to the traditional role of women in rock music.

NEW ROLES AND TRADITIONAL ROLES

Understanding the limited roles played by traditional-role female artists depends not just on examining direct lyric content but on accounting for a wide range of concerns. Five aspects affect the communicative roles of traditional-role female performers. The first aspect of the traditional role involves the relatively small numbers of female performers reaching a wide public. Historically, these numbers have been as low as 12 percent of even the *Billboard* Top 100 records of the year and have rarely reached more than a third of the *Billboard* Top 100 records of the year during the rock era. Second, female performers have typically worked in relatively limited musical styles with an emphasis on simple melodies and acoustic, folk, and pop-based ballads.

Third, the typical characteristics of vocal performance of female rock artists has tended to be much more limited than those of male rock performers. Female performers have continued to emphasize such traditional concerns as pitch, intonation, enunciation, and precision as opposed to the emphasis on sound and delivery for the purposes of emotional impact typical of male rock performers. In other words, in the rock music era in which male vocals are judged by their power and harshness, even ugliness in traditional musical terms, women have been expected to continue to "sing pretty."

Fourth, the limited subject conventions and basic viewpoints typical of female performers have emphasized such traditional "female" concerns as idealized romance, heartache if the idealized romance is not achieved, and vague sentimental generalizations expressed in moderation as opposed to the diverse subject matter and generally celebrated extremes of the rock music era. Finally, the traditional role is characterized by a relative lack of control over the final product in terms of the artist's control over material by writing it or actively choosing it, by playing instruments on the recordings, by arranging the material, or by producing the recordings.

The new communicative role, on the other hand, works in terms of a very different underlying pattern. The work of new-role performers is characterized by lyrical and musical rawness; by lyrical, musical, and emotional extremes and obsessions atypical of the moderation of the traditional role; by anger, bitterness, and irony as opposed to the simpler and "nicer" emotions of the traditional role; and by a viewpoint that tends to link power and love and sex. These artists have a control over the final product similar to that held by male artists since, like major male artists, these women often write their own material or choose it for themselves when they do not write it, play instruments, lead instead of front bands, and sometimes even do their own producing.

The work of these female new-role artists functions as declarations of independence empowering themselves and their audiences to enter into new and deeper experiential territory outside the normal pattern of the traditional role. These declarations of independence fall into two distinct categories: direct, even anthemic declarations of independence, and more indirect declarations.

The direct declarations function in one of three forms:

1. By making statements within the context of interpersonal, usually romantic relationships

2. By making declarations of a more general, often philosophical nature

3. By making statements stressing the importance and primacy of the artists' personal experience

The indirect declarations function in four different ways:

1. In terms of the music itself (just hearing a female voice in these musical contexts represents a new communicative role)

2. In terms of the nature of the rougher performance with an emphasis on emotional impact rather than prettiness or technique

3. In terms of transformations of previously recorded male-associated material often implicitly challenging traditional sex-role expectations (such as Aretha Franklin's version of "Jumpin' Jack Flash," in which a specifically male role disappears as it is appropriated by the female singer; Pat Benatar's "Sex as Weapon," which inverts the normal stereotype of which gender uses sex for power; or Joan Jett's covers of such male-oriented material as AC/DC's "Dirty Deeds," ZZ Top's "Tush," and the Doors' "Love Me Two Times")

4. In terms of the unexpected and untraditional, as well as frequently extreme, violent, and obsessive images, subjects, and language

A comparison of two well-known hit records from the 1980s, Whitney Houston's "The Greatest Love of All" and Janet Jackson's "Control," will help clarify the differences. Whitney Houston is in most respects a traditional-role performer, and "The Greatest Love of All" conforms to major aspects of the traditional role. Stylistically, the song is a conventional pop rock ballad with a pretty melody—exactly the kind of song stylistically that one would expect a traditional-role performer to sing. In terms of performance, Houston has a conventional "good" voice (and a very good one at that) that she uses to "sing pretty." In terms of control, Houston did not write the song, she does not play an instrument, and she did not arrange or produce the recording (and there is evidence to suggest that this song, like most of Houston's recordings, was hand-picked for her by Clive Davis, the president of her record company). In terms of content, the song is mainly a conventional ballad that is sentimental, inspiring, and general without speaking to specific, concrete situations. The song does contain a direct declaration of independence, stressing the importance of the singer's experience (the song suggests that what is necessary is faith in oneself: the "greatest love" is "learning to love yourself"), but that probably comes from the fact that the song was written about a male (Muhammad Ali—the song was originally the title song to a movie about Ali). It would be nice to see this as a transformation, but it is probably more or less an accident in this case.

On the other hand, Janet Jackson's "Control" differs in important ways although it is milder than many less-mainstream new-role recordings. Stylistically, the song is a much heavier funk style more typically used by male performers—however, since Jackson's commercial success, more women have used it. Jackson's vocal performance is rougher, more aggressive and distorted than Houston's. Although Jackson is capable of "singing pretty," that is not what she does here. In terms of control, Jackson co-wrote the song, she plays digital keyboards on the recording, and she has a co-producer and arranger credit for the recording. On the one hand, the song is typical of the Jimmy Jam and Terry Lewis production style, but on the other hand, she chose to work with them and had to fight both her family and her record company to be allowed to do so. Finally, in terms of content, this is a very specific song about herself and about concrete situations in which she needs to assert herself. The general attitude is tough, assertive, even obsessively so, and she makes direct declarations of independence in terms of her relations with her parents and with potential lovers (including an implied link between power and love and sex).

Even in terms of mainstream, Top 40 music, then, the new role marks a clear break in a variety of ways from the traditional role available to female recording artists. The most important point, though, is that the various characteristics of the new role suggest an underlying cultural construction that empowers women to engage in wider, more complex, more intense, if sometimes unpleasant, experience than the restricted lives implied by the limitations of the traditional role. The traditional role has not disappeared, but the new role continues to make progress in both more disguised forms used by "nice girl" performers and the more extreme forms exemplified by hard rock performers, hardcore rappers, and especially riot grrrl bands.

RIOT GRRRLS

"We want revolution grrrl-style now."
Bikini Kill, "Double Dare Ya"

In the early 1990s, a variety of new, young, female, and women-centered groups emerged playing various extreme rock styles influenced by hard rock, hardcore punk, heavy metal, and earlier new-role female performers such as Patti Smith, Chrissie Hynde, and Kim Gordon from Sonic Youth. The underlying cultural movement suggested by bands such as L7, Babes in Toyland, Bikini Kill, Brat-mobile, Hole, and PJ Harvey gets called by a number of different names associated with their different subcultural groups and musical styles, from *foxcore* (a somewhat offensive term used mainly by people outside the subculture to describe hardcore and heavy-metal-influenced bands) to *angry girl music*, to the most evocative, *riot grrrls*.

Riot grrrls is both an evocative term to label the larger underlying cultural phenomenon and a specialized term used by involved participants to label a specific youth subculture centered on groups like Bikini Kill and Bratmobile. The riot grrrls in this specific sense is an aggressive, post post-feminist feminist movement for teenage and early college-age women that is part normal teenage rebellion adapted for teenage girls, part punk, part traditional feminism, and part grassroots social movement centered on musical performers, clubs, fanzines (my favorite title is *Girl Germs*), and even exchanges of personal letters by involved participants.

Both the larger cultural movement and the specific youth subculture called up by the term *riot grrrls* share underlying cultural constructions concerning female empowerment and independence and evoke the new role pattern for female performers. (Indeed, the line between the larger cultural movement and the specific youth subculture can be difficult to draw—particularly over time; Polly Harvey of PJ Harvey has not identified herself as a riot grrrl and did not come out of the specific youth subculture, and yet women who do identify themselves as riot grrrls speak admiringly about PJ Harvey's music.)

The aggressive, even militant, if rarely didactically ideological, sound and language of these riot grrrl bands and recordings with an emphasis on female empowerment in one direction and the continued attraction of sex and even romance in the other direction highlight by their very difference from them the underlying constructions of both traditional gender roles and mainstream feminism. For example, when PJ Harvey complains disgustedly, even viciously, in "Dry" that "you leave me dry," the group generates a range of cultural messages from the literal to the metaphoric that invoke the declarations of independence typical of new role performers but that may leave some older, traditional feminists uneasy. The very term *riot grrrl* invokes images of aggressive independence and semantic reclamation in the one direction but also images generated by the word *girl* in the other. (Indeed, the single most reported riot grrrl incident is a New York club date in which Bikini Kill stopped the show to try to explain to an older female audience member why they use the term *girl* instead of woman.)

In some ways these messages are specifically feminist. Certainly most traditional feminists would have no trouble with the metaphorical, ideological implications of "Dry." Nonetheless, although most riot grrrl performers identify themselves as feminists (some, like Polly Harvey, refuse to accept the term, in part rejecting the chafings of ideological restrictions), some riot grrrls are troubled by the sense that traditional feminists and traditional feminist ideas are as potentially limiting as patriarchal controls. (For a good journalistic account of the clash between traditional feminists and the so-called lipstick feminists represented by the riot grrrls, see Powers, 1993.) Certainly many traditional feminists might feel uneasy with the literal level of meanings generated by "Dry" and by the use of such literal metaphors, as well as the extreme sexual and violent language and images, in much riot grrrl music. Likewise, the sexual bravado and sexual display involved in riot grrrl images and live performances might make some feminists uncomfortable. Members of Bikini Kill, for example, have appeared in bikini tops and bike pants with "slut" written on their abdomens; the cover of Babes in Toyland's *Fontanelle* features a crotch shot of an anatomically correct doll.

The most obvious new-role characteristics of riot grrrl recordings involve their sound and performance characteristics. Although such individual riot grrrl performers as PJ Harvey, Hole, L7, and Bikini Kill are readily identifiable as different from one another, they all feature harsh, loud, hard rock music made by distorted electric instruments being pushed to their limits (and in Polly Harvey, anyway, the riot grrrls produce the first genuine female guitar hero in rock music). The listener is literally bombarded by the sound of these recordings. The singers shout, scream, cry, whisper hoarsely, command, insult, insinuate disgust or disbelief or dislike. What they do not do is "sing pretty." The style of these records is not moderate or controlled or limited by the restrictions of the traditional role. The sound and the performance of these artists work to declare independence from all past limitations.

The language and the images used by these performers are frequently as extreme and obsessive as the sounds. Variations of such four-letter obscenities litter all these recordings. Bikini Kill tends to use these words almost as punctuation and intensifiers. Even Polly Harvey, the most traditionally literate of these performers, uses these types of words occasionally. Generally extreme images and language abound such as "slug me open and suck my scars," "you suicide bitch," and "when I was a teenage whore/I paid good money not to be ignored" from "Loaded," "Mrs. Jones," and "Teenage Whore" by Hole. Other examples include "this is a song about 16 year old girls giving carnies head for free rides and hits of pot" ("Carnival") and the teenager who tells her sexually abusive father to "suck my left one" both by Bikini Kill, as well as the man who rejects the singer by telling her to "put money in your idle hole" in "Sheela-Na-Gig," or the singer who demands of a lover that he "lick my lips of desire" in "Rid of Me" both by PJ Harvey.

In general, these artists construct a world in conflict in which various forces, sometimes more and sometimes less directly patriarchal, attempt to control the singer. This is a world in which violence, anger, sex, sleaze, even degradation are standard elements and a world in which power and self-assertion are important ingredients. The records by these riot grrrl artists are full of direct and indirect declarations of independence in which the singers assert themselves both in interpersonal relationships and against a series of restrictions. In "Double Dare Ya," Bikini Kill dares a "girlfriend" to "do what you want . . . be who you will" and tells her that "you've got to know what they are to stand up for your rights." In "Feels Blind," Bikini Kill complains, "As a woman I was taught to be hungry . . . we'd even eat your hate up like love . . . How does this feel? It feels blind," with the implication that independent self-assertion is the necessary antidote.

Hole asserts an independence from stereotypic female roles in "Baby Doll," first by worrying that the "baby doll" role is "sucking my energy" and then by claiming that "in the dark I destroy what I began" and rejecting a role in which "there is nothing you can feel but your chemical wedding and your chemical peel." Getting "Loaded" or being a "Teenage Whore" may sound negative, but they are ways for Hole to separate themselves from a type of life they abhor, relishing the mother's "repulsion" in "Teenage Whore" and telling her: "Don't want to live the type of life you put me through and I never would."

PJ Harvey similarly asserts in "Mansize": "I'll measure time/I'll measure height/I'll calculate my birthright/Good lord I'm big . . . mansize." In "Sheela-Na-Gig," the singer rejected after offering her lover her "child-bearing hips," her "ruby red lips," her "work-strong arms," and her "bottle full of charms" (apparently because she offers him this supposedly male wish-fulfillment-fantasy out of her own choice rather than his demand) not only is going to "wash that man right out of my hair" but also "take my hips to a man who cares." In "50ft Queenie," the singer wants "to be free/no one can stop me"; she is "second to no one/no sweat/I'm clean/nothing can touch me" because she is a "force 10 hurricane."

The work of these riot grrrl performers contains interesting variations on the transformation part of the new role model. PJ Harvey struts through a bravura version of Dylan's "Highway 61 Revisited," not so much reversing normal gender expectations as erasing them by implicitly suggesting that they can play anything. Recent live versions by Polly Harvey of everything from Willie Dixon's "Wang Dang Doodle" to the Rolling Stones' "Satisfaction" make the same implicit point. PJ Harvey's "50ft Queenie" marks an indirect transformation by playing off Chuck Berry's often covered "Little Queenie" by transforming the diminutive female role to a giant woman even bigger than the speaker in "Mansize." Hole transforms not male material but Joni Mitchell's "Clouds," turning the celebration of romantic possibility in the original into a cynical, hardcore dirge in which possibility becomes at best a desperate, impossible hope.

Riot grrrl songs frequently connect sex and power and violence. In "Rid of Me," PJ Harvey hoarsely commands her lover to "lick my legs/I'm on fire/lick my lips of desire" and threatens to "make you lick my injuries." In PJ Harvey's "Rub 'Til It Bleeds," the speaker offers her lover to "rub it until it bleeds," a promise that sounds more like a threat. Similarly, "Snake" constructs sex as a dangerous encounter, echoing the devil tempting Eve: "You snake/you crawl between my legs/said want it all/it's yours/you bet/I'll make you queen of everything/no need for God/no need for him . . . just take the brute/put it inside . . . I burn my hand/I'm on fire." Bikini Kill's "Suck My Left One" is the archetypal riot grrrl song that makes the sexual command of the title into an assertive declaration of independence. It combines an attack on restrictive social conventions (in the first verse the singer tells a "sister" they have got to show the "boys" that "we're worse than queer") with a criticism of incest (in the second verse, "Daddy comes into her room at night/He's got more than talking on his mind/My sister pulls the covers down/She reaches over, flicks on the light/she says to him: Suck my left one"—thus asserting power and control in a powerless relationship exactly in terms of the sexual power manipulation).

Riot grrrl songs such as "Suck My Left One," "Rid of Me," or "Teenage Whore" are, of course, serious business, with important messages about serious, even unpleasant subjects. But they are also liberating declarations of independence in the best tradition of rock and roll. As such, they partake of something very different from the seriousness suggested earlier. These riot grrrl bands suggest a deep, reckless sense of fun. There is a sense of playfulness in the way in which these performers pound out their ugly music, throw around their extreme and sometimes obscene language, and break social taboos. Bikini Kill enjoys showing us that they are "worse than queer." Polly Harvey loves insisting that she is not only "Mansize" but a "50ft Queenie" bending over Casanova. Riot grrrls do not want to "just" have fun, but they do want to have fun getting their own back in a serious world.

CONCLUSION: "YOU'RE NOT RID OF ME"

Women remain underrepresented on the *Billboard* charts, and the styles and cultural messages most often available from mainstream, frequently traditional-role female performers are limited. Nonetheless, different, less restrictive, empowering cultural messages and performances are available from female performers in a variety of styles. A range of less extreme but still clearly new-role performers exists in many somewhat more mainstream rock genres. But the riot grrrls remain the clearest contemporary examples of the new role.

Undoubtedly, many potential listeners (and perhaps some readers of this chapter) will find the musical style and performance, the extreme language, the unpleasant images and subjects, and even some of the underlying cultural constructions of these bands offensive. After all, even relatively mainstream new-role performers such as Sinead O'Connor and Madonna have had genuine problems with parts of the potential audience. It is almost always easier to experience hegemonic texts than it is to experience real cultural difference or deal with texts that generate genuine cultural resistance—even when one approves of the underlying ideas. Certainly, too, parts of the sound and message of these records are intended to be offensive to parts of the public; if they were not offensive, they would not be doing their job of breaking restrictive social norms.

Still, no matter how offensive the rough language or the violent images or the loud, obnoxious noise of some of these songs might be, the underlying pattern is positive and empowering. When Polly Harvey sings that "you're not rid of me," she is not talking just to a lover but to her audience, enjoining those who approve and threatening those who disapprove. Some of us hope that she means those lines as a promise not just for herself but for a whole range of strong, independent female performers with a variety of messages and styles who will continue to empower their audiences through their music and who we will not be "rid" of any time soon.

REFERENCES

Barnes, L. (1991). *Steel guitar.* New York: Dell.

Denisoff, R. S., & Bridges, J. (1982). Popular music: Who are the recording artists? *Journal of Communication, 32*(1), 132–142.

Hirshey, G. (1984). *Nowhere to run: The story of soul music.* New York: Penguin.

Powers, A. (1993, February 14). No longer rock's playthings. *New York Times,* Section 2, pp. 1, 34.

Stewart, A. D. (1987). *Declarations of independence or traditional sex roles: Female artists on the 1986 Billboard Hot 100.* A paper presented at the Tenth Annual Communication, Language and Gender Conference, Milwaukee, WI.

Whitburn, J. (1992). *1991 Billboard music and video yearbook.* Menomonee Falls, WI: Record Research.

While there are many ways to improve the portrayal of women and men to more aptly reflect our society, increasing the number of educated media consumers is the most important of all.

CONCLUSION

The 1990 census reveals:

- Nearly one out of every four American women is a member of a minority group.
- The median age of women has "increased from 31 years in 1980 to 34 years in 1990"
- "Only one-fourth of women over age 16 live in" a "married couple with children" household.
- "Women are more educated than ever" ("Here are the facts," 1994, p. 3).

Yet the media continues to portray fewer women, younger women, in less diverse roles than those assigned to men. In addition, there are fewer women than men working in the media, especially in powerful, decision-making positions (editors, directors, presidents of media companies, and so on), even though "women are a greater part of the American work force than ever" ("Here are the facts," 1994, p. 3).

The most recent studies on women and media do indicate an increase in the numbers; more women are working in media than in the past. In fact, based on much of the material within this book, one might argue that there is a direct correlation between the increase in the number and complexity of women's portrayals and the increase in the number of women employed in the media and the positions they hold. Not only are there more women working in the media, but a few are in powerful positions as prime-time television writers, television news anchors, film directors, owners of advertising agencies, and presidents of record companies.

Media content reflects the influx of women making decisions concerning media content. There has been an increase in the number of female bylines and references to women in newspaper stories. The number of women appearing in newspaper photographs was the "highest recorded on the front pages in five years" (Bridge, Chapter 1). On television, Pieraccini and Schell (Chapter 8) found fewer sexist ads in prime time than in past years. The analysis of network news (Foote, Chapter 14) indicated that women neither gained more visibility on networks nor lost it until 1992, when the percentage increased. Women now rank among the top 100 correspondents.

In the film industry, White women are offered more roles than in the past, but many of these roles are stereotypes of how and what a woman should be, while African-American women and Asian/Pacific American women are portrayed in even more limiting ways (Stubbs, Chapter 17; Goldstein, Chapter 19). In spite of the limited number of women film directors (women were less than one-fifth of the Director's Guild, directing less than 8% of the time in 1992 ["Director's Guild Study," p.7]), the influence of women in the field is obvious—Jane Campion won the 1994 Academy Award for Best Film Director.

Subtle changes in the portrayal of women appear in various media with a few exceptions. In Peirce's analysis of teen magazines (Chapter 5), "appearance" continues to be the central theme. Teen magazines cover male figures twice as often as they cover female figures. Only the category of "home" has dropped. What is seen, then, is an increase in the number of women portrayed in the media, the types of roles for women in the media, and more women working in the media. While this is important, one need only look at the numbers to realize there is a long way to go to gain equity.

SPEED OF CHANGE

Another pattern derived from these chapters is the amount of time each medium takes to respond to historical events. Some media are quick to change with the times. Television, for example, appears to hone in on issues of importance to society and produce programs that reflect, in some ways, safe topics. For example, the focus on families after the Depression and World War II produced a number of light sitcoms based on traditional family values. I emphasize the word *safe* in that, although television-produced programs took a new view of women in the 1960s when the women's liberation movement was beginning, its portrayal was superficial and, in some ways, just as stereotypical (Dow, Chapter 13).

Women's magazines, on the other hand, move very slowly in response to societal change. During the Depression, women's magazines lacked coverage of real issues impacting women and their readers turned away. With World War II women's magazines, having learned from the Depression, focused on real issues of the time.

HOW EMPLOYED WOMEN ARE PORTRAYED

The ebb and flow of employment of women affects the portrayal of women. For example, during World War II, more women joined the work force. During this time, positive portrayals of working women increased in films and women's magazines. When women returned to the home, their portrayal revolved around their function as homemakers/mothers while working women were portrayed as taking away men's jobs, being unfeminine, and without husbands.

In the 1970s, many women entered the marketplace again, and the media responded with some portrayals of women working. Mostly, however, the media continued to show women at home dealing with their families. If not married, their co-workers became their "family," with men continuing to play the role of father/husband and women as mother/wife (Dow, Chapter 13). The jobs women held outside the home were not portrayed as central to their lives.

In the 1990s, women are an ever-increasing part of the work force and have entered almost every arena of employment. Yet the diversity of women in the work force is rarely portrayed. Yes, Connie Chung, an Asian-American female, is co-anchor with Dan Rather. It was seventeen years since the last male–female co-anchor team. Is this progress? Yes, slow, incremental progress! Real progress is when it is commonplace for two women and/or African-American, Hispanic, and Asian-American men and women to co-anchor the network news.

SAME MEDIA, DIFFERENT AUDIENCE

Although one part of a specific medium might change, that doesn't mean the change is reflected throughout the medium. For example, while television ads in prime time are less sexist, one needs only to watch Saturday-morning cartoons to see the reinforcement of stereotypes within the commercials aimed at children. One must look beyond one single portion of a media form and investigate all aspects. While the content of teen magazines may continue to stereotype females as only interested in their appearance, other women's magazines may focus more on work problems or financial matters.

WOMEN OF COLOR

Across the board, the portrayal of African-American women in American media is rare; up until the 1980s, it was a series of stereotypes. Asian/Pacific American and Hispanic women are rarely seen in media, and when they are they are generally portrayed as stereotypes. Most positive portrayals of women of color come from pressure by their communities and by people of color who enter the industry and make changes. American media rarely change without this kind of influence.

ECONOMIC FACTORS

This brings me to a very important pattern embedded within the chapters in this book. Media changes occur most frequently because of political or economic factors. This has been most pronounced in the last twenty years, as advertisers have been forced to confront women as they are (diverse, independent, and so on), not as they have safely portrayed them. In general, the reason for change is not from media producers' desire to portray women realistically (although some producers do) but their confrontation with economic and political forces. The 1990 census shows that the incomes of American women have grown. Incomes of adult women increased 30% (average personal income of $12,200) from 1980. "Women living alone have the highest average income" ("Here are the facts," 1994, p. 3). Women are purchasing more high-ticket items and educated women not only care about portrayals, they are willing to use political clout to make changes (League of Women Voters and National NOW). Economic factors force media producers to discover why women aren't reading newspapers and spend less time watching television, because to maintain an ever-dwindling audience, they need to draw this group of purchasers back.

In addition, changes in the media usually occur when groups apply economic or political pressure to the media. Unfortunately pressure groups react to the media rather than lead the media to better content and portrayals. Usually an event sets the process in motion—an article, a book, a study—and then groups apply pressure, usually to advertisers.

WHAT'S NEXT?

Some media activists (Junior Bridge and Sally Steenland for example) examine ongoing trends within the media. The identification of trends is important in ascertaining shifts in the portrayal of women and women's employment status within the media. These studies are important because they gauge the changes in the media, both portrayal and employment.

It is also important that women who affect the media from inside be identified and discussed. There are too few role models for women in the field of media. It is much harder to think of yourself as a film director if you can't name another woman film director. Various groups across the country are documenting the lives of women in media. One such group, the Washington Press Club Foundation, recently completed an eight-year effort to document the lives and careers of fifty-four notable women journalists through an oral history project. This collection of audiotapes is accessible from various repositories, including Columbia University, the National Press Club, and thirteen university libraries across the United States. For all of us, young and old alike, role models help us determine what is possible and not possible in our lives.

Although progress for women in the media has been made, it has been incremental. In addition, progress has been made before, only to slip away. We can't rest on past achievements and say, "Oh well, it's OK now." Groups in the past have said just that. "Well, we've got the vote, it will be OK now," and it hasn't been. We need more proactive, not reactive behavior. Don't wait until a truly negative portrayal occurs before you say something. The mere absence of females or any group from the media is a warning sign. Examine the situation and ask questions. Recently, I wrote a letter to the manufacturers of LEGOs. My four-year-old daughter loves them, and we'd purchased a number of packages of LEGO people only to find very few LEGO females. While the male LEGOs were working construction, waiting tables (in a tuxedo), pumping gas, portrayed as firefighters, pirates, race-car drivers, astronauts, and knights—a diversity of roles—the female LEGOs were portrayed in leisure activities (riding bicycles, riding horses and sunbathing). I wrote and asked them to portray females in more realistic roles. I received a letter from the Consumer Affairs Department stating that their company was always interested in increasing their appeal, so they appreciated my comments on their products. In order to help my daughter enjoy her LEGOs, they included complimentary female wigs of various shapes and colors. Enclosed in the envelope were ten different-colored, long-haired wigs to replace the hats that usually fit over the heads of the various characters and a few little heads that had more made-up eyes (long lashes). Of course, LEGO's response didn't address the problem. Advertising, packaging, and so forth will continue to either discount females altogether or show them in leisure-only activities. Girls and boys whose parents do not write letters will not receive "female-looking" heads and wigs. The portrayal of LEGO females in the stores and ads will continue to show female LEGOs as less active than their male counterparts. Second, replacing a hat with a wig does not make a firefighter into a female firefighter. She no longer has the hat, a major indicator as to what the job is. Now she just looks like a firefighter in a wig. Of course, LEGO's response was less important than letting them know that somewhere among their purchasers is a person who can write a letter, purchase their products, and cares about the portrayal of females. Was the response disappointing? Somewhat, but it was a response (many times you receive no response). Will I write again? Sure.

While the above-mentioned activities are important, most crucial are people's awareness of the media and that if women are not fully represented, identified, and valued in the media, it is a problem. Last semester, one of the final projects for my Women and Media class was a content analysis of the portrayal of women in any media. Many chose women's magazines. Some compared them to similar men's magazines. In general, student response was the same. They couldn't believe they had been reading these magazines for years and not noticed the difference between the portrayal of women versus the portrayal of men in both types of magazines. They asked me, "How could I not notice the way women were shown in the ads or the types of articles written for women?" The students were upset, in part, because of the content, but more because they hadn't previously noticed the negative portrayal of women in their favorite magazines. Now that they were aware, they read the magazine more critically, no longer accepting the material without asking questions. While there are many ways to improve the portrayal of women and men to more aptly reflect our society, increasing the number of educated media consumers is the most important of all.

REFERENCES

Director's guild study: Action limited for women, minority directors. (1992, Summer). *Media Report to Women*, 7.

Here are the facts—But will they become stories? (1994, Summer). *Media Report to Women*, 3.

BIBLIOGRAPHY

GENERAL REFERENCES

Baehr, H. & Ryan. M. (1984). *Shut up and listen! Women and local radio: A view from the inside.* London: Comedia Press.

Beasley, M. H., & Gibbons, S.J. (1977). *Women in media: A documentary sourcebook.* Washington, DC: Women's Institute for the Freedom of the Press.

Busby, L. (1975). Sex-role research on the mass media. *Journal of Communication, 25,* 107–131.

Butler, M., & Paisley, W. (1980) *Women and the mass media: Sourcebook for research and action.* New York: Human Sciences Press.

Cramer, J. A. (1989). Radio: A woman's place is on the air. In P.J. Creedon (Ed.), *Women in mass communication: Challenging gender values* (pp. 214–226). Beverly Hills, CA: Sage.

Creedon, P. J. (1993). *Women in mass communication: Challenging gender values* (2nd Ed.). Beverly Hills, CA: Sage Publications.

Dates, J. L., & Barlow, W. (1993). *Split image: African Americans in the mass media* (2nd Ed.). Washington, DC: Howard University Press.

Douglas, S. J. (1994). *Where the girls are: Growing up female with the mass media.* New York: Random House.

Durell, A., & Lumsden, A. (1986). Sexual stereotyping in the media. In Curran, et al. (Eds.), *Bending reality: The state of the media.* London: Pluto Press.

Ewen, S., & Ewen, E. (1992). *Channels of desire: Mass images and the shaping of American consciousness.* Minneapolis: University of Minnesota Press.

Freidman, L. J. (1977). *Sex role stereotyping in the mass media: An annotated bibliography.* New York: Garland Press.

Gamman, L., & Marshment, M. (1989). *The female gaze: Women as viewers of popular culture.* St. Paul, MN: Real Comet Press.

Griffin, L., & McCann, K. (1992). *The book of women.* Holbrook, MA: Bob Adams, Inc.

Janus, N. Z. (1978). Research on sex-roles in the mass media: Toward a critical approach. In Janus, N.Z. (Ed.), *The uses of literacy.* London: Penguin.

Jewell, K. S. (1993). *From mammy to Miss America and beyond: Cultural images & the shaping of U.S. social policy.* New York: Routledge.

Karpf, A. (1980). Women and radio. *Women's Studies International Quarterly, 3* (1), 41–54.

Kent, S., & Moreau, J. (1989). *Women's images of men.* Winchester, MA: Pandora Press.

King, J., & Stott, M. (1977). *Is this your life? Images of women in media.* London: Quartet Books.

Knill, B. J., Pesch, M., & Pursey, G. (1981). Still typecast after all these years. *International Journal of Women's Studies, 4*, 497–506.

Kranich, K. (1989). Women's media. *Women and Language,* 7 (1), 19–22.

Lent, J. (1991). *Women and mass communication: An international annotated bibliography.* New York: Westport, CT: Greenwood Press.

Lull, J., Mulac, A., & Rosen, S. L. (1983). Feminism as a predictor of mass media use. *Sex Roles, 9* (2), 165–177.

Marzolf, M. (1991, 1992). *Women in media: Course outlines.* Ann Arbor: The University of Michigan.

Marzolf, M., Rush, R. B., & Stern, D. (1974–1975). The literature of women in journalism history. *Journalism History, 1* (4), 117–128.

Muramatsu, Y. (1990). Of women by women for women?: Japanese media today. *Studies of Broadcasting, 26,* 83–104.

National Council for Research on Women (1992). *A directory of women's media.* Susan A. Hallgorth (Ed.). New York: The National Council for Research on Women.

Ogundipe-Leslie, M. (1990). The image of women and the role of the media in a new political culture in Nigeria. *Africa Media Review, 4* (1), 52–59.

Pribram, D. (1988). *Female spectators: Looking at film and television.* London: Verso.

Rapping, E. (1994). *Media-tions: Forays into the culture and gender wars.* Boston: South End Press.

Robinson, G. J. (1992). Women and the media in Canada: A progress report. In Holmes & Taras (Eds.), *Our own reflections: Mass media and Canadian identity.* Toronto: Holt, Rinehart & Winston.

Rush, R., & Allen, D. (1990). *Communications at the crossroads: The gender gap connection.* Norwood, NJ: Ablex Publishing.

Sochen, J. (1987). *Enduring values: Women in popular culture.* New York: Praeger.

Steeves, H. L. (1987). Feminist theories and media studies. *Critical Studies in Mass Communication, 4* (2), 95–135.

Steeves, H. L., Becker, S., & Choi, H.C. (1988). The context of employed women's media use. *Women's Studies in Communication, 11* (2), 21–43.

Steiner, L. (1992). The history and structure of women's alternative media. In L. Rakow (Ed.), *Women making meaning: New feminist directions in communication.* New York: Routledge.

Strainschamps, E. (1974). *Rooms with no view: A woman's guide to the man's world of the media.* New York: Harper & Row.

Toronto Women in Film and Television (1991). *Changing focus: The future of women in the Canadian film and television industry.* Toronto: Toronto Women in Film and Television.

Tuchman, G. (1978). The symbolic annihilation of women by the mass media. In Tuchman, Daniels, Kaplan & Benet (Eds.), *Hearth and home: Images of women in the media* (pp. 3–38). New York: Oxford University Press.

Tuchman, G. (1979). Review essay: Women's depiction by the mass media. *Signs: Journal of Women in Culture and Society, 4* (3), 528–542.

Tuchman, G., Daniels, A. K., & Benet, J. (Eds.). (1978). *Hearth and home: Images of women in the mass media.* New York: Oxford University Press.

Tulloch, P. (1991). *Directory of women's media, 1991–92.* New York: National Council for Research on Women.

Van Zoonen, L. (1991). Feminist perspectives on the media. In Curran & Gurevitch (Eds.) *Mass media and society.* London: Edward Arnold.

Washington Press Club Foundation Oral History Project "Women in Journalism." (1994). National Press Building, Washington, DC.

Wilson, J. G. (1988). *Taking stock: Women in the media before the 21st century.* Gannett Foundation.

Women's Institute for Freedom of the Press (Annual, 1972–). *Index/Directory of women's media.* Washington, DC: Women's Institute for Freedom of the Press.

Yodelis Smith, M. (1982). Research retrospective: Feminism and the media. *Communication Research, 9* (1), 145–160.

PART I: NEWSPAPERS

Biographical

Barnes, K. (1990). *Trial by fire: A woman correspondent's journey to the frontline.* New York: Thunder's Mouth Press.

Beasley, M. H. (1976). *The first women Washington correspondents.* Washington, DC: George Washington University.

Beasley, M. H. (1983). A "front page girl" covers the Lindbergh kidnaping: An ethical dilemma. *American Journalism, 1* (1), 63–72.

Belford, B. (1986). *Brilliant bylines: A biographical anthology of notable newspaper women.* New York: Columbia University Press.

Bennion, S. C. (1990). *Equal to the occasion: Women editors of the nineteenth century West.* Reno: University of Nevada Press.

Brady, K. (1984, 1989). *Ida Tarbell: Portrait of a Muckraker.* New York; Pittsburgh: Seaview/Putnam.

Clabes, J. (1983). *New guardians of the press: Selected profiles of America's women newspaper editors.* Indianapolis: R. J. Berg.

Collins, J. (1980). *She was there: Stories of pioneering women journalists.* New York: J. Messner.

Demeter, R. L. (1979). *Primer, presses, and composing sticks: Women printers of the Colonial period.* Hicksville, NY: Exposition Press.

Dickerson, N. (1976). *Among those present: A reporter's view of twenty-five years in Washington.* New York: Random House.

Duster, A. M. (1970). *Crusade for justice: The autobiography of Ida B. Wells*. Chicago: University of Chicago Press.

Edwards, J. (1988). *Women in the world: The great foreign correspondents*. Boston: Houghton Mifflin.

Elwood-Akers, V. (1988). *Women war correspondents in the Vietnam War, 1961–1975*. Metuchen, NJ: Scarecrow Press.

Freeman, B. M. (1989). *Kit's kingdom: The journalism of Kathleen Blake Coleman*. Ottawa, Canada: Carleton University Press.

Geyer, G. A. (1983). *Buying the night flight: The autobiography of a woman foreign correspondent*. New York: Delacorte Press.

Goodman, E. (1979). *Turning points*. New York: Doubleday & Co.

Goodman, E. (1989). *Making sense*. New York: Penguin Books.

Gruber, R. (1991). *Ahead of my time: My early years as a foreign correspondent*. Tarrytown, NY: Wynwood Press.

Hudspeth, R.N. (1983). *The letters of Margaret Fuller*. Ithaca, NY: Cornell University Press.

Kroeger, B. (1994). *Nellie Bly: Daredevil, reporter, feminist*. New York: Times Books.

May, A. (1983). *Witness to war: A biography of Marguerite Higgins*. New York: Beaufort Books.

Quindlen, A. (1988). *Living out loud*. New York: Random House.

Quinn, S. (1975). *We're going to make you a star*. New York: Simon and Schuster.

Rhodes, J. (1992). Mary Ann Shadd and the legacy of African-American women journalists. In L. Rakow (Ed.), *Women making meaning: New feminist directions in communication*. New York: Routledge.

Ricchiardi, S., & Young, V. (1991). *Women on deadline: A collection of America's best*. Ames: Iowa State University Press.

Rollyson, C. (1990). *Nothing even happens to the brave: The story of Martha Gellhorn*. New York: St. Martin's Press.

Schilpp, M. G. (1983). *Great women of the press*. Carbondale: Southern Illinois University Press.

Sheppard, A. (1994). *Cartooning for suffrage*. Albuquerque: University of New Mexico Press.

Smith, W. M., & Bogart. E. A. (1991). *The wars of Peggy Hull: The life and times of a war correspondent*. El Paso: University of Texas at El Paso Press.

Solomon, M. M. (1991). *A voice of their own: The woman suffrage press, 1840–1910*. Tuscaloosa: University of Alabama Press.

Streitmatter, R. (1994). *Raising her voice: African-American women journalists who changed history*. Lexington: University of Kentucky Press.

Wagner, L. (1989). *Women war correspondents in World War II*. Westport, CT: Greenwood Press.

Wells, I. (1969). *On lynching and a red record*. New York: Arno Press.

Woodruff, J., with Maxa, K. (1982). *This is Judy Woodruff at the White House*. Reading, MA: Addison-Wesley.

General

Abremson, P. E. (1990). *Sob sister journalism*. New York: Greenwood Press.

Arnold, J. (1976). Feminist presses and feminist politics. *Quest: A Feminist Quarterly, 3* (1), 18–26.

Barrett, G. H. (1984). Job satisfaction among newspaperwomen. *Journalism Quarterly, 16* (3), 593–599.

Beasley, M. H., & Gibbons, S. J. (1993). *Taking their place: A documentary history of women and journalism*. Washington, DC: American University Press in cooperation with the Women's Institute for Freedom of the Press.

Beasley, M. H., & Theus, K. T. (1988). *The new majority: A look at what the preponderance of women in journalism education means to the schools and to the professions*. New York: Lanham.

Bennion, S. C. (1986). Woman suffrage papers of the West, 1869–1914. *American Journalism, 3* (3), 125–137.

Blackwood, R. E. (1984). The content of news photos: Roles portrayed by men and women. *Journalism Quarterly, 60,* 711–714.

Brabant, S. (1976). Sex role stereotyping in the Sunday comics. *Sex Roles, 2* (4), 331–337.

Brabant, S., & Mooney, L. (1986). Sex role stereotyping in the Sunday comics: Ten years later. *Sex Roles, 14* (3/4), 141–148.

Braden, M. (1993). *She said what? Interviews with women newspaper columnists*. Lexington: University of Kentucky Press.

Buchanan, E. (1992). *Contents under pressure*. New York: Hyperion.

Chavez, D. (1985). Perpetuation of gender inequality: A content analysis of comic strips. *Sex Roles, 13,* 93–102.

Cooper, A. M. (1983). Suffrage as news: Ten dailies coverage of the nineteenth amendment. *American Journalism, 1* (1), 73–92.

Cooper, A. M., & Davenport, L. D. (1987). Newspaper coverage of the International Women's Decade: Feminism and conflict. *Journal of Communication Studies, 11* (1), 108–115.

Davis, J. (1962). Sexist bias in eight newspapers. *Journalism Quarterly, 59,* 456–460.

Eberhard, W. B., & Meyers, M. (1988). Beyond the locker room: Women in sports on major daily newspapers. *Journalism Quarterly, 65* (3), 595–599.

Epstein, L. K. (1978). *Women and the news*. New York: Hastings House.

Foreit, K. G., Agor, T., Byers, J., Larue, J., Lokey, H., Palazzini, M., Patterson, M., & Smith, S. (1980). Sex bias in the newspaper treatment of male-centered and female-centered news stories. *Sex Roles, 6,* 475–480.

Fornoff, S. (1993). *Lady in the locker room*. Champaign, IL: Sagamore.

Guenin, Z. B. (1975). Women's pages in American newspapers: Missing out on contemporary content. *Journalism Quarterly, 52,* 66–69.

Holly, S. (1979). Women in management of weeklies. *Journalism Quarterly, 56,* 810–815.

Kramarae, C., & Rakow, L. (1990). *The revolution in words: Righting women 1868–1871.* New York: Routledge.

Kramarae, C., & Russo, A. (1990). *The radical women's press of the 1850s.* New York: Routledge.

Krieling, A. (1977–78). The rise of the Black press in Chicago. *Journalism History, 4,* 132–136, 156.

Luebke, B. F. (1985). News about women on the A Wire. *Journalism Quarterly,* 329–333.

Luebke, B. (1989). Out of focus: Images of women and men in newspaper photographs. *Sex Roles, 20,* 121.

Mann, J. (1994). *The difference: Growing up female in America.* New York: Warner Books.

Marks, P. (1990). *Bicycles, bangs, and bloomers: The new woman in the popular press.* Lexington: University Press of Kentucky.

Marzolf, M. (1977). *Up from the footnote: A history of women journalists.* New York: Hastings House.

McLendon, W., & Smith, S. F. (1970). *Don't quote me: Washington newswomen and the power society.* New York: Dutton.

Merrit, S., & Gross, H. (1978). Women's pages/Life style editors: Does sex make a difference? *Journalism Quarterly, 55,* 508–519.

Meyer, K., Siedler, J., Curry, T., & Aveni, A. (1980). Women in July fourth cartoons: A 100-year look. *Journal of Communication, 30,* 21–30.

Miller, S. H. (1975). The content of news photos: Women's and men's roles. *Journalism Quarterly, 52* (1), 70–75.

Mills, K. (1988). *A place in the news: From the women's pages to the front page.* New York: Dodd, Mead.

Morris, M. B. (1973). Newspapers and the new feminists: Black out as social control? *Journalism Quarterly, 50,* 37–42.

Ogan, C. L. (1980). On their way to the top? Men and women middle-level newspaper managers. *Newspaper Research Journal, 1,* 51–62.

Ogan, C. L. (1983). Life at the top for men and women newspaper managers: A five-year update of their characteristics. *Newspaper Research Journal, 5* (2), 57–68.

Ogan, C., & Weaver, D. H. (1978–1979). Job satisfaction in selected U.S. daily newspapers: A study of male and female top-level managers. *Mass Comm Review, 6* (1), 20–26.

Okigbo, C. (1988). Sex in the newsroom: Male–female differences in perceptions of media professionalism. *Communications: The European Journal of Communication, 14* (1), 7–22.

Orwant, J. E., & Cantor, M. G. (1977). How sex stereotyping affects perceptions of news preferences. *Journalism Quarterly, 54*, 99–108, 139.

Potkay, C. R., & Potkay, C. E. (1984). Perceptions of female and male comic strip characters II: Favorability and identification are different dimensions. *Sex Roles, 10*, 119–128.

Robertson, N. (1992). *The girls in the balcony: Women, men and the New York Times.* New York: Random House.

Ross, I. (1936, 1974). *Ladies of the press: The story of women in journalism by an insider.* New York: Harper & Arno Press.

Saenger, G. (1955). Male and female relations in the American comic strip. *Public Opinion Quarterly, 19* (2), 195–205.

Schultz-Brooks, T. (1984). Getting there: Women in the newsroom. *Columbia Journalism Review,* 25–31.

Sohn, A.B. (1981). Women in newspaper management: An update. *Newspaper Research Journal, 3* (1), 94–106.

Sohn, A.B. (1984). Goals and achievement orientations of women newspaper managers. *Journalism Quarterly, 16* (3), 600–605.

Streicher, H. W. (1974). The girls in cartoons. *Journal of Communication, 24*, 125–129.

Tuchman, G. (1978). *Making news: A study in the construction of reality.* New York: The Free Press.

Wachsberger (Ed.), *Voices from the Underground* (pp. 124–130). Tempe, AZ: Mica Press.

White, H. A., & Andsager, J. L. (1991). Newspaper column readers' gender bias: Perceived interest and credibility. *Journalism Quarterly, 68* (4), 709–718.

Whitlow, S. S. (1979). Women in the newsroom: A role theory view. *Journalism Quarterly, 56*, 378–383.

PART II: WOMEN'S MAGAZINES

Bailey, M. (1969). The women's magazine short-story heroine in 1957 and 1967. *Journalism Quarterly, 47*, 364–366.

Ballaster, R, Beetham, M., Frazer, E., & Hebron, S. (1991). *Women's worlds: Ideology, femininity and the woman's magazine.* London: Macmillan.

Bathen, S. (1992 August). Time to rewrite the women's page. *California Republic,* 14–15.

Braithwaite, B., & Barrell, J. (1979). *The business of women's magazines.* London: Associated Business Press.

Cancian, F. M., & Gordon, S. L. (1988). Changing emotion norms in marriage: Love and gender in U.S. women's magazines since 1900. *Gender and Society, 2*(3), 308–342.

Evans, E., Rutberg, J., Sather, C., & Turner, C. (1991). Content analysis of contemporary teen magazines for adolescent females. *Youth and Society, 23*, 99–120.

Ferguson, M. (1978). Imagery and ideology: The cover photographs of traditional women's magazines. In Tuchman, G., Daniels, A. K., & Benet, J. (Eds.), *Hearth and home: Images of women in the media.* New York: Oxford University Press.

Ferguson, M. (1983). *Forever feminine: Women's magazines and the cult of femininity.* London and Exeter, NH: Heinemann.

Flora, C. (1971). The passive female: Her comparative image by class and culture in women's magazine fiction. *Journal of Marriage and the Family, 33,* 435–444.

Franzwa, H. (1975). Female roles in women's magazine fiction, 1940–1970. In Unger, Kester & Denmark, *Women dependent or independent variable* (pp. 42–53). New York: Psychological Dimensions.

Geise, L. A. (1979). The female role in middle class women's magazines from 1955 to 1976: A content analysis of nonfiction selections. *Sex Roles, 5,* 51–62.

Goffman, E. (1976). *Gender advertisements.* New York: Macmillan.

Humphreys, N.K. (1989). *American women's magazines: An annotated historical guide.* New York: Garland.

Hynes, T. (May 1981). Magazine portrayal of women. *Journalism Monographs, 72.*

Inoue, T. (1989). *Reading women's magazines: Comparepolitan-studies of Japanese, American and Mexican women's magazines.* Tokyo: Kakiuchi Publishing.

Kranich, K. (1990). A bibliography of periodicals by and about women of color. *Feminist Teacher, 5* (1), 26–41.

Lisenby, F. (1985). American women in magazine cartoons. *American Journalism, 2,* 130–134.

McCall, L. (1989). The reign of brute force is now over: A content analysis of *Godey's Lady's Book,* 1830–1960. *Journal of the Early Republic, 9,* 217–236.

McCracken, E. (1983). In search of the female consumer: Latin American women's magazines and the transnational model. *Studies in Latin American Popular Culture, 2,* 226–233.

McRobbie, A. (1991). *Feminism and youth culture: From 'Jackie' to 'Just Seventeen'.* London: Macmillan.

Massey, J. (1992, October). Girl talk mags. *School Library Journal,* 54.

Mather, A. (1974–1975). A history of feminist periodicals. *Journalism History, 1* (3), 82–85.

Miller, C. (1987). Who talks like a women's magazine? Language and gender in popular women's and men's magazines. *Journal of American Culture, 10* (3), 1–10.

Petersen, T. (1964). *Magazines in the twentieth century.* Urbana: University of Illinois.

Phillips, E. B. (1978). Magazine heroines: Is *Ms.* just another member of the family circle? In G. Tuchman, A. K. Daniels, & J. Benet (Eds.), *Hearth and home: Images of women in the mass media.* New York: Oxford University Press.

Ruggiero, J. A., & Weston, L. C. (1985). Work options for men and women in women's magazines: The medium and the message. *Sex Roles, 5,* 321–328.

Shevelow, K. (1989). *Women and print culture: The construction of femininity in the early periodical.* New York: Routledge.

Steiner, L. (1983). Finding community in the nineteenth century suffrage periodicals. *American Journalism, 1* (1), 1–16.

White, C. (1970). *Women's magazines 1693–1968.* London: Michael Joseph.

Winship, J. (1981). *Woman becomes an "individual": femininity and consumption in women's magazines.* Birmingham: Centre for Contemporary Cultural Studies, University of Birmingham.

Winship, J. (1987). *Inside women's magazines.* London: Pandora Press.

Zuckerman, M. E.(1991). *Sources on the history of women's magazines, 1792–1960: An annotated bibliography.* Westport, CT: Greenwood Press.

PART III: ADVERTISING

Barthel, D. L. (1988). *Putting on appearances: Gender and advertising.* Philadelphia: Temple University Press.

Baxter, M. (1990). *Women in advertising.* London: Institute of Practitioners in Advertising.

Bonelli, L. (1989). Sex-role stereotyping in fragrance advertisements. In C.M. Lont & S. F. Friedley (Eds.), *Beyond boundaries: Sex and gender diversity in communication.* Fairfax, VA: George Mason University Press.

Clarke, C. V. (1993, June). Industry Overview: Redefining beautiful—Black cosmetic companies and industry giants vie for the loyalty of Black women. *Black Enterprise,* 243–252.

Courtney, A. E., & Whipple, T. W. (1980). *Sex stereotyping in advertising: An annotated bibliography.* Cambridge, MA: Marketing Science Institute.

Davis, S. (1990). Men as success objects and women as sex objects: A study of personal advertisements. *Sex Roles, 23* (1/2), 43–50.

Eanshaw, S. (1984). Advertising and the media: The case of women's magazines. *Media, Culture & Society, 6* (4), 411–421.

Faulkner, M., Kokkeler, L., & Wesson, D. (1989). Advertising students see field as less gender-focused. *Journalism Educator, 43* (4), 4–10.

Ford, J. B., LaTour, M. S., & Lundstrom, W. J. (1991). Contemporary women's evaluation of female role portrayals in advertising. *Journal of Consumer Marketing, 8* (1), 15–28.

Fox, B. J. (1990). Selling the mechanized household: 70 years of ads in *Ladies' Home Journal. Gender & Society, 4* (1), 25–40.

Jaffe, L. J. (1991). Impact of positioning and sex-role identity on women's responses to advertising. *Journal of Advertising Research, 31* (3), 57–64.

Jones, M. (1991). Gender stereotyping in advertisements. *Teaching in Psychology, 18* (4), 231–233.

Kilbourne, W. E. (1990). Female stereotyping in advertisements: An experience on male–female perceptions of leadership. *Journalism Quarterly, 67* (1), 25–31.

Komisar, L. (1971). Women and advertising. In V. Gornick and B. Moran (Eds.), *Women in a sexist society* (pp. 207–218). New York: Basic Books.

Leigh, T. W., Rethans, A. J., & Reichenbach, T. (1987). Role portrayals of women in advertising: Cognitive responses and advertising effectiveness. *Journal of Advertising Research, 27* (5), 54–63.

Lundstrom, W. J., & Sciglimpaglia, D. (1977). Sex-role portrayals in advertising. *Journal of Marketing, 41* (3), 72–79.

Masse, M., & Rosenblum, K. (1988). Male and female created they them: The depiction of gender in the advertising of traditional women's and men's magazines. *Women's Studies International Forum, 11* (2), 127–144.

Melton, G. W., & Fowler, G. L. (1987). Female roles in radio advertising. *Journalism Quarterly, 64* (1), 145–149.

Millus, T. (1975). *Images of women.* New Jersey: Rowan and Littlefield.

Poe, A. (1976). Active women in ads. *Journal of Communication, 26* (4), 185–192.

Pokrywczynski, J. V. (1988). Sex in ads targeted to Black and White readers. *Journalism Quarterly, 65* (3), 756–759.

Rakow, L. F. (1992). Don't hate me because I'm beautiful: Feminist resistance to advertising. *Southern Communication Journal, 57* (2), 131–142.

Riddle, J. S. (1993). Mining the non-white markets. *Brandweek, 34,* 29–30.

Saunders, C. S., & Stead, B. (1986). Women's adoption of a business uniform: A content analysis of magazine advertisements. *Sex Roles, 15,* 187–206.

Solomon, B. (1992). The '90s woman makes strides down Madison Avenue, *Management Review, 81,* 11–15.

Sullivan, G. L., & O'Connor, P. J. (1988). Women's role portrayals in magazine advertising. *Sex Roles, 18,* 181–188.

Taylor, R., & Hovland, R. (1989). Women likely to face salary discrimination in advertising. *Journalism Educator, 43* (4), 11–16.

Venkatesan, M., & Loslo, J. (1975). Women in magazine ads: 1959–1971. *Journal of Advertising Research, 15,* 49–54.

Weller, S., and Associates. (1987). *Sex role portrayal of women in advertisements: A content analysis.* Canberra: Office of the Status of Women.

Television Commercials

Bardwick, J., & Schumann, S. (1967). Portrait of American men and women in TV commercials. *Psychology, 4* (4), 18–23.

Caballero, M. & Solomon, P. (1984). A longitudinal view of women's role in TV advertising. *Journal of the Academy of Marketing Science, 12* (4), 93–107.

Dominick, R. J., & Rauch, G. E. (1972). The image of women in network TV commercials. *Journal of Broadcasting, 16* (3), 259–362.

Downs, A. C., & Harrison, S. K. (1985). Embarrassing age spots or just plain ugly? Physical attractiveness stereotyping as an instrument of sexism on American television commercials. *Sex Roles, 13,* 9–19.

Ferrante, C. L., Haynes, A. M., & Kingsley, S. M. (1988). Image of women in television advertising. *Journal of Broadcasting and Electronic Media, 32,* 231–237.

Furnham, A., & Voli, V. (1989). Gender stereotypes in Italian television advertisements. *Journal of Broadcasting and Electronic Media, 33,* 175–185.

Geis, F. L., Brown, V., Jennings, J., & Porter, N. (1984). TV commercials as achievement scripts for women. *Sex Roles, 10,* 513–525.

Gilly, M. C. (1988). Sex roles in advertising: A comparison of television advertisements in Australia, Mexico, and the United States. *Journal of Marketing, 52* (2), 75–85.

Jennings, J., Geis, F. L., & Brown, V. (1980). Influence of television commercials on women's self-confidence and independent judgment. *Journal of Personality and Social Psychology, 38* (1), 203–210.

Knill, B. J., Pesch, M., Pursey, G., Gilpin, P., & Perloff, R. M. (1981). Still typecast after all these years? Sex role portrayals in television advertising. *International Journal of Women's Studies, 4,* 497–506.

Lovdal, L. T. (1989). Sex role messages in television commercials: An update. *Sex Roles, 21* (11/12), 715–724.

McArthur, L. Z., & Resko, B. G. (1975). The portrayal of men and women in American television commercials. *The Journal of Social Psychology, 97,* 209–220.

Mamay, P. D., & Simpson, R. L. (1981). Three female roles in television commercials. *Sex Roles, 7,* 1223–1232.

Myers, P. N., & Biocca, F. A. (1992). The elastic body image: The effect of television advertising on body image distortions. *Journal of Communication, 42* (3), 108–133.

O'Donnell, W. J., & O'Donnell, K. S. (1978). Update: Sex-role messages in TV commercials. *Journal of Communication, 28,* 156–158.

Scheibe, C. (1979). Sex role in TV commercials. *Journal of Advertising Research, 19,* 23–27.

Schneider, K. C., & Schneider, S. B. (1976). Trends in sex roles in television commercials. *Journal of Marketing, 43,* 79–84.

Whipple, T. W., & Courtney, A. E. (1980). How to portray women in TV commercials—realistically. So said both viewers and practitioners. *Journal of Advertising Research, 20* (2), 53–59.

PART IV: ENTERTAINMENT TELEVISION

Acland, C. (1990). The "space" behind the dialogue: The gender-coding of space on *Cheers. Women and Language, 13* (1), 38–40.

Adelson, A. (1990, November 19). Study attacks women's roles in TV. *New York Times,* p. C18.

Alexander, A. (1985). Adolescents' soap opera viewing and relational perceptions. *Journal of Broadcasting and Electronic Media, 29,* 295–308.

Allen, R. C. (1985). *Speaking of soap operas.* Chapel Hill: University of North Carolina Press.

Atkin, D. (1991). The evolution of television series addressing single women 1966–1990. *Journal of Broadcasting and Electronic Media, 35,* 517–523.

Atkin, D., Moorman, J., & Lin, C.A. (1991). Ready for prime time: Network series devoted to working women in the 1980s. *Sex Roles, 25,* 577–585.

Atwood, R. A., Zahn, S. B., & Weber, S. (1986). Perceptions of the traits of women on television, *Journal of Broadcasting and Electronic Media, 30,* 95–101.

Babrow, A. S. (1987). Student motives for watching soap operas. *Journal of Broadcasting & Electronic Media, 31* (3), 309–321.

Bacon-Smith, C. (1992). *Enterprising women: Television fandom and the creation of popular myth.* Philadelphia: University of Pennsylvania Press.

Baehr, H. (1980). The "liberated" woman in television drama. *Women's Studies International Quarterly, 3* (1), 29–39.

Baehr, H., & Dyer, G. (1987). *Boxed in: Women and television.* New York: Pandora.

Brown, M. E. (1994). *Soap opera and women's talk: The pleasure of resistance.* Thousand Oaks, CA: Sage.

Brown, M. E. (1991). Strategies and tactics: Teen-agers' readings of an Australian soap opera. *Women and Language, 14* (1), 22–28.

Brown, M. E. (1990). *Television and women's culture.* Beverly Hills, CA: Sage.

Brown, W. J., & Cody, M. J. (1991). Effects of a prosocial television soap opera in promoting women's status. *Human Communication Research, 18* (1), 114–142.

Brunsdon, C. (1987). Feminism and soap operas. In Kathy Davis (Ed.), *Out of focus: Writings on women and the media* (pp. 147–150). London: Women's Press.

Buerkel-Rothfuss, N. L., with Mayes, S. (1981). Soap opera viewing: The cultivation effect. *Journal of Communication, 31,* 108–115.

Byars, J., & Dell, C. (1992). Big differences on the small screen: Race, class, gender, feminine beauty and the characters at Frank's Place. In L. Rakow (Ed.), *Women making meaning: New feminist directions in communication.* New York: Routledge.

Cantor, M. G. (1977). Women and Public Broadcasting. *Journal of Communication, 27,* 14–19.

Cantor, M. G. (1979). Our days and our nights on TV. *Journal of Communication, 29,* 66–72.

Cantor, M., & Pingree, S. (1983). *The soap opera.* Beverly Hills, CA: Sage.

Chaudhary, M. (1987). Images of women through television. *Communicator,* 29–31.

Copeland, G. A. (1989). Face-ism and prime-time television. *Journal of Broadcasting and Electronic Media, 33* (20) 209–214.

Cummings, M. S. (1988). The changing image of the Black family on television. *Journal of Popular Culture, 22* (2), 75–85.

Dambrot, F. H., Reep, D. C., & Bell, D. (1988). Television sex roles in the 1980s: Do viewers' sex and sex role orientation change the picture? *Sex Roles, 19,* 387–402.

Dates, J. L. (1987). Gimme a Break: African-American women on prime-time television. In A. Wells, *Mass media and society.* Lexington, MA: D.C. Heath Co.

Davis, D. M. (1990). Portrayals of women in prime-time network television: Some demographic characteristics. *Sex Roles, 23* (5/6), 325–332.

Dominick, J. R. (1979). The portrayal of women in prime time, 1953–1977. *Sex Roles, 5,* 405–412.

Downs, A. C. (1981). Sex role stereotyping on prime-time television. *The Journal of Genetic Psychology, 138,* 253–258.

Downs, A. C., & Harrison, S. K. (1985). Embarrassing age spots or just plain ugly? Physical attractiveness stereotyping as an instrument of sexism in American television commercials. *Sex Roles, 13,* 9–19.

Eddings, B. (1980). Women in broadcasting. *Women's Studies International Quarterly, 3* (1), 1–13.

Epstein, R. (1992, May 28). Empowerment is the name of the game for actresses. *Los Angeles Times,* p. F4–7.

Fine, M. G. (1981). Soap opera conversations: The talk that binds. *Journal of Communication, 31,* 97–107.

Gade, E. M. (1971). Representation of the world of work in daytime television serials. *Journal of Employment Counseling, 8,* 37–42.

Geraghty, C. (1991). *Women and soap opera: A study of prime time soaps.* Oxford: Polity.

Goff, D. H., Goff, L. D., & Lehrer, S. K. (1980). Sex-role portrayals of selected female television characters. *Journal of Broadcasting, 24,* 467–477.

Greenberg, B. S., Abelman, R., & Neuendorf, K. (1981). Sex on the soap operas: Afternoon delight. *Journal of Communication, 31,* 83–89.

Greenberg, B. S., Neuendorf, K., Buerkel-Rothfuss, N., & Henderson, L. (1982). What's on the soaps and who cares? *Journal of Broadcasting, 26* (2), 519–535.

Gunter, B. (1986). *Television and sex role stereotyping.* London: John Libbey.

Gutman, J. (1973). Self-concepts and television viewing among women. *Public Opinion Quarterly, 37* (3), 388–397.

Hanson, C. A. (1990). The women of China Beach. *Journal of Popular Film and Television, 17,* 155–163.

Haskell, D. (1979). The depiction of women in leading roles in prime-time television. *Journal of Broadcasting, 12* (2), 191–196.

Henderson, L., Greenberg, B. S., & Aitken, C. K. (1980). Sexual differences in giving orders, making plans and needing support on television. In B.S. Greenberg (Ed.), *Life on television: A content analysis of U.S. TV drama.* Norwood, NJ: Ablex.

Hill, G. H. (1990) *Black women in television: An illustrated history and bibliography.* New York: Garland Publishing.

Intintoli, M. J. (1984). *Taking soaps seriously: The world of Guiding Light.* New York: Praeger.

Kalisch, P. A., & Kalisch, B. J. (1984). Sex role stereotyping of nurses and physicians on prime-time television: A dichotomy of occupational portrayals. *Sex Roles, 10,* 533–553.

Kaniuga, N., Scott, T., & Gade, E. (1974). Working women portrayed on evening television programs. *Guidance Quarterly, 23* (2), 134–137.

Katzman, N. (1972). Television soap operas: What's been going on anyway? *Public Opinion Quarterly, 36,* 200–212.

Kimball, M. M. (1986). Television and sex-role attitudes. In Williams (Ed.), *The impact of television: A natural experiment in three communities.* New York: Academic Press.

Lemon, J. (1977). Women and Blacks on prime-time television. *Journal of Communication, 27,* 70–79.

Lemon, J. (1978). Dominant or dominated? Women on prime-time television. In G. Tuchman, A. Kaplan-Daniels, & J. Benet (Eds.), *Hearth and home: Images of women in the mass media* (pp. 51–68). New York: Oxford University Press.

Lowry, D. T., Love, G., & Kirby, M. (1981). Sex on the soap operas: Patterns of intimacy, *Journal of Communication, 31,* 90–96.

McGhee, P. E., & Frueh, T. (1980). Television viewing and learning of sex role stereotypes. *Sex Roles, 6,* 179–188.

Marc, D., & Thompson, R. J. (1992). *Prime time, prime movers.* Boston: Little, Brown and Company.

Matelski, M. J. (1985). Image and influence: Women in public television. *Journalism Quarterly, 62* (1), 147–150.

Matelski, M. J. (1988). *The soap opera evolution: America's enduring romance with daytime drama.* Jefferson, NC: McFarland.

Mayerle, J. (1987). Character shaping genre in Cagney and Lacey. *Journal of Broadcasting and Electronic Media, 31,* 133–151.

Meehan, D. M. (1983). *Ladies of the evening: Women characters of prime-time television.* Metuchen, NJ: Scarecrow Press.

Mellencamp, P. (1992). *High Anxiety: Catastrophe, scandal, age and comedy.* Bloomington: Indiana University Press.

Nochimson, M. (1992). *No end to her: Soap opera and the female subject.* Berkeley: University of California Press.

Peevers, B. H. (1979). Androgyny on the TV screen? An analysis of sex role portrayal. *Sex Roles, 10,* 797–809.

Prabha, K., & Dighe, A. (1990). *Affirmation and denial: Construction of femininity on Indian television.* New Delhi/Newbury Park/London: Sage.

Press, A. L. (1991). *Women watching television: Gender, class, and generation in the American television experience.* Philadelphia: University of Pennsylvania Press.

Reep, D. C., & Dambrot, F. H. (1987). Television's professional women: Working with men in the 1980s. *Journalism Quarterly, 64,* 2–3, 376–381.

Reep, D. C., & Dambrot, F. H. (1988). In the eye of the beholder: Viewer perceptions of TV's male/female working partners. *Communication Research, 15* (1), 51–69.

Rhodes, J. (1991). Television's realist portrayal of African-American women and the case of "L.A. Law." *Women and Language, 14* (1), 29–34.

Robichaux, M. (1993). Lifetime aim: Be all things to all women, *Wall Street Journal (Eastern ed.)*, p. B1.

Rose, B. G. (1985). *TV genres: A handbook and reference guide.* Westport, CT: Greenwood Press.

Rosen, M. (1981, October). Cagney and Lacey. *Ms., 4*, pp. 47–50, 109.

St. John, M. (1978, October 2). Debbie Allen swings on a star. *Encore American & World News*, pp. 26–29.

Sanders, C. (1983, March). Debbie Allen. *Ebony*, pp. 74–79, 84.

Schlesinger, P. (1992). *Women viewing violence.* London: BFI Publishers.

Scott, V. (1983, March 10). Debbie's a driving force to fame. *The Washington Times Magazine*, p. 7D.

Seggar, J. F. (1975). Imagery of women in television drama: 1974. *Journal of Broadcasting, 19*, 273–281.

Seiter, E. (1986). Stereotypes and the media: A re-evaluation. *Journal of Communication*, 14–26.

Signorelli, N. (1985). *Role portrayal and stereotyping on television: An annotated bibliography of studies relating to women, minorities, aging, sexual behavior, health, and handicaps.* Westport, CT: Greenwood Press.

Signorelli, N. (1989). Television and conception about sex roles: Maintaining conventionality and the status quo. *Sex Roles, 21*, 341–360.

Sklar, R. (1980). *Prime time America: Life on and behind the television screen.* New York: Oxford University Press.

Spigel, L., & Mann, D. (1992). *Private screenings: Television and the female consumer.* Minneapolis: University of Minnesota Press.

Stark, J., & Alexander, M. (1988, November 14). It's a different world for dancer and choreographer Debbie Allen: She's moved to prime-time directing. *People*, pp. 105–106.

Steenland, S. (1988). Ten years in prime time: An analysis of the image of women on entertainment television from 1979 to 1988. *Celebrate the Changing Image of Working Women*, pp. 1–22.

Steenland, S. (1982). *What's wrong with this picture? A look at working women on television.* Washington, DC: National Commission on Working Women.

Steeves, H. L., & Smith, M. C. (1987). Class and gender in prime-time television entertainment: Observations from a socialist feminist perspective. *Journal of Communication Inquiry, 7*, 44–63.

Stroman, C. A., Merritt, B. D., & Matabane, P. W. (1989–1990). Twenty years after Kerner: The portrayal of African-Americans on prime-time television. *The Howard Journal of Communications, 2* (1), 44–56.

Waters, H. F. (1991, November). Whip me, beat me . . . and give me great ratings. A network obsession with women in danger. *Newsweek*, pp. 74–75.

Weigel, R. H., & Loomis, J.W. (1981). Televised models of female achievement revisited: Some progress. *Journal of Applied Social Psychology, 11* (1), 58–63.

Zeck, S. (1989). Female bonding in Cagney and Lacey. *Journal of Popular Culture, 26,* 143–154.

Zemach, T., & Cohen, A. A. (1986). Perception of gender equality on television and in social reality. *Journal of Broadcasting and Electronic Media, 30* (4), 427–444.

Entertainment, Television, and Children

Aitken, J. (1989). The Transformers: An analysis of messages in a product-driven cartoon. In C.M. Lont & S. Friedley (Eds.), *Beyond boundaries: Sex and gender diversity in communication.* Fairfax, VA: George Mason University Press.

Bergman, J. (1974). Are little girls being harmed by Sesame Street? In J. Stacey, S. Bereaud, & J. Daniels (Eds.), *And Jill came tumbling after: Sexism in American education.* New York: Dell.

Busby, L. J. (1974). Defining the sex-role standard in network children's programs. *Journalism Quarterly, 51,* 690–696.

Dohrmann, R. (1975). A gender profile of children's educational TV. *Journal of Communication, 25,* 56–65.

Durkin, K. (1984). Children's accounts of sex-role stereotypes in television. *Communication Research, 11* (3), 341–362.

Durkin, K. (1985). *Television, sex roles and children: A developmental social psychological account.* Philadelphia: Open University Press.

Feldstein, J. H., & Feldstein, S. (1982). Sex differences on televised toy commercials. *Sex Roles, 8,* 581–588.

Feshbach, N. D., Dillman, A. S., & Jordan, T. (1979). Portrait of a female on television—some possible effects on children. In Kopp, C.B. & Kirkpatrick, M. (Ed.), *Becoming female: Perspectives on development.* New York: Plenum Press.

Goldreich, G. (1973). *What can she be? A newscaster.* New York: Lothrop, Lee & Shepard.

Mayes, S. L., & Valentine, K. B. (1979). Sex role stereotyping in Saturday morning cartoons. *Journal of Broadcasting, 23* (1), 41–45.

Miller, M., & Reeves, B. (1976). Dramatic TV content and children's sex-role stereotypes. *Journal of Broadcasting, 20,* 35–50.

Nolan, J. D., Galst, J. P., & White, M. A. (1977). Sex bias on children's television programs. *Journal of Psychology, 96,* 197–204.

Peirce, K. (1989). Sex-role stereotyping of children on television: A content analysis of the roles and attributes of child characters. *Sociological Spectrum, 9,* 321–328.

Pingree, T. (1978). The effects of nonsexist TV commercials and perception of reality on children's attitudes about women. *Psychology of Women Quarterly, 2,* 262–277.

Remafedi, G. (1990). Study group report on the impact of television portrayals of gender roles on youth. *Journal of Adolescent Health Care, 11,* 59–61.

Riffe, D., Goldson, H., Saxton, K., & Yu, Yang-Chou. (1989). Females and minorities in TV ads in 1987 Saturday children's programs. *Journalism Quarterly, 66* (1), 129–136.

Signorelli, N. (1990). Children, television, and gender roles: Messages and impact. *Journal of Adolescent Health Care, 11,* 50–58.

Sternglanz, S., & Serbin, L. (1974). Sex role stereotyping in children's television programs. *Developmental Psychology, 10,* 710–715.

Verna, M. E. (1975). The female image in children's TV commercials. *Journal of Broadcasting, 19,* 301–309.

Wartella, E., & Reeves, B. (1985). Historical trends in research on children and the media: 1900–1960. *Journal of Communication, 35,* 118–133.

Welch, R. L., Huston-Stein, A., Wright, J. C., & Plehal, R. (1979). Subtle sex-role cues in children's commercials. *Journal of Applied Social Communication, 29* (3), 202–209.

Women on Words and Images. (1975). *Channeling children: Sex stereotyping in primetime TV.* Princeton, NJ: Women on Words and Images.

NOTE: Sources dealing with television commercials are found in Section III, Advertising: Television Commercials, on p. 388.

PART V: TELEVISION NEWS

Blair, G. (1988). *Almost Golden: Jessica Savitch and the selling of television news.* New York: Simon and Schuster.

Epstein, L. K. (1978). *Women and the news.* New York: Hastings House.

Lemish, D., & Tidhar, C. E. (1991). The silenced majority: Women in Israel's 1988 television election campaign. *Women and Language, 14* (1), 13–21.

Media Studies Journal. (1993, Winter/Spring). A field guide for women in media industries, 81–98.

Nash, A. (1988). *Golden girl: The story of Jessica Savitch.* New York: Dutton.

Peisner, D. (1989). *The imperfect mirror: Inside stories of television newswomen.* New York: Morrow.

Rakow, L. F., & Kranich, K. (1991). Woman as sign in television news. *Journal of Communication, 41* (1), 8–23.

St. John, J. D. (1978). Sex role stereotyping in early broadcast history: The career of Mary Margaret McBride. *Frontiers: Journal of Women's Studies, 3* (3), 31–38.

Savitch, J. (1982). *Jessica Savitch: Anchorwoman.* New York: Putnam.

Trotta, L. (1991). *Fighting for air: In the trenches with television news.* New York: Simon and Schuster.

Van Zoonen, L. (1991). A tyranny of intimacy? Women, femininity and television news. In Dahlgren & Sparks (Eds.), *Communication and citizenship: Journalism and the public sphere in the new media age.* London: Routledge.

Whittaker, S., & Whittaker, R. (1976). Relative effectiveness of male and female newscasters. *Journal of Broadcasting, 20,* 177.

PART VI: FILM

Acker, A. (1991). *Reel women: Pioneers of the cinema, 1896 to the present.* New York: Continuum.

Basinger, J. (1994). *A woman's view: How Hollywood spoke to women, 1930–1960.* New York: Alfred A. Knopf.

Bielby, W. T., & Bielby, D. D. (1989). *The Hollywood writers' report: Unequal access, unequal pay.* West Hollywood, CA: Writers Guild of America.

Blonski, A., Creed, B., & Freiburg, F. (1987). *Don't shoot, darling: Women's independent filmmaking in Australia.* Richmond, Australia: Greenhouse.

Born, P. (1982). Sexual imagery and the Black woman in American cinema. In G.L. Yearwood (Ed.), *Black Cinema Aesthetics* (pp. 42–51). Athens: Ohio University Center for Afro-American Studies.

Bruckner, J. (1985). Women behind the camera. In Ecker (Ed.), *Feminist aesthetics.* London: The Women's Press.

Brunsdon, C. (1986). *Films for women.* Bloomington: Indiana University Press.

Burchill, J. (1986). *Girls on film.* London: Virgin Books.

Carroll, N. (1990). The image of women in film: A defense of a paradigm. *Journal of Aesthetics and Art Criticism, 48,* 349–360.

Clover, C. J. (1989). Her body, himself: Gender in the slasher film. In R.H. Bloch & F. Ferguson, (Eds.), *Misogyny, misandry and misanthropy* (pp. 187–228). Berkeley: University of California Press.

Clover, C. J. (1992). *Men, women, and chain saws: Gender in the modern horror film.* Princeton, NJ: Princeton University Press.

Davis, Z. i. (1991). Woman with a mission: Zeinabu irene Davis on filmmaking. *Hot Wire: The Journal of Women's Music and Culture, 7,* 18–19, 56.

Doane, M. A. (1987). *The desire to desire: The woman's film of the 1940s.* Bloomington: Indiana University Press.

Erens, P. (1979). *Sexual stratagems: The world of women in film.* New York: Horizon Press.

Fischer, L. (1989). *Shot/countershot: Film traditions and women's cinema.* Princeton, NJ: Princeton University Press.

Fitzgerald, T. (1989). Now about these women (British women film directors). *Sight and Sound, 58,* 191.

Fort, D., & Skinner-Jones, A. (1991). Filmmaking. In K. A. Foss & S.K. Foss (Ed.), *Women speak: The eloquence of women's lives.* Prospect Heights, IL: Waveland Press.

Galerstein, C. (1989). *Working women on the Hollywood screen: A filmography.* New York: Garland.

Gledhill, C. (1987). *Home is where the heart is: Studies in melodramas and the woman's film.* London: British Film Institute.

Jacobs, L. (1991). *The wages of sin: Censorship and the fallen woman film, 1928–1942.* Madison: University of Wisconsin Press.

Kaplan, E.A. (1989). *Psychoanalysis and cinema*. New York: Routledge.

Kirkham, P., & Thumin, J. (1993). *You and Tarzan: Masculinity, movies and men*. New York: St. Martin's Press.

Kuhn, A. (1982). *Women's pictures: Feminism and cinema*. Boston: Routledge & Kegan Paul.

Leveritt, A. L., & Meyers, E. (1989). Women in the director's chair: Eighth annual women's film and video festival. *Hot Wire: The Journal of Women's Music and Culture*, *5*, 30–31, 56.

Mayne, J. (1990). *The woman at the keyhole: Feminism and women's cinema*. Bloomington: Indiana University Press.

Molitor, F., & Sapolsky, B. S. (1993). Sex, violence, and victimization in slasher films. *Journal of Broadcasting and Electronic Media, 37*, 233–242.

Movshovitz, H. (1979). The delusion of Hollywood's "women's films." *Frontiers: A Journal of Women Studies, 4* (1), 9–13.

Muir, A. R. (1987). *A woman's guide to jobs in film and television*. London: Pandora Press.

Noriega, C. A. (1991). *Chicanos and film: Essays on Chicano representation and resistance*. Hamden, CT: Garland Publishing.

Pribram, E. D. (1988). *Female spectators: Looking at film and television*. London: Verso.

Rosenberg, J. (1983). *Women's reflections: The feminist film movement*. Ann Arbor, MI: UMI Research Press.

Rubinson Fenton, J. (1990). *Women writers from page to screen*. New York: Garland Publishing.

Sinclair, M. (1988). *Hollywood Lolitas: The nymphet syndrome in the movies*. New York; London: Henry Holt; Plexis.

Todd, J. (1988). *Women and film*. New York: Holmes and Meier.

Traube, E. G. (1992). *Dreaming identities: Class, gender and generation in the 1980s Hollywood movies*. Boulder, CO: Westview Press.

Walsh, A. S. (1984). *Women's film and female experience, 1940–1950*. New York: Praeger.

Williams, L. (1980). Type and stereotype: Chicano images in film. *Frontiers: A Journal of Women Studies, 2*, 14–17.

Zagula, J. T. (1991). Saints, sinners, and society: Images of women in film and drama, from Weimar to Hitler. *Women's Studies, 19* (1), 55–77.

PART VII: MUSIC

Armstrong, T., Jr. (1984). *Women's music plus: Directory of resources in women's music and culture*. Chicago: Armstrong.

Armstrong, T., Jr. (1989). An endangered species: Women's music by, for, and about women. *Hot Wire: The Journal of Women's Music and Culture, 5* (3), 17–19.

Armstrong, T., Jr. (1990). A personal chat with Holly Near about her new autobiography. *Hot Wire: The Journal of Women's Music and Culture, 6* (3), 2–5, 53–54.

Azzerad, M. (1993, October 28). The real new deal. *Rolling Stone*, p. 18.

Bangs, L. (1972, August). Women in rock: They won't get fooled again. *Ms.*, pp. 23–26.

Bufwack, M., & Oermann, B. (1987). Women in Country Music. In P. Buhle, *Popular culture in America* (pp. 91–101). University of Minnesota Press.

Butruille, S. G., & Taylor, A. (1987). Women in American popular song. In L. P. Stewart & S. Ting-Toomey (Eds.), *Communication, gender and sex roles in diverse interaction contexts*. Norwood, NJ: Ablex.

Carey, J. T. (1969). Changing courtship patterns in the popular song. *American Journal of Sociology, 74*, 720–730.

Cooper, V. W. (1985). Women in popular music: A quantitative analysis of feminine images over time. *Sex Roles, 13*, 499–506.

DeTurk, D., & Poulin, A. (1967). *The American folk scene: Dimensions in the folksong revival*. New York: Dell Publishing Company.

Dew, J. (1977). *Singers and sweethearts: The women of country music*. Garden City, NJ: Dolphin.

DiPrima, D. (1990). Beat the rap. *Mother Jones*, pp. 15+.

Dlugacz, J. (1988). If it weren't for the music: 15 years of Olivia Records. *Hot Wire: The Journal of Women's Music and Culture. 4* (3), 28–31+.

Dlugacz, J. (1989). If it weren't for the music: 15 years of Olivia Records—Part II. *Hot Wire: The Journal of Women's Music and Culture, 5* (1), 20–23.

Endres, K. L. (1984). Sex role standards in popular music. *Journal of Popular Culture, 18*, 9–17.

English, D. (1982). Women as singers. *Mother Jones*, pp. 5–6, 15–16.

Gaar, G. G. (1992). *She's a rebel: The history of women in rock & roll*. Seattle, WA: Seal Press.

Garofalo, R. (1994). Crossing over. In J. L. Dates & W. Barlow (Eds.), *Split Image: African Americans in the Mass Media* (2nd ed.). Washington, D.C.: Howard University Press.

Hesbacher, P., Clasby, N., Clasby, M. G., & Berger, D. (1977). Solo female vocalists: Song shifts in stature and alterations in song. *Popular Music and Society, 5*, 1–16.

Hesbacher, P., Simon, E., Anderson, B., & Berger, D. (1978). Substream recordings: Some shifts in stature and alterations in song. *Popular Music and Society, 6*, 11–26.

Hinely, M. B. (1984). The uphill climb of women in American music: Performers and teachers. *Music Educators Journal, 70*, 8, 31–35.

Hooke, H. (1990). Twenty years of making music. *Hot Wire: The Journal of Women's Music and Culture, 6*, 42–45.

Koskoff, E. (1987). *Women and music in cross-cultural perspective*. Champaign: University of Illinois Press.

Ladyslipper catalog and resource guide. (1993). Durham, NC: Ladyslipper, Inc.

Lont, C. M. (1988). Redwood Records: Principles and profit in women's music. In B. Bates & A. Taylor (Ed.), *Women communicating: Studies of women's talk*. Norwood, NJ: Ablex.

Lont, C. M. (1990). The roles assigned to females and males in non-music radio programming. *Sex Roles, 22* (9/10), 661–669.

Lont. C. M. (1992). Women's music: No longer a small private party. In R. Garofalo (Ed.), *Rockin' the boat: Mass music & mass movements.* Boston: South End Press.

Meade, M. (1970). Women and rock: Sexism set to music. *Women: A Journal of Liberation, 2,* 24–26.

Near, H. (1990). *Fire in the rain . . . singer in the storm: Holly Near, an autobiography.* New York: William Morrow & Co.

Orlean, S. (1987, March 26). The Bangles. *Rolling Stone,* p. 64.

Orloff, K. (1974). *Rock 'n' roll woman.* Los Angeles: Nash Publishing.

Rodnitzky, J. L. (1975). Songs of sisterhood: The music of women's liberation. *Popular Music and Society, IV,* 77–85.

Saucier, K. A. (1986). Healers and heartbreakers: Images of women and men in country music. *Journal of Popular Culture, 20,* 147–166.

Swartley, G. (1982). Girls! Live! On stage! *Mother Jones,* pp. 26–31.

Tilchen, M. (1984). Lesbians and women's music. In Darty & Potter (Eds.), *Women identified women.* Palo Alto, CA: Mayfield Publishing.

Wilkinson, M. (1976). Romantic love: The great equalizer? Sexism in popular music. *The Family Coordinator,* pp. 161–166.

Hot Wire: The Journal of Women's Music and Culture is filled with short articles that relate to women and music and women and film. There are too many to list.

Music Videos

Kalis, P., & Neuendorf, K. (1989). Aggressive cue prominence and gender participation in MTV. *Journalism Quarterly, 66* (1), 148–154, 229.

Kaplan, E. A. (1988). Feminism/Oedipus/postmodernism: The case of MTV. In *Postmodernism and its discontents.* London: Verso.

Lewis, L. A. (1987). Form and female authorship in music video. *Communication, 9,* 355–377.

Lewis, L. A. (1990). *Gender politics and MTV: Voicing the difference.* Philadelphia: Temple University Press.

Roberts, R. (1990). "Sex as weapon": Feminist rock music videos. *NWSA Journal, 2* (1), 1–15.

Sherman, B. L., & Dominick, J. R. (1986). Violence and sex in music videos: TV and rock'n'roll. *Journal of Communication, 36* (1), 79–93.

VIDEOGRAPHY

GENERAL REFERENCES

Women, Men and Media (1991). *Sex, lies and politics,* a 60-minute videotape of December 1991 conference. New York: New York University, Department of Journalism.

PART I: NEWSPAPERS

Ida B. Wells (videorecording): A passion for justice. (1990). Alexandria, VA: PBS Video. *Suggested preview due to violent scenes.

PART II: WOMEN'S MAGAZINES

Throughly modern Millicent: A profile of Millicent Fenwick (1982). Fashion model, editor of *Vogue Magazine* and elected to Congress at age 64. Authur Mokin Productions.

PART III: ADVERTISING

Kilbourne, J., and Cambridge Documentary Films (1981). *Killing Us Softly.* Cambridge, MA: Cambridge Documentary Films.

Kilbourne, J., and Cambridge Documentary Films. (1987). *Still killing us softly: Advertising's images of women.* Cambridge, MA: Margaret Lazarus.

Media Watch (1990). *Warning: The media may be hazardous to your health.* Santa Cruz, CA: Media Watch.

OASIS (1988). *Stale roles and tight buns: Images of men in advertising.* Brighton, MA: OASIS.

PART IV: ENTERTAINMENT TELEVISION

Lazin, L. (producer) (1986). *The 20th anniversary of the National Organization for Women.* Los Angeles: Peg Yorkin Production. There is a short section on women and media.

Media Watch (1992). *Don't be a TV: Television victim.* Santa Cruz, CA: Media Watch.

PART V: TELEVISION NEWS

Lazin, L. (producer) (1986). *The 20th anniversary of the National Organization for Women*. Los Angeles: Peg Yorkin Production. There is a short section on women as news anchors.

Newswomen videorecording. (1988). Princeton, NJ: Films for the Humanities.

Women and the media. (1987). Linda Ellerbee speaks before National Council of Jewish Women. C-SPAN: Purdue University Public Affairs Video Archives (40 minutes).

Women in the media. (1990). American University, School of Communication (panel includes Betty Friedan, Nancy Woodhull, Eleanor Randolph, Renee Poissant as well as others). C-SPAN: Purdue University Public Affairs Video Archives (97 minutes).

PART VI: FILM

Alfaro, R. Y., & Hagemann, L. (1992). *Japanese American women: A sense of place*. New York: Women Make Movies, Inc.

Ching, Y. (1991). *Is there anything specific you want me to tell you about?* New York: Women Make Movies , Inc.

Cole, J., & Dale, H. (1989). *Calling the shots*. Video. Direct Cinema Limited.

Edith Head (1981). Blackwood productions.

From Hollywood to Hanoi (1992). Tiana/Thi Thanh Nga.

Hope, A. (1994). Reel Women. 1–213-850–8588/213–852-1972.

Ingrid (1984). On Ingrid Bergman. Wombat Productions.

Krishnan, I. (1990). *Knowing her place*. New York: Women Make Movies, Inc.

Smith, S. (1975). *Women who make movies*, New York: Hopkinson and Blake.

Tanaka, J. (1992). *Who's going to pay for these donuts, anyway?* San Francisco, CA: Cross-current Media.

PART VII: MUSIC

Alberta Hunter: Blues at the Cookery. (1982). Media Network.

But then . . . She's Betty Carter. (1980). New York: Women Make Movies.

Davis, T. (1990). *Indigo Girls: Live at the Uptown Lounge*. New York: CBS Music Video Enterprise.

Girl groups. (1983). MGM/UA Home Video—Delilah Films.

Gould, Ron. (1991). *Holly Near: Singing for our lives*. Oakland, CA: Redwood Cultural Work.

Janis Joplin: The way she was. (1989). Universal City, CA: MCA Home Video Inc.

*Jhally, S. (1990, 1994). *Dreamworlds videorecording: Desire/sex/power in rock videos.* Amherst, MA: Foundation for Media Education. (Suggested previewing due to violent scenes).

k.d. lang: Harvest of seven years. (1991). Burbank, CA: Sire Records, Inc.

Madonna: Justify my love. (1990). Burbank, CA: Sire Records, Inc.

Public Affairs TV. *Bernice Johnson Reagon/Sweet Honey: The songs are free.* (1991). New York: Mystic Fire Video.

Reid, F., & Dlugacz (1991). *The changer: A record of the times.* Oakland, CA: Olivia Records.

Ripp, A. (1991). *Shindig! presents groovy gals.* Santa Monica, CA: Rhino Home Video.

INDEX

ABC, 219, 221, 223, 235, 254. *See also* Prime-time television; Television news; *specific shows*
Abolitionist movement, 7, 8
Abortion, 93–94
Abortion: Stories from North and South, 300
Abt, D., 332
Abyss, The, 265
Academy of Motion Picture Arts and Sciences. *See* Oscar awards
AC/DC, 365
Acker, A., 265
Activism, 30–39
Adam, Margie, 326
Adams, Bryan, 324
Ad Council, 160
Adele and the Ponies of Ardmore, 299
Adventures of Ford Fairlane, The, 265
Adventures of Ozzie and Harriet, The, 168, 169
Advertising, 111–116
  and censorship, 147
  content study methods, 124–125
  and desensitization, 144
  and economic factors, 376
  and favorable context, 102–103, 108, 146–147, 185
  history, 111–112
  important women, 118–119, 135–137
  organizations, 119
  and prime-time television, 167–168
  regulation of, 159, 160–161
  women's employment, 113–114
  and women's magazines, 102–103, 106, 107, 108, 147
  See also African Americans and advertising; Portrayal of women in advertising
Advertising Age, 116
Advertising Women of New York, Inc., 119, 137
Advocate, The, 44
African Americans and advertising, 132–142
  backlash, 139–140
  cigarette and alcohol advertising, 140–141
  employment, 135–137, 138, 139
  political activism, 137–138

  target audiences, 132–135, 138–139, 140
African Americans and prime-time television, 194–195
  early portrayals, 169, 170
  increase in visibility, 171, 182–183
African-American women, 375–376
  models, 92–93, 132, 134
  and newspapers, 2, 8
  rock music, 321–322
  in woman suffrage movement, 38
  and women's magazines, 70
  See also African Americans and advertising; African Americans and prime-time television; African-American women and film; Racism; *specific people*
African-American women and film, 266, 274–290, 374
  background, 274–277
  biographies, 282–283
  class status, 288–289
  and employment in film industry, 274, 288, 289–290
  gender bias, 281–282
  location, 287
  portrayal of women's employment, 283–284, 286–287, 289
  study methods, 278–280
Afro-American Council, 38
After the Montreal Massacre, 301
Age
  and advertising, 151
  and prime-time television, 184–185
  and television news, 236, 257
Ain't I a Woman, 44, 46
Albuquerque Journal, 17, 23
Alcohol, 140–141, 150–151, 161
Aldridge, H. B., 173
A League of Their Own, 267
Alexander, M., 193, 194, 195
ALF, 185
Alfaro, R., 311
Alice, 170, 181, 186, 202
Allen, D., 194, 240
Allen, Debbie, 192–197
  A Different World, 194–196
  early career, 192–193
  Fame, 193–194
Allen, Dede, 268
Allen, Gracie, 167, 176
Alley, R., 203, 204

Alligood, D., 134, 135
All in the Family, 181, 186
Allnighter, The, 354
All Over the Place (Bangles), 352
All the President's Men, 264
Alpha Suffrage Club, 38
Alrop, R., 123
Alter, J., 231
Alternative newspapers, 7–8. *See also specific publications*
Amanpour, Christine, 225
Amateur Athletic Foundation of Los Angeles, 6
A.M.E. Church Review, 32
Amen, 183
American Women Composers, Inc., 329
American Women in Radio and Television (AWRT), 173, 226
Amos 'n Andy, 168, 195
Andersen, K., 223
Anderson, Laurie, 328
Anderson, S., 132
And the Winner Is: The History and Politics of the Oscar Awards, 278
Andy Griffith Show, The, 169
Anheuser-Busch, 141
Anna, 266
Ann-Margret, 171
Anorexia, 153, 162
Anthony, Michele, 328
Anthony, Susan B., 8
An Unmarried Woman, 266
Apocalypse Now, 264
Appearance, 374
  and advertising, 114–116, 145–146, 147, 151, 152–154, 155–156, 162
  and newspapers, 20–21
  and prime-time television, 209
  and teen magazines, 82, 83
  and television news, 222–223, 244, 256–258, 259
  and women's magazines, 94
Arbuckle, Fatty, 263
Armatrading, Joan, 322
Armstrong, Gilliam, 270
Articulation, 314
Arzner, Dorothy, 268
Ashton, Ruth, 225
Asian/Pacific Americans, 375
  and film, 308, 310–318, 374
  and prime-time television, 183
  and television news, 223, 253
  See also People of color
Association for Anorexics and Bulimics, 153

Association for Women in Sports
  Media, 12
Atkin, C., 278
Atlanta Constitution, The, 17, 18
Attakiska vodka, 151
Attention: Women at Work!, 298
Aufderheide, P., 332
Avenoso, K., 158
Avery, Margaret, 287
Ayres, Mary, 118
Azzerad, M., 351

Babes in Toyland, 361, 367, 368
"Baby Doll" (Hole), 369
*Backlash: The Undeclared War
  Against American Women*
  (Faludi), 116, 123
Back to the Future, 264
Baird, Zoe, 23
Baker, LaVern, 328
Ball, Lucille, 169, 176
Ballard, Bettina, 75
Ball-Rokeach, S., 84
Bananarama, 353
Bangles, 324, 348, 350–356
"Bang Zoom" (Salt-N-Pepa), 324
Bark, Ed, 257
Barlow, W., 193, 255
Barnes, Linda, 358, 360
Barnett, Ferdinand L., 36–37
Barnouw, Erik, 168
Bassin, Amelia, 118
Bathrick, S., 203
Batten, Barton, Durstine, and
  Osborn Advertising, 134, 136
Bauder, D., 332
Baywatch, 185
BBDO Special Markets, 134, 136
Beaches, 267
Beacon-News, The, 17
Beasley, M. H., 7, 8, 171
Beatles, 264, 322
Beatty, Bessie, 75
Beauty. *See* Appearance
Beauty Myth, The, 123
Becker, S. L., 3, 167
Beers, Charlotte Lenore, 118
Be Good My Children (Chang),
  314, 316–317
Behind the Oscar, 278
Behind the Veil: Nuns, 300, 303
Believe it or not, 172
Belly, 351
Benatar, Pat, 324, 365
Benny, Jack, 167
Benokraitis, N. V., 255
Benson, 185
Berg, Gertrude, 176
Berger, John, 146, 149
Berle, Milton, 167
Berry, Chuck, 369
Berson, Ginny Z., 48
*Best Times of Our Lives, The:
  Portraits of Women in Mid-
  Life*, 299

BET (Black Entertainment
  Television), 334, 335–336,
  342
Better Homes and Gardens, 71
Better Living, 90–91
Bewitched, 169
Bigart, Alice Weel, 221
Big Chill, The, 266
Bikini Kill, 361, 366, 367,
  368–370
Bill Cosby Show, The, 195
Black, D., 333, 342
Black Enterprise, 133
Black Entertainment Television.
  See BET
Black Mother, Black Daughter, 302
Blackwell, Betsy, 75
Black Women on Television, 171
Black Women's Club Movement,
  37
Black Women-Talk, 226
Blakely, Mary Kay, 75, 147
Blinn, Bill, 194
Blockbuster, 149
Bloodworth-Thomason, Linda,
  176
Bluebelles, 323
Bly, Nellie, 7
Blyth, Myrna, 75
Bodroghkozy, A., 169
Bodyslimmer's, 149–150
Bogdanovich, Peter, 264
Bogle, Donald, 274
Bombeck, Erma, 59
Bond, James, 266
Bondage, 155
Bonnie and Clyde, 268
Booth, Margaret, 270
Boruszkowski, L. A., 335
Bosley, D. H., 230
Boston Globe, 62
Boudreau, F., 80
Bowser, P., 274
Boycott Action News, 161
Boycotts, 161
Boyz n the Hood, 267
Braden, M., 59
Bradshaw, Thornton, 219
Brandt, Pamela, 328
Brassard, C., 296
Bratmobile, 367
Braver, Rita, 223, 235
Breeders, 350, 351
Brennan, Christine, 11
Bridal Trends, 105
Bridge, Junior, 376
Bridges, J., 322
Brinkley, David, 219
British Anti-Caste Society, 36
Broadcast News, 266
Brokaw, Tom, 219
Bronx Zoo, The, 196
Brooks, James, 203
Brooks, T., 168

Brown, Helen Gurley, 75, 92,
  118, 147
Brown, Hilary, 226
Brown, I. B., 203, 204
Brown, J., 334, 335, 342, 343
Brown, Ruth, 328
Buchwald, E., 157
Buckingham, Bonnie, 321
Buell, Marge Henderson, 11
Bullock, P. L., 70
Burning Times, The, 300–301, 303
Burns, George, 167
Busby, L., 81
Business Week, 132
Buss, Frances, 225
Butler, M., 81, 335
Butterflies, 323
Butterick, Ebenezer, 101
Butts, Rev. Calvin, 141
Buy Nothing Day, 161

Cabaret, 283
Cagney and Lacey, 171, 181
Calloway-Thomas, C., 8
Campbell, K., 334, 335, 342
Campbell, Mary, 91
Campbell's, 149
Campion, Jane, 268, 374
Cancian, F. M., 122
Carbine, Pat, 76
Carey, Mariah, 360
Carmen Jones, 278, 287, 289
"Carnival" (Bikini Kill), 368
Caroline Jones Advertising, Inc.
  (CJA), 137, 142
Carpenters, The, 322
Carrie, 194
Carroll, Diahann, 169, 286
Carsey, Marcy, 176
Carstens, P., 258
Carter, Maybelle, 325
Cary, Mary Ann Shadd, 8, 11
Cavett, D., 203
Caxton, William, 111
CBS, 171, 219, 221, 223, 235,
  236. *See also* CBS Evening
  News; Prime-time television;
  Television news; *specific shows*
CBS Evening News, 223, 252–253,
  256–257
Censorship, 51
Center for Media and Public
  Affairs (CMPA), 172, 223
Cervenka, Exene, 328
Chang, Christine, 312, 314,
  316–317
Chaplin, Charlie, 267
Chapman, Tracy, 324
Charlie's Angels, 170, 171, 181
Chase, Edna Woolman, 76
Chase, Sylvia, 230
Chaua-Eoan, H., 154
Cheers, 171
Cher, 266
Cherry, Neneh, 361

Chesler, P., 43
Chicago *Defender*, 38
Chicago Tribune, 17, 21, 36
Children of Canada Series,
    298–299
China Syndrome, The, 266
Chinatown, 264
Ching, Y., 308
Chisholm, S., 136
Choy, Christine, 270
Christenson, P. G., 337
Christian, Meg, 326
Chung, Connie, 223, 230,
    252–253, 256–257, 375
Cigarettes, 140–141, 147
Ciriello, S., 157
Civil rights movement, 38
Clairol, 147
Clark, Chris, 288
Clark, Petula, 321
Clark, R. L., 72
Clarke, C. V., 134
Clarke, D., 158
Class of '96, 125
Class status
    and film, 288–289
    and prime-time television,
        185–187
    and women's magazines, 73
Claudine, 278, 286, 287, 289
Clayburgh, Jill, 266
Clibbon, Peter, 146
Close, Glenn, 266
"Clouds" (Mitchell), 369
Club Carnell, 157
CMT (Country Music
    Television), 335
Cochrane, Elizabeth. *See* Bly,
    Nellie
Collins, R., 144, 146, 159
Color Purple, The, 266, 278, 288
    marital status in, 289
    portrayal of women's
        employment in, 283, 284,
        286, 287
    stereotypes in, 266
Coming Home, 264
Como, Perry, 167
Compton, Ann, 230
Concrete Blonde, 350
Condé Nast, 91, 96. *See also specific*
    magazines
Condit, C., 214
Connolly, Vera Leona, 76
Consensus decision making, 51
Conservator, 36, 37, 38
Consumerism
    and advertising, 145–146
    and female bonding, 353
    and prime-time television,
        200–201
    and women's magazines,
        102–103
Consumers Report, 107

Consumers to Stop Sexist Alcohol
    Advertising, 161
Content studies
    advertising, 148–149
    film, 274–291
    music, 332–346
    newspapers, 16–24
    prime-time television, 180–189
    teen magazines, 82–85
    women's magazines, 100–103,
        106–108
    See also African-American
        women and film; Portrayal
        of women *headings*; Study
        methods
"Control" (Jackson), 365, 366
Cook, D., 263
Cook, S. L., 222
Cooleridge, Martha, 268
Copeland, Miles, 352
Coppola, Francis, 264
Cosby, Bill, 171, 194, 195, 196
Cosby Show, The, 171, 181, 183,
    185, 186, 195, 220
Cosby, William, 3
Cosmetic surgery, 153–154, 162
Cosmopolitan, 92, 147, 157
Coston, Julia Ringwood, 70
Country Woman, 104
Couric, Katie, 225
Courier, The, 17
Courtney, A. E., 115, 122, 170
Cover Girl, 133
Cover Girls, The, 353
Craft, Christine, 222–223
Craig, Jean, 114
Crain, Jeanne, 284
Crane, Ruth. *See* Schaefer, Ruth
    Crane
Crenshaw, K., 152
Croly, Jane Cunningham. *See*
    June, Jennie
Cronkite, Walter, 219, 220, 252,
    256, 257
Crosby, Bing, 167
Cross Creek, 278, 283, 286, 287,
    288, 289
Cry Freedom, 283
Crying Game, The, 267
Crystals, 323, 362
Cubbins, L., 150
Cultural identity, 311–312
Current Affair, A, 220
Curtis, Charlotte, 11
Cutex, 148, 151

Daar, G. G., 322
Daily Camera, 17
Daily Commercial, The, 35
Dallas, 181, 184
Daly, Tyne, 171
Dandridge, Dorothy, 287, 289
Dangerous Promises Campaign,
    161
Daniels, Faith, 225

Danson, Ted, 289
Dark Lullabies, 300
Darling, L., 157
Dash, Julie, 270
Dates, J., 193, 255
Dave Clark Five, 322
Davis, Bette, 284
Davis, Clive, 365
Davis, D. K., 335
Davis, Louise Taylor, 118
Davis, Madelyn, 176
Davis, Paul, 244
*Days and Nights of Molly Dodd,
    The*, 171
Days of Thunder, 265
Deadly Nightshade, 322
Deal, Kim, 351
Dear Phoebe, 169
Deerhunter, The, 264
DeFleur, M., 3, 4, 84
Dejanikus, T., 51
Delgado, R., 152
Delineator, 70, 71, 101
Demarest, J., 73
Democratic National Convention,
    253
DeNeffe, Lisa, 116
Denisoff, R. S., 321, 322, 323
Denmark, F., 80
de Palma, Brian, 264
DePasse, Susanne, 288, 328
Depression, 158
Designing Women, 171
Desperately Seeking Susan, 268
Detroit Plaindealer, 32
De Vries, H., 214
Dickerson, Nancy, 230
Dickinson, Angie, 170
Dick Tracy, 265
Dick Van Dyke Show, The, 169
Die Hard, 2, 265
Dieting, 145–146, 147, 152–153.
    See also Appearance
Dietrich, Marlene, 265
Different Light (Bangles), 352, 353
Different World, A, 183, 192,
    194–195, 196, 197
Dignam, Dorothy, 118
Direct Effect, 159
Director's Guild Study, 268
"Dirty Deeds" (AC/DC), 365
Dismemberment, 154
Dix, Dorothy, 7
Dixon, Willie, 369
DKNY, 157
Dlugacz, Judy, 328
Doctor, Lawyer, Indian Chief, 298
Dog Day Afternoon, 268
Dominick, J., 123
Donnerstein, E., 144
Donovan, R. J., 219
"Don't Get Me Wrong"
    (Pretenders), 324
Doors, 365

"Double Dare Ya" (Bikini Kill), 368–369
Douglas, Carol Anne, 42, 43, 44, 45, 46, 47, 49–50, 51, 52
Douglas Edwards with the News, 219, 222
Douglass, Frederick, 36
Downing, M., 170
Doyle Dane Bernbach (DDB), 114
Dragnet, 56
Dream of a Free Country: A Message from Nicaraguan Women, 300
Dreyfuss, J., 170
Driving Miss Daisy, 287
"Dry" (PJ Harvey), 367, 368
Dubler, Nancy, 21–22, 39
DuBois, W. E. B., 38
Dumm, Edwina, 11
DuPlessis, R. B., 57
Dylan, Bob, 323, 362, 369
Dynasty, 181, 183, 184

Eastwood, Clint, 266
Easy Rider, 264
Eaton, C., 123
Ebony, 133, 134
Ebony Man, 133
Economic status. *See* Class status
Edie Brickell and the New Bohemians, 352
Educating Rita, 266
Edwards, A., 193
Elder, Lonnie, III, 288
Electronic newspapers, 4
Ellerbee, Linda, 222, 257
Ellman, Mary, 58
Elm, J., 203
English, Diane, 176, 214
Enid News and Eagle, 17, 18
Entertainment Tonight, 220
En Vogue, 361
Epi-products, 154
Epstein, C. F., 5
Equal Employment Opportunities Commission, 173
Equality Productions, 177
Equal Rights Amendment, 93
Ernst, Lois Geraci, 118
Esprit, 159
Essence, 71, 76, 106, 134
Estee Lauder, 133
E.T., 264
"Eternal Flame" (Bangles), 353
Etheridge, Melissa, 324
Evans, E., 82
Evans, G., 295
Evans, Sara, 48
Eve Lambart, 299
Evening Shade, 171
Evening Star, 31
Evening Stars, The (Matusow), 252
Everything (Bangles), 353

Fairbanks, Douglas, 267
Fairchild, H., 144
Fairfax, Beatrice, 7
Fairness Doctrine, 160
Fair Trade, 299
Faithfull, Marianne, 328
Faithful Women, 301
Falcon Crest, 181, 184
Fales, Susan, 196
Faludi, Susan, 116, 155, 208
Fame, 193–194, 195, 197
Family Circle, 71
Family Matters, 183, 185
Family Ties, 171, 181, 185, 186, 196
Fannin, R., 73
Fanning, Katherine, 11
Fanny, 322, 351
Fashion. *See* Appearance
Fashion Fair, 133–134
Fatal Attraction, 266
Fat Albert and the Cosby Kids, 195
Father Knows Best, 169, 185, 205
Faulty Products, 352
Fawcett-Ward, A., 145
FCC. *See* Federal Communications Commission
Feagin, J. R., 255
Federal Communications Commission (FCC), 160–161, 173, 222, 230
Federal Trade Association, 112
Federal Women's Film Program (FWFP), 297–298
"Feels Blind" (Bikini Kill), 369
Female rock/MTV performers
  Bangles, 324, 348, 350–356
  history, 321, 322–323, 361–364
  and portrayal of women, 324–325, 333–334, 339, 341–343
  riot grrrls, 52, 366–370
  traditional vs. new roles, 360–361, 364–366
Feminine Mystique, The (Friedan), 71, 73, 115, 124, 204
Feminism and prime-time television, 200–214
  and consumerism, 200–201
  and hegemony, 201–202
  and individualism, 201, 214
  Mary Tyler Moore Show, The, 202–208, 213, 214
  Murphy Brown, 202–204, 208–214
Feminist movement
  and advertising, 114, 115, 116, 122
  backlash against, 208
  and film, 294–305
  and newspapers, 8, 9, 42–52, 159
  and rock music/MTV, 351–352, 367–368

and women's magazines, 71, 93, 107–108
  See also Feminism and prime-time television; Women-made films; Women's music
Fern, Fanny, 59
Ferri, A., 259
Ferro, Nancy, 44
Ferron, 325
Feuer, J., 201
Few Good Men, A, 267
"50ft Queenie" (PJ Harvey), 369, 370
Film
  history, 263–265
  important women, 270–271
  organizations, 271–272
  portrayal of women in, 265–267, 310, 316, 317, 374
  women's employment, 262, 267–268, 274, 288, 289–290, 374
  See also Women-made films
First Amendment, 160
Fishburn, K., 71, 114, 115
Fisher, Gail, 176
Fish That Saved Pittsburgh, The, 193
Fiske, J., 213
Fisk Herald, 32
Fitzgibbon, Bernice, 113
Five Feminist Minutes, 297
Flamenco at 5:15, 296
Flander, J., 230
Flashdance, 266
Fleeson, Doris, 11
Fleetwood Mac, 322, 363
Fletcher, P., 157
Flora, C. G., 73
Flying High, 170
Foley, Ellen, 323
Fonda, Jane, 266, 284
Fonda, Peter, 264
Fontanelle (Babes in Toyland), 368
Foote, J., 231
Footloose, 268
Forbes, 123
Forbidden Love, 301, 304
Ford, John, 116
Fortune, 90
Fortune, T. Thomas, 33, 35
Foster, Jodie, 268
Fox, S., 112, 113, 114
Frankel, Max, 18–19
Franklin, Aretha, 322, 323, 324, 365
Frank's Place, 171
Franzwa, H. H., 72
Frederick, Pauline, 221, 225, 230, 253–254
Fredlin, E. S., 222
Freed, Fred, 255
Freedom Forum, The, 16

Freeman, M., 196
Free Speech and Headlight, 33–35
Fresh Prince of Bel-Air, The, 196
Freydberg, E., 284
Friedan, Betty, 16, 71, 73, 115, 124, 204
Fried Green Tomatoes, 265
Frieze, I. H., 150
From Hollywood to Hanoi, 314–315
From the Shore, 299
Front pages, 17–18
Fuldheim, Dorothy, 222
Fuller, Margaret, 7, 11
Full House, 185
Fung, V., 222, 257

Gaar, G. G., 324–325, 326
Gamble, M., 266
Gamble, T., 266
Gant, Liz, 274
Garber, Mary, 12
Garbo, Greta, 265
Garner, J., 73
Garofalo, R., 321, 323, 324
Garrels, Ann, 230
Garvey, Marcus, 39
Geiger, B., 150
Gelb, J., 47
Gender-role socialization, 80–81
General Custer's Revenge, 152
Gentlemen and Lady's Town and Country, 69
Gentlemen Prefer Blondes, 268
Get Christie Love, 170
G. Heileman Brewing Co., 140–141
Ghettoization, 5
Ghost, 267, 274, 278, 284, 287
Ghostbusters, 264
Gibbons, S. J., 7, 8, 172
Gibson, Mel, 289
Gilbert, Ken, 135
Gilday, K., 152
Gill, B., 193
Gillespie, Marcia Ann, 76
Gilmer, Elizabeth Meriwether. *See* Dix, Dorothy
Gimme A Break, 170, 185
Girl groups, 321–322, 323, 353, 361–362
"Girls Just Want to Have Fun" (Lauper), 324
Gish, Lillian, 267
Gitlin, Todd, 168, 201, 202, 214
Glamour, 72, 91–97, 157
    African-American cover model in, 92–93
    circulation, 71, 88, 91, 101
    controversial issues in, 93–94
Gleason, Jackie, 186
Glory, 283
Glover, Danny, 289
Goddard, Mary Katharine, 7, 12
Goddard, Sarah Updike, 7
Goddard, William, 7

Goddess Remembered, 300, 304
Godey's Lady's Book, 69, 72
Godfather, The, 264
Goffman, Erving, 115
Go-Gos, 324, 350, 351
"Going Down to Liverpool" (Bangles), 354
Goldberg, G. J., 219, 220
Goldberg, R., 219, 220
Goldberg, Whoopi, 267, 274, 275, 284, 287, 289
Golden, Michael, 68
Golden Girls, 171, 184–185
Goldie and the Gingerbreads, 322
Gomery, D., 220
Gone With the Wind, 274, 278, 287
Good Housekeeping, 70, 71, 72, 73, 90, 101
Goodman, Ellen, 58, 61–63, 64
Good Times, 170, 183, 186, 193
Goodyear Tire and Rubber, 136
Goold, Lucille, 118
Gordon, Dexter, 283
Gordon, Kim, 367
Gore, Leslie, 321
Gore, Tipper, 325, 333
Gould, Beatrice Blackmar, 76
Gould, Cheryl, 226
Gramsci, A., 312
Grand Canyon, 289
Grant, Lee, 270
Graves, Teresa, 170
Gray, H., 201
Great Depression, 8, 70–71, 112, 374
"Greatest Love of All, The" (Houston), 365
Great Grand Mother, 299
Great White Hope, The, 283
Greeley, Horace, 7
Greenberg, B., 278
Greenberg, Florence, 321
Greenwich, Ellie, 328
Gridiron Club, 2
Grierson, John, 294–295
Griffith, D. W., 267
Gritten, D., 193
Growing Pains, 181, 185, 186
Grube, J., 150
Guardian, The, 44
Guess, 155
Guess Who's Coming to Dinner, 278, 287, 289
Gulf War, 22
Guns and Roses, 160
Guy, Richard, 154
Guy-Blache, Alice, 270
GuyRex Associates, 153–154

Hagemann, L., 311
Haines, Randa, 176
Hale, Sara Josepha, 69
Half the Kingdom, 300
Hall, S., 308, 314
Hamilton, A., 43

Hanes, 154
Hangin' With Mr. Cooper, 183
Hannah and Her Sisters, 265
Happy Days, 181, 186
Haralovich, M. B., 169
Hard Days Night, A, 264
Harlem Nights, 267
Harlow, Jean, 265
Harper's Bazaar, 91, 148, 151, 155, 157
Harris, Susan, 176
Harry, Debbie, 328
Hartman, T., 123
Hart to Hart, 181
Harvard Alcohol Project, 160
Harvey, Polly, 367, 368, 369, 370, 371
Hatfield, Juliana, 361
Hawkins, R., 335
Hawn, Goldie, 268
Haynes, K., 157
Hays, Will, 263
Head, Edith, 267
Head, Sydney, 169
Head of the Class, 183
Head Start: Meeting the Computer Challenge, 298
Hearst, William Randolph, 4
Heart, 322, 363
Heckerling, Amy, 268
Hedgepeth, J. A., 7
Hegemony, 201–202
Heilbrun, C. G., 240
Hellman, Lillian, 266, 270
Helm, De Witt, 150
Henry, Alice, 51
Hepburn, Katharine, 266, 284
"Hero Takes a Fall" (Bangles), 352, 353, 354
Hersay, 226
Hershey, Lenore, 76
Heublein, 136
Hewson, Barbara, 90
Higgins, Marguerite, 12
"Highway 61 Revisited" (Dylan), 369
Hill, M., 195, 196
Hill, Mabel, 118
Hill-Thomas hearings, 63, 116
Hirshey, G., 362
Hispanic Americans, 183, 375. *See also* People of color; Racism
History
    advertising, 111–112
    film, 263–265
    newspapers, 3–4
    prime-time television, 167–168
    rock music/MTV, 321–323, 361–364
    television news, 219–220, 252, 253–255
    women's magazines, 69–72
History and Memory (Tajiri), 312–314

Hoffs, Susanna, 348, 350, 352, 353–354, 355
Hogan, L., 278
Hogan Family, The, 185
Holden, A., 278, 284
Hole, 351, 367, 368, 369
Holiday, Billie, 283
Holm, Ethel, 118
Holsten, C., 256
Holston, N., 254
Home Improvement, 125, 171
Honeymooners, The, 186
"Honky Tonk Woman" (Rolling Stones), 323
hooks, bell, 274, 301, 310
Hooters, 156
Hope, Bob, 167
Hopper, Dennis, 264
Hopper, Hedda, 59, 267
Horowitz, Bruce, 114
Horowitz, J., 204
Hosley, D. H., 253
"Hot, Cool & Vicious" (Salt-N-Pepa), 324
Hotel, 181, 183
Hough, Arthur, 203
Houghton, Katherine, 287
Houston, Whitney, 360, 365–366
Houston Chronicle, 17
Howard, Lisa, 230
Howard's End, 267
How to Be a Successful Advertising Woman (McBride), 113–114
Hubert, N., 297
Huck, J., 203
Hume, Brit, 223
Hume, Emily, 116, 133
Hunter College Women's Studies Collective, 80, 81
Hunter-Gault, Charlayne, 225
Hunter, Holly, 266
Hunt for Red October, The, 265
Huntley, Chet, 219
Hurst, Fanny, 288
Huston, A., 144
Hutton, Lauren, 151
Hyden, C., 324
Hynde, Chrissie, 323, 360, 363, 367

Ida B. Wells Club, 38
"If She Knew What She Wants" (Bangles), 354–355
If You Love This Planet, 296, 300, 303
I'll Find a Way, 296, 298
I Love Lucy, 168, 169
I Married Joan, 169
Imitation of Life, 278, 286, 287, 288, 289
Important women
  advertising, 118–119, 135–137
  film, 270–271
  newspapers, 11–12, 30–39

prime-time television, 176, 192–197
rock music/MTV, 328
television news, 225–226
women's magazines, 75–76, 88–97
Impossible Takes a Little Longer, The, 298, 300
Indecent Proposal, 158
Indiana Jones and the Temple of Doom, 264
Indianapolis World, 32
Indigo Girls, 324, 361
Individualism, 201, 214, 353, 354
Indochine, 267
Industrial Revolution, 3–4
In Living Color, 183
In the Heat of the Night, 264
Investigative journalism, 7, 30–39
Ironweed, 266
Ishtar Films, 271
"Is That It?" (Katrina and the Waves), 324
"It Ain't Me Babe" (Dylan), 323
"It's Only Love" (Turner & Adams), 324
Ivory, S., 193, 194
I Want to Be an Engineer, 298

Jackie, 81
Jackson, Janet, 324, 360, 365, 366
Jackson, Rev. Jesse, 137
Jackson, Wanda, 321
Jacobson, M., 144, 146, 159
Jaggar, A., 204, 209
Jam, Jimmy, 366
James, Etta, 321
Janes, B., 303
Japanese American Women (Alfaro & Hagemann), 311
Japp, P., 202
Jasper, C. R., 116
Jaws, 264
JAWS (Journalism and Women Symposium), 12
Jazz Singer, The, 263
J.C. Penney, 133
JEB, 326
Jeffersons, The, 170, 181, 183
Jennings, Peter, 219, 223, 256
Jeopardy, 219
Jerome, V., 284
Jet, 133, 134
Jett, Joan, 322, 361, 365
Jewell, K. S., 170, 171, 266, 267
Jhally, S., 332, 333, 343
Jim-Crow laws, 32
Johnson, Angela, 48
Johnson, John, 133–134
Johnson, P., 196
Johnson, William, 160–161
Jo Jo Dancer, Your Life Is Calling, 193
Jolson, Al, 263
Jones, Caroline R., 135–142

Jones, Gerard, 168
Jones, James Earl, 283, 286
Jones, Leslie Ann, 326
Jones, Patricia, 176
Jones, Peggy, 321
Joplin, Janis, 322, 323
Joplin Globe, The, 17, 20
Jordan, Bob, 247, 248
Journalism and Women Symposium. See JAWS
Joyful Woman, The, 100
Joy Luck Club, 265
Julia, 169, 266
"Jumpin' Jack Flash" (Franklin), 324, 365
June, Jennie, 12, 76
Jungle Fever, 267
"Just a Minute," 296, 297
J. Walter Thompson Company, 113, 114, 135, 138, 146

Kahne, David, 352
Kamp, John, 150
Kaplan, E. A., 201, 332
Kate and Allie, 171, 181
Katrina and the Waves, 324
Kauffman, L., 156
Kaufman, D., 81
Keirman, Mindi, 6
Kelly, J., 51
Kenar, 154
Kennedy, John F., 60
Kentucky Fried Chicken (KFC), 136
Kerr, Deborah, 284
Kerrigan, Nancy, 149
Kilbourne, Jean, 116, 147
Kinder, M., 332
KING-TV, 247–248
Kirkland, Sally, 266
Kironde, Katiti, 92–93
Klassen, M. L., 116
Klute, 266
K mart, 134
KMBC, 222–223
Korda, Reva, 118
Kovacs, M., 123
Kramarae, C., 301
Kreiling, A., 37
Kristeva, Julia, 351
Kroll, J., 193
Kurtz, Gary, 264
Kushner-Resnick, S., 156

L7, 350, 351, 361, 367, 368
Labrys, 159
Lacayo, R., 265, 267
Ladies' Home Journal, 70, 71, 72, 73, 90, 100
Ladies Magazine, The, 69
Lady from Grey County, The, 299
Lady's Circle, 100
Lady Sings the Blues, 278, 282, 283, 287, 288, 289
Ladyslipper Distributors, 329

Lady's Magazine, The, 102
Laila, 298
Lakatos, I., 343
Landers, Ann, 59
Lane, Gertrude Battles, 70
lang, k. d., 361
Langer, Judith, 116
Language, 19–20
Lansing, Sherry, 268
Last Exit to Brooklyn, 265
Lauper, Cyndi, 324
Laverne and Shirley, 181, 186
Lawrence, C., 152
Lawrence, Viola, 270
Lazier-Smith, L., 115
Lazin, L., 222
Leadership, 45, 47, 48
League of Women Voters, 376
Lear, Frances, 106
Leave It to Beaver, 169, 185, 205, 207
Lee, Jessica, 2
Lee, M., 160
Lee, Spike, 267
Lefkowitz, M., 72
Legacy of Mary McEwan, The, 299
L'eggs, 154
Lennon, John, 362
Lennox, Annie, 324
Lesbianism, 94
Leslie, Mrs. Frank, 76
Lesser, Norma, 44
Lethal Weapon, 289
Letter, The, 310
Levine, Ellen, 76
Levy, E., 277, 278, 280, 281–282, 283, 286
Levy, S., 323
Lewinson, Minna, 12
Lewis, Lisa A., 323, 324, 333, 334, 335, 343, 344, 350–351
Lewis, Terry, 366
Libel, 3
Liberation News Service, 44
Lichty, L. W., 220
Liebowitz, Annie, 118
Life, 90
Life Goes On, 185
Liggett & Myers Tobacco, 136
"Like a Virgin" (Madonna), 324, 325
Little House on the Prairie, 181, 186
"Little Queenie" (Berry), 369
Livingstone, S., 334
Living Way, 32
"Loaded" (Hole), 368, 369
Lockeretz, S., 122
London Fog, 155
Long Time Coming, 302
Long Walk Home, The, 287
Loos, Anita, 268
Lootens, Tricia, 45, 47–48, 49, 52
Lorenzo's Oil, 267

Los Angeles Advertising Women, 119
Los Angeles Times, 17, 268
Loughlin, B., 73
Louise Drouin, Veterinarian, 298
Love, Darlene, 328, 362
Love Affair with Politics, A: A Portrait of Marion Dewar, 299
"Love Bizarre, A" (Sheila E), 324
Love Boat, 193
Love Field, 267
"Love Is a Battlefield" (Benatar), 324
"Love Me Two Times" (Doors), 365
Lowe, Joan, 326
Lubowitz, Shirley (Wershba), 226
Lucas, George, 264
"Luka" (Vega), 324, 351
Lulu, 321
Lupino, Ida, 173, 268
Luria, Z., 80
Lynch, Monica, 328

MacDonald, P., 257
Mackin, Catherine (Casse), 222, 230
MacKinnon, Catherine A., 43, 157
Mad, 107
Made in America, 289
Mademoiselle, 71, 91, 96, 100
Madonna, 160, 343, 350, 351, 360
and audience, 370
criticisms of, 325
female fans, 324
and traditional vs. new roles, 361
Maidenform, 103, 116
Male gaze, 332–333
Mallory, M., 132
Manhattan, 266
"Manic Monday" (Bangles), 352
Manning, Frank, 196
Manning, Marie. See Fairfax, Beatrice
"Mansize" (PJ Harvey), 369, 370
Mapp, Edward, 274
Marin, R., 223, 252, 253, 256
Marion, Frances, 271
Marital status, 20, 184–185, 189, 289
MarketData Enterprises, 152
Married . . . With Children, 185, 186
Marsh, E., 168
Marshall, Penny, 268
Martha and the Vandellas, 322
Martin, 183
Martin, Janis, 321
Martin, Judith, 12
Marvelettes, 322
Maryland Journal, 7

Mary Tyler Moore Show, The, 170, 200, 204–208, 213–214
age in, 184
and feminist movement, 203, 204
Mary as daughter in, 205–206
Mary as wife/mother in, 206–207
portrayal of women's employment in, 181, 202
Marzolf, M., 5, 8, 254
Maser, Wayne, 155
Massey, J., 82
Masterson, P., 134
Matabane, P., 278, 288
Matsuda, M., 152
Mattel, 133
Matusow, Barbara, 252, 254
Maud Lewis: A World Without Shadows, 299
Maybelline, 133
McBride, M. M., 113–114
McCall, James, 101
McCall's, 68, 70, 71, 72, 73, 101, 147
McCandless, N. J., 324
McCann-Erickson Advertising, 114, 136
McCarthy, E. J., 123
McCarthy, Joseph R., 252, 264
McClellan, S., 223
McCloy, Terrance, 288
McCormick, Anne O'Hare, 12
McCracken, E., 71–72
McCreadie, M., 266
McDaniel, Hattie, 274, 275, 284
McDonald, J. R., 333
McGrath, Nedda, 118
McGrory, Mary, 58, 59–61
McLaughlin, Marya, 230, 236
MC Lyte, 361
McNeil, J. C., 170
McRobbie, A., 81
McVie, Christine, 363
Media Foundation, 159, 160, 161
Media Studies Journal, 123, 255
Media Watch, 119, 161
Media Women Poll, 9
Meehan, D., 203
Merritt, Bishetta D., 195, 196, 278, 288
Messick, Dale, 12
Messner, Vetere, Berger, McNamee, and Schmetterer, 135
Meyjes, Menno, 288
MGM, 265
Miami Blues, 265
Miami Herald, The, 17
Miami Vice, 183, 186
Milius, John, 264
Miller, A., 146
Miller, C., 116
Miller, Norma, 196
Miller Brewing Company, 136

Millington, June, 326
Mills, K., 8, 9
Milton Berle Show, The, 168
Mingo, Frank, 136
Mingo Group, The (TMG), 137
Mingo-Jones Advertising Agency,
    Inc. (MJA), 136–137
Minnelli, Liza, 283
Minorities. *See* People of color
Mintz, Lawrence, 205
Mirabella, 76, 100
Miss America contest, 154
"Missionary Man" (Lennox), 324
Mitchell, Andrea, 223, 230, 235
Mitchell, Joni, 369
*Mob Rule in New Orleans: Robert
    Charles and His Fight to the
    Death* (Wells-Barnett), 37
Moira, F., 43, 44, 45, 46, 47,
    49–50, 51
Molson Brewery, 150
Moment by Moment, 266
Monroe, Marilyn, 265
Moonlighting, 186
Moonstruck, 266
Moore, Demi, 287
Moore, Juanita, 286
Moore, Mary Tyler, 176
Morgan, K., 149, 153
Morgan, Lucy, 12
Morgan, Robin, 107
Moseley-Braun, Carol, 21
Moss, Thomas, 34
Mother Jones, 44
Motion Picture Producers and
    Distributors Association of
    America, 263
Motown, 322, 362
Moving Beyond Words (Steinem),
    103
Mr. Belvedere, 185
"Mrs. Jones" (Hole), 368
Ms., 44, 71, 72, 85
    content study of, 107–108
    on advertising, 103, 122, 147
MTV (Music Television), 317,
    323, 324. *See also* Portrayal of
    women in rock music/MTV;
    Rock music/MTV
Murder, She Wrote, 171, 184–185
Muro, M., 157, 161
Murphy, Brianne, 176, 271
Murphy, Eddie, 267
Murphy Brown, 200, 202–204,
    208–214
    age in, 184
    femininity and masculinity in,
        209–210
    and feminist movement, 204
    portrayal of women's
        employment in, 171, 182,
        202
    professional vs. personal success
        in, 211–213
Murrow, Edward, 252

Musician Magazine, 325
Music videos. *See* Portrayal of
    women in rock music/MTV;
    Rock music/MTV
Myers, Lisa, 223
My Little Margie, 169
My Two Dads, 185

Naether, C. A., 115
Naked Gun 33 1/3, 264
Nardone, Ferguson, 222
Nash, A., 223
Nash, M. T., 294, 296
Nash, Terri, 297
"Nasty" (Jackson), 324
National Afro-American Press
    Convention, 33
National Association of Colored
    Women, 37, 38
National Boycott News, The, 161
National Commission on
    Working Women, 170, 171,
    180–189
National Federation of Press
    Women, 12
National Film Board of Canada
    (NFB), 294–295, 303. *See also*
    Studio D
National Institute for Mental
    Health, 154
National Organization for
    Women (NOW), 5, 122, 171,
    231, 376
*National Lampoon's European
    Vacation*, 268
NBC
    early years, 168
    news, 219, 220, 221, 223, 235
    See also Prime-time television;
        Television news; *specific
        shows*
Near, Holly, 325
Negro Fellowship League, 38
Network news. *See* Television
    news
New Day Films, 271
New England Journal of Medicine,
    147
New Initiatives in Film, 297
Newman, J., 153
New Republic, 157
Newspapers
    and advertising, 112
    alternative, 7–8
    and feminist movement, 8, 9,
        42–52, 159
    history, 3–4
    important women, 11–12,
        30–39
    organizations, 12–13
    portrayal of women in, 5–7,
        16–24, 373–374
    study methods, 16–17, 24–28
    See also Women's employment
        in newspapers

News-Times, The, 17
Newsweek, 241
Newton, Helmut, 155
New Woman Magazine, 85, 104
New York Age, 32, 33, 35, 38
New York Gazette, 3
New York Ledger, 59
New York Times, The, 17, 18, 22,
    64, 241, 256
New York Tribune, 7
New York Weekly Journal, 3
Nga, Thi Thanh (Tiana
    Alexander), 312, 314–315
Nicks, Stevie, 363
Nielsen Media Research, 196
Nightingale, V., 200
Nike, 116
Nixon, Agnes, 176
Noble, J., 150
Norman, B., 264, 265
Norma Rae, 266
Norris, J., 150
Northern Exposure, 171
Not a Love Story, 300, 303, 304
Null, G., 287

Objectification, 148–149, 154,
    337, 341
Occupational status. *See* Portrayal
    of women's employment
O'Connor, J., 203
O'Connor, Sinead, 351, 360, 370
Office of Production Code
    Administration, 263
Officer and a Gentleman, An, 266
off our backs (oob), 42–52, 159
    future of, 52
    history, 44–46
    organizational structure, 45,
        47–50
    overview of, 42–44
Ogilvie, Lana, 133
Ogilvy & Mather, Inc., 114, 123
Older, Stronger, Wiser, 302
Oliver, 240
Oliver, S., 194
Olivia, 326
Omission, 125, 127
One Day at a Time, 170, 202
Ono, Yoko, 328
On Our Backs, 52
On the Waterfront, 265–266
oob. *See off our backs*
Operation PUSH, 137
Oppenheimer, Jerry, 255
O'Reilly, J., 203
Organizations
    advertising, 119
    film, 271–272
    newspapers, 12–13
    prime-time television, 177
    rock music/MTV, 329
    television news, 226
    women's magazines, 76–77
Orlean, Susan, 354

Oscar awards, 275, 276–290
Oulahan, R., 193
Our Miss Brooks, 168
Our Women and Children, 70
Outrageous Fortune, 267
Ozzie and Harriet, 185, 207

Page, Geraldine, 284
Paisley, W., 81, 335
Palcy, Euzhan, 271
Palley, M. L., 47
Palmer, Volney B., 111
Palmolive, 147
Panitt, M., 203
"Papa Don't Preach" (Madonna), 325, 343
Parallax View, The, 264
Parents Music Resource Center (PRMC), 325, 333
Paris Beacon News, 243
Parrish, Charles, 70
Parsons, Louella, 59
Passion Fish, 267
Patriarchy, 202, 207, 353. *See also specific topics*
Patricia's Moving Picture, 299
Patty Duke Show, The, 169
Pauley, Jane, 226, 230
Pavletich, A., 323
Peirce, K., 81, 82
People of color, 375–376
    and prime-time television, 172, 182–184
    and Studio D, 302
    and television news, 223, 253
    See also African-American, Asian/Pacific-American, and Hispanic American *headings*
Pergament, A., 256
Peterson, Debbi, 350, 354, 355
Peterson, J. B., 337
Peterson, Lori, 110
Peterson, P. V., 8
Peterson, R. A., 321, 323
Peterson, Roberta, 328
Peterson, Vicki, 350, 352, 354
Phair, Liz, 361
Philip Morris, 136, 141
Phillips, C., 133
Phillips, Irna, 176
Phranc, 325
Phyllis, 170, 202
Piano, The, 268
Pickford, Mary, 267
Pictorial Review, 70, 71
Piirto, R., 123
Pillsbury, 133, 134
Pine Bluff Commercial, 17
Pingree, S., 335
Pinky, 278, 284, 286, 287
Pixies, 351
PJ Harvey, 361, 367, 368, 369
Planned Parenthood, 325
Playboy, 156

Pleiades Records, 329
Poitier, Sydney, 264, 275, 287
Polemus, Gretchen, 154
Police Woman, 170
Pollitt, K., 166
Polly!, 196
Polykoff, Shirley, 118
Pornography, 50, 51, 156–157
Portrait of the Artist—As an Old Lady, 299
Portrayal of women
    in advertising, 114–116, 122–129
    in film, 265–267, 310, 316, 317, 374
    in music, 323–325
    in newspapers, 5–7, 16–24, 373–374
    in teen magazines, 83–85
    in prime-time television, 169–172
    in television news, 220–221
    See also African-American women and film; Portrayal of women *headings*
Portrayal of women in advertising, 122–124, 126–128, 144–162, 374
    and ageism, 151
    and alcohol, 150–151
    and consumerism, 145–146
    and cosmetic surgery, 153–154
    and dieting, 145–146, 147, 152–153, 158
    influence, 147–148
    objectification, 148–149, 154
    overview of, 114–116
    political implications, 157–159
    and pornography, 156–157
    and portrayal of women's employment, 149
    and racism, 152
    sexual exploitation, 125, 128, 144–145, 149–150, 158
    and sexual harassment, 110, 150
    solutions to, 159–161
    and violence against women, 144, 150–151, 154–156, 157–158
Portrayal of women in rock music/MTV, 323–325, 332–344
    criticisms of, 332–334
    empirical literature review, 334–336
    study methods, 336–338, 344–345
Portrayal of women in women's magazines, 72–73, 106–108
    changes in, 68
    and consumerism, 102–103
    diversity, 100–101
    teen magazines, 83–85

Portrayal of women on prime-time television, 56–57, 169–172
    age and marital status, 184–185, 189
    and consumerism, 200–201
    economic status, 185–187
    and journalism, 56–57
    overview of, 169–172
    and portrayal of women's employment, 180–182, 188, 202
    and race, 182–184, 189
    Smurfette principle, 166
    See also Feminism and prime-time television
Portrayal of women's employment, 375
    and advertising, 122, 149
    and film, 283–284, 286–287, 289
    and prime-time television, 180–182, 188, 202
    and women's magazines, 72, 73
Post, Emily, 59
Poussaint, Renee, 226
Powers, A., 368
Prescriptives, Inc., 133
Pretenders, 324, 363
Pretty Woman, 267
PrimeTIME LIVE, 204, 223
Prime-time television
    hegemony of, 201–202
    history, 167–168
    important women, 176, 192–197
    organizations, 177
    speed of change, 374
    women's employment, 172–173, 187–188
    See also Feminism and prime-time television; Portrayal of women on prime-time television
Prince, 352, 354
Procter & Gamble, 103, 113
Proctor, Barbara, 118
Proetz, Erma Perham, 119
Profit, 71–72, 88
Provenzano, F., 80
Pryor, Richard, 193
Publick Occurrences Both Foreign and Domestick, 3
Pulitzer, Joseph, 4
Punky Brewster, 185

Quaker Oats, 133
Quantum Leap, 196
Quart, B., 268
Queen, Penelope, 146
Queen, The, 101. *See also McCall's*
Queen Latifah, 324, 361
Quicksilver Times, 44
Quindlen, Anna, 58, 64–66
Quinn, Martha, 328

Racism, 152, 160. *See also* African-
    American *headings*
Radiance: Magazine for Large
    Women, 77
Radio, 167, 168, 221, 253, 254
Ragtime, 193
Raiders of the Lost Ark, 264
Raitt, Bonnie, 322, 360
Rambling Rose, 268
Randazzo, S., 122
Randolph, L., 195, 196
Rap, 324
Rapping, E., 266, 266–267
Rashad, Phylicia, 196
Rat, 44
Rather, Dan, 219, 223, 252–253,
    256–257, 375
Ratterman, Debbie, 42, 48
Rawlings, Marjorie Kinnan, 283,
    288
Reagan/Bush administrations,
    140, 160
Reasoner, Harry, 223, 254
Reason Why the Colored American Is
    Not in the Columbian
    Exposition, The (Wells), 36
Rebel Without a Cause, 265–266
Redbook, 71, 72, 101, 103
Redd Kross, 350
Red Record, A (Wells), 36
Red Skelton Show, 169
Reed, B., 222
Reel Women, 268
Reeves, J., 145
Regards de Femmes, 298
Reid, Coletta, 44
Reiniger, Lotte, 271
Remington, B., 255
Remler, Emily, 325
Resor, Helen Lansdowne, 113,
    114
"Respect" (Franklin), 323
Revlon Corporation, 133, 147,
    151
Revolution, The, 7–8
Reynolds, Debbie, 243
Rhoda, 170, 181, 202
Rhodes, J., 8
Rice, Linda Johnson, 134
Rich, Adrienne, 202, 207
Rich, Frank, 256
Richards, Beah, 287, 289
Richardson, B., 81
Richardson, Midge, 76, 92
Richmond, D., 123
"Rid of Me" (PJ Harvey), 368,
    369, 370, 371
Right Candidate for Rosedale, The,
    299
Ringwood's Afro-American Journal
    of Fashion, 70
Riot grrrls, 52, 366–370
Ritter, Thelma, 284
Rix, S., 158

R.J. Reynolds Tobacco Company,
    140–141
Roadwork Inc., 329
Roberts, C. L., 3
Roberts, Cokie, 226
Roberts, Julia, 265
Robocop II, 265
Roc, 183
Roches, 361
Rock, M., 218, 222, 230, 252
Rock music/MTV, 320
    and feminist movement,
        351–352, 367–368
    history, 321–323
    important women, 328
    organizations, 329
    women's employment, 325–326
    See also Female rock/MTV
        performers; Portrayal of
        women in rock
        music/MTV
Rocky, 264
Rogers, Gerry, 297
Rogers, Will, 152
Rolling Stone, 350–351
Rolling Stones, 323, 362, 369
Romer, N., 80
Ronettes, 323, 362
Roosevelt, Eleanor, 8, 59
Roosevelt, Franklin D., 59, 264
Roots II, 193
Rose, B. G., 168
Roseanne, 144, 171, 182, 185
    economic status in, 186, 187
Rosellini, Isabella, 151
Rosen, Marcella, 114, 171, 268
Rosenzweig, Barney, 171
Ross, B. L., 122
Ross, Diana, 283, 287, 362
Ross, Ruth N., 76
Roth, M., 157
Rothenberg, R., 139
'Round Midnight, 283
Rountree, Martha, 226
Rozema, Patricia, 271
Rubin, J., 80
"Rub 'Til It Bleeds" (PJ Harvey),
    369
Ruggiero, J., 81
Russell, D., 156
Russell, Rosalind, 266
Rutberg, J., 82

Saatchi & Saatchi, 146
Sade, 361
Sadker, D., 80
Sadker, M., 80
Sadomasochism (S&M), 155–156
Salt-N-Pepa, 324
Sanders, C., 192, 193, 194
Sanders, Marlene, 218, 222, 230,
    236, 252, 254, 258
Sanderson, S., 123
Sanford and Son, 183
Sassy, 82

Sather, C., 82
"Satisfaction" (Rolling Stones),
    323, 369
Savitch, Jessica, 226, 230
Sawyer, Beverly, 196
Sawyer, Diane, 223, 230, 253
Sayonara, 310
Scent of a Woman, 267
Schaefer, Ruth Crane, 172
Schau, C., 85
Scherer, R., 219
School, 80–81
School Daze, 267
Schulze, Jennifer, 240–249
    early years, 240–242
    internship, 242–244
    KING-TV, 247–248
    WGN-TV, 248–249
    WLS-TV, 244–247
Schwartz, A. M., 116
Schwartz, Phyllis, 245–246, 248
Scorsese, Martin, 264
Scott, J., 124
Scott, V., 194
Screen Actors Guild, 170, 265
Screen Actors Guild Women's
    Committee, 177
Seagrams, 136
Seattle Times, The, 17, 22, 23, 257
Seaver, 73
Sedition, 3
Seggar, J. F., 170, 278
Seidelman, Susan, 268
Seidman, S. A., 335
Seinfeld, 125
Self, 71, 96, 100, 116
Sennott, R., 80
Seventeen, 81–85, 91
"Sex as a Weapon" (Benatar), 324,
    365
Sexism. *See specific topics*
Sexual exploitation, 125, 128,
    144–145
Sexual harassment, 110, 150
Shaffer, Beverly, 298–299
Shampoo, 264
Shangri-Las, 323
Shannon, Kathleen, 296, 297,
    298, 302
Shapiro, S., 320
Sharkey, Betsy, 147
Shear, Jules, 354
"Sheela-Na-Gig" (PJ Harvey),
    368, 369
Sheila E, 324
Sherr, Lynn, 230
Shirelles, 321
Shocked, Michelle, 324, 361
Shore, Dinah, 167
Shriver, Maria, 223
Signorielli, N., 81
Silverman, J., 157
Silverman, Trera, 176
Simmons, K., 278
Simmons, William, 70

Simon, J., 193
Simpson, Carole, 230, 255
Simpson, J., 132, 134
Simpsons, The, 185, 186
Singleton, John, 267
Singleton, L. A., 222
Sisters in the Struggle, 301, 302
Sloan, Margaret, 274
Smith, C., 222
Smith, Jessie Wilcox, 76
Smith, Lucy Wilmot, 76
Smith, Patti, 363, 366
Smolowe, J., 156
"Snake" (PJ Harvey), 369
Snyder, Joan, 226
Socialist Workers Party (SWP), 50
Socioeconomic status. *See* Class status
Sojourner, 44
Solomon, N., 160
Some American Feminists, 301
Sondergaard, Gale, 310
Sonic Youth, 367
Sontag, Susan, 145
Soren, Tabitha, 328
Sorenson, Erik, 256
Sorrel, L., 45, 49
Sounder, 278, 287, 288, 289
Sound of Music, The, 240
South Carolina Gazette, 7
Southern Horrors: Lynch Law in All Its Phases (Wells), 35
Spare Rib, 77
SPEAK, 46
Speaking Our Peace, 303
Specter, Arlen, 20, 21
Spector, Phil, 361–362
Spencer, Susan, 235
Sperber, A. M., 252
Spielberg, Steven, 264
Sports coverage, 6, 23
Springfield, Dusty, 321
Squier, Miriam, (Mrs. Frank Leslie), 76
Stahl, Leslie, 226, 230, 235
Stamberg, Margie, 44
Stanton, Elizabeth Cady, 8
Stark, J., 193, 194, 195
St.-Arnaud, M., 296
Star Trek, 125
Star Wars, 264
Statistical Package for the Social Sciences, 125
Steel, Dawn, 268
Steele, Alison, 328
Steele, Michael, 350, 352, 354
Steel Guitar (Barnes), 358, 360
Steel Magnolias, 265
Steenburgen, Mary, 286
Steenland, Sally, 376
Steffens, Heidi, 44
Steffens, Nan, 44
Stein, M. L., 9
Steinberg, C., 266

Steinem, Gloria, 92, 103, 147
Stereotypes. *See* AfricanAmerican, Asian/Pacific-American, and Hispanic American *headings*; Portrayal of women *headings*; *specific topics*
Sterling, D., 33
Stern, Howard, 160
Stewart, A. D., 322–323, 324, 362
Stewart, Sharon, 9
Stikeman, Ginny, 298, 303
St. John, M., 193
St. Louis Post-Dispatch, 17
Stoddard, Alice, 119
Stompin' at the Savoy, 196
Stone, Lucy, 8
Stone, V., 222, 255, 258
Stovall, J. G., 4
St. Pierre Ruffin, Josephine, 70
"Straightening Our Hair" (hooks), 310
Streep, Meryl, 265, 266, 284
Streisand, Barbra, 266, 268
Stroh Brewery, 110, 150
Stroman, C. A., 278, 288
Stubbs, F., 284
Students for a Democratic Society, 44
Studio D, 295–305
  conflicts within, 302
  creation of, 295–296
  feminist goals, 299–300
  filmmaker training, 296–298
  success of, 303–305
"Stupid Girl" (Rolling Stones), 323
"Suck My Left One" (Bikini Kill), 368, 369–370
Sun-Journal, 17
Superman, 264
Supremes, 322
Swayze, Patrick, 287
Swedish bikini team ads, 110, 150
Swisshelm, Jane, 12
Swit, Loretta, 171

Tajiri, Rea, 312–314
Tapper, J., 333, 336, 342
Tarbell, Ida, 7
Target audiences, 127, 132–135, 138–139
Taxi, 186
Taxi Driver, 266
Ted Bates Advertising Agency, 170
Tedesco, N. S., 170
'Teen, 82–85
"Teenage Whore" (Hole), 368, 369, 370
Teen magazines, 81–85, 91, 101, 374
Teichner, Martha, 230
Teinowitz, I., 150, 151
Television. *See* Prime-time television; Television news

Television news
  history, 219–220, 252, 253–255
  important women, 225–226, 240–249
  organizations, 226
  portrayal of women in, 220–221
  See also Women's employment in television news
Televison News Index and Abstracts, 231–235
10,000 Maniacs, 352
Tetzlaff, D., 332
Tewkesbury, Joan, 271
That Girl, 169, 204
Thelma and Louise, 265, 267, 289
Thomas, Helen, 12
Thomas, June, 47
Thomas, Marlo, 176
Thompson, Dorothy, 12
Thompson, J. Walter, 112
Thorson, E., 333, 342
Thorton, L., 255
Three Days of the Condor, 264
3 Girls 3, 193
Three's Company, 170
Thrunher, Jeffrey, 155
Time, 89, 90, 151
Timothy, Elizabeth, 7
TNN (The Nashville Network), 335
To a Safer Place, 300, 304
Today Show, The, 255
Too Dirty for a Woman, 298
Top Gun, 264, 268
Total Recall, 265
Toward Intimacy, 300
Towering Inferno, The, 264
Toying with Their Future, 301
Toys-R-Us, 134
Trachtenberg, J., 123
Trahey, Jane, 119
Trauma Foundation, The, 161
Tremblay, M., 296
Trip to Bountiful, The, 289
Trotta, Liz, 230
Tsiantar, D., 146
Tucker, Maureen, 328
Turner, C., 82
Turner, Kathleen, 265
Turner, Lana, 286
Turner, R., 171
Turner, Tina, 322, 323, 324
Turning Point (television program), 223
Turning Point, The (film), 266
Tuscaloosa News, The, 17
"Tush" (ZZ Top), 365
TV Guide, 171, 256
2 Live Crew, 160
227, 170, 185
Two Nice Girls, 325, 361
"Typical Male" (Turner), 324
Tyson, Cicely, 287

Ulrich's International Periodicals Directory, 73
"Under My Thumb" (Rolling Stones), 323
Unforgiven, 267
United Artists, 267
United Nations, 144, 149
U.S. Commission on Civil Rights, 172–173, 220–221
USA Today, 17

Vachss, A., 156
Van Bloem, Eddie, 149
Van Buren, Abigail, 59
Vanderbilt, Gloria, 156
Vanity Fair, 96
Van Upp, Virginia, 271
Van Valkenburg, N., 256
Varda, Agnes, 271
Vega, Suzanne, 324, 351
VH-1 (Video Hits-1), 335
"Video Soul" (BET), 334, 342
Vietnam Summer, 44
Vietnam War, 314–315
Vincent, R. C., 335, 343, 344
Violence against women, 144, 150–151, 154–156, 157–158, 162
Virginia Slims, 149
Vogue, 71, 91, 96, 155
von Trotta, Margarethe, 271
Vreeland, Diana, 76

Waiting for Prime Time (Sanders), 252
Waldo, Ruth, 113
Walker, Alice, 286, 288
Walker, Bree, 226
"Walk Like an Egyptian" (Bangles), 324, 350
Wallis, C., 151
Wall Street Journal, 138
Walsh, Williams, 150
Walt Disney Productions, 136–137
Walters, Barbara, 222, 223, 230, 231, 242, 253, 254–255, 257, 258
Waltons, The, 181, 186
"Wang Dang Doodle" (Dixon), 369
War coverage, 22
Warrenton, Lizzie, 30–31
Washington, Booker T., 37–38
Washington, Denzel, 275, 283
Washington, Margaret Murray, 38
Washington Blade, The, 44
Washington Post, The, 5, 17, 20–22, 59
Washington Press Club Foundation, 376–377
Waters, Ethel, 176, 284
Waters, H. F., 203
Weather, D., 231
Weaver, D. H., 222, 253

Webb, Marilyn, 44, 45
Weil, Mathilde C., 119
Weitzman, L., 81
Welch, Raquel, 171
Wells, Jim, 30–31
Wells, Mary, 328
Wells, Mary (Bunny), 119
Wells-Barnett, Ida B., 7, 30–39
early years, 30–31
Northern exile, 35–37
Southern work, 31–35
and Washington, 37–38
Wertmuller, Lina, 271
West, Mae, 263
Westinghouse Electric, 136
Weston, L., 81
WGN-TV, 248–249
"What Have You Done for Me Lately?" (Jackson), 324
What's Happening!!, 170, 183
"What's Love Got to Do With It?" (Turner), 324
When You're a Boy (Hoffs), 354
Where Credit Is Due, 299
Whetmore, E. J., 173
Whipple, T. W., 115, 170
Whitburn, J., 363
White, A., 231
White, Pearl, 271
Whitney, Ruth, 88–97
Better Living, 90–91
early years, 88–90
Glamour, 91–97
Seventeen, 91
Whittler, T. E., 132
Who, 362
Who's the Boss, 185
WHYS Crack Records, 329
Wicks, Marlene, 44
Wilhoit, G. C., 222, 253
Williams, Lucinda, 361
Williams, Mary Alice, 223
Williamson, Cris, 326
Willis, E. E., 173
Will Rogers' Follies, 152
Wilson, Amrit, 308, 312
Wilson, M., 80
Wilson, Nancy, 322
Wilson, Phyllis Starr, 92
Wilson sisters, 363
Window Dressing on the Set (U.S. Commission on Civil Rights), 172–173, 220–221, 222, 253
Wine Institute, 161
Winfrey, Oprah, 283, 286
WINGS: Women's International News Gathering Service University of Texas at Austin, 226
Winter, Kate, 326
Wisehart, B., 203
WLS-TV, 244–247
WMM. *See* Women, Men and Media

Wolf, M., 147
Wolf, N., 153
Woman's Day, 71, 101
Woman's Era, 70
Woman's Era Club, 70
Woman's Home Companion, The, 70, 90
Woman's Journal, 8
Woman's Place, A, 122
Woman suffrage movement, 5, 7–8, 38, 69
Woman's World, 104
Women, Men and Media (WMM), 6, 16–24, 221
Women Against Pornography, 122
Women and media
economic factors, 376
future of, 376–378
increased numbers, 373–374
speed of change, 374
women of color, 375–376
See also specific topics
Women at the Well, 302
Women directing, 222
Women in Cable, 177
Women in Communications, Inc., 9, 12, 119, 137, 221
Women in Film, 271
Women in Film, Atlanta, 272
Women in Media, 177
Women in the Shadows, 300, 301
Women-made films, 295–305
Asian American, 308, 310–318
conflicts, 302
filmmaker training, 296–298
Studio D creation, 295–296
and women's voices, 303–305
Women Make Movies, 272
Women Make News, Inc., 226
Women Readers Task Force, 6–7
Women Reporters Make Gains on TV News, 223
Women's Advertising Club of Chicago, 119
Women's Club, 70
Women's employment
advertising, 113–114
film, 262, 267–268, 274, 288, 289–290, 374
prime-time television, 172–173, 187–188
rock music/MTV, 325–326
women's magazines, 73, 90, 104
See also Important women; Women's employment in newspapers; Women's employment in television news
Women's employment in newspapers, 2, 7–9, 56–66
alternative papers, 7–8
columnist overview, 57–59
and emotionality stereotype, 56–57

Goodman, Ellen, 61–63
McGrory, Mary, 59–61
positive changes, 18, 373
Quindlen, Anna, 64–66
and war coverage, 22
Wells-Barnett, Ida B., 30–39
Women's employment in
  television news, 221–223,
  230–237, 252–259
and appearance, 222–223, 244,
  256–258, 259
audience reactions, 254
correspondents, 218, 230–237,
  374
historical context, 253–255
improvement in visibility,
  235–237
previous research, 230–231
Schulze, Jennifer, 240–249
statistics, 232–235
study methods, 231–232
Women's Institute for Freedom of
  the Press, 13
Women's liberation movement.
  See Feminist movement
Women's magazines, 68
criteria for, 103–106
history, 69–72
important women, 75–76,
  88–97
organizations, 76–77

speed of change, 374
teen magazines, 81–85, 91, 101,
  374
women's employment in, 73,
  90, 104
See also Portrayal of women in
  women's magazines
Women's movement. See Feminist
  movement
Women's music, 325, 326, 363
Women's National Abortion
  Action Coalition, 50
Women's Video Collective, 177
Wonder Years, The, 185
Woodard, Alfre, 283, 286
Woodhull, Nancy, 6, 16
Woodruff, Judy, 226, 230
Word usage, 125
"Working Mothers," 296, 298
Working Woman, 77
World Columbian Exposition, 36
World of Suzie Wong, The, 310, 316
World War II
and advertising, 113, 115
and Asian Americans, 312–314
and film, 263–264, 265,
  294–295
and newspapers, 5, 8
and television, 167, 374
and women's magazines, 71
Worth Every Minute, 299

Writer's Digest, 101
Writing style, 56–58, 60–61, 63,
  64–66
Wuornos, Eileen, 43
Wyndham, D., 144

Yamada, G. K., 230, 253
Yeakel, Lynn, 20
Yearling, The, 283
Yearwood, Gladstone, 195
Yellow journalism, 4
YM, 82
Young, Darlene, 288
Young, Neil, 362
Young and Rubicam, 114
Young Guns II, 265
Yovovich, B., 122
Yo Yo, 361
Yugoslavia, 43, 157

Zacks, R., 231
Zahn, Paula, 226
Zehme, B., 203
Zenger, Anna, 3
Zenger, John Peter, 3
Zetterling, Mai, 271
Zettl, H., 338
Ziegler, D., 231
Zilinskas, Annette, 352
Zukor, Jerry, 274
ZZ Top, 365

415